A LIFE OUT OF LINE

Fumblefinger

A LIFE OUT OF LINE

OUT OF LINE

A LIFE

OUT OF LINE

A LIFE

Fumblefinger

A LIFE OUT OF LINE

Stan Hart

Abeel Publishers

Cambridge, Massachusetts

OUT OF LINE

A LIFE

The chapter on Lillian Hellman was first published, in different form, in
The Sewanee Review CVII (summer 1999) under the title "Lillian Hellman
and Others." Copyright 1999 by the University of the South and by the
author.

Abeel Publishers
148 Pleasant Street
Cambridge, MA 02139
(617) 491-3410
(800) 478-7090

Interior and jacket design: Linda Manly Wade

Printed in the United States of America

Library of Congress Catalogue-in-Publication Data
Hart, Stan.
    Fumblefinger: a life out of line / Stan Hart.
      p.   cm.
    ISBN 0-9650357-3-5
    1. Hart, Stan. 2. Editors—United States—Biography. 3. Martha's Vineyard
(Mass.)—Biography. 4. New Britain (Conn.)—Biography.
I. Title.
CT275.H38675A3 1999
974.4'043'092—dc21
[b]
                                           99-11834
                                            CIP

1 2 3 4 5 6 7 8 9 0

FOR MY FATHER

No Man's Land: "…like a gnashing of teeth
…the abode of madness."

Wilfred Owen

•   •   •

From this "abode of madness" my father emerged
to marry and raise a family.

AUTHOR'S NOTE

I have tried to write an open story of my life. This may offend some people. They will have to understand that I cannot bear to travel on toward the end of my life without knowing where I've been, what I did, whom I did it with, and what I may have missed along the way. I do not intend to die a mystery to myself.

Throughout I have employed fiction to protect the privacy of the many friends with whom I had relationships, people who enlivened my life. Often, my story depicts events that are composites, a combination of scenes and people that obscures the facts, but does not alter the essential truth of how I lived.

CONTENTS

Preface   ix

Part I   New Britain and Martha's Vineyard   1

Part II   Brook Hall   81

Part III   Work and the Air Force   159

Part IV   The Adult World   205

Part V   Publishing and the Time of My Life   241

Part VI   Lillian and the End of My Beginning   327

Epilogue   351

By the time I was ten years old I was riding to school on my glowing *metallic lustre* aqua-colored, two-speed, Columbia bike. My bike had balloon tires and I could coast for a very long time. The Vance Elementary School was down Shuttle Meadow Avenue, just before the two- and three-decker houses began and before Brown's Market where I purchased candy and pop.

During school hours no one ever took another student's bike, so we could leave them unchained outside in the yard. After school I'd ride home (there were no buses in those days), whizzing along, finally pumping and coasting down Lincoln Road. By the time I was ten I was playing football and baseball in the schoolyard or across the road in the field by Doerr's Pond. Often I'd ride home in the dark to our large white house, entering through the kitchen door, inhaling the odors and steam of the kitchen, arriving just before the meal was to be served. *Hurry now, wash your hands, you're late again*, someone would say, and in a few minutes my mother, my father, and I would be dining on meat and potatoes with junket for dessert. Usually I'd let my mind drift back to the school-yard, oblivious of the adult conversation and the tension that was often present.

One day my parents decided to go down to Martha's Vineyard for Easter weekend and open up our bungalow. It was suggested that I might go swimming, so a bathing suit was packed for me, and on Easter Sunday I ran to the beach and toed the water, but Nantucket Sound was frigid. Shivering, I ran home to get ready for our motor trip back to New Britain.

Anyway...on the day we were to leave for the Vineyard, rather stupidly, I had ridden my bike to school. I say this was stupid because at the end of the day my parents would be picking me up. They'd arrive in the new Buick Roadmaster convertible sedan, red as a fire engine. I loved that car. The top was white, the enamel on the body glowed. It was the kind of car you'd see on

Movietone News—President Roosevelt riding in one, waving his arm, doffing his fedora to the crowd that lined the thoroughfare. When my father drove that Buick, I thought he was the grandest man who ever lived, and there was joy in the land.

But that's not the story I'm telling: a celebratory touring car marking the end of the Depression was part of my life in those days, but it was only marginal to what happened that Easter weekend in 1940. It began at the end of class, when my heart sank. With a startling revelation I realized my error! What do I do with my bike? I didn't blame my parents, who should have foreseen this problem: I blamed myself. A fumblefinger, I'd done a really dumb thing: Now I'd have to leave my bike at school for a whole weekend. The bike was like the Roadmaster, its metal agleam with a shiny finish, a treasure to catch the eye, and now it would be stolen. Any bike left alone on the playground on a Saturday night would be deemed abandoned. Who wouldn't take such a bike and keep it? I had no time to ride home and park it safely in our garage. With my heart beating wildly, I rode it quickly over to a fence separating the property of an abutting homeowner from the schoolyard.

Sure enough, just as I was walking back from the fence, I saw the Buick pulling up in front of the school, reflecting the afternoon sun, a smattering of students and a teacher or two agog, watching its approach. I saw my mother, looking very stern, in the front seat. *Who are those people staring at us?* Then I saw her break into a smile as I approached. I loved my mother and I loved my father, but I was extremely self-conscious when they intercepted the course of my everyday routine with their presence, a presence often accompanied by the glow of money.

As we rode along they may have known that something was bothering me. I stayed silent in the back seat, holding our Welsh terrier, the two of us, boy and dog, partners in life. I didn't dare tell them about the bike.

All weekend I worried. The thought of my bike being stolen lived in my mind like a cancer and dug itself into my imagination. All I recall about that weekend is the roaring fire that warmed our very cold little summer home and the numbing sea. My mother and father went to a cousin's house for a party. I suspect they argued later on until my father shouted, *Now shut up, Lu. Goddamn it. Shut up!*

The silence as we rode home from the island was claustrophobic. Even now I can feel it. Silence spells tension, and tension cut into my soul and worried me terribly. Hugging our dog in the back seat, I carried the weight of my crime with me. Never once did it occur to me to tell my parents, to ask their advice right at the start, as I entered the Buick: *Hi, Mom and Dad. Guess what? I rode my bike to school. Do we have time to take it somewhere for safekeeping?*

Sadly, we did not live that way. In my home we never spoke if doing so would cause embarrassment. In the case of my bike-in-jeopardy, all three of us would have felt foolish, then embarrassed by the feeling. Getting upset because of feeling foolish was something we avoided at all costs. Any untoward, uncomfortable emotion was to be buried at once.

Riding home, I wiggled and worried in the back seat. What made matters worse was that as we rode up West Main Street, the door of a parked car opened in front of us and my father's bumper hit it. Already I was aware of a class system, and true to form, the hapless man, once he observed my father and the Buick, was quick to admit that he should not have opened his door into the oncoming traffic. I could see his door knocked cockeyed. My father hardly spoke. The other man assumed all the blame. There was no confrontation, no passing of telephone numbers, no talk of insurance, and certainly no police.

Quickly my father drove away; it was not his fault. Yet I felt the fear, I felt the nearness of danger. I felt the hostility in my father begin to surface. But the other man had known his place and retreated to his old Dodge or Plymouth, the door loose on its hinges.

As we pulled into our driveway, I worried even more because I sensed my father's ire over *some fathead who opened his car door right in my path.* Another fumblefinger. Over and over I asked myself: What do I say in the morning about not having a bike? I could hear the questioning from my father: *You left the bike at school? For the whole weekend? Why didn't you tell me? We could have driven down and picked it up. Why didn't you just call Mom from school?*

How could I tell my father that I was afraid to call home? I *never* called home about anything. How could I tell my father that the few times I opened my mouth to ask for anything I sensed quite profoundly that I was a nuisance? How could I tell him that I would never say anything to him that indicated I had done something stupid? If I was stupid, somehow that made my parents stupid. If I was a stupid boy, then my father was stupid, too. I could not stand that notion. I could not carry in my heart the shame and blame of my parents.

My father opened the garage door and returned to the Buick and drove into our garage, which smelled of gasoline. There was a workbench along the back wall. Against it, out of the corner of my eye I saw the aqua luster of my bike. Rejoicing as I had never rejoiced in my short life, I ran to it. Amazed, I looked it over. Down by the pedal was a piece of paper: *I saw your bike and rode it home for you. Farmer.*

A school chum named Farmer Gantner, who lived in a triple-decker down past Brown's Market, knew I was going away. He saw my bike, gave the matter some thought, and then pedaled it home for me. Farmer did not want me to lose my bike to a thief. He was my friend.

I did not know it at the time because I was too young to put such an alarming thought into words, but later I began to see that the good people were the Farmer Gantners. I should not have venerated people like my parents. In later years I understood that I'd been raised all wrong. I should have been raised like Farmer Gantner, who didn't have a nickel to his name.

PART I

New Britain and
Martha's Vineyard

Chapter 1

I was twenty-two during the Christmas season of 1952 when I was on furlough from the Air Force. Although my parents had moved, I had a cousin who lived in Hartford and I drove up to visit him. Within a day or so I attended a dance at the Hartford Golf Club where my cousin was a member. I knew some of the young men and their dates from childhood as I had lived until the age of 12 in the neighboring town, New Britain. By 1952, I was pretty much a stranger from Maryland so I was not part of any group and so I did not sit at any particular table. I floated around, spending most of my time at the small bar, now just an extra young man without a girl. I harbored few expectations: I'd get drunk, try to kiss the occasional wife of some junior executive who might be losing his ardor, and then return to my cousin's. I hadn't thought of Margaret Kelly; she was older than I, and came from Dover, Delaware, a young woman whom I had last seen at college before I quit. She'd been dating a veteran. I remembered her from that one meeting in college: she was good-looking and she had smiled at me. In 1952 I was still a kid, of course, although over a year in the service had probably given me a measure of self-assurance.

I was absorbed with my drink, listening to the dance music, gleeful to be home and in civilian clothes. Under the influence of the alcohol I felt almost cocky, and I probably postured as a man of the world. I was quite full of myself when I saw her. She was turning toward me, her face alive with joy, her figure sculpted inside a black dress with considerable cleavage. Her hair was perfectly bobbed, lustrous and brown and it glistened when she laughed as it caught the rays of light shining above the bar. I was a yard away when she turned toward me and walked right into my arms, stepping directly up to my chest, her face against mine and her lips kissing my lips.

It seemed that all the good feelings I'd ever felt in my life were focused on our kissing. I floated on air from her affection, so brazen and freely given. I returned her kisses, pressing in on her lips to open them more; finally they were open wide and wetting my face.

When we broke apart I asked if she was alone, which was unlikely, and she said there was a man somewhere, probably dancing. It was platonic, she told me, just friends. Could we meet inside the doorway to the club? I asked. I wanted to get her outside and into my car. She said yes, and we agreed to meet at eleven. This is wild, she told me. Who would have thought it would be you, she said. I tried to read a message in her brown translucent eyes, so expressive and shining, as she tried to read one in mine. This would not be a simple flirtation. She had been attracted to me since our one meeting at my fraternity house, a couple of years before. She thought I was cute. She had seen me as I had seen her—just in passing, but we both remembered each other.

At eleven she saw me leaning against the wall and she hustled to get to my side and kissed me immediately. I held her against me until I felt my erection pressing her, and as she raised herself on her tiptoes I pushed her clothes back inside of her just enough to soak her panties. Later in the back seat of my car I'd feel the wetness with the palm of my hand as I cupped her crotch over the damp, thin nylon, and soon we were both undressed.

She was silent for a few moments. When she began to speak, her voice was tentative, almost weak. "I was so excited," she said. "Was it good for you?" she asked and I said, "Oh shit." Good? I was in love. I told her as much and said I was falling in love with the most wonderful girl in the world. She claimed coyly that she'd been carried away; then she kissed me again and said we'd better go back inside. She did not mention love.

In the parking lot I held Margaret close, all the while brushing myself off and conscious that I reeked of our lovemaking. She'd smoothed her hair and looked as lovely as ever. I had an impulse to strip off her clothes and behold her totally naked. I sensed that I had become involved with someone truly wonderful. Her sexuality had overwhelmed me, and inexperienced as I was, I was nevertheless aware of that. I had fallen head over heels in love, and much later, when I finally drove home alone that night, I was afraid that I could lose her. I'd always been aware of the bigger, stronger, handsomer, more mature lover. Now, I was also conscious of my low standing as an Air Force enlisted man. How could I hold on to such a woman?

Once inside the vestibule of the club we parted. She went back to her platonic date, and I headed to the bar. One of Meyer Davis's society bands was playing a medley of Cole Porter songs. A local boy home from Colgate went to the bandstand and sang "In the Still of the Night." Everyone applauded, and I saw Margaret leaning into a tall middle-aged man and clapping as she nestled against him. Who in hell is he? I asked myself, already jealous. She said he was a friend of the family. Two years later she told me he was her first lover, her cousin's husband, a womanizer of note. Every young woman needs a man like that once in her life, she would say, teasing and fooling with my shirt buttons but hurting me all the same. She could not know how painful it was for me to imagine her with some local Don Juan whom she once used just for sex. But that night when I first saw her and the tall middle-aged man, I had a strong intimation of who Margaret really was. I knew she could be far too much woman for me, far too exciting. Yet, emboldened by drink, I was competitive and ready to do battle. I was in both camps at once: I was retreating and also on the attack. The drink seemed to keep everything in balance.

Before she left the club I was able to maneuver one dance with her, a slow fox-trot to "All of Me," the Colgate boy back again doing the vocal. I asked her if she would go to New York with me the next day. For the night, I said, brazenly and with confidence as we danced cheek to cheek, her hair brushing against my face. I had anticipated having to do a good deal of coaxing, but she answered at once that she would go anywhere in the world with me. "Why not New York?" she said, and she laughed. "As man and wife?" I told her we'd check in as Mr. and Mrs. Ben Billingsley, a name that popped into my head. Sherman Billingsley owned the Stork Club, and the music we were dancing to must have brought the Stork Club to mind.

"A good name," she said. "Margaret Billingsley. It beats Kelly." And we danced and arranged a time for me to pick her up in the afternoon. I had my father's car, a little money. There was joy in my heart and a wild expectation as to my future. I had made love to Margaret Kelly. I belonged to her. I did not feel—nor did I put into thought—the notion that she belonged to me. *Oh, God, I can't believe this is happening,* I thought, as I drove home tipsy. With the car radio on, I listened to a love song sung by Tony Bennett and I felt that I'd joined the adult world of love and romance and desperate longing.

•   •   •

We drove to New York on the Merritt Parkway, a two-hour ride. Margaret was wearing a brown tweed suit with a green and orange pattern woven into the material. She wore low-heeled brown shoes with a brown leather handbag and a white blouse under her jacket. She looked sensible, almost prim, very competent and adult. I by contrast was overwrought with anxiety and was sweating slightly in my blue blazer and gray flannel trousers. In the trunk I'd put a little carrying bag with a clean shirt and a toothbrush. She had a small suitcase—Amelia Earhart luggage. Our overcoats were thrown across the back seat. Thoughtfully, we'd even brought our overshoes in case it snowed.

Margaret did most of the talking. She told me about her job, supervising a large office of women employees at the Aetna Life and Casualty. It was wonderful in a way; she was pretty much her own boss. But what she really wanted was to sell insurance, and she was taking a sales course that met two evenings a week. At the moment her mother thought she was visiting a college roommate. Her mother had no idea that she had become Mrs. Benjamin Billingsley. And I was cute. She said that twice: "I always thought you were cute." And later, "You were so cute last night, waiting by the door."

I was young and maybe "cute" but I would have preferred another word, something to connote manly stature. Still, I warmed inside when she called me cute, not realizing then that her reason for responding to me so strongly was that I was noncompetitive, nonthreatening, adoring—and cute. As I grew to know her, I realized that strong men might attract her, and often succeeded with her, but what stirred her sexually was someone less aggressive, someone with whom she could let down her guard, drop all pretenses, and turn sensual without fear. She would let her pleasure move through her whole being until it reached a crescendo of ecstatic joy. With me she didn't have to worry about measuring up. She owned me.

I would learn all that in time, but in those first few hours in New York I was too full of adoration and love to think. We entered our small bedroom at the Commodore and fell in each other's arms, falling together onto the double bed. I was undressed and was undressing her, finally pulling her transparent white panties down over her dense growth and finding her oil-coated to the touch of my fingers. I played with her small breasts as she examined me. She noticed I was not circumcised, which surprised me, because I was unaware that young women knew about such things. I was very naive about women, and the fact that Margaret knew so much about life and life's pleasures fascinated me—and gave me pause.

That night we went to Greenwich Village, where we had dinner in a small bar called the Paddock; later we drank for several hours at Eddie Condon's. We sat against the wall and I thumped my feet and sometimes waved my arms and oohed and aahed in mock ecstasy to the trombone solos of Jack Teagarden and the delicious flights of melody on Pee Wee Russell's clarinet, like any college boy getting carried away with the music, an infectious brand of Dixieland in the heyday of the Dixieland revival. Everyone sooner or later went to Eddie Condon's, where the patrons were rich and good-looking and tried to recapture the Roaring Twenties.

Television was rudimentary in those days, but everybody read the vibrant novels about wealthy and successful Americans who pursued lives full of promise that ended in disenchantment. People who read *The New Yorker* and *Esquire* went to Condon's. So, too, did movie stars and what was called Café Society. Career girls two years out of Wellesley and young men who had gone to Yale, served in the armed forces, and were now carving names for themselves also went to Condon's. At Condon's there was that aura that comes when successful people with money get together and let their hair down. Condon's reminded me of the movie *Elephant Walk* in which a group of British colonials in Ceylon get drunk and play polo in a spacious house, ripping everything up. Hijinks amid good rousing music was a combination I fancied and responded to and I imposed it on Margaret. I was emboldened by the wine at the Paddock, and in any case Margaret had mentioned Condon's. She'd never been there. Condon's was her idea but to my taste.

It was nearly two in the morning when I became impatient over Margaret's long delay in the ladies' room. Finally I walked toward the back hallway and saw her leaning up against the wall, bending her fine head and her lustrous hair toward a tall man much older than I.

Astonished and frightened, I felt my face turn red, and I approached them, my heart pounding. He was staring into her eyes, himself quite drunk, a cigarette in his mouth, his own eyes telling her things about his sexual ability. I could see she was drawn to him. I've set her up for this, I thought. She warmed up with me, and now she's ready for him.

I didn't say anything, but that's what I felt. I felt my face go scarlet and tears welled up in my eyes; I was sure I'd lost her. But then she turned, as though she'd known I was there all the time, and introduced me. "I want you to meet my date," she said, and then, looking at the stranger, "I didn't catch your name?" I shook his hand, knowing I was the interloper, stumbling on a flirtation. They told me they'd met coming out of the restrooms. He'd said hello and she'd thought he was a co-worker at the Aetna, had him mixed up with someone else. It was all presented as something very routine, and when she and I returned to the table, I quickly ordered another round of drinks. In my panic I was sure she'd picked him up, that she wanted to dump me. I drank quickly, and so did Margaret, and the drink helped muffle the terror of betrayal. On the one hand I was in love and imbued with the power of a lover, and yet on the other I was fearful of losing everything.

We drained our drinks, then we left Condon's and returned to the Commodore where again we made love. Before I turned out the light I asked Margaret to hold still and not to move as she lay spread open on her back. I knelt down by her toes and looked up her body. Her stomach was sunk into her ribcage, and her small breasts lay flat on her chest like a boy's. The hair of her head was tousled and her eyes were once again like shining gems. Her legs were slender. Not to forget her feet, I kissed both of them and then turned off the light and curled up against her. It's time for the Billingsleys to go to sleep, I whispered in her ear. She giggled like a teenager and rolled up against me.

• • •

By August, now stationed in Sacramento, I was able to take a month's furlough. After many letters back and forth I was still in love with Margaret, having lost my heart to her in New York, although Margaret was not yet in love with me. Images of our lovemaking haunted me in the old World War II barracks where I crawled into my top bunk every weekday night at about ten. I'd tried picking up women during that winter and spring but often failed, and one time when a pretty secretary who wore braces on her teeth took me back to her apartment, I was impotent. I blamed it on the braces which gave her a lisp, but I suspect it was my love for Margaret. Something inside—my conscience—was keeping me true to her.

I did have an affair with another secretary, Evelyn Slade, who took me home and then after a few encounters tried to trap me into marriage. She drove me up to Reno in her Buick coupe, and once we got there she tried to get me drunk. I'd never met a woman who insisted that I drink, so I was on my guard. I pretended to be drunk when I wasn't and heard her suggest that we go to a justice of the peace. We could be married immediately, she said, and live together in a house off base and not in a barracks and if I made a career of the Air Force we could travel all over, maybe have some children, all medical expenses paid for, and we would have friendships with other airmen and their wives. Down deep I winced and led her on a bit before taking her to a room at the Mapes Hotel where I took her to bed, she all compliant and full of hope. Later she sat in a chair by the one bureau in the room, smoking a Kool, told me that we had to get a move on if we were going to get married. I pretended that I didn't know what she was talking about; I must have been drunk when I led her to believe that we might get married. She smoked and drank some beer we had ordered and talked and cajoled and then she gave up. "I knew I shouldn't have let you fuck me. You got what you wanted and now you don't want me. You're lying on that bed all satisfied. You're thinking, why pay for the cow when the milk is free? I know men," she said. She was not really furious, more resigned. "Oh why was I so stupid?" she said all of a sudden, castigating herself, her face distorted, her hand clutching the back of her neck.

We stopped for a drink on our way back to Sacramento. We pulled into a bar in Placerville where I drank too much and told her about Margaret. I ventured that I was already in love and that I could never marry anyone but Margaret, who was waiting for me back in Connecticut. She told me that I was a shithead who had misled her. "I didn't know you had a girl back home," she said, looking at me suspiciously. I assured her that I did, and eventually she came to believe me. We stopped at her place before she drove me back to the gate at the air base. She gave me some coffee and a sandwich and then we tumbled into bed, where I found quite suddenly that there were no holds barred any longer, no holding back things that might offend a sensitive and naive easterner such as myself. Her old phonograph was playing country western music, and we rolled about in her bed for what seemed to be forever as she moaned and cried out. I'd had so much to drink up in Placerville that I was able to contain myself until she turned me over and flung herself down on me with such force that she made my nose bleed.

Evelyn Slade was the last woman I would be with before my return to Margaret. The next day when I thought of her I was aghast, as unsettling images of her flashed across my mind. She had long, unkempt brown hair that billowed out, and when she fell on my chest and face, her hair was all over my head and in my mouth. Everything tasted so rich and ripe, her juices carried strong, pervasive odors, and my image of her was of a scary woman who appeared wildly out of control. We'd gone at it for a long time. Years later it occurred to me that the image of sex is more purely erotic than the event, as the event in itself can be unsettling. A woman out of control is like a mother gone mad. The sexual act should reach that climactic level of total passion, but it cannot cross the line where it produces panic. That day Evelyn crossed the line where passion goes mad, and when that happened I felt everything too much. I was attracted to the violence yet fearful of falling to my death, out of control and consumed alive by a woman who had lost all civilizing restraints. For decades a woman out of control was something I would fear.

• • •

At last my month-long furlough arrived. Since it was August, I went to Martha's Vineyard and Margaret came down every weekend to visit me. Each Friday she drove from Hartford to Woods Hole on Cape Cod and took the ferry over. She was granted a two-week vacation at the end of August so we could share our summer holiday, almost as husband and wife, although neither of us had yet dared to mention marriage. Though it was wrenching to see her leave on those first two Sunday nights before her vacation began, catching the last ferry to the mainland, it was far worse when I departed for Sacramento. I wept, as did Margaret, on the tarmac at the island airport, where I would fly down to La Guardia in a small Cessna. Events and necessities were tearing us apart. With our feelings for each other so exposed, ourselves so vulnerable—our parting was nevertheless, in hindsight, a grand melodrama, she waving as the Cessna banked over the airstrip, her figure diminishing to a dot and then gone amid the drone of the engine. Later, half asleep, somewhere over the Great Plains, I thought of Margaret as a partner for life, going with me wherever I went, enjoying herself through my joy, knowing that what was good for me would be good for her. She was a part of me and I would not let her down.

During our vacation Margaret slept in the stateroom of my father's forty-two-foot Alden schooner which he moored at the end of his dock in Harthaven. In theory, I slept in my own room upstairs in the house; there was no guest room in the converted boathouse that was our summer home, and young people who visited us would sleep on the boat, as did Margaret that summer. And so, after an evening out at a party in Harthaven or up in Chilmark, I would walk Margaret down to the schooner and we would quickly commence touching and undressing each other. Although Margaret had surprised me with her expressiveness in New York, she was even freer on the Vineyard. I told her that only the word *bliss* could define what I felt. "A surging bliss," I said. "It was just the most fantastic thing," she said, curling against me, her body limp and soft. And though I had been pleased by Evelyn Slade, even the time she had turned wild and bloodied my nose, I had never felt anything like I did with Margaret. I knew it was because I was in love and I suspected she had fallen in love with me.

Over her two-week vacation we were seldom apart. We sailed on a friend's yawl for an overnight cruise to Nantucket, and we went to parties and to the yacht club, but mostly we went off to the great white dunes up at Zack's Cliffs in Gay Head where we left our car off at the side of the old trail and then trespassed down to the beach. We'd walk up into the hollow of the dunes, and then naked, we'd amble above the high-water mark and look for driftwood. We always made love the same way, with her below me, her eyes closed and her legs wrapped around me. After it was over she would open her eyes and the bright overhead sun would burn into them and she would shut her eyes and shield them with the back of her hand and turn her face to the side and I would kiss her cheek.

Her soft stomach became tan and red as an Indian's and the furry triangle I liked so much would puff up in the sun, and the salt water would make it curl so I could toy with it as I kissed her breasts.

I must have kissed her several hundred times a day during our holiday. We were so young and so healthy, and with the Korean War now over, and with my father's money and her good looks and my discharge a year and a half away, we could project a rosy future. The gods could not have been more beneficent than they were in that summer of 1953. My parents thought we were in love, and there wasn't much we couldn't do with our lives.

I went back to Sacramento in a buoyant mood, secure in my trust in her. I had Margaret Kelly who swore to be faithful to me as I swore to be faithful to her and I had no reason to doubt her. Margaret had a small apartment in West Hartford that she shared with a fellow employee named Maggie Flanagan, whom I met only once—a big-boned woman with black hair in a bun. Everyone thought Maggie should have been a nun. Religious, hardworking, and not interested in men, Maggie was nevertheless a career woman who marched off to the insurance world every morning carrying a briefcase, walking on strong legs, full of pride. Maggie Flanagan eventually married her boss, but there was no intimation of any sexual life when I knew her, and thinking of her as Margaret's roommate was comforting. She was like a guard for Margaret. I had imbued Maggie with a strict moral code which I was sure she would impose upon her roommate.

And so the fall and winter went by. I carried out my duties for the Air Force, Margaret kept at her job, and we wrote long, loving letters to each other. Amazingly, Margaret had not become pregnant, which had been a concern of mine although we never discussed it. I did not want to use the pack of Trojans I had bought almost as a joke a year or so before meeting Margaret. I was afraid I would not do it right and would seem stupid at a critical moment. As for Margaret, she was Catholic and never mentioned birth control. I knew little about the rhythm method, and in any case we did not talk about such matters as we loved with high ardor, and because everything worked so well we never thought to question what we did.

I returned briefly over the Christmas holidays and we spent our last night at a motel on the highway outside Hartford, having dined holding hands over the table in front of a roaring fire at the Avon Tavern. Over the ensuing weeks our letters heated up, and in May, Margaret flew to California. We had not seen each other in four months and she had never been west. I took two days off, combined with a three-day pass, and on a bright California day I drove down to San Francisco and out to the airport, where I parked my Chevy Bel Air and went to meet her, the woman who held my heart.

I was nervous after the long separation, and she, being far away from home, was now in my care. I felt responsible for her, and she sensed my worries as I spoke evasively and suggested that we drive south and find scenic California and act like tourists. Knowing I was constrained and nervous, Margaret, who seemed so happy to see me, agreed that anything I wanted to do was fine with her. She snuggled up to me as I drove, her eyes smiling and shining like pure brown marbles. Her lips were lightly colored and her soft brown hair was in its accustomed bob, falling about two thirds of the way down her long, fetching neck. She was wearing a white blouse with a tan cardigan sweater over her shoulders. In the back was her Amelia Earhart suitcase about medium size, and I told her that I was impressed by the economy of her packing.

"It was cold back home," she said, "but I wanted to dress for California. I didn't take very much, just some money to get around on if you should leave me stranded some place," she said and she hugged closer to me.

I felt very grown-up, like my father. It seemed that I was reliving my father's life back when my mother was young and pretty like Margaret and so very loving, just as Margaret was. I had everything I would ever need right with me in the car, and in my pride I felt very accomplished. I lit up one of my infrequent cigarettes and settled back in my seat. The radio was playing Les Paul and Mary Ford, "Vaya con Dios, My Darling." Margaret, who did not smoke, opened the car window on her side and let the fresh California air blow in upon us as we drove on.

We found a motel down by the harbor in Monterey. It was past midnight by the time we registered at the desk and followed a sleepy middle-aged woman down a cement walk to our room. We were Mr. and Mrs. Benjamin Billingsley again, and once the door closed we jumped on the king-sized bed and began to undress each other. Margaret was wearing stockings and garters that attached to a garter belt, and when I removed her skirt I could see the bristly, almost fluffy pressure underneath the thin covering of her underwear. Margaret excited me as though I had just discovered a treasure; we made love at once and once more in the middle of the night when I rolled over on her and she instinctively, in a half-sleep, opened her legs for me and began to moan softly, asleep and dreaming. She gripped me up inside herself and I could feel the contractions and pressure she applied. I asked her how she was able to do that. This was the first time I had been squeezed up inside a woman. "I learned it at home. I practiced," she said.

"What?" I asked. Practiced! I couldn't imagine it. What did she mean? With a broom handle? A banana?

"I used a Coke bottle," she said. "Benjamin Billingsley, you know how boys give themselves pleasure for release? Well, so do girls. A friend told me that girls who can grip a man like I was doing—oh, Benjamin," she said, laughing, using our Billingsley alias. "It is so hard to talk about this kind of thing. Anyway, she said that girls who could do that held their lovers and were good in bed. So I practiced. Anyone can do it. I think a lot of girls do it."

"My God," I said. We were walking down by the pier at the harbor and I could see sea lions out on the jetty barking like crazed dogs. You could hear the barking from a mile away, I thought. And at the same time I was hearing this extraordinary news about how Margaret had practiced with a Coke bottle. While I loved the eroticism of Margaret's disclosure, it prompted pangs of jealousy. She had been with other men many times, I assumed, as we walked down the pier. So many men, all bigger and better than I. Big dicks going up inside Margaret was what I was thinking. I didn't even look at the sea lions. I stood beside her and let her enjoy them and then she left me to buy some fish carcasses to feed them and she threw out big bony slices of fish scraps and I watched her, simultaneously confused and excited.

We drove to Carmel and then across the state to Fresno before heading north again to Yosemite National Park. We stopped along the way for a long lunch consisting of Mexican food and steins of beer. At night we ate pheasant and drank two bottles of Almaden Grenache Rose, which was a California wine that had won a prize somewhere and Margaret knew about it and thought that in California we should drink California wines. We probably drank too much, but we were so young and so full of sexual need that it didn't seem to matter. Earlier we had pulled off the highway near Oakhurst and another time she played with me while I drove, causing the car to swerve toward the guard rails. Margaret was laughing afterward, saying I was cute down there and I remembered that word from our earlier days together. I was sated and felt unclean as I drove, and her use of "cute" irritated me.

At Yosemite we ambled arm in arm near our cabin, ate, and made love. We did not take any adventurous tours, although we walked about the park and got some idea of its grand beauty. I remember quite clearly the small cabin we shared at Yosemite and how it was connected to another cabin where a middle-aged couple with Missouri license plates on their Pontiac were staying. The walls were thin and we could hear them talk, just barely but distinctly. Margaret's sexual cries in the afternoon after our longest walk and at night and again in the morning were doubly exciting to me because I knew that other people were hearing her. It was almost like doing it in public, and because she was enjoying it so much, by extension I was perforce a great lover and I enjoyed having others know about that. But we were running out of time and soon would leave each other. Quickly we were on the road again, Margaret anxious to see San Francisco. Driving into Stockton we began to fool with each other, and I almost went off the road, much to Margaret's evident amusement. We were lovers and reckless.

In those years I must have had some inkling as to the ways of women, but I was almost totally preoccupied with the give and take within my own sex and how I stood as a young man among peers. I had given very little thought to women in my pursuit of being accepted by the guys with whom I had to contend on a daily basis. When I considered Margaret, I compared her to women in the movies, where she compared well indeed. And like the movie queens of the day, she had had love affairs with men. I tried to suppress all notions of her previous experience; I did not want them to vex me. While at the same time I allowed enough of her imagined past to give her a special allure that thrilled me, I elevated her to a level where no blemish or fault could exist.

We stopped for a beer somewhere near Livermore. We were both tired, and after our near-accident Margaret had tried to sleep. The bar seemed to be part of a motel complex, and as it was in the middle of the afternoon on a bright sunny day, we were alone with the bartender. Margaret was wearing one of my Brooks Brothers shirts, open at the throat. She had the sleeves rolled up and I could see veins on the inside of her slender arms. The bartender had his name, Mike, on a card pinned to his chest. He was a handsome man about Margaret's age—a year or two older than I—and was broad-shouldered, good-humored, and very Irish looking. I had noticed during my three years in the Air Force how Irish guys tend to compete with one another often to the point of fighting. While I could get along fine and most enjoyably with Irish men, the Irish among themselves seemed to be forever strutting about and one-upping one another in some ancient ritual. I had a friend named Kevin Baker who used to say that there wasn't any sense in being Irish if you couldn't be stupid, and with that he'd go off and pick a fight with another Irishman.

At the bar near Livermore I heard Margaret say to our bartender that she was out here in the West to set up a branch office for the Aetna Life and Casualty Company. "I'm from Hartford," she said. "They're sending me out as a regional manager. I'll be running things for Aetna just south of San Francisco, near Palo Alto," she lied, remembering the name from our trip down from the airport. I had pointed out the sign and said that Stanford University was nearby. I remember telling her about Ernie Nevers, the great legend of Stanford football. Now she was lying to a total stranger about opening up an office there. I saw him nod with appreciation and respect. "Well, I will have my own tavern some-day," he said merrily, wiping a glass with a towel, looking into Margaret's wonderful eyes.

"I am sure you will, Mike," she said to him. I sensed the old com-petition and a patronizing tone in her voice, she so obviously assimilated in the American dream machine, working her way to the top, destined to be the first woman president of a large insurance company. She was a star who could dispense kindness toward the bartender whose aspira-tions could only reach the ownership of his own bar.

I held my tongue. Let her lie to him, I thought. Perhaps under-neath the lies and the bragging she was flirting. Did she find him hand-some? He *was* handsome, I admitted to myself. He could whip me easily, I thought, and I quickly drank my beer. I ordered another and contin-ued to listen to Margaret.

"The trouble with the West," she was saying, "is that people here don't have the sophistication we have back east. Oh, sure, there are uni-versities and so forth and so on," she said, "but you see what I mean? Too much Hollywood and beaches and surf and sun and hanging around. It's probably the fault of the weather," she said. "At home, it's so damn miserable in the winter that we have to get out and bust our bot-toms, so to speak, to keep warm."

"Yeah," he was saying, agreeing with her. What was her point? Was she trying to impress him? I was getting edgy. I hated this. I hated Margaret. I had never seen her behave this way. She was always agreeable, a support to my thoughts and opinions and my own ramblings. I had never heard her just go on like this, winging it. It was obvious that she was building herself up at the bartender's expense and he must have been wondering why she was telling him about her successful life unless it was to impress him for her own needs, which would be her sexual needs. *And what's wrong with the guy she is with? Can't he get it up?* I could read his mind and I felt foolish.

I did not like show-offs, probably because my father didn't either. He had served in the trenches in the First World War, from June 1917 until he was unable to fight anymore, gassed by the Germans, his life saved by a comrade who pulled him back from no-man's-land. My father retained his "thousand-yard stare" for the rest of his life, often looking out into space as though searching for the sight of the Hun, the deadly Boche whom he had chased with his eyes narrowed to slits over his rifle for two years in France. A corporal in the infantry, he had attacked through the Argonne, until somewhere in the battlefield he collapsed from the deadly gas. Back when I was a child my father seldom discussed his own war, turning his attention to the Second World War as it was building in Europe and beginning to threaten us from the Far East. For reasons not too hard to fathom, the battle and the bestial conditions in the trenches had brought a gravity to my father's nature and he did not tolerate puffery, tomfoolery, or braggadocio. He liked the term "straight shooter" and employed it often as a symbol of respect. To my father, patronizing someone was a lapse in character, and while he might overlook a simple white lie, he wouldn't give a chance to anyone who was full of vainglory and pretension unleavened by wit.

Margaret Kelly was hurting my feelings with her flirtations. Her self-promotion was sickening, and I was doubting her loyalty. My father had learned the meaning of loyalty from "the lads," as he called them— the troops with whom he served. You never knew what he was thinking about when he stared into space, but you could guess that it was serious business. Outside, not too far away, was the Hun, and my father might just have to slide over the edge of the trench and go into no-man's-land again and find him and silence him and then return. To do that he had to depend on his lads absolutely, and because they had never failed him, his memory would lead him back to the place where people could be relied on and didn't lie or brag or make a fuss. Because of my father, whenever I saw poppycock coming my way I bridled. Margaret and her bartender irritated me no end.

We returned to my car and I stayed silent on our way to Oakland and over the Bay Bridge. Margaret listened to the radio and dreamed out the window, her thoughts far from me. She must have sensed my irritation and was drifting away until my mood would change with time. Bent as we were on the grand time in San Francisco, I carried with me a discomfort, almost a loathing that I could not shake. Margaret's senseless chatter may not have been in itself anything to worry about, yet it troubled me. She was a four-flusher and a flirt and potentially disloyal. I was pierced with disappointment and I was taking the episode in the bar very personally. I was twenty-four years old and I didn't know how to work through my feelings. I could not probe my reaction. The only thing I could do was stew about it. But beside me, Margaret was now animated and full of anticipation.

"Baghdad by the Bay," she said. "I have heard about San Francisco for so long, Ben. So long, and now the two of us can really see the city. I want to see Chinatown, and Nob Hill, and my mother told me to visit a restaurant called Julius' Castle. Also the St. Francis Hotel. Did you know that General MacArthur stayed there after he was recalled from Korea? Can we stay there?" she asked.

"It's kind of expensive," I answered, "but, what the hell, I have some money left. We might as well go all the way."

"We've already done that," Margaret said, leaning against me and trying to find my penis withdrawn under the folds of my trousers.

I pushed her hand away and told her that I had to concentrate, which was true, but I did not feel amorous. Maybe I was overtired. I began to think that she was all over me too much and too often. Why couldn't we just have quiet, neat sex without the loud crying, the thrashing, and the wetness and the smell and the feral cast in her eyes? I imagined her odor on me, even through my clothes, and I could not wait to take a shower. I felt unclean and rumpled and very disorganized, and I decided that I didn't look right for the opulent St. Francis. I opted for a smaller hotel, completely nondescript, behind the St. Francis on Geary Street, called the Ardmore. It would save me money. "It's for salesmen and weary travelers like the two of us," I said. "I don't think we are elegant enough for the St. Francis," and Margaret nodded and said that we could at least go over for a drink. "I want to be able to tell Mother that I was there," she said.

I looked at her and almost responded, *Then why don't you just lie and say that you stayed there? We don't even have to go near the place, just lie about it.*

I don't think Margaret knew that I was upset; she may have thought I was tired as I found a place off Mason to park my Chevy Bel Air, locked against the night. It was almost seven as we carried our luggage with us around the corner and down the street to the hotel. They had plenty of rooms and we took one on the fourteenth floor. "Enjoy your stay, Mr. and Mrs. Billingsley," said the bellhop, an older man who momentarily brightened me because he looked Italian and reminded me of Fisherman's Wharf and DiMaggio's Restaurant and the Buena Vista, which was a bar I had been to. If I show Margaret all those places maybe I'll feel better, I thought, as I tipped the bellhop.

"So this is San Francisco," Margaret said, looking out the window at a cityscape of buildings and then down to the street full of people still leaving work, going into bars, meeting boyfriends and girlfriends and already partying and moving on into the weekend. It was Friday night and we would have until 6:00 A.M. on Monday when I had to return for duty.

I lay on my side of the double bed and closed my eyes. Soon Margaret was next to me. "Time for a shower and then let's go on the town. Remember Chinatown and the St. Francis. But we must have dinner at Julius' Castle. Mother really insisted. I think she and Dad went there early in their marriage. Or maybe just before he died. I can't remember. Dad was always going to conventions for bankers and whatnot. He was away a lot and sometimes took Mother. Can we call for a table? Am I boring you?" she asked after a pause.

"I'm sorry," I said. I rose from the bed and went to the phone. I couldn't shake my mood. Why did she have to be so enthusiastic? As I talked with a man at the restaurant and made our reservation, I was thinking about the Kellys and told myself that I didn't give a shit about the Kellys.

Talk of her mother was tiresome and her brother Jim, whom I didn't know, looked like one of those tall, bony guys who could be all knees and elbows on a basketball court. I'd seen Margaret's snapshot of him and decided he was not someone I would warm to.

I was still irritated by Margaret's attentions toward Mike, the bartender. Whenever I thought of how she had acted, I boiled inside. It was such a minor thing, yet it seemed she had gone out of her way to make me mad. If that was her nature, we would be in trouble. As Margaret took her shower, I kept thinking that she had tried to hurt me.

•   •   •

We sat at the bar at the St. Francis. The top of the bar was covered with what looked like at least a thousand highly shined silver dollars that were neatly inserted into the wood. The St. Francis was not celebrating the Gold Rush but was inspiring thoughts of silver mines, Nevada, and gambling with silver dollars everywhere and lusty saloon dancers with their heels high in the air wearing garters and black stockings. As I finished my second martini, I was alive with lusty thoughts about the Old West. As I drank, good times with Margaret and even Evelyn Slade poked into my memory, and though my experience in saloon society was slight, I felt randy again and I squeezed Margaret's hand. We had made it to San Francisco. My mood had changed and I was my old self, full of adventure. Margaret responded and kissed me impulsively right on my lips as we sat at the bar.

After Julius' Castle, where we both ate pheasant and drank another bottle of Grenache Rose, I took Margaret to hear Turk Murphy's Dixieland band. We were in the nightclub of the old Fairmont and I tipped the maître d' well enough to get us seats up front. The room was crowded, and as Dixieland filled the room my feet pounded the floor, my voice rising with the pitch of the music, almost yelling at the conclusion of one trombone solo. Suddenly I was a wild man, totally released from the mood that had previously dogged me. Loud, half-drunk, I was clapping and stomping to all the old numbers—"Panama," "That's a Plenty," "Chinatown," "Muskrat Ramble," "The Saints Go Marching In." "You won't find this in Hartford," I yelled at Margaret over the din.

We had more drinks in the intermission, and then as Turk Murphy began his second set I realized that Margaret was anxious to leave. She had a good capacity for liquor; she was tall and rangy and seemed to have the kind of metabolism that could soak up alcohol. I, on the other hand, did not. I could drink in those days and did, but whenever I tried to extend an evening or a party I was in dangerous territory. I was at my best at the dinner hour. I could get sloppy after dinner, and as Turk Murphy played "After You've Gone" with me singing, "You'll feel blue, you'll feel sad, you'll miss the bestest pal you ever had, and..." Margaret began to make little gestures. She held my arm at the bicep and squeezed ever so slightly as though to say, "There, now, you'll be all right." Twice she rested her foot on mine to keep me from stomping on the floor of the nightclub. Her expression became severe on those occasions when I sang so loud that people at other tables turned to stare as if to admonish me. The band members, themselves, could not miss me at that front table, clapping and stomping, and they, who had probably seen everything, would not mind. But Margaret did, and finally she came out with what she had been suggesting in other ways. She asked me directly if we could go back to the hotel.

We walked back to Geary, our arms interlocked. I felt reckless and dangerous and brave as I strode through the dark night almost inhaling the thrill of San Francisco. It had been such a raucous and free-feeling evening, and I, thinking I was in charge, was leading my woman to our bed.

I fell sound asleep soon after my head found the pillow. Margaret was leaning into me and was naked, her right breast pressing against my left arm. Once she climbed on top and covered me with her body, but I was too tired. Just as I fell into a deathlike darkness I heard her say, "I love you" and I answered, "I love you, too," and dropped out of consciousness like a man struck on the head with a baseball bat. I had no dreams; I was so dead to the world a surgeon could have amputated my leg, or the atomic bomb could have fallen on Oakland. I slept lifeless, inert in one place, on my back and probably snoring loudly until sometime near dawn when Margaret again crawled over me. She couldn't sleep any longer, she told me, speaking softly through a partially closed mouth, her lips almost touching mine. Her skin was so soft and yet her body was athletic and firm and her small breasts were touching mine, nipple to nipple. I was erect, and when she sat back on me I went into her slippery opening and felt her contractions as she grabbed me so I could not slip out, she gently rocking back and forth on top of me. I could feel myself swell as I do just before I come and she must have felt it too because she cautioned, "Not yet, darling," and she climbed off and lay down beside me and then turned on her stomach. "I want you there," she said and I did not know what she meant. My first thought was that she wanted me up her anus—buggery or bungholing, I'd heard it called—and I shuddered. I couldn't do that. But then she said, "Go in me from the rear," and she raised her round curvy bottom to me so I could see in the half-light of dawn and the light from the bathroom her sex exposed with a profusion of hair, and I could not help but think of wild beasts in the rutting season.

"Oh, please," she was calling to me, so softly and urgently and breathlessly. I was new to all of this and startled and I was sure her awkward position would make it impossible for me to guide myself into her. She couldn't reach around with her hand to help and I was feeling increasingly foolish. I began to panic. "I can't do it," I finally said, and fell on my back. Margaret turned over then and began kissing me and when I was aroused once more she guided me into her and in our accustomed way we made love. Shortly I heard her cry so loudly that someone nearby could have justifiably called the police. I was fearful that she had died in my arms, and at the same time I felt the blood drip down from my right ear where she had bitten me in concert with her cries. I had been deeper inside her than ever and I felt, without putting it in words, that she was a professional at lovemaking and I was now her servant.

Late in the morning, as I lay on the bed amid the tossed sheets and blankets and drank beer ordered from room service, I watched Margaret pose for me. She was walking around the room naked, and then she sat before the mirror that hung against the wall over the bureau. She was brushing her hair and I could see her reflected in the mirror. Her nipples pointed upwards, which was something I hadn't noticed. Her waist was thin, but her rump was round and wide and before long, perhaps not too far off, it would begin to spread. I couldn't see her legs but I knew that they were very thin. Slim and shapely, she looked wonderful when she wore high heels. I loved it when she wore stockings and a garter belt. Once when I'd taken her out on Martha's Vineyard, to a party up in Gay Head, she had worn no underwear at all, just stockings and a garter belt. I recalled how she'd sat across from me, and when she shifted her legs in a practiced way, you could see up her skirt to her tangle of dark brown hair. I was sure that some of the women had noticed her pussy while men might miss it, involved as they were with making an impact and clever conversation. Women check out other women, I thought, and yet a man or two could have seen it. I certainly did, but I was looking for it. With her sitting in front of the mirror I thought of that and felt myself get aroused again. I moved from the bed and went over to her and pressed myself against her back. She turned and then began sucking me in front of the mirror. It took several minutes before I came into her mouth as I watched her do it. I could see this beautiful woman sucking me, naked and wanton and eventually draining me. The image of me standing there was very strong and followed me for years; I was showing off in front of the mirror and Margaret Kelly's lips were around me in admiration and lust. I had often posed naked, alone. Now I was posing with a woman. I held that memory of myself and Margaret for a long time.

When I was done she took me to the bed and spread her legs and guided my head down to her. I had already tried that back in Sacramento with Evelyn Slade and I performed well enough to once again raise her cries, and when Margaret's twitches had subsided, I went to the bathroom and brushed my teeth and took another shower. When I was drying myself, I felt a tremble in my right arm. I couldn't hold it still. I looked in the mirror in the medicine chest and saw that my eyes were sunk in their sockets like dark wounds. I don't know about other men but I can't handle this, I said, talking to my pained face in the mirror. One hell of a woman, I was saying, repeating it over and over again. I checked my ear where a scab was forming. I turned sideways trying to get a view of my back. There were dried scratch marks as though a cat had clawed me. I looked down at my small penis and wondered how I could keep going like this. Margaret would have to find someone else sooner or later. I remembered the bartender and then looked at my worn member: I was too puny, I thought, and looked again at myself and then raised my fingers to my forehead and began rubbing it, trying to rub away the tired look on my face.

•   •   •

I showed Margaret Chinatown, Fisherman's Wharf, the Coit Tower, and North Beach where we drank at Barnaby Conrad's Matador Bar. We had dinner at DiMaggio's down by Fisherman's Wharf, but what could have been a wonderful experience for me was boring to Margaret. She had no interest in baseball, and so the athletic grace of the brothers Dom, Vince, and Joe DiMaggio, all playing center field, was lost on her. The photos on the wall and the general ambience of the place— a shrine to the great Joe DiMaggio—escaped Margaret's attention. DiMaggio's was juvenile to her, and matters were not helped much when the veal parmesan that we ordered arrived tough and tasteless. I had two beers with dinner and vowed to stay very sober. The previous night's frantic drinking at the Fairmont, followed by sex, had made me very fragile. I told Margaret that she'd taken away my legs and she smiled at me lovingly and said, "It's not my fault that you have so much sex appeal that I can't stay away from you. You were so handsome at Julius' Castle. I could look out over all of San Francisco or so it seemed and then see you sitting across from me and it was as though I owned the world. Did you feel that way?"

I said that I had. In fact, the night before at Julius' Castle that was exactly how I'd felt. It was like owning a kingdom, and when Margaret said, "It's like being master of all you survey," she was speaking my mind. Lovely in the soft light, she was wearing a red blouse buttoned at the throat, and her mother's pearls shone splendidly in the silvery half-light of the restaurant. We had been sitting by the window on the second floor of what I gathered was once a private mansion perched on top of a hill. The restaurant offered sweeping views of the city and San Francisco Bay and Alcatraz and, far off, the Golden Gate Bridge. As dusk turned to night, hundreds of lights began to flash below us, and up there with money in our pockets and good looks and youth and as much Grenache Rose as we could drink, we did feel like a king and a queen, and the citizens who lived and worked and scurried about below us were serfs.

Alas, the evening at DiMaggio's was a letdown. Try as I might to instill spirit into the dead tone of the night, I kept drawing blanks from Margaret. She aspired higher: the St. Francis, Nob Hill, and Telegraph Hill. These were areas of the city that resonated with class and were places where wealthy men and stylish women would appreciate her beauty. As I looked at her with a growing sense of dismay, I guessed that all our lovemaking had turned her head. She was beginning to see her-self in queenly terms, as some grand lady who was also a femme fatale who lusted openly, suggesting pleasure in the flush of her face and the allure of her eyes. As a woman who could turn the heads of the most sophisticated men, she was understandably unsuited for DiMaggio's, a place that attracted tourists and sports fans, a middling restaurant with the most common of menus. Time was running out. Was this the best that I could offer?

Margaret wore a slinky black cocktail dress that night. I remember wondering if she wore panties. It pleased me to think she was reckless, with nothing underneath except a garter belt and flesh-colored nylon stockings hitched halfway up her thighs. She was wearing her mother's pearls again, and while she looked a bit overdressed at the Matador, where we had cocktails, she was extremely overdressed for DiMaggio's. I told her I would take her to the Buena Vista afterward for Irish coffee and she could pretend that she had just come from a snappy party somewhere. "Anywhere but here," she said, and she looked around with her nose slightly elevated like Myrna Loy in the *Thin Man* movies. Her bright eyes had turned dark, and she tapped the table with the fingertips of her left hand to show her unease. "I feel as if tourists are staring at me," she said. "They are," I answered, and for the most part we dined in a strained silence.

I felt the tension slip away at the Buena Vista as the Irish coffees took effect. We sat at the bar and Margaret was able to swing around on her seat, showing a flash of thigh when she felt like it to two men who were at the table behind us, sitting at a lower level and looking up at us at the bar. We seemed to get quite chummy in a very short time, Margaret wiggling on her seat and joking with the two of them about their work. "I want to know if you are famous," she teased. "I like to discover talent," she was saying, and though I was now in a relaxed mood and ready to go along with almost anything in the aftermath of the difficult dinner at DiMaggio's and the rather unpleasant afternoon walking about Chinatown, which had not impressed Margaret—too dirty and too crowded and too American—I could still sense a phony comment when I heard one. She did look terrific and by now her eyes were reflecting the light of the bar and sparkled like glass. She'd brushed her hair in the ladies' room and it was lustrous; her nails were slippery red like a Revlon ad. She was running on about art and a show she had apparently seen at the Guggenheim in New York. The two men knew of it and were impressed. They bought us drinks and we in turn bought them a round. Jolly at the bar but not without some disapproval, I listened to Margaret extol a group of artists—the Ashcan School in New York—and then chastise her new companions that the West Coast could not produce great art. "Name me one," she challenged. "Name me a great California artist."

In the cab back to the Ardmore I reached up inside her dress and felt her stomach from the garter belt south. Her thin panties would not hide her sex and though not naked, she had nevertheless exhibited herself on the bar stool. I asked her about showing her sex to her friends at the bar and she responded that they'd seen it all before. "But not yours," I said. And then quite suddenly I began to weep. It was all too much for me. I could not stop crying, and Margaret told the cab driver to keep driving around the city. Finally I stopped. The crying jag had lasted almost twenty minutes. Margaret held me to her bosom and I shook against her. My chest was heaving and tears were streaming down my face and through my shirt. I had fallen apart.

•   •   •

I'm not sure what I told myself. In those days I would not have prodded too deep below the surface in order to find the cause of my collapse. I do know that I did not write to Margaret. She flew back to New York while I was en route to Sacramento in my Bel Air. Neither of us talked about my breakdown in the taxi. Back on the base I turned my attention to my job and getting on with Air Force life. I was ashamed of myself for breaking down. I did not know what had got into me back there in the city. I must have been exhausted and overwrought. I only knew that I wasn't going to write her. I was afraid to. I knew that much. But I didn't know why I was afraid.

Margaret wrote me several times, the last two letters chiding me for failing to respond. "Are you on a secret mission?" she asked in one letter. "Are you involved in the Cold War in some secret way? If so, find a means to let me know so I will stop worrying." At my end I just let her blue envelopes pile up in my footlocker. I read each letter once and then filed it away.

Five months went by and still I did not write her. I started seeing Evelyn Slade on occasion, and every time I saw her I realized how different she was from Margaret. When I thought of Margaret, it was only in relation to Evelyn. Whereas Margaret was slender, Evelyn was lumpy. Her breasts were larger and drooped and she was not as lush below as Margaret was. On my drives back from her tiny little house on a side street behind the Ford dealership in Sacramento, I did think how, compared to Evelyn, Margaret was really unique and how very pretty she was, but down deep I also felt relief that I was not with Margaret. It was fun to fool around with Evelyn now that I had disabused her of the idea of marriage. It was not very romantic, and there was no great passion, but Evelyn allowed me to be a rather slapdash lover. In fact, with Evelyn I could just lie there in the dark and listen to the country western music that she loved. Though I never knew which singers I was listening to, her hi-fi record machine kept dropping LPs into the late hours. I could lie on her bed with her beside me and smoke my Marlboros and sip on a Budweiser and let the night pass into morning. I didn't have to do anything or be anybody with Evelyn Slade. She just liked my company. It was a relief.

In October I heard from Margaret again and this time I did not file her letter away. She was five months pregnant, she told me. And "quite frankly" she wanted to know what I was going to do about it. I hadn't written. "What are you trying to pull?" she asked.

•   •   •

The Korean conflict, as it was then called, was over. By April in Sacramento the sun, rising in the sky, would shine on the tarmac of the aprons that led to the long runways, and through the warm months it was a joy to work at seven in the morning. In autumn it was still warm though breezy and wet but not yet biting cold and raw as it gets in winter. In winter, when we went out to the big converted bombers at dawn we had to bend into the wind and keep our hands deep inside the pockets of our field jackets. Had it not been for Margaret's condition, perhaps some enthusiasm for duty would have persisted, but with the war long over, men being discharged, and everything being scaled down, military esprit had disappeared and my job, almost civilian in nature, was becoming increasingly casual. No more parades. No more practicing on the firing line. Even saluting was falling by the boards. A little tennis on weekends. Evelyn Slade to lie beside three or four nights a week. Saturday nights were followed by long, lovely slow-motion Sundays when we would drink Bloody Marys at the Onyx Room and buy the *San Francisco Chronicle* to read over an expansive brunch at Caulfield's Cafeteria and finally go back to her place for a nap and some fooling around. "Let's go home, honey, and fool around," she would say as I was working my way through the sports section of the paper. Dinner at the Capitol Tamale Café in downtown Sacramento and then a movie and at about 11:30 I would drive my Bel Air back to the base for another week of relaxed work on the flight line. Although Evelyn had a scary, wild streak in her that I had experienced after our abortive trip to Reno, she was basically a woman who wanted comfort. And she wore a diaphragm. "If I was to get pregnant, everything I'm working for would go down the drain," she said. "No siree Bob! It's obvious you aren't a man for marriage," and she would look down at her formidable bosom for confirmation. I liked Evelyn Slade. How could I not like her?

When Margaret sent me her terrifying letter I was reminded of Dreiser's *American Tragedy*. I was aware that knocking up a girl was serious business with much attendant misery. I knew that this was not your standard case of serviceman meets girl at bar and gets her pregnant. In that scenario one is dealing with two strangers. In my case I was dealing with a woman whom I had loved madly. Though she irritated me with her phony posturing and wore me down with her sexual appetite, it was conceivable that I could overcome my fear that she was too much for me. Though Margaret was from Delaware, her father had been a vice president of a bank and my father had heard his name. I was not involved with some secretary I had picked up at the piano bar of the Capitol Tamale Café. The honorable thing, indeed the only thing, for me to do was to marry Margaret. But deep down I was afraid. I couldn't marry anybody. Deep down I knew I couldn't handle it.

•   •   •

The chaplain was calling me "son." He was a handsome man about forty years old who wore his uniform with campaign ribbons that showed he had been in the European theater in World War II and in Korea. One ribbon had a cluster that indicated something very special and honorable, but I did not ask what it was. Had he not worn little chaplain insignia on his lapels I would have taken him for some ground control officer; he did not wear wings.

"Son," he said. "I know what you're going through. You fall for a girl, you think you are in love, and the next thing you know the girl is with child. Yours. Now, our position on this is, it is better for one person, in this case the child, to suffer a little bit than to have three people—both parents and the child—suffer a lot over the course of a lifetime together due to a forced marriage. And we can hope for the best as to the type of adoptive parents the baby will be living with. Properly placed, the child in question should have a fine, normal, and healthy family life. It may be a blow to your girlfriend's ego, but the people who will end up raising the child will be far better and more loving than she could ever be. Of course, I have not met her, you understand, and you say that she is a wonderful girl, but how wonderful is it to get pregnant like she did? And now she wants to force your hand and drag you to the altar."

"I don't want to get married," I said. "I can't tell my father, for one thing. I can't tell him that I screwed up like this," I said, and my eyes were welling with feelings of shame. I had never said that before, not even to myself. But it was true: I couldn't face my father with this. I had already screwed up in college and had to leave. I was inept at the things that he valued such as carpentry and trout fishing. I was a fumblefinger, he said. I was maladroit. I couldn't even have an affair with a nice Catholic girl from the Aetna Life and Casualty Company without knocking her up. Why, he would think, would you have sex over and over again with someone who never protected herself and you don't even wear a rubber? I couldn't tell him that I had never used a rubber and was afraid of them, afraid that I would fumble and be a fumblefinger—and fail.

"No," I said after a pause, "I won't marry her. I can't do it," I said, knowing that I couldn't face it—my father, Margaret, the whole horrendous mess I'd gotten myself into.

"Then it's settled," the chaplain said. "We've met three times now and each time we have come up with the same result: you do not wish to marry Miss Margaret Kelly. And our policy," he said, staring at me with his very clear blue eyes, "our policy is to assist you in maintaining your freedom. If need be, we will send you to another base. We are prepared to do that and have done it before and we do not leave forwarding addresses. If need be, we can shelter you here while you do your nation's work. Let's see," he said, as he looked at a sheaf of papers on his desk stuck into the blotter holder. "You are due for a discharge the beginning of 1955. You can go back to civilian life or you can reenlist if this thing doesn't die down. If Miss Kelly wants to make trouble in some way…if that happens, we can take you back, probably with a promotion, and send you to one of our bases in Germany. I don't see why that can't be arranged."

I studied the chaplain, who was a major and though perhaps a spiritual person at heart was all business and seemingly very secular in this kind of situation. I knew I had lucked out. First, he was a Protestant of some kind and not a Catholic, who might have sided with Margaret. And he seemed to have no interest other than to protect his men from outside complications. He showed no pity for Margaret. He had been to war and he thought with a military mind. Now he was telling me what we would do. "You take this name and address and I will arrange that you get all the three-day passes you need and even some emergency leave time if you need it. You take this address and this name and you go over to the Department of Social Services in Sacramento and they will send you to someone in San Francisco and you follow their suggestions. I will have it all arranged so that the baby will be born at the St. Francis Memorial Hospital. The agency people will be there at the time of birth. The mother will never see the child, and the baby will be with adoptive parents almost instantly. We have gone through this before. There is a demand, a considerable demand, for children from parents such as you and Margaret Kelly. All you have to do is to go through the procedure and sign certain papers and get Margaret to sign her papers and get Margaret a room somewhere to recover in and do anything else you think you can afford to do to make her comfortable and to keep her from making trouble, and I underline that last part, and this whole thing will be over. I can arrange for the processing of the paperwork from here. You just be sure that you do what you can do to help her. She is flying in soon, you say. You say she has given notice at her job. So far no one knows that she is pregnant. She will need an apartment or a room in the city to wait for the time to come. You will need your days off. No sweat," he said encouragingly. "We have handled many, many cases like yours, although, as I said, this one seems a bit different in that the woman was your girlfriend from home. The point here is that you can't change your mind on this. This sort of thing entails a lot of work. Don't blow it."

"Margaret will be coming in two weeks or so," I said. "I will have to meet her at the airport. I can get her a room next weekend. I should stay with her for a day or two. I'll have to call my father for money. I'll just have to face him over the phone," I said, feeling the full impact of my words.

"As the base commander said the other day, he said to a group of us at the club, 'Gentlemen, the war is over. Now let the civilians go home and let *us* get back to the old days. Here's to the old days,' he said and we all toasted the old days. We know. In the old Army Air Corps we took care of each other. Let's say we are back in the Army Air Corps again and we're in this thing together. And don't worry about your father. You are an airman. Think about it." He stared at me then and finally concluded by saying, "I hope you appreciate all this, son. If God can forgive you, so will Margaret Kelly," and as he mentioned God I noticed for the first time a stainless steel crucifix standing behind him on a long table covered with manila folders.

"What about myself?" I asked looking at him, suddenly emboldened by his pep talk. "Can I ever forgive myself?"

"You will never forgive yourself," he said. "You can only try to forget about it."

·　·　·

She was about midway down the line of passengers coming through the door: everyone angled toward the exit, some in fine clothes and others dressed casually as though a plane trip from New York was like going to the market. Margaret was carrying the same handbag she always carried and she was wearing a tan trenchcoat that she had purchased in Hartford soon after we started our affair. She walked with a distinctive forward bend, as though she were leaning into the wind. I had forgotten how tall she was—five feet nine, nearly six feet in heels. But it was her face that threw me off: I had always thought of her as having an oval face, and now within five months it had grown round and chubby. She showed the beginnings of a double chin, and the overall impression was not of a tall and slender woman who might be a fashion model if she got rid of her bob and did something fashionable with her hair. Rather she gave the impression of being a physical education teacher or maybe a female basketball player who had grown soft now that she no longer ran the court. She had lost her graceful ways and was lumbering up to me.

I had been waiting for her, having arrived early. I'd drunk a couple of vodka and tonics as I waited and was thus bolstered somewhat, but I could not shake the notion that I was a traitor. In my head was the idea that I should not have gone to the chaplain and said what I'd said. If I were looking for spiritual guidance, I should have gone to a priest because Margaret was Catholic. The whole idea of talking behind her back to a Protestant chaplain was now odious to me, and though I was committed to following his directions, I did not like it. I felt duplicitous, sneaky, and disloyal. Soon we were sitting in my car talking about the weather and how things were back in Hartford and Delaware and other mundane subjects, dodging the main topic, and all of the time I felt very uneasy. I was a traitor, but worse, I was a coward.

"I have taken steps," I said finally, staring straight ahead, my eyes on the road.

"Steps?" she asked. "Look…no one at home except Mother knows why I am out here. All they know is that I have put on some weight. I've quit my job.…What steps? What have you arranged?"

"I went to the base chaplain and talked our situation over and he was the one who set things up for you, you know, helping me get a place for you to stay until the baby is due and then for some time afterward and he is the one who set things up with the various agencies and the woman, Mrs. Restelli, who is sort of your case manager."

"Various agencies?"

"I wrote you about that. In order to put the baby up for adoption you go through a lot of paperwork. The state of California will take over the whole project and the baby will have a very fine home."

Margaret stared at me in disbelief: "You haven't changed your mind? You haven't budged? And I don't like the word 'project,'" she said, and she continued to look at me and I could see her dark, almost lidded eyes. "I don't like the word 'project,'" she said again. "This is our baby and we should raise it in a good home of our own. You have only a short time to go and we will be back home again. We can stay at Mother's. Her house has plenty of room. Only while you are finishing college, of course. Then we can move out and start our own life. We can have a great life. We love each other. I just don't understand you."

I was not sure I understood myself. Yes, I loved her. But I couldn't marry her because I was not ready for it. I couldn't handle it. It was all so lame, but that is what I would tell her. At the time, though, riding in my car, I said nothing. She could believe what she wanted to believe. I had to get her into her small one-room apartment and get her organized. I would take her to dinner. Maybe we would sleep together. It was in the back of my mind all of the time. I did not want to be told after dinner that I had to drive back to Sacramento.

Margaret's apartment had a bedroom and bath with an alcove in which there was a refrigerator, a stove, and a small table with four chairs for eating. A bay window bellied out over Jones Street. She was about an equal distance from the St. Francis Hotel and the St. Francis Memorial

Hospital. She could walk to the delivery room if she was able to do so. I assumed she would call a taxi when the time came, but I wanted her nearby so the cab ride would be short, as would a potential police car ride or a ride from a total stranger. She would be alone with her condition—what one called a "delicate condition" in 1954.

I was able to park out in front of the apartment building, and I carried her two suitcases up the one flight of steps to her room. I had been given the key by the landlord, and earlier I had brought over a vase of roses and bottle of scotch, two bottles of wine, and four bottles of Lucky Lager beer. I poured two scotches after we were settled in, and we sat at the table and drank in silence as Margaret's eyes scanned the out-of-doors through her bay window.

"Well, here we are," she said. "You and me in San Francisco, once more."

I was nervous about where she might be going so I intervened and asked her about money. I wanted to be helpful: "Do you have enough money for yourself?"

"I brought a check for three thousand dollars and I have some money in my bag—a couple of hundred. I cleaned out my checking account at home. I didn't get a nickel from the Aetna because I quit. Had I been fired, I would have received some very nice severance pay, thank you. But no. I had to quit. I left some people back there who are very upset with me. You know how it goes: 'We train you and get you on your feet and get you doing a good job and then you quit with no explanation and all of our training is down the drain.' That sort of thing. Of course, Mother knows why I am here and we know what she expects of you."

"Let's wait on that," I said, weakly trying to dodge the bullet that I knew was already in the chamber ready to fly. "I want to take you to dinner and get you all relaxed and adjusted to California after that long flight. You look very well, by the way," I lied. I did not like her so full in the face. She looked like a typical housewife, and I suddenly couldn't imagine her in New York or anywhere else that was interesting.

"I have been covering up my tummy for all this time," she said. "I strap myself in with a corset. Look here," she said and with that she rose and turned from me, and after kicking off her low-heeled shoes and wiggling and bending and going through contortions, she was able to free herself from the corset. It lay on the floor, a white blob of elastic and cloth looking like something worn by older women who lived in factory towns and who tried to look slim even though they had fat stomachs from eating greasy food. I had seen ads for corsets and I could imagine the women who wore them. But there she was now facing me and I could see the swelling in her middle.

"We'll have to buy some maternity clothes," I said. "Maybe tomorrow. I'll buy them for you," I said. "My father sent me some money."

"You told him about us?"

"I had to. I had no money for all of this," and I waved my hand in a gesture of helplessness.

"What did he say... I mean about us? What was his opinion?"

"My father's opinion was that I was a damn fool. Those were his words. 'Damn fool,' he said. He didn't go any further. He sent me some money so I could set you up here and get back and forth to the city to facilitate matters and all."

"He didn't tell you to marry me?"

"I told you he just called me a damn fool."

"A damn fool because you weren't going to marry me or a damn fool because you got me pregnant?"

"I don't think of myself as getting you pregnant," I said.

"Then who did?" she countered.

"You got yourself pregnant. You were the—what would I call it?—the leader in all of this."

"I'm a good lay? Is that what you are trying to tell me? But it takes two to tango. I didn't get myself pregnant. *You* got me pregnant. Your father didn't say anything about that? You mean he didn't address that?"

"No. Tell the truth, I can't remember. I was too shook up. I blurted it all out to him. He said he would send some money. I don't really know what he said. Or thought, or meant, by 'damn fool.'"

"Great," Margaret said with sarcasm. Her eyes were dark again and her eyelids were beginning to lower. I rose up and went for another drink. "Let's eat," I said. "I don't want to get into all of this now. Let's try to relax after your trip. I'm your friend. I want to help," I added, looking at her, a drink in my hand, both of us pitiable and lonely in her small apartment.

That night after many glasses of wine, and feeling the effects not only of the wine but also of San Francisco—I had taken her to the Top of the Mark for more drinks before dinner at the Blue Fox, a classy, well-known restaurant where we ate pheasant once again and drank on and on and made moon eyes at each other as we had so often in the past—after a wonderful warm and tender evening we tumbled into each other's arms in her freshly made queen-sized bed. We could sense the dark night below us right outside our window, we could hear voices and feel the emotions of other people as we held each other.

We were on familiar ground. Loving each other was so normal and enfolding and enclosing; it was as though she just took me way up inside herself and squeezed me and held me firmly and brought me to her so that I was deep within her soul or her inner life. It was far more than sex. It was timeless possession. Within her I fell into her ownership.

In the morning she cooked us breakfast from a small supply of groceries we had hurriedly purchased the day before. She'd even remembered to get me marmalade, which I liked on my toast, along with a slice of bacon wrapped up inside to make a little sandwich. We sat there eating runny eggs and toast and bacon and drinking cup after cup of coffee. She was wearing a nightgown and I was in my shorts with my shirt unbuttoned and open at the chest. That last breakfast was so intimate and yet, under the circumstances, it was confining, too, and it made me feel claustrophobic. I felt trapped in the room with the smell of sex and bacon and eggs and toothpaste and perfume coming from the bathroom. I was on my third cup of coffee when she brought up the forbidden subject again.

"Well, Benjamin Billingsley, what will it be?" she asked.

I was already on my guard. I was gulping my coffee, readying myself for my departure now that I had got her settled on Jones Street; she had an apartment and money and all of San Francisco to explore while she waited for the baby to come. I said as naively as possible, "I don't know what you mean. What do you mean?"

"The baby. We should keep it and we should get married. I looked into Reno. We can be there in four hours or so. Just drive over and get married."

"I've been through that already," I said, deflecting her plea.

"What are you talking about?" she asked, and there was an edge to her question.

"Back some time ago this woman I knew tried to get me drunk and then tried to get me to a justice of the peace. I outfoxed her," I said.

"I didn't get drunk, I just acted drunk to see what she would do, see how far she would go. Her name was Evelyn…"

"I don't give a fuck what her name is. I am trying to be serious. I don't care about your dumb adventures with some girl you picked up in a bar in California somewhere. I am talking about us."

"I'm sorry," I said. "I can't do it. I just can't."

"Last night you said you loved me. Doesn't that mean anything?"

"We were making love, we said it to each other like we used to do, but you never wanted to say it. I was the one that said it."

"I didn't love you until our trip together. I came out here to see you, to be together, to find out how I really felt. I fell in love with you all the way, deeply in love on that trip. I couldn't believe it when you didn't answer my letters."

"When I was so in love with you, you were playing me along?"

"We had great sex together. I don't mind saying that. Originally I went along because I liked you so much and we seemed so free with each other. I thought you were so cute. When we were alone out here and traveling together and just being a couple like a married couple, I fell for you all the way. I want you," she said, and her eyes were pleading with me and were welling up with tears.

"I can't do it," I said again. I rose and began buttoning my shirt. My pants and sport jacket were on a chair and I walked over to get them.

"Are you leaving me then? Are you leaving me like this? Are you walking out on me? Almost six months pregnant and you are leaving me? Some kind of a skunk sneaking out of sight, some lizard ducking away like a snake in the grass…"

"Look," I began.

"Look, bullshit," she said.

She was standing now and her stomach was pressing out against her nightgown. "If you leave me I'll kill you," she said and her eyes were now on fire like shiny coals, glistening and burning from beneath her forehead.

"I can't help it." I was stumbling toward the door.

"Some day you'll pay for this, you asshole." She was yelling now. As she lunged at me, I slipped out the door and made a quick exit down the flight of stairs. From the sidewalk I saw her in the open window. Her round face looked absurd. Her unbrushed hair was wild, sticking out from her head on either side and her black eyes were burning at me. "Come back, you bastard!" she yelled.

I waved and as I stepped into my car I heard her say, "I hope some woman does to you what you did to me. You bastard!" she yelled again and then her last words: "You're breaking my heart, come back." But I was already away from the curb and gaining momentum.

•   •   •

For many years I chose to justify my actions concerning the pregnancy of a young woman I once thought I loved and to the daughter who was born of our union. I rationalized my retreat from the affair in very simple terms: I didn't love her, the marriage wouldn't have worked, and in any case it was her fault. I did not allow myself to probe any further. I did not allow my mind to tell me the truth: I should have done what was honorable. I should have done what was right.

I was a callow youth with deep fears. Behind my smiling face was a mind wracked with a sense of ineptitude. I thought I could never cope with a wife and child. And I could not cope with Margaret's sexuality, a sexuality our lovemaking had unleashed. I was too timid. She was too strong. I could get swallowed alive by her. I wasn't up to the job. I'd never make it as husband, father, wage earner, or lover. I was best at having affairs and doomed to fail over the long haul. Or so I told myself.

To understand my early adulthood and how I arrived at my decision to walk out on Margaret, I must go back to New Britain, Connecticut, to the 1930s and how it was.

Chapter 2

Toward the end of the Depression, when I was eight or nine years old, I imagined myself growing up to become a very brave man, an American hero. I habitually scanned a set of books my father owned on the Great War. The illustrations depicted handsome men either in combat or preparing for the fighting in France, a magical land. The Marne, the Argonne Forest, Verdun...exciting place-names jumped off the pages like cannon shot. In a book titled *Fixed Bayonets* there were pictures of more great-looking, straight-featured Americans. I liked the American helmet, a saucer-shaped object that had a sleek look. In contrast, the German helmet looked like a heavy bonnet clamped down over the ears. Thick and ponderous, it was like the Teutonic personality I had noticed in German maids and cooks in my hometown. The saucer-shaped American helmet was neat, light, and fast, as if made for a half-back. Furthermore, it was daring in that it exposed the sides of a soldier's head. One illustration showed a soldier using his helmet as a cooking pot. He appeared to be stirring a bowl of stew, and I thought of how the men roughed it in the great adventure of the trenches. It would be like camping out, only with artillery blasts piercing the quiet chatter of the day and bullets going ping-ping over the trenches, often hitting some object—maybe human—a thud against flesh and leather and a ping against metal.

I liked the idea of war. My friends and I played war games. I fashioned wooden swords and my father made me several wooden pistols. I loved the smell of powder from a cap gun. Always, we chased one another about waving a war club or a toy gun. *Bang,*...You got me, and then an exaggerated fall to the ground. Sometimes when I fell, the victim of a mortal wound, my dog Brownie would come over and lick my face. I was saved by my dog the way an Alpine hiker is saved by a Saint Bernard or a real soldier is saved by a buddy, rushing through shot and shell to lend aid.

Overhead an airplane could fly by and we'd all strain our necks to see it. Our maid, Anna, would run out into the yard at the sound of its drone in the sky. Once the dirigible *Hindenburg* was scheduled to glide above us on its way to Europe from New Jersey. We had been alerted, and we waited outside our house to see it pass. My mind tells me that we waited to no avail, yet I do seem to remember seeing it, a great gray shadow, cylindrical and scary like some unknown, unimaginable *thing* in the sky, sure to trigger acrophobia as I could imagine it falling with a hundred passengers in full scream. Though hard evidence is lacking, and though I doubt my memory, I can feel, even now over fifty years later, the fear when I imagined it dropping from so high aloft. Now, as I ask myself why the *Hindenburg* would fly over New Britain, Connecticut, I can only conclude that the dirigible was advertising itself as it journeyed on to Hartford and Boston and then out to sea. In any case, it was uncommon to see an airplane then, much less a dirigible.

The *Hindenburg* exploded in 1937 when I was seven years old, so my memory of seeing it must date close to that year. As for acrophobia, I have suffered that affliction for a lifetime. It may have started with the *Hindenburg* or with nightmares about the doomed airship. Or perhaps it started on the high cliffs on the way into Hartford, near Trinity College. There was a crevice that my father would skirt, driving along its edge in our Packard. I remember hiding against the door, away from the dreaded drop. What would happen if a tire blew so close to the edge? I hid against the door and shrank from my fear.

• • •

I venerated my father, who had served in the trenches in 1918. He'd earned the Verdun Medal, which I discovered in his belongings after his death in 1963. He also had a Purple Heart to his credit and the distinction of giving away his corporal's rank to another soldier who needed the extra pay. That, too, I learned after his death. During his life I was aware only that he'd seen a good deal of fighting within the confines of trench warfare. Finally, I learned from someone else who'd served in Europe how my father had gone time and again into no-man's-land on errands of great danger, the details of which I did not pursue.

In fact, he never spoke of the Great War and eschewed all parades on Armistice Day, although on two occasions I persuaded him to take me to watch. I recall a fellow veteran of the Yankee Division seeing my father in the crowd and calling, "Hey, Bill," and that was it.

Modest in his silence, my father inadvertently instilled in me a strong tendency toward hero worship. I often thought of him in his brown army uniform, his helmet spattered by mud and perhaps dented from a rifle shot, and I revered him. I glorified his strength and his return from the war even though I never said a word of this, nor did he. My father was usually in view, and I could touch him if I chose, yet he was aloof, and through my childhood there was not much touching or hugging. When we walked together on Main Street, he did not hold my hand. He never came to a school play or a school conference. He wanted me to learn how to fish, to catch trout (which was a fatherly gesture on his part), but he was not tactile with his affection. Affection showed in his face but journeyed no farther, and lessons in trout fishing were very painful. I never knew what to do and always snagged my line on a twig. One day as I stood there on the verge of tears he told me to go for a swim. Forget fishing, he said. I went upstream where there was a small dam and a pool of cold brook water and I swam in the chill of late April. My father caught two trout while I shivered in defeat by the dam.

If my father was inaccessible, which is to say remote, even though he was at home each evening, a presence before my very eyes, his modesty and disdain of attention intensified my hero worship. But I had to look elsewhere for someone in whom I could lodge my fantasies. I looked to the newspapers for subjects of adulation. If there is a psychological profile of a fan, surely I filled it. Not being able to get my silent father to play the hero role, I looked to Robin Hood and then to the Knights of the Round Table. From these worthies I moved on to the sports pages of the *Hartford Courant* and found Larry Kelley and Clint Frank, football stars at Yale. In 1940, at ten years old, I discovered Tom Harmon of Michigan. Sergeant York came next. And then the floodgates opened and so many great men, young and old, filled my imagination: oh, to be a Texas Ranger! to fly the Atlantic like Lindbergh! to clean up the Wild West like Wild Bill Hickok! In those days before television, I ran with my fantasies.

Usually I was alone in my bedroom or the playroom or in our mysterious rathskeller where my father had a mounted stuffed pheasant that he had shot years earlier and where he kept German beer steins and a captured German helmet and an old flintlock rifle mounted against the wall. Below in the rathskeller you could smell angostura bitters and cocktail cherries and whiskey and gin. My parents hosted parties down there and everyone got "tight," which was my father's word for it. He seemed to mean it as a compliment when he described someone as being tight. It was a joyous state, and tight people were popular.

By 1939 I had formed a pretty good idea of evil, and it resided in the German soldier. Germany had been and still was the enemy. The Boche! Americans were lean and brave; the Germans were bulky and oppressive. Our maid, Anna, who came from Austria and looked German, was someone who defied my image. Although she was strong and buxom and could have been domineering, she was not. Instead she was warm and affectionate and I loved her. On still nights I could hear Hitler from her Emerson radio in the room next to mine. His voice was beamed to America via shortwave, and somehow or other it ended up on her small Emerson. At night Hitler's frantic, strident, stentorian tone cut the air. I lay in bed and heard raving in German, but the intent behind those words needed no translation: he was making war with words, a wild leader of Germans, the hated Boche, and men like my father would have to stop him. Anna, whom I adored, was an innocent pawn in all of this. Surely my father would show her the light in due course.

On occasion I would go into Anna's room to hear the voice up close. She would be in bed and I'd sit beside her while Hitler screamed at the world. I can still see her eyes shine as the Führer spoke his magic words. *A new world order...* The enthusiasm would rise in Anna's eyes as Hitler challenged my parents and all the other people who had already beaten him once before. Now he was back like a nightmare. To Anna, though, it was not a nightmare at all. She worked as a maid in a large house. When Hitler and Germany conquered the world, maybe the house would be hers. Her eyes glowed in the half-light of the room. I was eight years old, dreaming of Clint Frank, but I knew that evil was afoot and was possessing Anna. With my father nearby, however, I had nothing to worry about.

•   •   •

I could never be a nature writer. I was never one to lend language to the elm or the maple or the oak. Wildflowers and lichen-covered rocks caught my eye, but I was loath to explore their botanical heritage.

Who cares what they are called so long as they exist to be seen and promote good feelings when you are standing nearby and sharing the same sky? And yet, for some reason, many people feel the need to analyze the raw beauty of vegetation. As a boy I would ask: Who cares what a flower is called? Why punish a great tree with impossible language? By ten years old I carried an anti-academic bias. Even now I am incapable of learning the proper names of plants or fish in the sea (*Morone saxatilis* for striped bass), and it disturbs me that I have never learned to differentiate between the puma, the jaguar, the mountain lion, and the Florida panther. I see one or the other on my television screen and I become befuddled.

But in those last years of the Great Depression I was not befuddled. In my innocence I roamed New Britain on my two-speed Columbia bike from the center of the city out into the hills, halfway to Southington. I felt like Tom Sawyer as I scooted about town, even riding to Plainville at night to go to the movies with Augie Bross, the son of a maid who worked for my aunt and uncle Alice and Stan Eddy.

Quite possibly, much of Connecticut looked at New Britain with skepticism and even dislike. It was a polluter, sending sooty coils of dark smoke rising into the sky from tall smokestacks. Industrial debris flowed into the streams of the area, extending into the Farmington River and off to Hartford to the great Connecticut River, where New Britain's detritus would drift slowly to the Long Island Sound and thence to the open sea. All true, of course, but I was immune to any censure of my hometown. My heart sprang with delight at the leafy smell of autumn as well as the heavy verdancy of late spring and the musk of nature as I explored the hills and vainly sought signs of fox and stared into streams running down from the reservoir or Hart's Pond, looking for trout. As Robin Hood, I loved the woodlands and the long sweep of the golf course near my home. The greensward of a newly mowed fairway held an odor that equaled the smell of a forest glade. A free spirit, I recall coasting through those years, 1937 to 1941, like the gliders made of balsa wood that I scaled across the playground at the Vance Elementary School.

Though the picture I paint is accurate, and indeed I was free to enjoy all the amenities of the out-of-doors, the undeveloped beauty near our home, the school yard where I excelled at games, my classmates with whom I roughhoused, my dogs, my house, my privileged life, there were dark currents in all of this, underground currents that could and would cause sinkholes in my life. I think of them now, sixty years after the first moment of bewilderment and hurt. I shall sketch a few of them lest they vanish from the forefront of my memory.

•   •   •

One day on Martha's Vineyard, where we summered, we were all returning in my grandfather's sloop, the *Ferry Quahog*, having enjoyed a family outing, sailing off toward Chappaquiddick and then back again. We had eaten a picnic lunch of stuffed eggs and ham and cheese and wonderful English cookies from a tin, and before long we were secure in the harbor at Harthaven. Only three years old, I decided to step from the boat onto the dock. The grown-ups were drinking in the cockpit and their voices were rising in enthusiasm and intimacy. The family was together: my parents, my grandparents, my sister and brother and me. I placed one foot on the dock with the other securely planted on the ship's gunwale and the boat drifted outward to the end of its tether. So very secure in the vicinity of both father and grandfather, I felt detached from danger as I split spread-eagled, and then, when I could split no wider, in total astonishment I fell. I heard the merriment behind me but I did not call out. I simply fell like a stone. As I entered the water, I carried only one thought that came as a terrible shock and it haunted me on and off for many years: the grown-ups didn't care. Because they didn't care I did not call out. I plunged downward in silence, in the third person. Using my nickname, I said to myself, *Buster's going to drown*. I saw myself from outside of myself. So very young, I did not know enough to evade death. If I possessed a survival instinct it had not yet been sharpened; dying had never crossed my three-year-old mind. I knew I was slipping away and no one was paying heed because they had better things to do. I was underwater when my sister, who was eleven years old, grabbed me by my hair and pulled and eventually lifted me up to the cockpit. Someone gave me a towel to dry off. No one hugged me. No one seemed to realize how close I had come. I had not caused a stir in the flow of merry talk and good cheer. Only my sister, who had spotted my plunge between boat and dock, ever knew how near I'd come to death. My coming and going without impact upon my parents' life was evident even at the age of three. They had each other and their life in New Britain, Connecticut, and on Martha's Vineyard. That evening I sat with Anna in the kitchen listening to the radio, to Lannie Ross sing his theme, "Moonlight and Roses." I am guessing at the song but it's a safe guess. Where else would I be at so young an age in the summer of 1933? And Lannie Ross sang every night during our supper.

I can go back and forth during the '30s looking for clues. I was seldom recognized and often ignored. Doubtless I'd been an after-thought, the result of a strong sexual attraction, not the result of two people's hunger for children. They already had a girl and a boy, my sister and brother, one seven and a half and the other six years older than I. When I came into the world the thought was, *Well, that's done, that's good, that's peachy fine* (my father's favorite expression); *now let's get back to having fun.* They hired Anna, a young woman from the "old country." They also hired Helen, again from the old country, a bit younger than Anna and quite pretty. Helen had a niece who came one summer to stay with us in the bungalow and took my brother's room (he was away on a cruise—the Tom Wadlow Cruises—trying to learn the ways of men and the sea). Helen's niece took the room next to mine, and unbeknownst to her, there were cracks in the wall through which I could spy. I would lie in wait after swimming and I would peek at her as she dropped her black bathing suit—a Jantzen—onto the floor. I saw strong, graceful legs and a very lush underbelly and round buttocks and soft round breasts the size of grapefruits. But it was the underbelly that stirred me. From then on, from the age of five or six, I would forever look for that same luscious jungle wherever I went. Helen's niece fired my loins and my heart and my young life, and forever what a woman had a few inches beneath her navel would be the most daring temptation in my well-fed and well-housed life.

I often think of Helen's niece and of other women and their soft or wiry places. And I should think that one can trace this kind of atten-tion back to one's mother and the long-forgotten sexuality of an infant or toddler. There is a corporeal freedom with a naked woman, your mother, being hugged and cuddled against skin, and the short, crisp hair of the pubis as well as the long hair of the head brushing across you and the musk of maternity, the visibility of it, the total woman nursing, hold-ing, finally dressing in front of your eyes. Naked. You would have seen your mother thus and many times. In the bath? Surely. On the bed? Surely. In the bedroom, dressing, while the infant voyeur espies the ten-der areas for love. From one's mother proceeds a long list of substitutes adding to or accentuating what began at the beginning of life.

That was the way it is for most of us, and the way the stage is set for what is to ensue: a glimpse of the inner thigh as a woman shifts in her chair, the fuzz around the edge of a bathing suit. For centuries people knew about this voyeur streak, the immediate prod to the nervous system. We are forever lookers. We try to deny it, skirting the edges of it, allowing a hint, a peek, a wayward thought to become a moment's luxury. A fashion designer plays with human lust to sell a dress, a bathing suit. A novelist backs off describing the graphic particulars of sexual tension. The moviemaker calls for a fade-out as the shoulder straps of a nightgown are loosened prior to the gown itself slipping to the floor. Titillation. One can wonder how deep it goes in a boy and how much it determines his life. Where does it lead him? How far will he travel, what jobs will he take, what rituals will he endure in order to return to the titillation and then break through to its source? I am sure that the titillation is of itself the heart of the matter and that what often follows is anticlimactic.

• • •

From the fall of 1929 to the late summer of 1942 I lived in New Britain, Connecticut, a city of approximately sixty-thousand people. Our geography book at the Vance School described New Britain as "The Hardware Center of the World." It was and still is the home of the Stanley Works, makers of Stanley tools. My great-grandfather went to work at Stanley in his teens, when it was a very small manufacturer with only twenty-five employees. He assumed higher office in 1854 (secretary and treasurer) and eventually became president and chairman. When he started with Stanley, they made wrought iron straps and T-hinges. When he left in 1919, they were at the center of The Hardware Center of the World.

Now, as I write the above, I feel an old sense of pride in family. To some degree it is a family I rejected, and a family in which I can find stupidity and sloth and awkwardness, but it is a family that framed my life, set me apart, and produced a deep and enduring sense of being special.

In the Great Depression into which I was born, industrial cities like New Britain were filled with unemployed workers, and bread lines materialized and soup kitchens were formed to serve emergency meals. Those of us from the "better families" began to stand out. There is no doubt that I felt I was a special case from the day I first began to think of myself in terms of those other people, unrelated, whom I saw lining up in town for food. I always felt different, too, from fellow citizens crowding the sidewalks on Armistice Day to watch the parade of Yankee Division veterans. I was apart from those fans who filled the stadium at Willow Brook Park to watch the New Britain High School Hurricanes play football, usually a team of greatness with players who were lucky enough, even in those straitened times, to get football scholarships to major universities. Indeed, every time I ventured beyond the circle of my large extended family I felt special, and as my grade school years began to slide by, I felt a call to lead, to be better than those to whom I felt alien. There was no doubt in my mind that I would grow up to become a great football star or a hero in some future war.

Where I lived on Lincoln Road I was surrounded by cousins. Beyond this home territory there was downtown, into which I made sorties. Because I was always special, I was also immune to harm. I had a license to do what others could not. I had a license to be an adventurer, a poet, an all-star athlete, an iconoclast. I had a license to do what I pleased, and everything that happened in my life would be unique and intense. Being very shy, I would lie in wait and let life take me into its maelstrom where I would find greatness. I did not think I had to *do* anything in order to be a success among lesser men and women.

In truth I was a repressed boy who lived on dreams, who saw himself haloed in glory. In real life I would wait in the shadows, but I fooled myself into thinking that before long the light of stardom would scan my face and then halt its beam just where I stood. Like Lana Turner, supposedly discovered in Schwab's drugstore at the corner of Sunset and Vine, I, too, was going to be discovered. I had no thought of earning my rewards. I was a youngster of destiny. Such was my thinking as I held fast to my bedroom or the playroom, toying with wooden blocks and metal soldiers or little cowboys and Indians made of plaster. I was Tom Mix, Buck Jones, a Texas Ranger. Later I was Tom Harmon. Later than that— by two years—I was Sammy Baugh. I was a Marine at Wake Island going to my death as I fired at the heinous invading Japs. I was a pilot on a Flying Fortress. By fourteen I was a war hero back home on leave and my hand was on Rita Hayworth's thigh under the table in a San Francisco restaurant. I was feeling her up—that's what the older boys told me would happen when I had a real date. I'd make her come, is what they said. In my dreams and fantasies I would see Rita Hayworth naked and my hand was always toying with the soft curls between her legs. In my dreams I was defending America, chasing bandits, scoring touchdowns. Dreams were to become as important as life.

• • •

Back in the spring of 1938 I'd lie in bed at night, waiting for Anna to walk home from the bus stop about a half mile from our house. Usually I would be asleep by the time she returned, about eleven o'clock. Anna got Thursdays and Sundays off, starting after the midday meal. Her entertainment was found at the German–American Club and a roadhouse at a bend in the road on the way to Newington, the Blue Danube. Whom she met on her evenings off and who romanced her I never knew. My father wondered if Anna had a membership in the Bund, a national organization of Hitler enthusiasts who supported the return of German power and German pride. When my father mentioned the Bund, I imagined Nazi armbands and the dreaded straight-arm salute followed by *Heil, Hitler!* I'd seen it in the newsreels and, as mentioned, I'd heard the hated voice beamed into our house.

On the night in question I lay in bed tossing and turning. For some reason I feared for Anna. I knew she was in danger. I thought of the Bund and Europe already gripped in tension and rioting and overthrow. It was in the newsreels and coming in over our stand-up Philco. That spring night it was quiet save for the night sounds of ground frogs and the fluttering of leaves or the bay of a dog far off in Kensington somewhere. In the morning during my very early years I would hear the clip-clop of a horse and the groan of a milk wagon as the Ferndale Dairy delivery buggy meandered down Lincoln Road. But that night I heard another clip-clop; I heard the quick steps of Anna hurrying along the road. My heart stopped, however, when I heard another set of footsteps trailing to her rear. I could hear both pairs of feet, and very soon the second set was immediately behind Anna. My ears were like sonar as I picked up pulses, one closing upon the other. A collision was in the offing—or was it an attack? I held my breath as both sets of feet clopping on the dark macadam became one set of four feet, and then I heard the shriek. Anna's scream of terror pierced the night air like a rocket. I had been lying in bed awaiting just such a feral screech, but when it sliced through my open window it struck my heart and took away my breath. I loved Anna more than my mother and I was losing her to a madman at the foot of our driveway. I heard the thud of his fist on her head and she screamed again. Where was my father? He was in the living room with my mother having a nightcap. I wanted to call "Help!" but I lay frozen in my bed. I waited, and in a moment I heard a hideous laugh, a lunatic's hilarity, and with it I heard Anna's sobs. Then there were the footsteps of someone running toward the house, up our gravel driveway. Anna was free of her attacker and was coming to the kitchen door.

I did not call my father. I lay mute and very still, petrified by what I'd heard and more…what I had foreseen. Wasn't it true that I had lain awake with my imagination full of dire possibilities, my mind a pit of worry for Anna? I had known that she was in danger and had felt her attack coming. Now that it was over I was held by a paralysis while Anna sobbed uncontrollably in her bedroom next door to mine.

I waited half an hour before I summoned the courage to call down to my parents. I left my room and went to the landing at the top of the stairway and called "Dad!" and he hurried to me and I told him about Anna's attack and then I heard the police and I could hear them all talking down in the kitchen. At some point, before the police came, while I was still out of bed, my father asked me why I had not called him at once, the minute I heard the first cry out on the street, even before the horrible thud as Anna was struck. Why did I wait so long? The attacker would be gone now, he said.

I had no answer to that, and my father studied me for a moment and sent me back to my bed. It would be many years before I could answer his question. The answer lay in fear: I was afraid to interrupt my parents. I believed they were arguing. I was afraid to bring them such terrible news, so harsh an intrusion. I did not want them to yell at me. The first jarring note of a scolding was always something I felt personally, deeply and painfully. Rather than confront them with Anna's assault, I lay in straits, a nervous wreck, unable to move. The truth was, I was so in awe, if not actually afraid, of my parents and so fearful a child that at eight years old I was ready to endure the death (if need be) of the woman I loved like a mother rather than call attention to the dreadful affair as it unwound before me. Shy? I was beyond shy. Inhibited? Indeed. Pathologically so. That was why I lay frozen while Anna cried behind her door.

I developed a stammer soon after that. By the fourth grade I couldn't speak up in class until recess when some activity like dodgeball gave me pride. Now, as I think back to that night, I am full of wonder at the shame I felt and at my profound embarrassment in being a witness to the affair. Was my shame tied to my prior knowledge of disaster and of not doing anything about it? Should an eight-year-old boy run out into the street at 11:30 at night to signal the alarm? Should I have gone to my father? In my original and continuing silence I felt a penetrating shame. And I was embarrassed as well. Raw emotion embarrassed me; crying embarrassed me. I was embarrassed by my own needs as a child. I could not turn to my own mother and father and call for help. I've often asked myself: *What kind of family did I grow up in? Why was I so frightened in my own house?*

• • •

I did not know that my world was fearful. On the contrary, I thought of myself as very happy and I took my fearfulness as a natural condition of life. If I ever thought about my little world at all, and I did, I thought that my life was ideal. I adored my father and I loved my mother, especially when she was affectionate and loving to me. And I had Anna to whom I was a steady sidekick, hanging out in her kitchen, eating with her in the little kitchen alcove that overlooked our backyard. I had friends at school, and as a small boy I was surrounded by familiar territory. My relatives were sprinkled throughout my end of New Britain, and those who were not relatives were in any case friends of my parents. Yet, beneath these accommodating features of home and parents and money, friends and social position and access to nature, there lay enough terror to render me speechless and trigger such a burst of imagination that in the case of Anna's assault I could actually foresee the danger to her. Paranoia was close at hand. In my happy mind there was nevertheless always an image of disaster: the *Hindenburg*, the Lindbergh kidnapping, children from school falling through the ice at Doerr's Pond and drowning—a terrible misfortune that actually occurred when I was in the fourth grade.

Fear was joined with love from the beginning; happiness and projected calamity lived in my heart, side by side. The fear began before I could walk, and certain particulars intensified a basic wariness in my nature. First, there was my mother who drank and did not handle it well. That was in the beginning. Later on, in her forties, she became a drunkard, incapable of drinking without emotional outburst, bad temper, or loose tongue. And though I cannot pinpoint a concrete example, I retain the impression of sexual passion and overt sexual activity boiling over after a drink or two. All my life I have thought of my parents as tactile, huggy, kissing lovers; even toward the end when my mother lay very ill with multiple sclerosis and was incontinent, even then my father slept at her side, surely feeling the seep of urine against him. Volatile and sexy, my mother had been very beautiful as a girl—"a humdinger" was my father's name for her—with an earthy and often lovely presence. Although on most occasions she was warm and responsive, she was also emotionally unstable: her behavior was always loaded with feeling, and this side of her nature lent a theatrical quality to my life. As I grew in age, I matured within the confines of a melodrama.

And then there was my brother, Bill. Older by six years, he roamed the shadows of my childhood, striking out at random, always *there*—but where? At one or two or three I shrank from his presence, flinching at his approach. One of my earliest memories is of being left alone with him in the house. Anna was outside somewhere and I was in our playroom. I heard scary noises from somewhere close by. I'd already been made to cry that day so I was very apprehensive when I heard his scary voice off in another room. I heard him searching for me, and when I could not stand it any longer, I called out for help. I cried toward the walls of our playroom where I was crouching in a corner. I heard Bill come into the room and saw his predatory face red with hate. Suddenly Anna burst through another door across the playroom and scooped me up. I cried into her bosom and she comforted me. But she did nothing about Bill. No one ever did. Later in life I assumed that my parents must have known that their elder son was unbalanced but they chose to ignore it. My father had a way of saying, "When things get better..." usually referring to my mother's tribulations, but he could have thought the same way about Bill. Nobody wanted to approach Bill to his face and tell him the truth, which was that he needed help.

Bill was never called Billy. *Can you bake a cherry pie, Billy Boy, Billy Boy?* is the opening line to an old song, and in, say, 1934, when I sang it to him, to test him, he flew into a rage. My mother told me never, never to sing that song to Bill. In the fall of 1934 he was sent away to the Indian Mountain School in Lakeville, Connecticut. That same year I entered kindergarten at the Vance School, where Bill, had he stayed, would have been in the fifth grade. When I learned that Bill was not going to be at home except on vacations, my heart leapt. Walking to school with Bill would have been unbearable. Playing with Bill in our yard as I grew older would have invited torture. Just to see him in the hallways at school and hear stories of him, to be thought of as Bill Hart's brother, would have ruined everything. The only other time I felt such joy as I did when my mother told me that Bill was going away to school was when Anna, who had quit our employment, changed her mind and stayed on. The sense of relief and joy in each case has never been equaled.

Because Bill's years at the Indian Mountain School were never discussed, I have no idea how he fared. At the Berkshire School, where he went next, it was the same thing. No comment. To my knowledge no one broached the subject: *How is school, Bill?* He just went off and returned for holidays. The Berkshire School, like the one before it, meant nothing to my parents or to me. Both institutions were custodial, and that apparently was their whole purpose. They took Bill in and kept him busy for most of the year. In the summer he was let out and he came to Martha's Vineyard with the rest of us, but I have few precise summer memories of him. I blotted him out like an accident involving pain and blood. After all, one did not dwell on what was upsetting. Essentially, most of what I can recall from the early days is a feeling of dread.

I do remember that in the late '30s my parents rented a house on Vineyard Haven Harbor for the summer. We had our own cottage, our bungalow, in our family community, Harthaven. But things were amiss, and the idea was to get my mother away from bad influences; get her out of town, as it were, to where it was hoped she'd cut down on her drinking and end her flirtations. By 1938 my mother was gaining a reputation for getting tight and flirting—how seriously I don't know, but I can guess *very* seriously—with other men in the crowd, cousins and friends of my father's. Leave Harthaven with its private beaches and harbor and rent a small shingled house right on Vineyard Haven Harbor; that would be the ticket. There was too much temptation for my mother back in Harthaven, with my father away during the work week and the cocktails flowing and, well...who can say what was to blame? In Vineyard Haven the bad influences would be absent.

Perhaps in Vineyard Haven Bill would make friends. He had no real friends in Harthaven. Our cousins Mike Pease and Howard Eddy, for example, were too old for him, and Al Pease and Russ Hart were too young. In Vineyard Haven he would have pals at the Yacht Club. Or so it was hoped. But such was not to be the case. Bill stayed at home playing cards and listening to the radio, day after day. He was a sullen presence in our house along with my mother, now isolated and removed from temptation. Both brother and mother acted as though they were being punished. My father came on weekends. My older sister, Bideau, of whom I have the fondest of memories, was touring Europe. Lonely, lost to his fantasies, my brother spooked our home, bedeviled by a bad temper. I remember nothing particular about him except for the time he exposed himself to me and I fled down the stairs without looking. I shrank from him. Sadly, his situation was not assayed by my parents until one day in early August when my father spoke harshly to my mother: "We moved here so Bill would make friends. He never leaves the house. He's never raced once at the Yacht Club. And you..." He glowered at her, unable to continue. She, by then, had been drifting back to Harthaven, where the cocktail crowd welcomed her and at night the old gang would sing "Let's Put Out the Lights and Go to Sleep" or "Yes, We Have No Bananas" as the sea surged against the shore and hearts filled with feelings of camaraderie.

A deep affection filled those Harthaven living rooms, and a need for sexual attention, loosened by drink, was palpable even to a child— perhaps especially to a child, who could peek into the good-natured groupings that drifted his way during a party or after the late morning swim when a small knot of cousins and friends would meet on our porch for "a snort or two," as my father would put it. Almost naked in their bathing suits, they appeared loose-limbed and touchable and peek- able to me: breasts and thighs and a flash of hair. Everyone always seemed to be on the very edge of sex. As I kept my eager eyes glued to the joyous crowd that laughed and flirted beyond the screen door, my heart would fill with their happiness. The women in particular were like actors in a play or slow-motion dancers choreographed to move and twist and throw back tender shoulders, to toss their hair, to raise an eyebrow, to lift lips to the rim of a glass, to slip the strap of a bathing suit sideways. I was witness to a dance of grown-ups on display, and my heart raced.

Once the others had left, my mother and father would go to their room to change out of their bathing suits. They'd linger there while I sat in the kitchen with Anna, waiting to go to our beach—the beach where the servants went—for the rest of the afternoon. Other than that one outburst, back in Vineyard Haven in our rented house, my father remained mute on personal matters and went along with the summer fun. Sometime that August we returned to our own house in Harthaven. There was little point in trying to stay away from the crowd to which they belonged, those intimates who claimed them and to whom my mother was so warmly drawn. Neither she nor Bill had made a single friend in Vineyard Haven.

When I was very young, my parents raced an eighteen-foot Vineyard Interclub with the Edgartown Yacht Club, where my father was a member. Every time they came home after the Saturday race my parents would spread the sails around our porch to dry. As they flopped the canvas about, they would argue over the race. My mother's temper flared, for she was not a good sailor, and every Saturday she vented her complaints: "You didn't hear me when I was caught by the jib sheet. You didn't see me almost fall overboard. When you are going to come about, you've got to warn me!" From my father would eventually come his cutting retort: "Oh shut up your trap, Lu."

Always in the residue of a race acrimony would grow. A vitriolic monologue would issue from my mother while my father went on his way, draping the sails and pretending he did not hear his wife. Anna told me that my mother was a nervous wreck. Once I repeated that at dinner. I was four or five years old and I said, "Anna says Mom is a nervous wreck." My mother flew into a rage and told my father to fire Anna. Assuming it was 1935, this would have been the middle of the Depression. Anna, an immigrant, would have had nowhere to go. My father ignored my mother, as he so often did, and dinner progressed in silence.

But going back to those Saturday race days…I hated everything about racing. Even today I can see the sails draped over our porch furniture and railing and wince inside because when the postmortem began—they usually finished last or close to last—my mother's harsh tongue would fire blame at my father. She wanted to be a good sailor, but she had not been raised on boats and had little experience with the sea, and though she tried to be a good sport, she couldn't make the grade. She was terrible crew: nervous, petulant, and scared. Of course, neither parent would properly address the situation, and as a result they suffered. My mother pretended she could sail though she couldn't. My father called her a good sport when she wasn't. By denying the truth, my father grew sadder each year. The sailing interlude—it lasted only five years or so—is a good example of how my father refused to see the truth, read the facts, learn anything at all. He lived with blinders on: Lucy was a good sport who had the makings of a good crew. Soon they'd win a race. "Oh boy, oh boy," he'd say rubbing his hands. There was no chance whatsoever of their becoming a polished racing team. Yet he promoted the dream that it was so.

In the aftermath of a quarrel, all dressed for dinner, with whiskey glasses raised high and with lovemaking just completed, their eyes would sparkle and life looked grand. Nobody would have to worry about racing again for a week. But then it would start all over and I would wonder to myself: *Why don't they just stop racing and sell the boat?*

•   •   •

In one important way my father was just like every other man in his crowd: he hated Roosevelt. He detested "that man" so much that when he actually contemplated FDR and his presidency he grew ill. The term *visceral reaction* is very apt. My father saw the New Deal as colliding with the entrenched beliefs of Republican Party–business as usual–rugged individualism that he venerated. But below the surface lay a deep-seated resentment of Roosevelt's lofty pretensions, his Harvard arrogance, his preening vanity (the cigarette holder, for example), and his snobbery. For some reason this man who had avoided the Great War by serving in the Navy Department had the gall to lord it over the manufacturer, the man who maintained the engine that kept the country running. An aesthete! A sissy! Roosevelt was the epitome of the dreaded Harvard dilettante, a man of the drawing room and lounge who never got his hands dirty but who dared to instruct the man of the shop, the inventor, the person who could shape things with his own hands. While the benighted lower-class worker might be swayed by his grand manner, anyone from a shop foreman on up could recognize the fraud and the balderdash in this counterfeit of a person. So my father thought, and because it made him sick when he thought about it, he limited himself to simple outbursts of venom, covered up by a scoff. Beyond "that damn man in the White House," he swallowed whole paragraphs of derision, although I knew that in the late evening after many drinks he would let fly. By then I was usually sound asleep, but sometimes I'd hear his voice coming up the staircase in New Britain and I knew he'd been carrying on at length about the President whom he found so loathsome.

Almost all of my father's friends, the men and women of his generation who had been to prep school and college, recoiled almost in panic at the thought of socialism. It was the God-given right of all Americans to work hard, to produce something, to invent, to package a product or a process with no interference from the government. Those who could not run things worked for those who did. Unemployed Americans received the largess of an unfettered economic system. The role of government was to stay out of the way yet keep a watchful eye out for monopolies. Teddy Roosevelt was a good man. T.R. took on the monopolies, which operated against fair play. After all, my father and his friends were from the playing fields of Taft, Hotchkiss, and Choate, schools where competition ruled. Monopoly was an evil word. It would never do for Henry Ford to buy out a rising star like General Motors.

And that was it: America's strength lay in its manufacturing, and the men who took the gambles, raised the money, and went ahead and made something were the heroes in his book. The manufacturer and his plant were the American equivalent of a duke and his duchy.

All that said, it must be noted that New Britain was small potatoes and far out of the social mainstream. The social set that met at the Shuttle Meadow Country Club were ungainly, unsophisticated, and dim-witted. I can recall them in the Men's Grille: midlevel executives, salesmen, insurance brokers, deep in their cups, the room resounding with a bonhomie born of a common background and a good deal of gin. My grandfather, who founded the Fafnir Bearing Company and other concerns in New Britain, would never have been seen in such company. My father and mother often dined at the club on Thursday and Sunday evenings, but I never saw my father in the Men's Grille or anywhere other than the dining room. He eschewed bragging and banter as his own father would have. When he played tennis, he played on the club courts or on a private court across the street from our house.

He did not hang about, engaging in witless exchanges. Nor, to my knowledge, did the other leaders of New Britain industry. It wouldn't do to be caught in the gaucherie that obtained at the Shuttle Meadow Club. One used it for golf and tennis and an occasional meal. Otherwise it was left to the wiseacres and the men and women who did not dream, or if they did, dreamt only of New Britain: the tawdry love affairs still to come, the money to be made, the new car.

Even so, if New Britain, Connecticut, was small potatoes compared to Pittsburgh or Detroit, those of us who grew up in New Britain did not know in our early years of the other cities. Therefore New Britain *was,* to us at least, as big and important as Pittsburgh. In our ignorance we saw the men in dark overcoats and felt fedoras drive by in Cadillacs and Packards, some with chauffeurs. We saw the older women from my grandfather's generation in mink, and these women in pearls and white gloves gave no hint to a six- or ten-year-old that they were small-time. "The Hardware Center of the World" read the geography book—and this, we were reminded, was a nationally published textbook.

And so as a little kid I thought New Britain was the grandest place to live, a major city. My father had a term: "the cat's meow." I thought along those lines whenever I thought of New Britain, when I saw my grandfather drive up in his Pierce Arrow and my grandmother came into the room, a loop of real pearls brightening her formidable bosom.

Chapter 3

I recall Christmas in New Britain and my extended family, of whom my favorite was my father's first cousin—a woman named Betty Cooley—who wore black dresses with plunging necklines. I was usually chosen to deliver presents to the assembly of relatives, and when Betty Cooley bent over to unwrap her gift I could easily see down her dress, and I could see her naked chest softly and loosely held by a brassiere of thin and scanty proportions. I stood before her and she knew that I was seeing her bare breasts and she blushed beautifully. The two of us, therefore—she in her thirties and I not even pubescent—would play this sexual game, I am sure to the delight of the older relatives who must have seen me at my mischief.

Outside everything was so white. The tall cedars would be heavy with snow, and behind them in the deeper woods there were tracks of dogs and the smaller prints of rabbits or raccoons that ventured from their lairs, padding about in the snow looking for food. My memory picks up talk of ski trips into Vermont and college vacations and liquor, and I can see the flushed faces of relatives as they entered the vestibules of large homes. Add to this the aromatic hotel lobbies and lounges and beautiful young women, girls really, in polo coats and radiant stocking caps and long scarves in college colors and bright red kissable lips. Sex was at full throttle at Christmas when young people came home for vacation. But older people, too, became more affectionate and physical. It was all part of this time of goodwill when everyone hummed carols and hoped for peace on earth.

In 1936, as was our custom, we all convened at Al and Stan Eddy's house where my grandfather, now a widower, presided over a sumptuous banquet. As usual, Betty Cooley exposed her chest and Jack

Kirkham, my aunt Lois's brother, became drunk. Jack Kirkham, the son of a judge, was the first male drunkard I'd known. He arrived tipsy. Then he began slurring his speech and stumbling about. I felt he was a threat to the group. I wanted my father to banish him, but instead he was accepted as he was. This puzzled me because he was frightening and needed to be expelled; but no, he was just drunk, apparently an accepted condition. Jack eventually bought an old tavern in Plainville—Cook's Tavern—and played a good deal of tennis, at which he excelled.

I remember that Christmas as the year my mother was sent to Austin Riggs's sanitarium at Stockbridge, in the Berkshires. She'd been there before but never over Christmas. Our local doctor, "Doc" Kinsella, was unsure as to what ailed my mother. For some reason she was unable to cope with social life, family life…events as they unfolded in New Britain. Her complaints seemed real—pain, fatigue, numbness—yet they could have been symptoms of mental illness, something wrong with her emotions. In those days alcoholism was not an available diagnosis. In the mid-1930s it was not yet recognized as a disease, nor was it a term applied to people of money and position who lived in large houses with a staff. To label any woman an alcoholic was surely to assault her moral stature. A well-bred woman did not suffer such castigation in those days. It was simply not done. As for multiple sclerosis, that disease was new to the medical community. Doc Kinsella had yet to read of it, and so by 1936 there appeared to be nothing else to do but send my mother away for "a rest." She was overwrought; she needed to get away and get a hold of herself.

I remember when my father broke the news. It was on Christmas Eve, at dinner. He was uncomfortable, as was I. "Mom won't be back by tomorrow," he told us. "Mom needs more rest. She'll be home soon, by golly. Until then, just around the corner, we'll just go on and have our own Christmas." Not his exact words, but close enough. My father always slipped into expressions of hope such as "by golly" or "oh boy, oh boy." There was always good news in the offing. Mom would miss Christmas, but so be it. We'd see her as soon as she felt better, and by gosh, by golly, oh boy, oh boy, that wouldn't be long to wait.

That day at dinner my grandfather lifted his glass and proposed a toast: "To Lucy, who can't be with us today, who will be home soon in fine fettle." I was sitting far down the table, perhaps with other younger children—Barbara and Judy Hart or my cousin Dick Smith, who often had Christmas dinner with us. I recall the acute embarrassment of hearing my mother's name in a toast. I so wanted her absence to go unnoticed. I was full of shame. I wanted no one other than my own family to use her name, to know where she was or guess why she was there. I wanted to keep it a secret. That was the way we did things.

•   •   •

My mother returned from Stockbridge with an exercise plan. She was to take long walks. Exercise was the cure. I remember her brown walking shoes made in England. She gave it a try but then gave up after the two of us became lost. I'll explain. On a Saturday in February during a thaw my mother suggested that I accompany her on an extended hike, far up into the woods. She wanted to test herself, she said: doctor's orders. So we drove down to the old icehouse that abutted the golf course behind the Stanleys' house and left the car. We crossed the little dam and walked into the woods. I had already been up there exploring old trails, pretending I was a man of the frontier. Strangely, though in some ways my mother worried about me to an excessive degree, I was allowed great freedom as a boy. Almost as soon as I could walk, I began exploring, both in New Britain and on Martha's Vineyard. In any event, on that day the two of us struck out on an afternoon journey through the damp forest, our feet wet, dodging little heaps of melting snow. We walked for an hour or so, my mother determined to press on, to push herself, until suddenly she stopped and with panic in her voice admitted she was lost. She'd never been up in the forest, had only walked on sidewalks alongside the road. Where were we? Where was help? Who would save us? Such were her fears, her words tumbling out in the dark glade. Heroically, I led her out of the forest to safety and eventually onto a road near Rogers' Orchards. I'd seen a rock-bedded canal that I knew led to the reservoir and we followed it downhill to something I could recognize. Once we had our bearings, I could lead my mother to civilization.

Over the ensuing years my mother would smile and laugh softly as the two of us reconstructed our adventure. "You were *so* young," she'd say, smiling at me. "No more than a tot." And she'd say that I should feel very proud of myself, very proud of how I had helped her.

We never took another walk together. We did play board games and bridge until 1946 or so, but never did we share a real experience again. Being with my mother (who was a much softer person than my father), just the two of us on that long ago day when I led her to safety, being a teammate with my mother, lives warmly in my heart as I write this memoir. Her troubles and her self-centeredness, her carping at my father, her drunken behavior and her crippling illness twisted my feelings over the ensuing decades from unqualified love to pity and even to scorn, yet there was that time when I loved her and was proud of myself for being such a good companion.

•   •   •

As a young child, I thought New Britain had everything. I knew no better. I was impressed by the grandparent generation that was still very much alive when men like my grandfather looked powerful and accomplished to young and old alike. The women were grand in furs and jewels; as a group they formed a knot of dignity and demanded privilege. Alas, by 1940 style had deteriorated and the crowd that my parents (not my grandparents) partied with was quite ordinary and those below them who met at the Shuttle Meadow Club Men's Grille never had a clue, just bodies hanging on in a backwater, looking forward to the next game of golf. But there was one man who took it upon himself to puncture the New Britain balloon. His name was Roger Pease. I never met him, but I knew of him and had heard of his great skills and charm. Roger Pease was the headmaster of a small day school at which most of the children from the "better" families matriculated. Back in the '30s the Shuttle Meadow School was a stepping stone between the Lincoln School and prep school, from grades seven through nine. Mr. Pease was beloved. By all accounts he was a fine teacher and a gentle leader of faculty and students.

Mr. Pease was also a Marxist. He may even have been a full-blown communist, though party membership would have been very risky in such an environment of free enterprise zealots. Yet surely he subscribed to the ideal of a cooperative and classless society. He must have looked at the class system in New Britain, seen the soup kitchens, and felt the suffering of the unemployed. A bright man, he would have read *Das Kapital* and other writings of Karl Marx. At least somewhat sophisticated, he may have been caught up in the glamour and the intellectuality of the left as it stormed through the Great Depression. And, suddenly, there he was, plunked down in New Britain, in a veritable sea of bigotry and boosterism and blind belief in business, along with the standard contempt for organized labor.

Mr. Pease was fired from the Shuttle Meadow School at the end of my sixth grade year, so I was denied his presence when I entered that school the next fall. He did, however, teach my sister for three years, as well as our cousins Norman and Howard Eddy and Betsy Chamberlain and Pete, Mary, Dave, and Russ Hart. These and many others flew by our house each morning in a whoosh of stocking caps and pumping legs, the girls with tan knapsacks on their backs and their hair flying, straining at the pedals of their bikes so as not to be late and garner demerits. For eight years or so, youths from our side of town were placed in the care of a left-winger, a pacifist, a believer in the overriding value of art, literature, and love. Roger Pease cared about human dignity, and in subtle and, one imagines, non-subtle ways he inculcated in his students a sense of social responsibility. He tried to give them all a conscience.

My cousin, Howard Young, who graduated in 1934, remembered visiting Mr. Pease for a weekend at his farm in Vermont. The atmosphere there was very different from his home in New Britain. There was hard outdoor work, chores and teamwork and affection and a sense of being part of nature and the forces of growth. There was a love of life, a simple hardworking life, evident in that farm. It had nothing to do with factories or products or salesmanship. There was no competition. You learned to respect honest toil. My sister described Mr. Pease exploding in class and throwing down his blackboard eraser and addressing his students: "The next time you see a dirty fisherman on a boat or on a dock, smelling of fish and covered with scales, just remember that he is as fine a gentleman as any industrialist. Just remember that!"

Howard Young was taught fair play by Mr. Pease when he borrowed, without consent, a fellow student's bike and proceeded to wreck it in a stunt performed by riding up the large roots of a tree, then up its sloping trunk before sailing into the air. Howard sailed off the tree and landed clumsily, destroying a wheel. Upon hearing of this, Mr. Pease grabbed the hapless youth and sat him in a corner. There he was admonished as "Bung the Bike Buster," Bung being the lad's nickname. For some time he was greeted thus, as Mr. Pease's scorn hung in the air. It was not long before Howard realized that he could never simply take what was not his and put it to his own use. Such was Mr. Pease's way of addressing the arrogance of the rich during the Great Depression: *You can't get away with it anymore, so don't get into the habit as your parents did before you.*

Another recollection of entitlement is my sister's memory of my Aunt Minnie Cooley, who was a Stanley, the New Britain version of aristocracy. Both Minnie Cooley and my grandmother often assumed a royal bearing: no one would mistake either woman for anything other than a grande dame. My sister's account of going to the movies with Aunt Minnie Cooley is instructive. As they approached the movie theater, they saw a line. To my sister's surprise, Aunt Minnie walked up to the ticket window, bought two tickets, and led my sister inside to their seats. It never dawned on her that she should wait in line and take her turn. Mr. Pease would have drawn a lesson from her behavior had he been there. He would have seen it for what it was, a naive arrogance in the landed gentry that was loathsome. He would have found no redeeming features inherent in the elegance and composure of my Aunt Minnie.

Aunt Minnie's sense of class was persuasive, and in my house it was unmentioned but assumed. You paid lip service to democracy as a form of government, but not to equality. People belonged to classes. There were the Vanderbilts and the Astors who were high class and were bigger than everyday life. My father and his friends belonged in a social stratum considerably below the very rich. These were the Americans who ran factories and went to private schools, had summer homes but not estates, and belonged to the country club. This crowd did not speak any foreign languages, were frightened of intellectuals, hated opera and loved the movies. My father's Americans joined the armed forces, voted Republican, and assumed leadership if they chose. In New Britain there was a place at the top for names such as Hart, Cooper, Moore, Chamberlain, and Stanley. My father may never have felt completely at home in such an environment, but he embraced the class system totally. As *his* father's son, he had his inherited the right to live near the top of the heap. This way of thinking would erode during World War II and fade away by the 1970s, but it was still very much a fact in the 1930s. Howard "Bung" Young never doubted that it was his right to take, unasked, another's bike and then carelessly break it. Mr. Pease, a robust, fiery man of 5'7", would set him straight, and Bung the Bike Buster grew up eschewing manufacturing, going into journalism and then to work for the government. "Bung" went to Harvard—Roosevelt's university—and became a lifelong Democrat.

I was only a small boy when Mr. Roger Pease had his heyday in New Britain. All I remember is that my sister and her friends were bright, creative, joyous, and free. Because my sister shone so brightly in contrast to my difficult brother, I saw her as symbolizing the joys of life and extended her glow to her school. I just knew that the school to which my sister and her crowd pedaled each morning was a magical place because of what it produced. Miss Goodwin, Mr. Tarr, and Mr. Pease were the faculty, and their names were celestial. They floated out of my sister's mouth and ascended airily in our living room or in the backyard or wherever she was when she invoked their names, as in "Mr. Pease said today that..." By four years old I had right in my home a lightness and a darkness, with a disturbed ten-year-old on one hand and a smiling, bright-eyed, twelve-year-old sister on the other.

My family had no religious life, no formal concern with God or the Bible. I think that this lack of any real belief beyond a belief in our family name led my sister and her crowd to an almost reverential attitude toward their school. I had no knowledge of art, music, free thought. But my association with my sister's gang of gentle rebels placed me under the spell of Mr. Pease without knowing it. In later life I hankered for the bohemian lifestyle, the freedom to bust loose. At five years old I was already alert to a freedom of thought and the uplift of spirit that my sister carried with her. I wanted to be part of that happiness.

Someone might say, "But you were so young." True. But in a home where no one ever confronted anything, where adults mindlessly derided the course of the nation and Franklin Roosevelt, where danger lurked in a brother driven by demons, where a mother drank to drunkenness and a father stared off into the distance—in such a world one fantasizes and dreams and notices and becomes a watcher. And as a watcher I began to learn a good deal about other people long before I was old enough to understand what I was learning and could put what I was watching into words.

• • •

I do not wish to complain, to whine. The out-of-doors in and around New Britain, coupled with the beach, harbor, and pine woods of Harthaven on Martha's Vineyard, gave me a glorious opportunity to run free with the wind, to explore and make believe and sparkle in the glare of the sun. I adored my father, loved and pitied my mother, had a strong attachment to Anna which I unhesitantly call love, and in my private moments I hugged and caressed our dog Brownie, whom I considered my best friend. In retrospect I see myself as a loving boy who was happiest outside his home, coasting along on his Columbia, aiming for a playground or the woods. I was also a needy kind of kid, circling behind my father as he sat reading in his chair, hugging him from behind and feeling the coarse skin of his face brush mine. Things never seemed wrong at home because I knew no other life.

Raised as I was, I moved toward oddity and, later in life, a modest eccentricity. Sometime in the late '40s my father and I saw the play *Harvey* by Mary Chase. At once I saw myself in the character of Elwood P. Dowd, the sweet eccentric who has a six-foot-tall pretend rabbit for a friend. Of course, so did thousands of others see themselves in him, or else the play would never have been a success. Madcap characters strike chords in a good many of us. Therefore, it does not serve me well to think of myself as being particularly different in this regard. Like so many, I was susceptible to eccentricity simply because of the way I was formed. Secrets produce counterparts in the imagination. I lived in a house of secrets and naturally I spent hours pretending and dreaming and hanging back in the corners, holding my dog or pushing a toy soldier across the floor. But none of that interfered with the glee I felt at being a boy in New Britain out on a bike, at play with pals, lying in the grass by a small stream and thinking I was in a glen in Sherwood Forest, about to ride against a hated king.

•   •   •

My father hated his job. He was, after all, a manufacturer of heating vents and related equipment. For escape he would read on weekends and sometimes in the evening. Usually what my father read could have been serialized in the old *Saturday Evening Post,* and often was. I recall around 1938 that he wrote and presented a paper on Africa. He'd read *Out of Africa*, and that book excited his interest in the Dark Continent. He took me down to the Museum of Natural History in New York, where he studied the exhibit composed by Carl Ackley, a leading Africanist. If you saw my father sitting before his shelves of books with a volume in his lap, or working on material related to Africa spread about him as he prepared for his address before the Saturday Night Club of New Britain—if you saw him in such a pose, then you might have inferred wisdom. To stretch a point, you would have been correct.

My father did garner knowledge from his readings, and he knew a great deal about human experience. His weaknesses stemmed from his attitude. Deep in the core of his thinking there existed a rigidity of thought and a pattern of reaction that were undisturbed by the life he had led or the information he received from books. Nothing penetrated that inner core of his being. He was William Hart, his father's son, a Connecticut Yankee. He did what he thought he had to do. He relied on common sense. What he received from his reading was informative and pleasurable to pursue, but it did not alter his innermost thinking one iota.

The great issues of our time such as racial prejudice and segregation, communism and fascism, the emerging role of women, the recognition of the sex drive as basic to one's psychology...from all of this his mind would dance away, his eyes drift off. My father knew that the Hun was on the rise in Europe, and America would have to fight again. He thought that the labor movement was frightful and that all communists intended to dismantle America. Naturally a woman belonged in the home unless she was too unattractive to get a man. In that case she became a schoolteacher, a nurse, or a librarian. The world was a man's world and women needed to be protected from it. Marriage and a home were a woman's best bet.

Colored people in the South (seemingly there were no colored people in Connecticut) were of no concern to him. The dreaded New York Jew who spent his winter vacations in Miami was someone to avoid. Jews from outside New York didn't trouble my father so long as they did not appear pushy.

Sex was a private matter. One never read about it, nor did he care what Freud had to say. He once pronounced Freud as "Frood" because he'd never heard the name spoken, only then reading aloud from the cover of a book I had brought home.

Down deep my father was immovable. In 1988, when I first began to listen to Vice President George Bush, who was running for President, I recognized the same unreachable core, the same implacable attitude about life, shared not just by my father (also of Connecticut and Yale) but by a large percentage of the upper-middle-class people I have known. These are the people who "don't get it." When that denigrating tag was applied to Bush, I could see at once how accurate it was. In him I saw my father and his friends.

My mother, whose maiden name was Upham, lived in my father's shadow, but unlike my father she was a talker. She talked when drinking, though now so many years later I cannot hear her words. Liquored language—even before my mother became a chronic alcoholic—carried no staying power. Her father was a Methodist minister, a Phi Beta Kappa graduate of Wesleyan University. My grandmother was a Williamson from Virginia. Her relatives had fought under Lee and Jackson for the Confederate Army of Northern Virginia. It was said that one of her female cousins lured a Northern sentry from his post so a Confederate spy could pass through and gain information for the South. My grandmother, née Fannie Williamson, smelled of age and looked very gray and tall and always seemed overdressed in shawls and long dresses that reached her ankles. She bored me to death. While her husband, whom we called Pop, was sprightly and full of zeal and sported a mustache, my grandmother looked aged and dead—like the cause her relatives had supported and which I knew had led to so many deaths and dismemberments. I was a Connecticut Yankee and was proud to be from a people who'd freed the slaves. Even at five or six years old I knew as much.

Pop loved to hear Paul Robeson sing "Ol' Man River," and as he'd play it on the upright Victrola in our playroom, his eyes would mist over and, filled with feeling, he'd silently weep. He was a very emotional man who gave moving sermons. His wife seemed stern and overwrought with impatience. They had a dog named Baldie who fought with my dog Brownie. My parents had to banish Brownie into the rathskeller against my cries. The whole Upham connection was very distasteful to me, and whenever they came to visit us in New Britain I felt a slight terror and tried to avoid their embraces and conversation. On Martha's Vineyard, Uphams were unavoidable since they also spent their summers there; it was where my parents first met.

• • •

Now, a word about the Hart boys of my father's generation. By 1922 or so there were eight Hart first cousins—young men from eighteen to their mid-twenties. They called one another by their shared last name, "Hart." In the summer they were all in Harthaven, outside Oak

Bluffs on the Vineyard, cutting their figures, so to speak. My great uncle George Hart was chairman of the Stanley Works. He had two sons, Tod and Merv. My great uncle Max, who worked for my grandfather's subsidiary at Hart and Hutchinson, also had two boys, Ted and Bob. My father and his brother Stan were the sons of Howard, an industrialist (like George) of some national repute. Uncle Walter, also at the Stanley Works, had a pair of boys named Val (Valentine) and Jerry (Jerroms), the latter too young to be part of the crowd that assembled in the early 1920s in New Britain and on the Vineyard.

Arguably, excepting Jerry, the other seven presided over the disintegration of their extended family. The eldest, Mervyn Hart, left his job at Stanley Works and settled in California. He divorced his wife, who, after he remarried, committed suicide. His eldest children (Bruzz and George Hart II) did not fare well in the long run and are now deceased. A younger batch, all with strange names (Bubbles was one), sired with his second wife, Saralyn, are out and about. Happy or not, reasonably well-off or poor, they have escaped my purview. Merv's brother Tod, however, had four children—all of whom were divorced, and one died from alcoholism. My father had three children, all of whom were divorced, and one—my brother, Bill—is dead from alcoholism. Ted had two daughters, both divorced. Stan Hart had two daughters, one of whom never married; the other was divorced from a stock car racer named Buddy, who is now dead from alcoholism. Apparently divorce was inevitable among the children of the Hart boys. By my count, the rate of divorce among the offspring of those seven cousins stands at thirteen out of fifteen or over 86 percent, and with an 86 percent divorce rate, the concept of family does not carry much weight.

This group of gay blades from the '20s certainly caught the attention of the young ladies who summered on the island, and joyous marriages were arranged between high-spirited, attractive young people. My uncle Stan comes to mind; Stan ran one of his father's companies and served on the boards of others. He was a field and stream kind of man who contented himself with skeet shooting (he became Connecticut state champion), boat handling (he owned a succession of powerboats for fishing out of Harthaven Harbor), and hunting for woodcock and other fowl. What he passed on to his daughters eludes me. I just remember his home to be very cold prior to the cocktail hour, at which time, as in our home, a human warmth would suffuse the room. At huge

Christmas reunions Uncle Stan would chafe at the bit, waiting to go out to shoot skeet, once bolting the room, not even waiting for the lavish turkey feast presided over by my grandfather, and served by two cooks and a maid who poured champagne until almost all of the grownups as well as I became tipsy. In those pre–World War II days I recall my uncle and his wife, Lois, as two especially attractive people just casually attentive to their daughters.

I suppose I am trying to paint a picture of men in clothes and equipment out of Abercrombie's in New York, most of them married to sprightly, sexy women. These men had boats and guns to play with, enough inherited income to give them a cushion, and a playful spirit not dampened by harsh economics, never having known penury on a personal basis. I see them as heirs to a family tradition of business and Yankee individualism going back to 1632, when Deacon Stephen Hart settled in the Connecticut Valley. I do not imagine this group as thoughtful; rather they assumed a way of life that happily placed them somewhere in the top third economically and socially. Of all of them, only my father saw combat in World War I. I do not know what the others thought about that, but I like to think that down deep they must have admired him. He returned damaged and married my mother in 1921, the year his cousin Ted was playing end on Yale's undefeated football team, the year that kicked off a "roaring" decade in which cousin Merv would disappear on binges and Tod Hart would be dispatched to find him. Young Val and Stan Hart teamed up to set hearts flying about that time, and Bob Hart commenced a long love affair with aircraft, becoming a pilot when such was very unusual. Tod, a handsome and wry man, was married to Elise Russell by then and raised an interesting family that produced a psychotherapist; an army colonel; an obscurist, brainy housewife/mother; and a son who drank himself to death in his early forties.

As for my generation, Martha's Vineyard was our playground. A pine forest rose behind our house; our harbor opened to Nantucket Sound where, during the war, I fished for scup and flounder from my rowboat. Beyond Nantucket Sound was the Atlantic and the whole wide world. Cousins my sister's age abounded, and I grew up hearing them call to one another through the hot, hazy daylight and again in the evening before Anna put me to bed: Howdie, Norm, Dave, Mary Jane, Bung, Dorsey, Phronsie, Patty, Betsy, Bill Abbe (called Blabby), Mike…so many for my sister to play with.

Today, no one with the name Hart lives in Harthaven. Four Moores—whose grandmother was Martha Hart, daughter of William—and my cousin Sam Low, the son of Virginia Hart Low and grandson of Walter, still have dwellings in the family compound. The classic summer homes still stand along the harbor where, in the '30s, my grandfather ran races for his grandchildren and grandnieces and nephews. The '40s and '50s, which I recall so vividly, saw the harbor fill with catboats, small powerboats, and larger sportfishing craft. My father's black schooner was tied up at the end of our own dock. We had large authentic family clambakes in those years, at which some family members got quite drunk. Once a fire started in the beach grass and almost burned Tod Hart, who'd passed out unnoticed amid the tall leaves, his head very close to the encircling flames. Just as my parents had failed to notice my fall off the boat when I was three, no one paid much attention to him. At the end of the clambake, boats tipped over in the harbor as merry-makers made their way back from the beach. In later years, with my Uncle Stan in charge, the clambakes became more organized, the whole affair performed up in front of the Peases' house where there was no harbor to contend with.

Although some of us still see one another, the family as I recall it from childhood has broken up. The closest thing we had to family reunions were the clambakes. I recall my tall, dark-haired cousin Joanne Hart Shepard stating, "What a grand family we have," as she surveyed the scene at the beach. That would have been around 1955. I also recall Harthaven cruises led by Uncle Stan in his powerboat and my father in his schooner. We'd go off to Tarpaulin Cove on Naushon Island. They'd set up a charcoal grill and a bar and we'd all drink, eat, and swim. On the way back I'd sleep on the deck of the schooner or take the helm, letting the sun color me as dark as hickory. That night I'd take my date out to a party or a bar or just for a ride, feeling the effects of the salt and sun and the lovely waters of Vineyard Sound as well as the glow from a huge family mulled by spirits. Casual as an old flannel shirt, life just took its time with me.

•   •   •

Martha's Vineyard became famous in 1969 when Senator Edward Kennedy drove his rented car off a bridge at Chappaquiddick. Carly Simon and James Taylor, Walter Cronkite, Lillian Hellman, William Styron, and Mike Wallace—all summer residents—brought additional notoriety to the island. When Universal Pictures filmed *Jaws* on the Vineyard, and then when Jackie Kennedy Onassis built a house in Gay Head, the island's celebrity was secured well into the future. Finally, President Clinton and his wife, Hillary, began to call for a summer fortnight. By now perhaps a majority of readers can visualize what the Vineyard looks like today and guess with some accuracy what it would be like to summer there.

What most readers will not be able to imagine is how the Vineyard was before the 1950s, when the first gaggle of newsmakers began to gather on its shores. The 1930s and '40s were the years of James Cagney, Katherine Cornell, and a few thousand Portuguese-Americans and Yankees joined by a few thousand businessmen and their families in the summer. The Vineyard had artists and writers in those pre-celebrity days: Thomas Hart Benton, Van Wyck Brooks, Max Eastman who loved the beach that was so immense. The beach meant freedom. As a boy, I walked the beach and often I came across a group of nudists, with Max Eastman at its center. Eastman, a vague figure of prominence, was very handsome and easily drew attention to himself. Seeing him on the beach, surrounded by naked women, filled my young heart with envy. Also, back before World War II, I never was quite sure who I was seeing along the roadways or in town or on the beach as other intellectuals and luminaries came to visit. Somerset Maugham, Jackson Pollack and Charles Lindbergh come to mind. We summer folks had the run of the island, and the few so-called important people garnished our lives and spiced things up just a bit. I could tell my parents that James Cagney sat in front of me at the movies or that I saw Katherine Cornell and a man who could have been Noel something or other at Darlings on Circuit Avenue in Oak Bluffs, buying popcorn.

"Coward," my mother had said. "You don't know who he is but he is English and in the theater and he writes. He is what the English would call 'very clever.'"

"Pooh!" my father exclaimed, sitting in a wicker easy chair, his head under a stand-up lamp, reading. *Pooh* was his word of derision for anything that implied culture with a capital C, as he put it. He detested pretension so much that any man who put on airs was a "big poobah" and a woman who did likewise would be a "Miss La de da!" A term of approval was "good scout" as in "He's a good scout." The worst thing to be was "a fathead." *Dunderhead* and *fumblefinger* were close seconds.

My father was happiest in his workshop back in New Britain. He loved wood and making things like a table or a cabinet. He once built a mahogany rowboat for me; heavy and russet colored, it took over our playroom for months as it progressed from a design on paper to the moment he inserted brass oarlocks and pronounced it ready for rowing. He trusted his hands and he had a blind faith in what he called common sense which was a kind of fraudulent wisdom that resided in the uninformed mind. He was like others in his crowd: half-educated at a New England prep school, distrustful of artistic people, big city folk who couldn't hunt or fish or sail, and do-gooders. Common sense was what you went by and it served you well, so it was thought. He read popular novels, popular histories and manuals of instruction. He abhorred Reds because Communists threatened the power of the industrialist. The industrialist was someone who could get the job done, get his hands dirty and fashion a product. His blind allegiance to the hierarchy of the factory and its spokesman, the Republican Party, coupled with a security that emanated from within—courage in war, potency in bed, and dexterity with mechanics and carpentry, hunting, fishing, building, and sailing boats—produced a wall of ignorance when it came to understanding the rest of the world. It was not surprising therefore that he did not care for actors or clever people like Noel Coward.

Once my grandfather, Howard, brought James Cagney over for a sail on my father's Alden schooner, which he kept at our dock in Harthaven. Later at dinnertime I asked how it went. I'd seen James Cagney from a distance and in movies for three years or so. I'd gotten the idea of a movie star from our maid, Anna, and I was thrilled that my father had one out on his boat. My father's response to my question was silence. I asked him again: "How did it go?" Finally he said, "Jimmy didn't say much. He did tell a couple of stories that weren't funny. The old man liked it. So I guess it was okay. It went peachy fine," he admitted in a resigned voice. And that was that. No buddy-buddy for me with an exciting actor. Cagney, who was a friend of my grandfather's and Uncle Stan's as well, never returned to our house. I don't think my father ever said more than a word or two to him again. Hollywood…pooh!

Disregarding my father's imprecations concerning art, the world of the mind, or any social scene that lauded wit and style, I, conversely, *did* think that there was something enviable about being clever. There was a theatrical streak in me that made me want to be witty and extemporaneous, to let words roll off my tongue with bite and spoof and even rhyme. I pictured myself as a virtuoso with words. Such was a natural reaction to my father, who could equate a spate of verbal acumen with balderdash. With or without my father's influence I was destined for verbosity by my stammer. Bound up as I was, whenever I was able to free myself and allow language to flow from my mouth, I felt a rush of joy and fell victim to compulsive chatter and was often scorned by my brother as a "blabbermouth." In the chaos of my upbringing I yearned for attention, hearing all of the time my father's contempt, lodged in the word "fumblefinger." I was busting at the seams. I wanted to shout to the heavens but I was too fearful to do it.

•   •   •

Each June we would go back to the Vineyard. I longed for that first familiar whiff of saltwater. We'd set out in my father's Packard, or later in his Buick, carrying with us a leather picnic case from Abercrombie & Fitch in New York. We always picnicked at Frog Rock, a halfway spot in eastern Connecticut. I luxuriated in the smell of the leather that gushed forth when the picnic case was opened. But the salt smell that greeted us in Fall River was the grandest of all odors as it signaled our final approach to New Bedford, a few miles down the road, and the steamer that would take us to the Vineyard. New Bedford evoked images of sailing ships, fishing boats, waves lapping against the shore, and that cool green saltwater along the wharf where the pilings smelled of tar and oil and marlin—a tough, oiled spool of line used for reefing sails and making things fast. The breeze carried with it the ripeness of harbor life, and from where the breeze came was the open sea.

In a back closet in our summer house J-Boat replicas awaited. I had two of them: *Yankee* and *Rainbow*. They tipped over in rough water as the ripples in our harbor were too large, but the wading pool down by the bandstand in nearby Oak Bluffs was ideal. In or out of the water, I loved to handle them and pretend that I was at the helm.

Smells. So intense were the odors that greeted me in my early days that they became a major source of comfort. Leather. Saltwater. Another smell I loved was the odor of mothballs in our bungalow, entered again after nine months away. My father would unlock the front door and the rush of camphor would strike us. His first move after bringing in our suitcases would be to start a fire to take the chill out of the house. Anna would stoke up the coal stove in the kitchen, and within half an hour I'd be blessed with the cozy smell of hot coals, the odor of scrub oak burning on a roaring hearth, and still strong in the back room the great first-day-of-summer smell of mothballs. As I went to find my toys, left in the back of my closet, my heart would sing. I was in the bosom of life.

Try as I may, I cannot extract from my memory events that occurred prior to my second birthday. I retain impressions of skin and hair and comfort with my mother and maybe Anna. I sense a closeness to my father and feel myself nuzzled by him, the bristle on his face and the hairs on the back of his neck touchable to my pudgy little fingers. After two, things begin to come into focus. My olfactory senses produce sharp images. Besides the smell of the sea and mothballs and burning coal, there was the smell of beach grass and dry sand. I would dig out a swirl of sand and press my face into it and smell the sand mixed with long-dead microorganisms from the sea and crushed shell and other material that once lived in the depths. The sand and the slim reeds that grew from it formed my bed when I napped beside Anna or Helen, our maids. I smelled the desiccation of the beach the moment we made the turn at the seawall in Oak Bluffs and headed into Harthaven. Other more noticeable odors came from the harbor itself, often dead calm and pungent. The muddy bottom at low tide produced a fishy aroma. I recall the smell of my father's closet in Connecticut where he kept his shotgun and rifle and gunnysacks and heavy hunting clothes. My aunt Al Eddy had a toolshed, earthy with large tools crusted with dirt.

As a toddler I'd smell everything, and well into my childhood I can remember the acrid smell of sweat mixed with a rich aroma of sex emanating from my parents' bed. As soon as I could walk, I'd toddle into their bed to cuddle with my mother, early, before she rose for breakfast. She slept late, my father gone to work, and I became accustomed to the odor of what decades later I knew as the inevitable aftermath of liquescent lovemaking. Later on I'd sense the same odor just passing down the hall. I knew that they had sex often up into their sixties. It hung in the air like a glue that bound them to each other.

•　　•　　•

Right from infancy I learned not to cry. Crying pained my father, and his pain turned to disgust and scorn. A "good scout" didn't cry, and it was always important to be a good scout. Back before kindergarten when I started going to the dentist, at first I'd cry but quickly learned not to. My father would look exasperated, and my mother always turned to him for guidance, staring into his eyes to see what he would do. Exasperated, he did nothing, but his disgust was evident. I detested and feared the dentist because he hurt me, but I feared my father's pained expression even more. I do not recall Novocain in 1933 or 1934, and the dentist's drill was a heavy instrument and hurtful. The whole process was a nightmare, but I had to go because my teeth were soft as mush. I'd developed a gaseous stomach, and the pediatrician had prescribed a childhood without milk or dairy products. As a result, my teeth became vulnerable to the slightest intrusion of food. As for brushing my teeth, nobody had ever shown me the right way to do it. As with most of what life demanded and held, I was supposed to get the picture on my own.

So I did not cry at the dentist's, but I did cry when I had to go to dancing school, and my father, exasperated, threw up his hands and said, "Lu, let him be. He doesn't have to go if he doesn't want to." I cried when Anna decided to quit in the spring of 1940. I cried when my fingers got slammed in a car door on our way to see a Tom Mix movie at the old Seabreeze movie theater in Oak Bluffs. I did not cry again until I was nineteen. I'd finally learned to suppress my emotions. If I was afraid, I cowered within my own skin. If I hurt, my eyes would well up, but I would never cry lest my father see me.

•   •   •

I think my parents had dirty minds. Because they avoided all mention of sex and were never seen in the nude, except in my infancy, and didn't ever use words like "pregnant," one can imagine how much they kept inside their heads and how it festered there. Certainly things festered within me: I recall walking down the beach in Chilmark, probably in 1938. We were at a family picnic at cousin Carrie Brainard's beach, about a quarter of a mile up from Windy Gates, where a crowd of artists and intellectuals swam. I remember leaving my parents and my mother's relatives who were having a drink or two before the picnic and walking east, down the broad beach that fronts the Atlantic. I rounded a slight promontory of clay cliff and my eyes filled with the most heavenly sight. I'd already watched Helen's niece undress through the cracks in our mutual wall, but to see an adult woman, perhaps forty, about my mother's age, lying on her back, fully nude, was a signal experience I shall never forget. She was golden brown from weeks in the sun, and there was a lush growth on her lower belly that struck me like a blow. To stumble on such a sight at eight years old was stunning. She exceeded my range of fantasy. Her beauty was beyond anything I had imagined. Seeing her as she was unnerved me, as I knew that we were totally alone, just she and I and the sand. Far down the beach I could see naked men and women running along the edge of the surf. Whoever she was, her image became indelible in my mind, and even though I was puny and a child, I wanted to stroke her and explore her.

She was far more exciting than Helen's niece. I think that all of my life I've been looking for a duplicate of such a body, such a coloring and configuration of skin and hair and fair features. I stared at her—she, no doubt, amused. After a few moments I turned and wandered back to my relatives, returning with a secret that pulsed within me. I never told a soul about my discovery. Off and on throughout my life I'd chance upon a woman like the one I saw that day. I'd find them in the movies and in photography books. I began to luxuriate in my fantasies and became a closet peeper, a looker at others, a scrutinizer, a scanner of art and photography books, a tramper of nude beaches. What had been a pleasing experience became a deep-rooted secret pleasure I yearned to repeat.

Nothing risqué stays healthy locked in the closet of the mind. As with my parents, my mind grew dirty. Female beauty and procreative activities turned licentious. Thus a woman's breasts became something to stare at. The pubis was charged with sharp temptation. Later I would go to military school for five years, an all-male college on and off for eight years, the overwhelmingly male U.S. Air Force for four years—all the while warping and twisting the loveliness of women into sexual images, while women themselves were often remote and beyond my reach, leaving me to obsess like a troubled voyeur. I lived in the gap between actual experience and fantasy, growing up confused and charged with longing. I came out of the darkness of a home where everything of real interest was suppressed. I never knew what meaningful living with other people entailed and was never encouraged to explore the origins of my ignorance. There were millions of people like me across America. When I finally began to mature, I would read about bigotry and sexual repression and anti-intellectualism, defensive snobbery and fear of intimacy and on and on, and I'd see myself and my early life.

•　•　•

In June of 1941, when I was eleven years old, my mother asked me if I would mind moving to Maryland. "I thought I'd ask," she said. And at once, without a moment's thought, I answered, "Sure, that's okay with me," actually amused that my parents had thought to ask me. I had no awareness of Maryland and did not know what I had agreed to. I was not sure that it mattered. They were going, and therefore so was I.

By 1941 I was in the seventh grade at what was now called the Mooreland Hill School, riding my bike all over our end of New Britain and down into the center of town. I had friends everywhere and could roam at will. I'd discovered hockey and was learning to skate well. Football was still a passion, and I competed with much success. There were girls in class whose presence I was beginning to notice, particularly Joanne Vance, about whom I daydreamed. Girls in the ninth grade were displaying breasts through their sweaters, and in the spring when they raised their arms I saw hair that drew me back to Helen's niece and the memory of the woman on the beach. The mysteries of life were teasing me, I thought, as at home I listened to Victor Herbert's "Ah, Sweet Mystery of Life," recorded on Victor Red Label and belonging to my sister, away at Smith College. When my brother returned on vacation from the Berkshire School, he'd play his Will Bradley records down in the rathskeller and he'd drum on wooden boxes, trying to look like Gene Krupa.

My life seemed to be running on its own, with or without my parents' help, with or without any opening of the closet where all true feelings and revelations were kept. Anna was in the kitchen, our new dog, Taffy, was bounding about our large house. With friends I lost my stammer, but it returned when I was forced to speak to an adult. I hated to pick up the telephone when I was alone in the house and expected to take a message of some importance. But apart from my stammer, my life ran smoothly.

By 1941, when I was at Mooreland Hill gazing at Joanne Vance and wondering how I could get her undressed—play house, post office, activities I'd heard of—I was already suppressing uncomfortable experiences and thoughts so that I could live free of personal vexations. My mother, now forty-one years old, was returning drunk from cocktail parties and fighting with my father. My brother was like a thundercloud far off in the distance. My sister was blond and vivacious and appeared extremely happy at Smith. She'd studied for a year in Switzerland, raced my father's old boat, *Mahomy*, fallen in love with Kingman Brewster, a sailing friend, later president of Yale, and was always bursting with motion and glee. I lived for school and sports and reading the newspapers. I followed the Battle of Britain even before turning to the sports pages. Occasionally I thought of Brownie, put to sleep by my father in 1938, but true to my habit of suppression, I would push Brownie from my mind. But Brownie is in my mind now as I write this memoir…

My mother never liked Brownie. Brownie was a mongrel who cowered and skulked and smiled with his head down when spoken to. Brownie was not a poodle or a cocker spaniel, America's favorite dog. He was not like Taffy, our purebred Welsh terrier. Brownie was in fact an embarrassment.

To me, however, Brownie was my best friend. I was closer to Brownie even than I was to Anna. Brownie followed me to school and was waiting in the driveway at home when I returned. When I was an infant, he'd lie beside my carriage and snarl at passersby. Brownie and I spoke to each other. He could understand me and I could understand him. I loved his smile which my mother saw as weak. If dogs had classes, Brownie would have been lower class. My mother, born to relatively poor parents, was always interested in class. So, as I figured it, one summer she pressured my father into killing my best friend because he did-n't *look* right for a woman of her position.

My father lied. He said Brownie was going to the kennel just for a while to be checked over. After a month went by he said that, yes, soon Brownie would come home. After two months, almost at the end of the summer, I mentioned that I'd be so happy to see Brownie again. We were going to return home from the Vineyard, and then we could retrieve him from the kennel where he'd been held so long, I thought.

"No," said my father, looking away. "We had Brownie put to sleep."

"But he wasn't sick," I protested.

"He was getting old," he said, and then there was silence.

•   •   •

It did not pay to dwell on Brownie, nor was it helpful to recall the time I almost lost Anna. It was in May, before the war, and Anna had heard enough complaints from my mother. There may have been trou-ble in the Bund which was unsettling her. All I knew was that one Saturday morning when I was still in bed I awoke to hear my mother screaming into the telephone at my father who was at work. (My father always worked in the factory on Saturday mornings; everyone worked on Saturdays, the Depression having lost its sting at last.) My mother was screaming that Anna had quit and would not be going to the Vineyard with us in two weeks' time. I flew from my bed and raced to her room, crying loudly, a boy in hysterics. I heard her tell my father, "Come home at once. Buster is having a fit."

My father returned and spoke to Anna and before long I could sense a truce settling over the house. Anna and my mother might detest each other but would make do for the greater good—for me, and beyond me, for my mother herself. By the end of the '30s she was already seriously infirm, and not just from alcohol and emotional instability. Her diagnosis of multiple sclerosis had been confirmed. She needed help. It was impossible to expect her to cook and clean house even if she knew how to, which she didn't. My mother, incapacitated, simply had to have Anna, who knew the family so well, and within an hour of my father's return, Anna had retracted her resignation. I truly felt that my life had been saved. Although everything was opening up for me, I still depended on Anna. Anna meant so much, and with Brownie gone by then, she was, in an emotional sense, all I had left.

None of this is to deny the love I felt for my father. But he was not soft. By the time I reached nine or ten we never embraced, and from ten on I ceased to touch him. But I did touch Anna, and beyond touching and holding her, she talked to me. She talked about the world we lived in, and with her I could discuss matters that I felt were important. I remember telling her about a man and a woman I'd seen on the beach at Harthaven. In 1940 there were still dunes on the beach where I used to play Prince Valiant, running about with a wooden sword and a round shield fashioned from the bottom of a barrel. Suddenly one day I nearly stumbled over a naked woman lying on her back with her legs spread akimbo and a young man rhythmically rising and falling above her, stomach pressed upon stomach. As I approached I saw her closed eyes open wide. I had never seen anyone so startled and so full of dismay. The man, sensing something, turned to see me. Astonishment filled his eyes. He pulled apart from the woman, emitting a suction sound. Frightened, I ran away. I was ten years old by then and still completely ignorant of the sexual act. I told Anna what I had seen and she looked at me for a second, then threw back her head and laughed as she spoke. "Why, Buster, you caught two people fucking," she said, her own eyes merry with the thought. I knew at once what the word meant. My imagination on fire, I could see them doing it on the beach, the woman so deep in her pleasure that the dismay in her eyes was close to pure hatred. She was on the verge of something I could not put words to, but I could sense it. What I'd happened upon was the most powerful thing I'd ever seen or imagined.

· · ·

I never said good-bye to Anna. It was September 1942. My sister was newly married and my brother was at the University of Chicago about to enlist in an Army Air Corps training program (from which he would be jettisoned and reassigned to the military police). There were now only four of us and Taffy. The house was closed and our belongings were loaded in a huge Mayflower moving van. I'd given away most of my toys including an electric train. In a daze I stood in front of my aunt and uncle's house, where we'd spent the night. I trusted in my father. That was all I knew as the reality of leaving New Britain began to settle in.

Soon my mother started to cry; she must have begun to see what some half-drunk, late-night conversation had gotten them into. Middle-aged, my parents were leaving their home and my father's heritage, the place where both his grandfather and father had become what were called captains of industry. All their connections, economic and social, were based in New Britain. Now, suddenly, almost as if on a whim, they were leaving town. And they were leaving at the start of a World War, plunging ahead during a state of emergency, private and public.

Anna reached down to pat Taffy who was beside me on a leash. Then she stooped to hug him. She rose and stared me in the eye. There were no tears, just her soft brown eyes looking into mine trying to tell me something I thought I already knew. She was saying: *Your parents are fools. You should stay here.*

But she did not speak. Then she turned on her heels and walked away, back toward the Eddys' cook, Emma Bross, the mother of my friend Augie, whom I used to bike to Plainville to see on my Columbia. Anna walked back toward the house as we all stood in silence. Neither my mother nor my father said good-bye. This woman who had been with us for twelve years and who had raised me was now being discarded. We got into my father's Buick and I took my seat in the back with Taffy beside me. As we pulled out of the Eddys' driveway, my mother began to weep. The enormity of it all struck home and I asked myself, *What in the world are we doing?* But I did not utter a word.

Something that has rankled my conscience for decades is my cowardice that day when I never said good-bye to Anna. I should have hugged her and wept and told her how much I loved her. I should have gotten her address and vowed to write and to visit when the war was over. Instead I was mute. I deflected my feelings in good style, a fine son to my father. I was being a good scout that day but I was a terrible human being. In the ensuing years when I could have found her, I never did. Not once in all the days I spent visiting New Britain did I search for Anna. I cannot forgive myself for being so callous.

Sometime much later, well into the 1950s, I heard that soon after leaving us Anna took a job in a downtown bakery. How many bakeries were there? If she were working in a New Britain bakery, I should have found her. I have no excuse for not going to Anna, to thank her for raising me and to tell her that I loved her.

PART II

Brook Hall

Chapter 4

Has anyone ever seen such dull and tired earth as extends south from the school once called the Brook Hall Military Academy? In southern Maryland in 1942 rutted roads disappeared into pine forests leading to Amish settlements or to the slatted barns of colored people who lived in forestial isolation within a county run by white people, the whites themselves isolated from the rest of the world. Sometimes you'd see them hunkered down along the walls of old barns where bullet-ridden Royal Crown Cola signs hung rusted and dangling.

People moved in slow motion through this odd somnolence. Coal-black roads snaked tar hot, mapped like rivulets toward the southern tip of St. Catherine's County; they made a network of narrow byways pushing south to Point Diamond, a dead end on the Chesapeake Bay.

Harold Hawkins, who was only twelve, had never seen swayback mules or their drivers: usually Negroes in coveralls, but sometimes white men, thin as sticks, plodding along the shoulders of the road, stepping past the litter that attends to a county too poor to clean itself. At night, when you rounded a bend in the road, it was common to come upon a man listing from too much beer, who'd got drunk in one of the tawdry roadhouses that appeared at intervals between Thomasville to the north of Brook Hall and Clark, a small intersection at the head of Old Man's Creek, which emptied into the Potomac where the river meets the Chesapeake.

Dodging lurching figures in the night was easier than dodging pickup trucks coming at you, their wheelbases straddling
the center of the narrow unlined pavement. As a result, there
were a good many deaths in this rural area; it was part of the
way life was lived. It was like the school. It was like the earth
itself, where there was only one money crop, tobacco, and
even the tobacco that hung like brown papyrus in the old
warehouses in Thomasville was third-rate. But even if you
could rate the tobacco, you couldn't rate the school. Supported by state funds, it existed without definition save for its
teams. If you defined a school by its football and boxing
teams, you could define Brook Hall. Otherwise it was too
amorphous for categorization, too lacking in most essentials
to be accounted a genuine preparatory school. A small,
dispirited faculty of teachers, called Captains, were paid to
teach a hundred and fifty students, or cadets. Harold Hawkins
thought the whole place scary and weird, but he kept his
feelings to himself. He did not want to report home that his
parents had made a mistake.

He remembered his mother waving at him from the
window of the Buick roadster, the car's snappy dark red
body and white convertible top a grand contrast to the
bleak, spartan, and weathered campus. The school bus, so old
it had to be hand-cranked to get it going, stood inert by the
side of the gymnasium. There may have been other vehicles
about, but Harold did not notice them as his parents drove
away. All he saw was this run-down bus, so battered and old
and his father's maroon Buick so sporty and new and his
mother looking at him out of the window, her eyes full of
tears and confusion and fear that she had erred— erred
badly. Watching them pull away, his father stoic behind the
wheel, Harold did not cry out. Instead he assumed their failure and guilt as his own. His mother's shame became his. His
father's, too, lived within him that day in mid-September
when he stood before his assigned barracks, holding a small
suitcase, somewhere forty miles south of Washington, D.C.
The old World War I cannon that rested on the lawn,
painted dark green and looking fit and ready for action,

reminded him that the war was on and was going badly. He decided to stand erect and take what was coming to him as he supposed the men at Dunkirk had stood beneath the diving Stukas. If his mother's tears had raised doubts and guilt, the cannon brushed them away. He would be a good scout and make do.

So it was off to the barracks and the smell of young boys hot from the white glaze of summer's end in the South when just about everything is burnt dry. His roommates were named Rawlings, Mayfield, and Braun. Both Rawlings and Mayfield had first names, although they were seldom called by them, but Braun was only Braun—Cadet Braun in class. He was fourteen and very strong for his age, and though kindly by nature, he had a dark side and chose to keep his first name to himself. One did not press him.

Harold met Braun on his first afternoon at Brook Hall and was informed that he came from "the streets of Baltimore." He was large-boned and had a full head of dark brown curly hair and well-developed biceps. He planned to try out for the varsity even though he was only in the eighth grade—a Prep like Harold himself. Jimmy Mayfield was also in the eighth grade and was thirteen, both of them a year older than Harold.

That first night at school, just after taps had sounded and the dusk of daylight saving time was still slightly illuminative, Harold was to get his first inkling of life as it was lived at Brook Hall. Apparently the idea was to see who could ejaculate first—Braun or Mayfield. Neither Harold nor, presumably, Rawlings knew what they were talking about, and so they watched from their cots against opposite walls. In the middle, standing on their own beds, were Braun and Mayfield, and at the word "Go," rendered timorously by an importuned Rawlings, they began a furious exercise in masturbation. Mayfield was able to come within ten seconds, while Braun, taking longer and enjoying it more, emitting deep groans of pleasure, finally was able to spurt "jissum" up against the chandelier which depended from the ceiling just above his bed.

Harold felt his stomach turn to knots and wondered in a state of panic who this Braun was. Mayfield was smaller and less frightening; there was something in Mayfield that reminded Harold of himself. But Braun was huge with a great pulsing cock extending from a lush tangle of brown hair. And he was right there beside Harold, his eyes closed, the veins in his neck, like the veins in his large organ, outlined and vulnerable to the edge of bursting.

Naturally Braun took credit for the victory because, though Mayfield was quicker, he was better. "I hit the light bulb," he said proudly, almost sneering at Mayfield's puny and shriveled equipment which hung for a moment outside his pajamas. Harold cowered beneath his covers which were soaked with sweat. Rawlings at the other side of the room did the same. Finally the two masturbators, each filled with his own sense of victory, curled into their beds.

That first night was quiet save for the padding of feet in the hallway—older boys going down to the one foul toilet, maybe for a smoke or to urinate, maybe to see Herman Fillmore, a Captain who had his room near the toilet and entertained after taps. Other than the padding of feet, the only sound was the sound of whippoorwills in the still Maryland night. Mayfield and Braun were breathing heavily by the time Harold finally fell asleep.

A funny thing about Braun. After maybe three weeks— after the time Rawlings tried to commit suicide—he just upped and left. He hit the tracks, which was what most boys did when they ran away. They were scared of being found by the headmaster, Major Walter Keller, should they get caught hitching along the road. So what they did was to walk down to the single-bed railway tracks that ran in front of the school and then follow them up past Thomasville, past an intersection at Yarborough, and finally to Washington. If they walked quickly, they knew—or had been told—that the tracks led straight to Washington, and if you left at night, you could be in the capital by the next evening. In the five years that Harold attended Brook Hall, only one boy who hit the tracks ever returned. Parents or guardians usually just sent for their sons' clothes. Anyway, off went Braun with no explanation, no warning, leaving only a kind of residue of personality that told Harold and the other smaller students who formed the Prep squad that he was too much for them: too grown-up. Harold figured that Braun would lie about his age and enlist. Someday Braun would avenge the country's losses in the Pacific. Everyone figured he'd be a hero.

When boys got in trouble and acquired "hours," they walked them off or worked them off. In the war years there was little outside help for campus maintenance, and those students who found themselves in trouble were the ones who did the clean-up and fix-up work. There were two ladies who doubled as nurses and seamstresses. Presumably they were also paid to oversee the kitchen, which was run by a hulking black woman, the color of India ink, named Willa.

The women, both approaching forty, were called Miss Stowell and Miss Ziegler. They were basically idlers who provided warmth to the healthier faculty members. Captain "Greaseball" Louden, who taught military history and the math teacher, Captain Lipsett, were often spotted nude back in the pine woods, lying on blankets with the two spinsters snuggled close to them. The women would also be nude but somehow more repulsive than sexy. The one time Harold sneaked up the narrow lane to "where the Captains go," he saw rail-thin Captain Louden lying on his side and pudgy Captain Lipsett resting on his back, his organ lost in a patch of tan pubic hair. The women were on their backs as well, and their white skin was ghostly and their white hair was sprinkled with pine needles and leaves. Miss Ziegler had a scar that went straight up her stomach. Neither one had tits. Harold might have been viewing a scene from a prison camp. No wonder more students didn't sneak along the path to spy. It was better to stare at pinup girls like Jinx Falkenburg and Ella Raines. With only women like the spinsters around, you needed pictures. That seemed to be the consensus.

There were two older boys, brothers, whose name was Westinghouse. Harold didn't know where they came from but assumed, mistakenly, they were somehow related to the family that was a household word. They were bright and deployed a cynical style that said "bugger off" to the beholder. They were always in trouble and spurned sports. And they too were from the North. Harold wanted to get to know them but was too young. The Westinghouses were over sixteen and talked dirty and were always walking the track, which was an oval cinder pathway that circled behind the pathetically meager grandstand used for parade watching and football games. Harold's friend Sanderman said: "The Westinghouses don't give a shit. They've seen the fickle finger of fate and laughed at it in its face." Harold, looking at their long necks, thought of cranes or swans or geese and nodded. Fuck-ups. He liked the Westinghouses and kept it a secret lest someone ask why and he would not know the answer.

Every afternoon, through all seasons, you would find the Westinghouse brothers walking the track, Springfields cock-eyed on their shoulders, their uniforms reminding you of a badly defeated army. And if they were not on the track, they'd be painting, scrubbing, sweeping, or even shoveling coal down a gaping hole in the floor of the gymnasium.

Sometimes, though, if you watched them closely while they were on the track, you'd see them suddenly duck under the stands. They'd sneak cigarettes there while a compliant Sergeant of the Guard would turn the other way. And if the Sergeant of the Guard was reliable enough to lie on their behalf, the Westinghouses would slip under the stands and sneak across the end of the football field, their long slender bodies angled against the wind, into the woods and thence to Gerner's garage or to a hillbilly bar named Robey's.

Early on, Harold came to romanticize the Westinghouse brothers, who inspired awe with their insolence and subdued bravado. Often Harold would be on the track with them, his Springfield so heavy as to dig welts in the flesh over his collarbone. Suddenly, like will-o'-the-wisps, the Westinghouse brothers would be gone. At the far bend of the oval track Harold could see them dash from the stands and then in quickstep hike it into the woods. At Gerner's garage the Westinghouses and another cadet, Karl Stackhouse, would talk atomic physics while sitting on crates of Nehi Orange or leaning up against a wall of beer cases, bottles of Arrow and National Bohemian. They also talked of test-tube babies and Alfred Einstein. Any local boy who might happen by would keep his distance from this kind of talk, tinkering with a Ford or a Chevy, unable to follow the line of excited patter. At five o'clock they'd be back, their fingers nicotine-stained and their eyes bleared by beer.

In that first fall what passed the time at Brook Hall—walking the track, drilling, studying after a fashion, eating improvised meals from meager rations, and of course going to football games—was not dull. Cadet Stackhouse got caught screwing in the chapel. He was a raffish, probably brilliant, seventeen-year-old who looked like the Joker in the Batman comics. He had very black hair and large ears and a broad mouth. He didn't talk very much and hated sports. Normally he'd have been hazed or picked on, but he was in the Westinghouse group, which took intellectual preoccupations as their due, and when Stackhouse began talking about the atom everyone would listen, even the Westinghouses, who would look down from their slender necks and nod approvingly. He was in effect outside the law. His indifference to mundane matters was his shield; his knowledge of the "roots of existence" was so arcane that it granted him the status of an admired untouchable.

After long weekends and holidays, Karl Stackhouse would return from his home in Washington with exotic-smelling cigarettes he'd got from jazz musicians, and everyone knew that he smuggled hard liquor into the barracks. But the night of the big dance, Alumni Day, he outdid himself by luring a pretty girl who attended Owen's City Junior College for Ladies down the lawn to the old church which was so covered with ivy that it looked camouflaged against air attack.

His lovemaking would have gone unheralded had he not been caught by Major Keller. Led into the night by some primal intuition, the Eagle, as he was called, strode into the dark chapel and, turning on his four-battery flashlight, he saw there on the altar behind the lectern the two bare legs of a girl wrapped vise-like around the naked, pimply rump of Cadet Stackhouse.

Back across the lawn, cadets and their dates from the junior college were dancing to "In the Mood" and "Chattanooga Choo Choo." Young Harold was darting about in the shadows, out after taps for the Preps, slipping along in the dark with Jimmy Mayfield. They hid pop-eyed near the gym where the dance was going on, watching alumni with students in tow slip out to their automobiles for a slug out of a bottle, hearing the giggle of older girls who had come as dates of the alumni and were therefore removed from the rules of both Brook Hall and Owen's City J.C., hearing them giggle in Packards and Pontiacs and even in the cabs of old pickups. This was heart-pounding material for the young voyeurs.

And then they saw the Eagle. The Eagle was holding the awkward Joker by the hair of his head, propelling him across the undulating lawn. And behind the two of them was the girl, as lovely as a flower but misty-eyed and sobbing and carrying her high heels and wiping the hair from her eyes. She looked like the actress Ann Rutherford to Mayfield and Harold, hidden behind a small truck as the Eagle led the two culprits back inside to the sounds of "Pistol Packin' Mama."

The Eagle was known to be strict but fair. If you'd been reported for pillow fighting—normal youthful hijinks—you might get twenty hours. With a bit of industry you could work that off in three days by shoveling coal, for which you were credited at triple time.

Offenses such as missing formation or being improperly dressed carried a punishment predicated upon the Eagle's mood. A first offense for oversleeping was dismissed lightly. If you made a habit of it, you could get full time. It all depended.

But unprovoked assaults meant dismissal. "We want no bad Bustahs here," the Eagle would roar. To coldcock a student without warning was the ultimate transgression, and any boy who beat up another boy in a fight that was not "fair" was sent home. Cadets were expected to square off behind the main barracks or at the smoker. Broken jaws and black eyes were allowable if the fight was fair. As for Stackhouse, getting laid in the chapel was an offense with no history. The cadet corps whispered about it and finally concluded that Stackhouse had received a private tongue lashing, but no other penalty.

Rawlings, who was Harold's age, never got into a fight; he was much too girlish. What he did do was attempt suicide. His mother, who came to collect him, rampaged through the barracks like a wild hen in a chicken house. She threw clothes and a radio and Victrola records down the corridor. She yelled, "Look what they've done to my boy!"

It all began when Rawlings received news concerning his father, a pilot in the Navy. Lieutenant Rawlings had been reported missing in action, and then quite suddenly the Red Cross sent on his name as a prisoner of war. When this was reported to young Rawlings, it should have brought him joy. But as Harold and Mayfield figured it, Rawlings had assumed his father was dead and had come to terms with it and, though surely joyful that he'd lived, he could not handle the image of a man he revered being prodded and beaten and starved in some horrible prison camp. He could not abide the thought of his father's humiliation. Or were they very wrong? Maybe the reason Rawlings tried to kill himself was that he hated and feared his father, and now quite suddenly the Red Cross had told him that his father would be back. When the war was over, his father, a Navy hero, would see him, see how he had grown. Lieutenant Rawlings would assess his son's progress into manhood. And Rawlings as Harold knew him would never wish to confront his father who had endured so much hate and pain in a Japanese prison camp.

At Brook Hall, Rawlings had turned girlish. With so many young men and boys and no way to compete with them, he soon gave up and affected the posture of a girl. He walked with his thumbs against his hips, his fingers facing backward, and wiggled in a provocative fashion. He had a sad face and wide hips and narrow shoulders that disappeared inside his uniform shirt. No one ever got to know Rawlings very well, although Harold had heard him speak of his father being shot down and then left for dead. They were walking back to Morris Hall where the Preps lived, and Harold felt a closeness to Rawlings and he could imagine Rawlings's father plunging into the sea. Older cadets said Rawlings was queer, but Harold didn't know what "queer" meant.

When it happened, it was a pleasant Sunday and Harold was in his room wondering what to do. He was looking out his window at a farm that abutted the school and where a large stallion stood still in the heat, something hanging from his underside that couldn't be what Harold thought it had to be. So his mind was slightly preoccupied. There was a box of Ritz crackers on the large table in the middle of the room and he was idly taking a cracker from the box when he heard a muffled scream coming from a room across the hall. Harold waited a moment and heard it again. It was the sound of a person trying to gargle. But he sensed panic in the sound, panic and pain and death, and he rose to investigate. As he entered the room, he saw Rawlings hanging from the over-head light fixture. A pile of schoolbooks had been kicked away and scattered. Above the disarray was Rawlings, dangling from the chandelier, his face the color of a ripe tomato, turning purple. He had tied himself by his necktie to the fixture above the table and then had kicked the books out from under him. Now with little breath left he was trying to untie the knot that had cinched up under his jaw. Rawlings had changed his mind, Harold thought, even as he grabbed at him and held him up, himself scrambling onto the table and hoisting Rawlings so that the pressure could be relieved.

Rawlings was heavy, and soon Harold was losing his strength. He didn't know how long he could hold him with both hands, with no third to try and rip the tie or to grope for scissors or a knife. But he held on and Rawlings kept making terrible noises in his throat and finally Mayfield came back from sneaking a smoke and, hearing Harold scream, ran to the rescue. Eventually he was able to find some scissors and the tie was at last cut and Rawlings fell to the table, bruising the side of his head. By that time his face was the color of a purple plum and his eyes were bulging from their sockets. Finally, Harold ran to find either Miss Stowell or Miss Ziegler and brought the latter back with him, hurrying her along. She had not been easily located, but at last he'd found her in the laundry room; the other woman was somewhere in the sunshine with Captain Lipsett and Captain Louden. Miss Ziegler was rumpled and red-faced as she heard her name yelled and came charging up from the basement of the main barracks. In the end she just checked Rawlings's pulse and called an ambulance from Crandallton, fifteen miles distant. He was carted away crying, and later that night Braun nodded mysteriously and said that Harold had acted like a man.

It was the day after Mrs. Rawlings came to collect her son's things that Braun hit the tracks. He sneaked out at about eleven o'clock. He never said good-bye. He'd had enough of this chickenshit place, or so he'd said a few days back—back before Rawlings tried to kill himself, which seemed to confirm everything.

•   •   •

My parents lived on a small chicken farm in southern Maryland, down toward the end of a peninsula. To the east of this peninsula was the Chesapeake Bay. On the west was the Potomac. St. Mary's City, where we lived, overlooked the St. Mary's River, a most beautiful meandering river that originates several miles inland from a plot of land between Great Mills and a town inexplicably called California. If you sailed down the St. Mary's, you'd reach the Potomac, thence to the bay itself, a magical body of water imbued with legend and history and, by 1942, a supposed haunt of German U-boats.

My father had over forty acres on the St. Mary's where he raised White Leghorns. He was a "gentleman farmer." A fringe benefit to his chicken business was a "T" (for "truck") gas ration sticker for his station wagon at a time when gasoline was severely rationed. There was an old flatbed truck on the farm as well, driven by the hired man, John Hopewell. That too had a "T." Gas, therefore, was theoretically not a problem, although getting it was always an inconvenience as the two or three service stations in St. Mary's County would periodically run dry.

John Hopewell was a towering black mountain of a man, surely six feet three and weighing at least two hundred fifty pounds. Some school-mates at Brook Hall who lived near St. Mary's City told me that John Hopewell was a champion wrestler. He took on all comers in the slanted, cinderblock-built roadhouses for colored folks. Men died in knife fights up in the hills behind crossroads towns of little account, men dark as pitch like John. John remained unscathed. *Huge* was my father's word for John.

John's wife, Nora, was built like a rectangle—seemingly almost as wide as she was tall. She was maybe five feet two in height and café au lait in color. Nora was very sweet and a good cook and she did all the cleaning as well as cooking grand southern-style dinners. In the spring, before we went north to the Vineyard, my parents were served crab cakes and deviled crabs at lunch. When so inclined, my mother would request soft-shell crabs, and John would take the rowboat and pole along the river's edge scooping as he went, his big brown eyes alert to any slight indication of a crab hiding in the muddy bottom of the river. A sizable network of raspberry bushes grew in the garden and John tended to these with loving care. This conglomeration of bushes bore a surfeit of berries, enough to eat like peanuts, enough for a hundred breakfasts and at least that many desserts.

Having my fill of crabs and berries made my early summer a gas-tronomic delight. I ate sparingly at school owing to a perceived food scam. On arrival, each student had to submit his food ration book, and someone apparently took them all—a treasure trove on the black mar-ket—and sold a large number of them, saving just enough for minimal fare. We dined on scrapple, Spam, and something called monkey meat, and on Sundays we ate boiled chicken that looked like survival rations in a lifeboat, badly plucked, naked, and obscene. Our milk was often rancid. We had no butter or margarine or sugar. I used to pour plain syrup on almost everything; into my coffee it went and over the tasteless hot cereal in the morning, and of course over the scrapple. I lost several pounds each year; in my first year I went from being a well-padded northern boy to looking like some southern cracker's child, deprived of anything nutri-tional. I could have gotten rickets. And yet the smell of the hot cereal and the bitter coffee as it wafted over our military formations for morning mess was heartwarming. Inside we'd get something resembling grits— maybe a cereal called Wheatina—ladled out in large portions, hot and ready for a covering of nondescript sweet syrup. We all drank syrupy coffee and in the heart of a cruel winter storm we huddled over breakfast like young soldiers going off to war, into danger. The hot food and the aroma of it and the excitement of the corps inspired me.

•   •   •

My parents' lives had changed too. My father would rise at eight for breakfast, served to him at our dining room table by Nora. He dined alone, reading the *Baltimore Sun*. He always slurped his coffee. Usually he ate hot oatmeal for breakfast, but sometimes he'd relent and eat eggs, as he had a world of them in his backyard. Nora made jam from our crawling raspberry patch. While others were concerned with shortages, my father started each day in fine shape; his small farm, a liability in ordinary times, was a godsend during the war. For example, in Washington, where fresh white eggs were at a premium, he could trade a few cartons for all the scotch whiskey he wanted. Vat 69 and Dewar's White Label were in plentiful supply, as were bottles of already mixed manhattan cocktails packaged by Heublein up in Hartford.

After breakfast he'd play the piano. I'd given him a large instructional booklet on how to play the piano by a man named LeRoy, and my father, who had a fine ear, learned by himself, utilizing the LeRoy method. Each morning when I was at home and sleeping late as I always did, I'd hear chords from "Beautiful Dreamer" and "Poor Butterfly" float up the stairs and into my room. Another favorite of his was "Girl of My Dreams." He played quite well, and my mother, down the hall in their bedroom, also a late sleeper, would hear the same refrain and draw pleasure from it; her husband played for her each morning.

Somewhere between piano playing and the noon cocktail hour my father would do his chores. He'd check on John to see how he was doing, inevitably leaving everything up to him, then go up to Bohanon's at Park Hall for supplies. Only once did I go with him. I could sense that he was ashamed of certain aspects of his life, including his trips to the old country store, where he had to converse with poor tobacco farmers, local politicians, and hangers-on who drank at the counter, which was also a bar. In the back, colored folks hooted and hollered as whiskey flowed. Arguments broke out. Probably my father took an occasional drink at Bohanon's just so the crowd there wouldn't think him stuck-up, or worse, a tenderfoot. He didn't want trouble in a country store peopled by what the postwar press would call "rednecks." Now in his mid-forties, my father had developed some girth, but he still had strong arms and shoulders and that troubling, icy stare where he'd look past people into the distance. I envision him as if always on guard.

By noon my mother would be ready to join my father for drinks. She'd have had breakfast in bed, served to her by Nora. It was clear to all of us that by midwar, 1943, my mother was becoming increasingly incapacitated. Her multiple sclerosis was paralyzing her and causing pain. She countered the pain with an opium derivative called Luminal; that, combined with liquor, hastened her into chronic alcoholism. Still ambulatory, she needed my father's arm to lean on, and each morning at eleven thirty the two of them would make their slow descent down the stairs into the dining area, actually part of our living room. ("Why did we buy a house without a genuine dining room?" she would ask, over and over again.)

My father would turn on the news at noon so they could keep abreast of the war as they drank their scotch or ready-made manhattans, always "sweetened up" with an extra ounce of straight whiskey. Lunch would be boozy, full of remembrances and complaints. My mother hated being in Maryland, I could tell. She had no positive knowledge of what my father did during his short absences from the home, though she suspected other women such as our neighbor next door, the rather attractive Lucille Cherbonnier. She fantasized slatterns along the roadside tempting my father on his daily run for supplies at Bohanon's. Certainly the postmistress in St. Mary's City must have a yen for such a good-looking Hotchkiss-Yale man, for my father did cut a handsome figure. In those days in the backwater of a backward state my father stood out. He dressed well in twill trousers, a heavy shirt from Abercrombie's or L. L. Bean, and a tweed jacket. A gentleman farmer, he wore cordovans and eschewed boots except when it snowed, and then he wore arctics or calf-high duck hunting boots from Bean's.

But what could my mother do? She had nowhere to go with her fears, her concerns, her hatred of what had befallen her. While my aunt Alice Eddy thought she had manufactured her illness just to control my father and ruin his life, the medical people at Union Memorial Hospital in Baltimore thought otherwise. She was very ill, they said, with what was then considered a rare debilitating illness. There was little anyone could do other than try to make her comfortable. And that job fell to my father. It became his lot in life to see that Lucy got all the comforts she would ever need.

My father traveled to Washington every Wednesday, driving his Chevrolet station wagon with its load of eggs the seventy miles up the peninsula on old macadam roads, past my school, past T.B. Junction, and over the John Phillip Sousa Memorial Bridge which arched into the nation's capital.

He sold his eggs to Brooke and Harry's, a prestigious grocery store with a distinguished customer list that included the White House. Brooke and Harry's valued my father's fresh white eggs. As an inducement they offered him whiskey and cigarettes and real butter and meat... all he wanted, some of which he bought, some of which was passed to him "on the Q.T.," as he would put it, some of it originally destined, no doubt, for the White House. He was always reminded that fresh eggs were like gold in those days and FDR himself had commented on their freshness. The folks at Brooke and Harry's beamed at my father when he drove the Chevy into their loading area in back of the store.

After his "Brooke and Harry business" my father had free time. He had hours to kill if he chose, as my mother always overestimated the length of the drive to Washington. To her it was a full day's trip. It was her good fortune if my father returned by dinnertime at seven. In truth, it was a four-hour round trip with an hour at most spent at the grocery store. If he dallied with loose women (and I think he did), I have no proof of it. Indeed, I had no direct evidence at the time that connected him to Kay Radford, but I knew in my bones that they were lovers and that Wednesdays—my father's egg day—were their days to be with each other.

Kay Radford was a tall woman with graceful legs and a finishing school carriage. She had soft brown hair and was quick-witted. She may have been all of thirty years old. It was easy to see what my father saw in Kay Radford who was chief administrator of the small hospital at the Navy base, called Cedar Point. She was good-looking, had a hearty laugh, and was very confident and very lonely. By her own admission she had been unable to connect with any young officer over at the Patuxent River Naval Air Station, a secret installation for advanced testing of aircraft and a hotbed of sexually deprived pilots and technicians. She was a skilled civil servant and too mature for them and too well educated. They bored her. My father, by contrast, was approaching fifty.

Though his formal education was limited to four years at Hotchkiss and a year and a half at Yale, he had seen life in the trenches of France, and in that lay his appeal. He looked and acted like a grown man who had lived. He was handsome and even courtly. A northern man whose rough edges had been smoothed, he appealed to Kay Radford. Kay saw herself as cast adrift in a backwater village at the bottom end of Maryland with no source of affection other than the young naval officers to whom she felt superior. She desired my father because he was mature and he, flattered by her attentions, must have responded with all his heart. My mother was not to receive proof of their affair for ten years or more. Though I could never prove that my father and Kay Radford were lovers during the war, I believe they grabbed at love while they could, each knowing that their affair would eventually end.

His private melodrama notwithstanding, my father believed that someday when the war ended and things got back to normal, my mother's health would be restored, and he would relish the return of his "humdinger." He'd often look at my mother and say, "You sure were a humdinger," and she'd beam at him, her face getting cockeyed from manhattans or scotch, her eyes teary as she remembered dancing with my father over weekends in New York, dancing to Vincent Lopez and his orchestra at the Hotel Pennsylvania, the Waldorf Astoria, or perhaps the old Lincoln. Each night, down in Maryland, they'd reminisce and remember when my mother was a knockout and how they'd loved to dance together.

•   •   •

With my home life such as it was, it should be noted that I carried on or made do at what I've called Brook Hall and came to enjoy it. I was a careless, rebellious cadet who couldn't seem to conform. I picked up penalty hours through indifference. I was heedless of discipline, and so I walked the track daily for the first three years. Despite my poor comportment I got high grades in school. At home my parents were neither dismayed nor impressed by my school activities. I was off in limbo somewhere. I was neither complimented nor criticized by them for anything I did during my whole career at Brook Hall.

By the fall of 1944 I was beginning to develop into young manhood. Although my parents did not notice it, some of the Captains at school did. The school, a homoerotic citadel, had a faculty composed primarily of two homosexuals and other men with physical problems that made them ineligible for the draft. Since my first day I had been exposed to the constant pulse of male posturing and raw lust, from simple horseplay in one of the large open showers, to teachers slipping into a student's room to stroke or fellate a cadet in the wee hours of the morning when he would be erectile and vulnerable. And though molesting minors was unlawful, the commonness of its occurrence legitimized it. It was the way things were. Custom overruled the law. The concept of child abuse was unheard of in the 1940s, certainly unheard of at Brook Hall. In five years at Brook Hall I never witnessed an argument related to homosexual conduct. When it happened, it felt good. No one vouchsafed opinions about it one way or the other, perhaps because the subject was so laden with guilt and so incendiary. No one dared stoke such a tinderbox.

Truth in Fiction: Harold Hawkins #2

On the morning of February 17, 1944, Harold awoke to find the whole campus frozen solid with ice. The sky was overcast, and when he walked to the bathroom to take a leak at one of the urinals, he found that the lights were off. One of the boys was running down the corridor screaming that the school was going to be shut down. "There ain't no electricity or nothing!" he cried, then added, "And there ain't no heat," which sent Harold back quickly to his quarters to check the cast iron radiator under the window at the far end of his room. It was cold.

Captain Sullivan was out in the hall, bundled in an Army officer's thigh-length polo coat with huge lapels. With no water to wash his face, his normally slicked-back hair was bushy on his head. "Calm down," he cautioned, but within minutes cadets were scurrying about yelling and hollering about their good fortune. "No school!" everyone seemed to be shouting, and by the time they got to roll call the whole corps was on edge, waiting for news. Then the Major appeared, a signal incident because he never attended the early formation. He stood in front of the long line of cadets and looked over to Mole Kelly and finally said, "Cadet

Captain Kelly, is Corporal Lott in your company?" When he was assured that Lott was indeed in ranks, the Major hollered, "Cadet Lott, get to the school bus at once and fire it up."

He then turned to the whole corps and said, "There is no water, no electricity, no telephone. We will shuttle cadets to Washington and T. B. Junction for connections north. Other cadets who live south of here are to line up outside the office as soon as possible. The school will close during this emergency."

Harold looked out at the ice. It was a half-inch thick on every limb of every tree. He could see power lines drooping in front of Bowman's General Store. The telephone line that ordinarily ran from the office in the main barracks out to the road was already down, one end buried in the two inches of snow and ice that lay between the school building and the railroad tracks. The sky was still gray but beginning to lighten, and in the half-light he could sense the full impact of the deep freeze that gripped the school. Major Keller, the Eagle, was dressed like Captain Sullivan, his own tan polo coat, very broad at his shoulders, made even wider-looking by the pointed lapels and the short cutoff below his waist. His dress cap glistened in the semidark, the gold disc over the brim large and resplendent in the gloom. A man of action, he had acted quickly. Everyone was to go home.

Everyone, that is, but Harold and some of the boys from Cuba and Ecuador and Harold's friend Doc Blanchard, who had no parents, both of them having been killed in a car crash in New Jersey. He had been sent to Brook Hall by an uncle, a traveling salesman, whom he hated. He had no real home, and although he would have been happy to go anywhere, the Eagle refused him. "We can't take the risk of just sending you out into America," he said.

The Spanish-speaking stayed by themselves. Talking in their native language, they huddled together in a unit. As for Harold, he was to stay because there were no school vehicles going as far as St. Catherine's City, which had been cut off from the world. There was no way to reach anyone down there, no way to get Harold home because the one long, curving road would be covered with ice. "Maybe tomorrow," the Eagle said. "Tomorrow, when we get the bus back and all the other cadets are home, perhaps then we can find you a ride to your house. But it is doubtful and I can't risk taking the academy station wagon down there for just one cadet, sliding every which way and that way," he said, and he looked at Harold, perhaps thinking: *This boy is in my office almost every night for some infraction. He is always on the track. If he can rough it here, maybe it will do him some good. In any case he is clearly too incompetent to get home by himself. All the boy does is blush.*

By nine o'clock a busload of cadets and faculty was off, clinking over snow-encrusted gravel, bound for the icy road to Washington, thus far devoid of traffic. "Be careful," said Mole Kelly, who was waiting for the bus's return so that he could ride up to T.B. Junction to get a Greyhound on to Baltimore. "If you get stuck, I'll have your ass, Lott!" he hollered, but Lott had already shut the door and did not hear him. Harold could see his friend Peanut Enderberry grinning out of a side window. Beside him, his neck craning for a farewell look at the school, was another pal, Rocky Ward. Then something past the bus caught Harold's eye. Coming out of the greenhouse was Captain Herman Fillmore, called Phantom Fillmore by the cadets. He walked so leisurely across the parking area, back toward his room, that Harold could tell he was in no hurry to leave. It was even possible that he was not going to leave. After all, someone had to stay on to help the Eagle. Harold watched the strange Fillmore, tall and slender, slowly stride toward his room. His long arms swung like pendulums at his side, the palms of his hands turned out the way the suicidal Rawlings used to do it. It had long been noted that Fillmore walked like a woman. Harold wondered for a moment and then turned back to the swirl of cadets. Someone had mentioned that the mess hall was open. There would be no scrapple and no coffee with cane syrup, but they could all eat cold cereal and peanut butter sandwiches, and there was a goodly store of number ten cans filled with Dole's pineapple juice so they could wash down the peanut butter in style. They pushed and shoved their way into the mess hall, all the time watched by Willa, the cook, who was shaking her head, a shawl over her round shoulders and long underwear running down her legs from beneath her cotton skirt.

•   •   •

On the second day of the great blizzard, after a bad night's sleep, huddling near the fireplace in the academy's spacious living room, Harold was set upon by Captain Fillmore shortly after breakfast. He had eaten cold cereal again and had nothing to look forward to but more cold Spam sandwiches for lunch and dinner.

"How would you like a nice meal tonight?" asked the Phantom, his long body stooped to Harold's height. All morning Harold and Doc Blanchard had been looking through a stack of movie magazines they had found in Mole Kelly's room, and when Harold was approached by Captain Fillmore, he was erectile from thinking about Rita Hayworth in a negligee and blushing and wondering where to go for privacy. His confusion showed in his face, and before he could answer, Captain Fillmore said, "I am going down to Casa Toledo till things get straightened out."

Casa Toledo was a refurbished plantation that sprawled inland from the north bank of the Potomac River. In 1944 this formidable holding of more than five hundred acres, complete with Negro tenant help and scattered outbuildings, themselves commodious enough to billet a regiment, was owned by the leading trustee of Brook Hall School, General Michael Crossley Long. In the late spring of every year at declamation time, he would drive up to the academy to present the prize for best oration, and in the middle of Christmas holidays he would meet with the other trustees to listen to the annual report rendered by Major Keller. Other than that he kept to his own business, which was running the plantation and leading a controlled social life centered around Casa Toledo and the Army-Navy Club in Washington.

General Long had impressed Harold at the end of the previous year's declamation contest when the elder Westinghouse brother had recited "The Woman I Love," otherwise known as the abdication speech of Edward VIII. The Westinghouse brother had spoken with such feeling that the audience was stunned and the few women in the back, notably Miss Ziegler, were heard to cry. Although the Westinghouse boy was anathema to Major Keller, General Long seemed genuinely pleased by his performance, and when it came time to present him with the scroll of excellence in oration, the Lieutenant General of the Army, Retired, strode to the podium and received Westinghouse's somewhat ill-managed salute and complimented the rebellious cadet. "A truly remarkable recitation," he had said.

Now, in the midst of an ice storm, Harold had an invitation to see the exotic-sounding Casa Toledo. "They probably don't have heat or electricity," Captain Fillmore was saying, "but there are fireplaces for cooking and fireplaces in the bedrooms and we can all be very warm. The General is in Washington—he left last week—and only his sister, Mrs. Cawley, is there. We should go to lend her support. She is probably beside herself, don't you think?"

Harold knew of Mrs. Cawley, a dark-haired woman of forty or so who was in charge of her brother's estate. She had a love of chess; this had come to the attention of Captain Fillmore who ran the Chess Club at Brook Hall. She often drove up to the school to assist him with his small group of cadets. Of course, a woman on campus was immediately noticed, and all the cadets had at one time or another seen Mrs. Cawley. But because the Phantom was womanish, her visits to him did not become the source of bad jokes or smutty talk; only the uncouth older boys could find anything dirty to say about Mrs. Cawley. When she was on campus, boys on the way to the smoker would note loudly that Mrs. Cawley needed "a good meat injection." The rest of the students saw Mrs. Cawley in simple terms: a chess nut who did-n't mind working with Captain Fillmore who was, after all, just like another woman and might as well be her sister.

Harold was deeply confused by Captain Fillmore's approach. First, he wondered if Fillmore had noticed his Rita Hayworth hard-on and if that were the reason for his invita-tion. Second, he had always been petrified of Captain Fillmore. Because Fillmore taught only English and ancient history to the juniors and seniors, Harold had yet to have him in class. Familiarity had not been achieved as it had with the other captains, and Harold still felt very tense and shy around him. Yet at the same time he was cold and hungry and tired from a fitful sleep in front of the fireplace in the large drafty living room. Then he wondered about Doc Blanchard. Why couldn't he come? Harold stammered, his head down and his eyes turned away from Captain Fillmore. He could still feel his erection making a slight bulge in his heavy twill trousers. He knew his face was red and he hoped that his uncontrol-lable blushing would send the older man away.

But Captain Fillmore bore on. "I don't think I can take two boys to the farm. It is already an imposition to ask Mrs. Cawley to keep us warm and well fed without bringing a third person."

He then looked down at Harold's fly and placed one arm on his shoulder and said, "Just get a pair of pajamas and your toothbrush. We should go around noon. I'll leave word for Major Keller. If you do chores for Mrs. Cawley, you know, it is triple-time credit against all those hours you have. I think you will be pleased when you see how you have reduced your hours." It was a bribe and Harold knew it when he agreed to go. Still, he was excited about going even though he knew his father would not approve. He could not help himself.

•   •   •

Captain Fillmore borrowed a car from a friend of his who lived in nearby Thomasville, a middle-aged man who taught English in the regional high school and apparently had known Fillmore for many years. Every other day the friend drove over to the school to have coffee with Captain Fillmore. Sometimes they walked around the campus and up into the pinewoods behind the watertower. More often they'd go out for a drive. Regardless of the ice that day, Captain Fillmore's friend arrived for his visit, and soon Harold was sitting in silence, wedged between the two men who were chatting in the front seat. Nervously he studied the school buildings and the campus and was struck by a sense of desertion. The whole place looked like an old abandoned fort, lost to the world, resting on a plane of ice in far-off Siberia. It was a wasteland of felled branches and bent or downed utility poles, hamstrung by lines. Nothing stirred. It was as though a raiding party had swept through and left only an ungodly stillness in its wake.

They dropped off the English teacher in Thomasville, and before long Harold was alone with Captain Fillmore, feeling the crunch of the tire chains on the frozen roads as the prewar Chevrolet rattled slowly down narrow byways toward the Potomac. The world was silvery and frozen. The sun had not come out, and the gray skies overlaid the wonderland of ice, turning everything to the color of a slightly tarnished silver tea set. Once it snowed lightly, and the car skidded a bit as Fillmore drove down the long dirt driveway that led to Casa Toledo.

Harold was led into the manor house and shown to his room upstairs. There was a small fireplace at one end of a bedroom as big as two classrooms back at Brook Hall. In the center was a four-poster bed raised a few feet from the floor. It had puffy down pillows under a clean white bedspread with a ribbed pattern that reminded Harold of his smaller bedspread at home. The closet was so grand that he walked into it and partly closed the door. It smelled slightly of moth balls and canvas, and once his eyes became accustomed to the dark, he saw a pile of duck decoys stacked neatly at the far end. Some marlin line curled about them emitting oily odors that reminded Harold of his father's gear back on the farm in St. Catherine's City.

Harold wondered about the plumbing and the shower. There was no water because there was no electricity. At school he had just gone about pissing in the various urinals, letting the acrid odor filter through the barracks. Fortunately he had showered the evening before the storm and so he was relatively clean. But soon he would have to go to the bathroom. He wondered about it and then threw back his head and walked out into the hall and then down the long curving stairs to the living room where a mighty blaze was sending a surge of heat throughout the house. An old colored man named Mr. Slye stood by the fire. He had just brought in some wood and was warming himself. In the familiar patois of the Hawkins's handyman in St. Catherine's City, Mr. Slye told Harold that there was an outhouse down by the stables. Harold thought that the old man had read his mind.

Captain Fillmore came into the living room along with Mrs. Cawley. They had been laughing out in the kitchen and had finally decided that what was in order for dinner were two large steaks to be cooked over the fire. They would rest a kettle on the grill to boil water for coffee and another pot to boil some peas and carrots that had been put by in storage for use throughout the winter.

It was five o'clock when Captain Fillmore opened up the bar and poured himself and Mrs. Cawley each a glass of whiskey with soda. He offered Harold some Dubonnet, which Harold took eagerly. He sat and listened to the two adults talk girlishly as the evening wore on and the steaks cooked over a broad bank of coals. He was not left out, as Captain Fillmore kept refilling his small glass and Mrs. Cawley inquired about the Hawkins's farm. She seemed very nice, Harold thought, and as he grew more brazen from the Dubonnet he began to converse with her. She had straight black hair that was brushed back from her head and tied behind with a bow. Her almost perfectly oval face was very white and she affected dark red lipstick and a touch of mascara. Her figure was trim and looked very hard from her gardening and managerial duties. She kept her legs crossed, so Harold could not really tell, but they looked thin. Her torso was cloaked in a heavy yellow turtleneck sweater that gave her a nautical look, and her Scotch plaid skirt bunched in her lap as she sat and talked, often throwing her head back to laugh.

By the time dinner was over, both adults were very merry, having drunk wine while Harold was given only one more Dubonnet lest, as Captain Fillmore said, he get giddy and then sick. Harold knew that in southern Maryland if you were big enough to stand at the bar, you were big enough to drink. No one worried about a fourteen-year-old being served some Dubonnet or a glass of wine. Captain Fillmore was becoming very loud, almost silly, as he carried on with his friend, Mrs. Cawley, whom he called Helen. They seemed to be content just to talk by the fire. Harold, uneasy and feeling the effects of the Dubonnet, decided to explore. He began pacing through the many rooms of Casa Toledo.

He held a kerosene lamp in his hand which cast odd shadows against the walls, and when he entered the General's study the light illuminated the many mementos with a ghostly glow. Mounted on the wall was an old Prussian helmet with a plume and a smaller American helmet beneath it. There were old photographs of men in uniform and battle scenes and trenches lined with American troops. There were inscribed pictures of General Pershing and Marshal Foch and a photograph of Siegfried Sassoon, a poet, and a tray of medals set against the wall. They were under glass and looked very impressive, and right above them was a bright Colonel's eagle set on felt in a frame. Over the General's desk was a large photograph of Mrs. Long, a serene-looking woman who was unsmiling and rigid, though she was quite pretty in her old-fashioned way, and Harold stared at the photograph for a moment or two wondering if she had died. There were boxes on the floor, overflowing with books, and a small radio on a stand next to the fireplace. The ceiling was low, no more than eight feet. Casa Toledo was probably as old as Brook Hall, which had been built before the Revolution. The house made him think of all the wars that embroiled America, and he even had a vision of Barbara Frietchie leaning out her window, challenging Stonewall Jackson to "shoot if you must." This was a military man's home and it exuded a long history of weathering conflict, of horses saddled to ride, of men-of-war on the river and long handwritten letters arriving in the mail from battlefields far away.

But Harold was getting tired. He wandered back toward the living room and then on into the spacious kitchen, which was the biggest room in the house. He looked out the kitchen door and saw a row of empty milk bottles resting on the ice. Walking out past the milk bottles, he quickly unbuttoned his fly and urinated. Silently he rejoined the others, then asked Mrs. Cawley if he could have a glass of milk and some crackers before going to bed.

"Of course, Harold," she said, and she jumped up to get him a box of saltines and a glass of partly frozen milk and some cheese. Though he ate as quietly as he could, he still crunched with his teeth and spilled a few crumbs on the great bearskin rug that extended back from the hearth. Finally he asked if it would be all right to go to sleep. Mrs. Cawley led him to his room where he would lie in the four-poster like a tired soldier. Mr. Slye had a fire going which he knew would burn out by dawn but it made the room cozy for the time being. He first stripped to his jockey shorts and then took them off to put on a set of red cotton pajamas. In no time he fell fast asleep, the ear that was not buried in the downy pillows picking up traces of laughter and effeminate chatter from the adults in the living room below and then a dark blank of non-being.

It was still night when he heard the door open. The door was made of oak and was thick and heavy. It had an old-fashioned wrought iron latch, painted black with a slim black handle. There was no lock, though Harold had not thought of using one. When he heard the door open with the squeak of an ancient hinge, he turned slowly toward it and saw the Captain standing there in his bathrobe, a Chinese affair with gold lamé and orange and gold dragons printed on the silk of the gown. He also saw his face, the long angular face under neatly combed black hair and the sharp nose that reminded the boys of General MacArthur. In fact the Phantom's other nickname was "Mac," so dubbed by the Westinghouse brothers. It was obvious to the cadets that Captain Fillmore never wore underwear. In study hall when he leaned over a cadet's shoulder to help him with his work, you could see the outlines of his pecker. Sometimes it was hard. The cadets would watch him and nudge one another and laugh or giggle as his pants filled out at the fly.

And there was Fillmore now, moving toward Harold, his eyes kindly and gray as the candlelight in the hall illuminated the room, sending eerie shadows across the rug toward Harold's bed. As he sat down on the edge of the bed, Harold, lying on his back, could feel himself becoming hard, simultaneous with the appearance of the Phantom's giant bulge under his thin silk robe. Then Fillmore opened his robe where it was untied and loose across the front. His member was very stiff and it was bent upward and was longer than Harold had imagined. It looked reddish in the half-light of the room. Deliberately, Fillmore reached under the sheet and began to caress Harold and then he drew the sheet back and bent his head to Harold and made him come within a minute or so.

Harold lay still, helpless and spent, staring at Captain Fillmore, who then masturbated in front of Harold, letting his own sperm fly over Harold's face and drip down upon the pillow and upon Harold's hair. And then it was over. Fillmore lowered his head and kissed Harold on his cheek and then quietly withdrew, softly closing the door behind him.

When Harold awoke, he briefly thought of Captain Fillmore and what had happened and automatically he was excited again. But it was after nine in the morning and he could smell bacon cooking and there was a strong odor of coffee in the air and he was starving. Turning untoward thoughts aside he dressed and went down to the living room where the fireplace was full of hot coals for cooking, and bacon had been set on a sheet of paper towels and the coffee was being served Western style, the grounds right in with the water, the taste very tart and very hot to the tongue. There was toast as well and Mrs. Cawley was in the process of scrambling six eggs in a bowl to slip on the frying pan. Taking the coffee in his hand Harold excused himself and went out the kitchen door to the same shrub behind the milk bottles he had found the previous night and again relieved himself. When he returned, Mrs. Cawley politely reminded him that there was a privy down by the stables. Captain Fillmore would show him where it was after breakfast.

They did it twice more that day. First in the stables and then much later, just before supper, up in Harold's room. The captain's girlishness almost made the enormity of their sex a natural occurrence and when Harold took Fillmore's pulsing, curving penis in his hand it was exciting and it seemed right and in any case Harold had no choice, now carried along by his own pleasure. In almost no time and without much provocation he had become receptive to the older man's gentle stroking and caressing and the grand excitement of impending orgasm.

But in the morning of the last day both adults were in his room. Mrs. Cawley was also in a dressing gown which she threw on the floor, and after Captain Fillmore had stroked Harold for a moment she slipped on top of him, sitting on top of his erection. Her crotch seemed meager and not as hairy as those of the few women he had spied upon, and her breasts were very small and conical and they slanted out from the center of her chest in an odd fashion that was not familiar to him, nor did they resemble any of the pinups he had ever seen. But he reached to touch them, and as Captain Fillmore watched, she rode up and down on Harold until he came and then Mrs. Cawley fell across his chest, her lips pressing upon his own and her black hair covering his eyes. Captain Fillmore, who was playing with himself, came across her bare rear end, his own eyes closed and his thin body in spasms almost like a jackhammer.

They ate breakfast as though nothing unusual had transpired. The sun had finally emerged from the dour overcast to grace the countryside. By ten in the morning the temperature was rising and the ice was already melting. Although it was Sunday, work crews were expected to restore the power. Every day was a workday during the war, and the increasing importance of the naval air station over on the Patuxent made it imperative that telephone and power lines operate in that part of Maryland.

On the way back to school, Captain Fillmore touched Harold on the thigh and said that he would like to see him from time to time but that he could not see him all of the time. Major Keller would surely find out, he said, and then added, "Besides I have other boys I must not forget. Their love I may not disabuse."

With his hat on he looked pompous and his sharp features pointed his face toward the road ahead. Harold would always remember Mrs. Cawley but vowed to forget Captain Fillmore if he could. He would tell tales of Mrs. Cawley, who was, after all, a general's sister, but he would tell nobody about Captain Fillmore. He wondered if what he had done would show on his face. He would take a shower as soon as the water came on. He could wash things away, but Harold realized that he had gone beyond the limit. What he had done would have made his father sick, though he had felt pleasure beyond imagining. Harold whirled inside. It was all wrong, he knew that, but it had been a weekend to exceed anything his young mind could have fancied.

He might try, but Harold would never forget Casa Toledo. For decades he would see himself walking across the land, his eyes scanning the partly frozen river and the broad reaches of tobacco fields. There was a large brick barn shaped like a huge boiler that had reminded Harold of an armory he had seen in Connecticut from the window of his father's car once when they were driving to New Haven to go to a football game at the Yale Bowl. And there was a tennis court and many shacks back past the stables where Negro women walked about, their men standing in groups talking and laughing and passing the bottle around. "With the General gone to Washington certain liberties are to be expected," Mrs. Cawley had said, and Harold skirted the crowd of colored folk as he explored the estate. In his mind's eye he saw them all—the colored people and Mrs. Cawley and Phantom Fillmore, too.

At first he could not forget Casa Toledo because that is where he lost his virginity in a "double play," as he would call it, first to the vulturous Captain Fillmore and then to the black-haired woman who was old enough to be his mother. Her splayed breasts and the feeling of being inside her were imprinted in his memory. As he finished the year, walking the track or later in bed before sleep, he'd remember her riding him and the way she fell upon him when he came. And when he thought of Mrs. Cawley he would remember the superior lushness of other women and he would guess about Rita Hayworth and Jinx Falkenburg, the pinups over his bed. Inevitably, too, he would think of Captain Fillmore, who still came to his room on occasion, almost stalking him in the dead of night, his long fingers like talons as they hung loosely along his legs, then turning soft and very practiced under the covers with a rhythm Harold could not resist had he wanted to.

By the end of the spring of 1944 Harold was always on the track and he was always daydreaming. Even so, he would get his Certificate of Scholarship, which was awarded to the academic leaders of the school. But nothing rivaled the awakening he had experienced by the Potomac and the monomaniacal bent that was now directing his young life. His imagination had linked him to incredible pleasures, and he dreamed endlessly of carnal encounters, dying to grow up, his conscious mind on the war and Washington and beautiful long-legged secretaries walking along Pennsylvania Avenue, and fantasized their thinking he hoped was like his own.

• • •

In the summers of our Maryland years—war or no war—my father, mother, our dog Taffy, and I would travel in a halting fashion up to Martha's Vineyard. In 1943 we journeyed by train, which was an ordeal. My father reserved two drawing rooms for the three of us, but Taffy was chained up in the baggage car and I worried over him the whole way. My mother, who by 1943 was at best wobbly on her legs, would be coaxed by my father down the rocking aisle of the train toward the dining car as I tagged along behind. Back in the drawing room they'd drink manhattans as we watched the camouflaged Glen L. Martin aircraft plant whizz by our window. Then New Jersey, and finally the flats that led into New York. But what I remember best was the tortuous trip to the dining car. Across slamming and shimmying connecting platforms, my father would hold my mother lest she carom against a half-opened door and fall out onto the railbed.

In Manhattan we had to get my mother from Pennsylvania Station over to Grand Central and onto another railroad, the New Haven, which would take us to Providence, where we could spend the night in a hotel. Cabs were scarce in New York during the war, and I recall my father's confusion and irritation as he tried to get us from Penn Station over to Grand Central. *Don't you know there is a war on?* was a familiar and annoying remark at the time, and I can hear people saying that to my father, who would scowl at the crowd. Impatience did no one any good. My stomach tightened as I stood beside my mother who was sitting on a large suitcase, our dog straining and scared out of his wits, pulling at my arm on his leash. It seemed unbearable because, at that moment, my father was impotent in his attempts to lead his family. Also my mother was clearly ill, holding her bladder, trying to control her tears...all of us helpless in the same city where only five years earlier my parents had danced the night away, slept in classy hotels, dined in good restaurants, and brought goodies home from a store called Rumpelmayer's. But no longer. My father looked old, and my mother, her face contorted, appeared crazed by the crowd of gesticulating servicemen and pressing civilians. And no transportation.

I had never seen my stalwart father stymied before. He'd always gotten his way, almost as an inherent right. Pacing nervously before Penn Station, I studied my father and realized that the crowd was indifferent to him. I had never imagined that anyone would ever treat my revered father with indifference. What was very wrong about this scene was that my father, too, was a hero. Why didn't this crowd of nondescript civilians and G.I.s make room and give him his due? Somehow, at last, we did get to Grand Central, disheveled and dismayed, but the war had caught up with us.

•   •   •

We had to return in September by train, but from then on my father, with a surfeit of gas coupons, drove his Buick or his station wagon whenever we ventured north in the summer. Yet even then it was awkward. My mother could not abide dirty restrooms, and because by now she had so little control of her bladder, restrooms quickly became an issue. Cheap restaurants were anathema to my refined mother. So were gas stations with the least bit of grease in the ladies' room. My mother would nudge my father when it was time to go to the bathroom, either at a clean gas station or down some country lane. We'd always bring toilet paper, and my father would pull off the road so she could sit on the front bumper as I averted my eyes. All of this made me extremely uncomfortable, though no one ever said a word to me about it.

It was on these yearly trips back and forth to the Vineyard that I became aware of my mother's drug problem. Traveling frightened her, probably because of her shaky carriage, her tendency to fall, but also because she was often in withdrawal from drinking, nervous and almost frantic. Hence the Luminal. My father, a stoic who never appeared to doubt the wisdom of the medical community, gave her the drug whenever her anxiety began to escalate. Doped-up, she traveled north or south with us with a sloppy expression on her face, a look of bewilderment in her eyes, her body limp. No one ever mentioned her condition until late one evening in 1948 or 1949, when I heard my father scream at my mother, "No more goddamn Luminal. You're a damn drug addict; that is what you have become," his voice cutting into me. Crying, she protested by invoking her illness, but my father would have none of it. He detested what she had become. The next day she drank heavily at lunch to overcome the effects of opium withdrawal. From then on until she was completely bedridden, alcohol would be her principal and usually her sole sedative.

•   •   •

By war's end my father's affair with Kay Radford was obvious to me. Three times he'd either missed appointments with me in Washington or left me abruptly to attend to other business. I suspected that the "other business" was Kay. Kay had been coming over almost every night for cocktails with my parents. My mother's heavy drinking did not keep her away and usually she brought her sidekick, a nurse named Claire Dent. During the nine months when my parents were not on the Vineyard, they were often with Kay and Claire, whom my mother called "Dentie." As Kay discussed the war with my father, my mother found in Dentie a boon companion. Claire Dent, who could talk of medical breakthroughs, befriended my mother with a genuine affection while covering for her friend Kay, who was drawn to my father. Everyone knew my mother had a drinking problem and was sick. Most people who knew us showed a great deal of sympathy for my father. I suspect they thought that he deserved some fun.

Kay and my father would look into each other's eyes over the dinner table. Often my father, who was the one with the gasoline coupons, would pick them up at the base and then return them at night, leaving my mother alone, still sitting in her chair before the fireplace. Suspicious by nature and extremely possessive, she must have surmised the truth. But she never said a word. Perhaps she gave my father a long leash just to see how far he'd go and what he'd do. If he went too far she could catch him, and with the power of a cripple she could invoke a cripple's revenge. She would strike with the righteousness of a martyr. Thinking back on it, perplexed, I am sure that my mother could not have been insensitive to the chemistry that was pulling my father and Kay together. Kay, for her part, was a cool customer, with her short fluffy hairdo and her glasses. But beneath that look of a librarian anyone other than a fool could sense a hidden agenda.

•   •   •

By 1943 my brother had dropped out of the University of Chicago and was in the Army Air Corps. A well-connected Chicago lawyer and distant cousin named Ronnie Boardman had gotten him into what was called the Great Books Program at the university under President Robert Maynard Hutchins. Accepted but unqualified, he quit. The draft was upon him and he enlisted, specifying the Air Corps and air cadet training, which was open to college students. He finally washed out after being downgraded from pilot trainee to navigator and was assigned to the military police. In 1944, after the invasion of Normandy, he went to France to direct traffic and keep order. What he did there and how he comported himself was always a mystery to me. While he was away he was never discussed. It was as though any discussion of my brother would ensure his death. No one wanted to jinx him.

My sister, whom we called Bideau although she was named after my mother, Lucy, lived in Charlottesville, Virginia with her husband, Frank Abbot. By 1942 Frank was in medical school. Occasionally we motored to Charlottesville, and on Christmas holidays Bideau and Frank drove over to St. Mary's City, burning scarce fuel. During those war years my sister and her husband brought merriment to our home. Liquor flowed and I was allowed to drink beer, as much as I wished, and sparkling wine at dinner. Our meals were sumptuous: Nora served fried or roast chicken and homemade rolls with real butter and I smothered everything in gravy. Frequently we'd have grand helpings of roast lamb, ham, or turkey but seldom steak. Steak was rare even at Brooke and Harry's.

My sister was the one bright spot in my home life as I was depending more and more on school for entertainment. She was always upbeat, pretty, and appeared to be genuinely in love with her husband. The Abbots offered companionship as my budding sex life stumbled along. I was glued to news of the war as it raged and MacArthur began rolling back the Japanese, island after island, but at the same time I fantasized about women. In my mind I saw a thousand naked bodies and enjoyed a thousand kisses from the loveliest of Hollywood stars. I heard the war news and said to myself: *Live today, for tomorrow you may die.* I did not know what I was thinking, I just relished the melodrama of my little world, and like a billion teenagers over the millennia I pined for a mate whom I could undress and fondle. I needed a girlfriend like MacArthur needed the Philippines. In my house of secrets, sex became an obsession with me, and I yearned to be a lover and a hero at the same time.

Chapter 5

By 1943 the Army was practicing its Normandy landings on the beaches of Martha's Vineyard, and the Navy was operating out of a naval air station constructed in the center of a state forest in the heart of the island. Young women danced with flyers and doughboys at the Country Club, a public golf and tennis club in Oak Bluffs. As a teenager riding my bike home from the movies in Edgartown, I'd hear the music from the club: "I'll Be Seeing You" and "Moonlight Becomes You" evoked images of a young man and his girlfriend saying good-bye—one going off to war, the other to wait for his return. The girl would keep his photograph on her dresser, his high school sweater in her chest of drawers, a hoard of memories in her mind. She would stay true to him, and when the war ended she'd take her hero into her arms.

As I rode by in the night, I could hear not only the music but also the sound of male voices, sometimes high-pitched or drunken, mingled with the laughter of spirited young women, raising their dresses as they jitterbugged to "In The Mood." Often I would pause and peek in the windows. I loved it. I was thirteen in the summer of 1943. By the next summer most of the G.I.s would be gone, off to Normandy and beyond. By June 1944 the LSTs that unloaded soldiers on State Beach on the Oak Bluffs–Edgartown Road and over at Katama were overseas getting shelled from Nazi fortifications.

In my mind I saw danger and a chance for bravery everywhere. The war years were rife with images, and as my body grew, so too did my urge to join the frenzy of men and women in a tangle of uniforms and swing music and a last chance to love someone before the killing began. Everyone was so trim and young and sexy. I almost hoped the war would last until I was seventeen. I could go from Brook Hall directly into the Marines, as older cadets at school had been doing...and when I thought like that I'd catch myself and say *almost*. Certainly I would not want the war to go on a minute longer if it meant that death would catch up to my brother. Although I had always feared the look of doom in his face, now that he was away I quickly forgot the unpleasantness, the dark side of his temperament. By 1943 he was a hero to me. Like the rest of my male cousins, Bill was in the service. In 1944 after the landing at Normandy he did his soldiering in France as my father had done twenty-six years before.

In part, wartime summers were spent shagging flies with my neighbor in Harthaven, Crosby Prizer. At night we'd listen to the radio, tuning in the Brooklyn Dodgers on WHN in New York, trying to hear through the static. Eddie Basinski and Eddie Miksis. Arky Vaughan. Tommy Brown. I loved the names. Especially Dixie Walker. How could you not love a man named Dixie? In New Britain we'd had a young neighbor my sister's age named Dixie Cutter, and "Dixie" had a soft feel to it the way I imagined the Deep South to be.

Fifteen years later "Dixie" would mean segregation and violence, and I suspect that even in 1943 I should have been cautious with the word. For I had seen subjugation in Maryland. Dark people lived with few rights and little hope. John Hopewell was lucky he worked for my father. In wartime, where else could he go? My cousins and sister who had been exposed to Mr. Pease were already rebels, and I was beginning to rebel also, but it had nothing to do with human rights. Brook Hall was stripping away my image of myself as a privileged Yankee temporarily slumming in Maryland. The drilling and the tough customers who filled our cadet ranks had begun to shape my romantic inclinations. Sometimes out on the track with a Springfield on my shoulder, walking mile after mile, I would feel a sense of mission. I felt hardened to the chill that swept across the track. I almost liked it. If the war should last, I'd be glad to do my part. Serious thinking had not yet set in, but I'd begun to see myself as different from the gang up on Martha's Vineyard and in New Britain. Occasionally resentments toward privilege would cross my mind and they steeled me. I did not want to be soft.

In the summer of 1944 I began working at Bill Jones's bowling alley in Oak Bluffs. Jones, a handsome square-looking man, asked me if I was sure my parents wouldn't mind. I was underage, but there was a war on and kids could spot pins, he said. Sure, I agreed, my head down, embarrassed at being addressed directly by an adult. Any boy my age could spot duckpins—set them up on numbered spots after they'd been bowled into the pit. My parents wouldn't mind at all, I told Bill Jones. In truth, they didn't seem to care what I did. They assumed I was a good boy and let it go at that.

I spent all of my childhood trying to get the attention of my parents. The only time I recall that they listened to me was when I returned from a movie. I remember having seen *It Happened One Night* with Clark Gable and Claudette Colbert. Both parents listened intently with broad smiles on their faces as I described the zany course of events that propelled the plot and how Gable and Colbert had to spend the night together, unmarried. Sometimes when I talked of other movies such as *The Hunchback of Notre Dame* or *Northwest Passage*—two of my favorites—I'd get a moment of attention. But, as always, the grownups would go back to their own affairs, their own experiences, their drinking. Years later, when I was in my late twenties, I'd often stay up into the late hours drinking highballs with my parents, bonding in a drunkard's way, but never did I recall upon awakening what we had discussed in the night nor what had drawn us together. Nor did my parents remember. It was as though our blurry evenings never occurred.

By 1944 my father had started bringing a large stash of whiskey up to the Vineyard from Brooke and Harry's. I recall the Dewar's scotch in wooden crates. The war raged and they had their snorts, as my father referred to his highballs. As they listened eagerly, I'd tell them in detail about a Robert Young or John Wayne movie I'd seen. As for actresses, I'd elaborate on Alexis Smith and Rita Hayworth and Susan Hayward, who were my favorites, but I always withheld the name Ella Raines. I did not tell anyone how Ella Raines had entered my life. It was late one morning when I swam out to a raft that floated in front of our community beach. Swimming quietly, I surprised a young woman sunning in the nude out on the raft, and when she looked up to see me ogling her I saw her face...just like Ella Raines. She was slow to cover herself and looked very tan and furry and full-breasted. I guessed that she was a friend of my cousin Geoff Young, who was 4-F as a result of a childhood accident which had blinded him in one eye. Lucky Geoff, I thought, fantasizing over her for days on end. For weeks I pretended that I had seen the real Ella Raines, and in my nighttime movie critiques I never mentioned her name for fear I would blush.

Bowling, as with the Air Force seven years later, quite probably saved me from going mad. I was a highly charged boy, aware that my sexual imagination knew no bounds. The total absence of young women at Brook Hall was producing an obsession with their body parts. At fourteen I was still a raw kid with a stammer, unable to speak to grown-ups other than my parents, and frightened to death of adolescent girls. My best chance for sexual delight, I figured, was to tarry on the way back from listening to the Dodger games with Crosby Prizer, stalling in my journey before a house rented to the Charles Stanleys that stood across the road from the Oak Bluffs Country Club that was usually alive with music and clinking glasses and the whoops of servicemen and their women. I would pause whenever I saw a light on in the upstairs bedroom that fronted the road. I knew that Sally Stanley and Mary Lewis slept up there and at night when they undressed they did not pull their shades though the front of the house was darkened by the wartime blackout. I never told Crosby, but I could see bodies up in the window—quick glimpses of enough skin and breast and what a fellow pinboy at the bowling alley called poontang—enough to make my night a success. One glimpse of bare skin meant I had scored.

Remembering how I lived as a boy, I am now struck by my ability to remain sane. Obsessed as I was, I could have set fire to our bungalow or accosted a woman sitting on the beach and ripped away her bathing suit. Were it not for my father, who was my conscience, I am convinced that I would have committed some terrible deed, born of intense sexual frustration and confusion. But I could not let my father down—at least not through my own initiative. Whatever happened to me at Brook Hall, though shameful, could not be charged to me. Any raw act of aggression in Harthaven, however, would require an unbearable recounting were my father to learn of it. So I desisted and held a lid on my emotions.

Bill Jones's bowling alley presented an outlet, a way for me to work off steam. I was pleased with my athletic ability. It took timing and hand-eye coordination to spot pins as you hopped back up on a sitting ledge or perch to await a speeding bowling ball that sent duckpins flying. A pinboy blocked the flying pins with the soles of his shoes. After all three balls had been sent into the pit below, you alighted quickly and grabbed the pins four at a time and set them on the spots, indentations in the wood where the pins could stand balanced and ready for the next frame. If a pin was spotted incorrectly, the bowler was apt to yell down the alley, calling for a correction. The better one did, the bigger the tip.

Because of the job I had change in my pocket and some confidence in my bearing. In that first summer of 1944, the bowling alley relieved me of my obsession. Thoughts of girls gave way to the satisfactions of work. Many afternoons at about two, I'd ride my Columbia into Oak Bluffs and rest it against the wall of the bowling alley. Inside I'd lounge about, awaiting action. Before too long some bowlers would appear—tourists or Army personnel—and I'd run down the alley to the deep pit at the end and hop on my perch to wait for the game to begin.

Only once did my father see me at work. On the last day of the summer, with the car packed and my parents ready to leave, I was again at my post at Bill Jones's. My father, astonished at my absence, had to ask where I was. My mother suggested the bowling alley and, agitated, he drove into Oak Bluffs to find me. I looked up from the pit where I was reaching for pins to spot when I caught his eye. He looked so out of place, so ill at ease standing by the door. I hated his intrusion into my world. He must have been stunned. He'd never been in a bowling alley in his life. More astounding, he'd never seen me work. At anything.

The war ended the next summer, in August 1945. My brother returned almost immediately. One day a collect call came from Fort Meade, Maryland, and I accepted it. It was Bill. His first words were: "Don't tell Mom who it is. I want to surprise her." My heart raced. All the years of fear and wonder about my brother were blown away. There was something in his tone that indicated he'd changed. Just the idea of wanting to surprise his mother suggested some new roguish sense of humor, a bit of imagination. I'd always seen him as a human volcano who'd spew his lava if you pressed him on anything. But now I had only kind thoughts in my head as I called to my mother in her bedroom, "Someone on the phone for you." A moment later I heard her cry out his name. Our hero had returned to America. He'd be home in a few days. He was being "mustered out," he said.

Once the U-boat scare was over, and certainly by the time Germany surrendered, the lights went on again all over the island. Blackout curtains and shades and black paint could be removed from the windows. At night I could ride home from Bill Jones's or the movies with a light on my bicycle. By the summer of 1945, with my brother returning miraculously unhurt, the Vineyard began to burst with postwar enthusiasm. The Army was gone, and the Navy was still on the island but thinned out. Civilians seemed prosperous as a result of wartime wages, and as far as we could determine not one of my cousins had been wounded in the war. Harthaven had been spared.

My grandfather had died in the winter of 1944, before the end of the war. In our family he had been all-powerful, making my father very uncomfortable in his presence. My father drove from Maryland to the funeral alone and never spoke a word to his children about it or what it meant to him. I do not know what he told my mother. I do know that with the "old man" gone, he felt some relief. Our lives were not to change, however. With my grandfather dead, I had thought we could finally leave Maryland and go back to Connecticut where we belonged. I'd been told that the reason we'd moved in the first place was that my father was under too much pressure from his own father, a controlling tycoon who was always looking over my father's shoulder and who, though semi-retired, kept interfering in the running of his business. My mother's illness was part of it, too. But instead of going home we stayed on in Maryland, I suspect because of Kay Radford.

•   •   •

During the late summer of my fifteenth year I misbehaved badly on the way back to Maryland from the Vineyard. It had all begun a few weeks earlier on the island on a hot summer's day when I was swimming in from the raft—the same raft where I had come upon my Ella Raines lookalike. I began to float on my stomach, in a sort of dead man's float, only I kept my legs going, paddling my way to the shore very slowly. I enjoyed floating along in shallow water with my eyes open so I could study the bottom. Sometimes I'd spy a whelk and dive down to scoop it up. But this time I was just coasting along the placid waters, searching the bottom, easing my way toward the beach.

I was floating into shore when I looked up from my study of the sea floor to see the exposed genitals of a woman who was sitting chest high in the water right in my path. Her bathing suit was hiked to one side, her reddish hair a giant tangle, magnified perhaps by the seawater, but in any case a thick expanse leading up her stomach. The pink lips of her labia protruded a bit, enticing me. I knew her—she was a guest of my cousin, Barb Pease, and I knew, too, that she was purposefully exposing herself to me. She had seen me floating my way toward shore and had gone down into the calm waters of Nantucket Sound to sit semi-naked, probably aroused, waiting for a fifteen-year-old boy to see her.

I was so startled that I swam quickly away, almost in a panic, and emerged from the water down the beach, several yards distant. I kept stealing glances at her until it was time to go home for lunch. She must have known I was watching her. My heart beat rapidly and I began to ponder the possibilities. I did not know her well, but I thought of her as being without a husband. Either he was in the service or they were estranged. In later years she showed up with a second husband, so I may have been correct about her marriage being over. Whatever her marital condition, she had succeeded in exciting me with the most blatant gesture imaginable. By the time I reached my late twenties I'd learned that women often had "accidents" on purpose: a strap would slip over a shoulder exposing a breast, or a bathrobe would fall open by mistake giving the viewer a quick glance. Indeed, over my later years such erotic enticements would come and go with some regularity. But in 1945, at fifteen, I was innocent of such fetching maneuvers and was astonished by what I'd seen and terribly stimulated by the scenarios I was concocting. Startled, I made no move toward her, a woman approaching middle age. I left the beach with my parents, my father helping my mother each step of the way, down a cut in the dune grass and to the car. My mother's legs were so weak that she wobbled and almost fell several times, and would have done so were my father not holding her. My father wore a pair of dark blue woolen bathing trunks, and his muscles were still well defined in his back, his shoulders and arms, and his strong legs. Like the "good scout" he honored, he soldiered on, carrying his wife along like a wounded buddy back from no-man's-land.

I dutifully walked behind them, slowly picking my way along the dry sand. I felt so childish trailing my parents to our car, especially having seen so much of the woman who'd displayed herself to me. I had watched her on the beach, and she must have seen my gaze and certainly knew what I was thinking, as I knew what she was thinking. I was the only boy around. Older men, obviously husbands, were sprinkled about on the beach, but no young males. I must have excited her, and knowing this excited me.

Because of my mother's condition we were to make two overnight stops on the way back from the Vineyard. The first night we stayed at the Sheraton in Providence, and the second night we stopped at the

Princeton Inn in New Jersey. On that night the air was heavy and it stayed hot well into the evening. Air conditioning was not in use, the war just having ended. Instead a big ceiling fan went round and round over my bed. Outside the street was silent, and as I looked out my window I saw streetlights and some solid two-story houses and shade trees. It looked like New Britain to me, like Lincoln Road where I had grown up, where cousin Tim Stanley lived across from me in an old house that predated the Revolutionary War, where elms and huge maple trees swelled into the sky each spring, bulging with life. I was so homesick that night, homesick for Connecticut and hurt that my parents had erred so badly and that we were once again leaving New England, not staying. To this day I recall the terrible loneliness I felt when I stared from my window and saw the quiet tree-lined street below and the lights and felt the soft still air outside my open window.

I undressed for bed and went back to pull the shade when I heard footsteps below. I peered out into the night and saw a young woman walking under the glare of a streetlight. She was wearing a skirt and blouse and probably stockings, a thought that excited me. Suddenly I recalled Barb Pease's guest at the water's edge, naked, only four or five feet from my face, so close I could have floated another second or two and kissed her on her sex. Now, fired by memory, I stripped and posed before the woman walking directly below my window on the second floor, in clear view. In my heart I knew that this grown woman would respond to me with more courage than I had only a few days before. I pictured her entering the hotel, finding my room, knocking on my door. I was fifteen and didn't know any better. Any minute she would be with me. I waited.

No one came to my room. The woman did raise her eyes to me and stared up at my lean fifteen-year-old body for what seemed a lengthy evaluation. But I would never know exactly what she thought, though evidence would mount that she had been unimpressed on the one hand and furious on the other. Apparently she reported me to the management of the inn. Rather than search me out for sexual intercourse, she turned me in as a sexual exhibitionist.

Naturally, in the secretive world of our family no one said anything to me directly, but I remember breakfast with my father the next day. Though his usual manner leaned toward preoccupation and dead silence, that morning I could feel added tension stemming from him. Later in the car, ten minutes or so out of Princeton, my father spoke to my mother clearly and with force so I could hear in the back seat where I rode with Taffy curled up beside me.

"You know, Lu," he said, "the people at the inn seemed to dislike us. I wonder why."

"What do you mean?" she said.

"They were anxious for us to leave," he said. "I could almost feel a hatred, as if we'd done something wrong."

"Why, what could that be?" she asked.

"I don't know, Lu, but we did something unpardonable that they didn't like. We can't go there again," he said.

"Never again?"

"No. They told me so," he said, and then there was silence in the front seat. My father had just let me know that he knew what I'd done and that it was bad. Very bad. My mother would have known, too. They may have rehearsed their conversation. Painfully, they made me aware that I'd been found out. What had worked so well for the woman on the Vineyard had not worked at all for me. I could get in real trouble for doing what I'd done, I thought, and yet I also remember the charge, the thrill it had given me. Now, driving back to Maryland and Brook Hall, I imagined young women in Washington, the war over, everything breaking wide open. I'd go out for football, hang around with the older guys, and sooner or later I'd have a woman like the one who turned me in, only instead of being offended she would be as desirous as I'd been for the lady who'd shown me everything.

Truth in Fiction: Harold Hawkins #3

In early March, Harold's father began to pick him up on Wednesdays for weekly trips to the dentist. Harold's teeth were throbbing terribly, and when Dr. Kaseby examined them he told Harold's father that he had seldom seen such a mouth. "It's a mouth of pain and decay," he said. Then he went on: "There are a dozen cavities to be filled, two teeth that are abscessed which must be removed, and at least six years of orthodontia that should be performed on this young lad." The orthodontia would be postponed and eventually forgotten, but there was no avoiding the other dental work, and plans were laid.

Harold's father usually arrived at the school right after noon mess, and by 2:30 Harold would be in Washington sitting in Dr. Kaseby's chair, squirming in blinding pain as he gripped the chair by its arms. For Harold, in a show of misplaced bravery and guilt, eschewed Novocain except for the extractions, which he could not have handled without it. Thousands of Marines had died on Iwo Jima; it wasn't much to ask, he thought, that he take a little drilling without anesthetic. Everything conspired to make him "take it like a man," just as he needed to walk the track. He would tell himself this as he sat quiet and stoic in his father's station wagon. In his mind he repeated over and over again that he was tough enough to take whatever tortures Dr. Kaseby could offer.

In 1944 a first-year student, a boy called Wedge Shapiro, had been holding court before the main portico. In his high-pitched voice he delivered broadsides to the corps of cadets. There would be a day of reckoning, he proclaimed. He talked of horrible Nazi experiments and ghastly pyres of bodies. Millions were dying or dead, he would cry into the waning daylight, almost wailing at the cannon which stood imperturbable behind the tall flag pole. He stood possessed, his hand filled with sheaves of paper, his bright blue eyes on fire with rage, his arms extended.

Harold often moved close to listen to Shapiro. Unmolested by either the cadet officers or the Eagle, the crusading Jew would appear daily in front of the portico one hour prior to formation for evening mess. His eerie speeches went unchallenged. On the first day a small crowd began to assemble, composed of cadets passing by on their way back from study hall in the Old Main. By the end of the week there was a crowd listening to the news Shapiro received in daily dispatches mailed from his home in Baltimore. Harold, upset by what was happening to the Jews of Europe, was fortified in his conviction that he too must suffer—all of his suffering a cover for that other knowledge that his mother was ill and his father was too quiet and maybe on Wednesdays, while Harold was with Dr. Kaseby, his father was doing something he shouldn't be doing.

At first, those evenings in Washington with his father were good fun. His father would pick him up at Dr. Kaseby's soon after Harold was through. Then the two of them would go to a movie after dinner at Hammel's, a small restaurant near the Justice Department which his father fancied. His father always ordered veal scallopini, and Harold usually had two club sandwiches and a large glass of fresh, cold milk—milk that did not taste of garlic as it did at Brook Hall, especially in the spring when the cows ate onion grass. Milk at Hammel's wasn't warm from sitting on the tables for an hour before the cadets marched into the mess hall. Once Harold even had a glass of port wine which his father ordered with a flourish. "You're fifteen," he said. "When I was fifteen, my father let me drink wine on occasions. This is an occasion," he said, and they smiled and beamed at each other, in itself an exception to the generally pleasant but uncommunicative dinners they shared.

One night they did not go back to Brook Hall but stayed at the Mayflower Hotel. Harold was not surprised. He'd seen her in the lobby, a woman dressed to the nines as his father would put it, her hair lightly touched up by a hairdresser so that it was radiant under the brilliant chandeliers that hung from the ceiling of the great corridor that ran the full length of the block. Officers in uniform gave her long looks as she crossed the carpet toward them. She was wearing a black silk dress with a V-neck and a diamond brooch positioned at the bottom of the V. It was clipped to her bra so you could not look down her chest, but her cleavage was still ample as her breasts pushed into the V, her white skin virginal and soft. Her gloves were off-white suede and they extended up to her elbows. Her dark suede shoes were high-heeled and gave her calves a graceful curve that would bring whistles on the street. She wore a small black felt cap on the back of her head with what looked like two felt rudders standing out on either side. The headgear did not take anything away from her hair, however; indeed the rudder-shaped appendages called attention to the soft flow of her tresses. She looked like a movie star, and the enormity of the thought that his father had lain with her naked and that they'd had sex was numbing. When she joined them, he could only stammer and blush.

Harold's father said that they were going to have cocktails, and he gave Harold some money to go to a movie.

Father and son would eat later at Hammel's and then go on up early to bed. Major Keller knew that Harold would be spending the night. "By Garry, you deserve it," his father said to Harold. Then looking at his elegant companion, he added, "Harold's so cooped up at that school, I thought that a full night in the city would be good for him."

As he walked to the Earle Theatre, Harold reasoned that the meeting had been no accident. She was all dolled up, anticipating his father. She was dressed the way ladies dressed in *Life* magazine, photographed at a fancy party, or the way women probably dressed when they went to the Army-Navy Club and danced with General Long from Casa Toledo. His mind awhirl with images, he realized that he was not supposed to know about his father and her, but he did know as soon as he saw her smile slip across her face like a lie slipping into a sentence. His stomach growled in anticipation of dinner at Hammel's and he turned quickly under the marquee. He would lose himself in the movie, all the while knowing that this meeting had not happened by chance. There'd been a host of other Wednesdays when Harold had not accompanied his father to Washington. They must have rendezvoused many times before.

•   •   •

He walked slowly through the gilded lobby under the filigreed ceiling that reminded him of a sultan's palace. He strode upon an endless carpet into the dark theater and heard the voice of Judy Garland. The movie was Meet Me in St. Louis, and she was singing "The Trolley Song," a song that Captain Sullivan often played on the piano at morning assembly. Harold sat down halfway back in the upper balcony and tried to follow the movie while he watched couples necking in their seats, their heads desperately glued together. That previous winter at Casa Toledo, Mrs. Cawley had kissed him, but with Captain Fillmore watching, Harold had not really felt the effects of the kiss. Now he gazed at Judy Garland and wondered what it would be like if she fell in love with him. He could kiss Judy Garland for an hour non-stop, he thought.

When the movie ended, he went back to the hotel. He was still thinking about Judy Garland when he saw his father sitting alone in the lobby with a newspaper in his hands. Harold could smell liquor on his breath. His father looked very happy. His gray-blue eyes lit up his face. There was life and adventure in those eyes and in the tone of his voice when he said, "Now tonight, Harold, I want you to try the broiled lobster. You can even have some special Chablis wine with it. Boy oh boy, Harold," he exclaimed, "we are going to eat!"

Hammel's was a small restaurant and very crowded, with a line at the door. Most of the men were in uniform, some of very high rank. There were perhaps a third as many women as men, all of them dressed well, wearing dark blue or maroon or black dresses which ended at the knees. They all looked young, but not fancy in their choice of clothes. These were working girls, not socialites, he thought. But the real focus of his attention was on the officers and their decorations.

In lectures at school he had learned how to differentiate combat ribbons from the different theaters of action. Suddenly finding himself so close to so many high-ranking military men, Harold was considerably awed, especially when his father was waved right through the line of waiting customers because of his position as a provider for Brooke and Harry's, a chief supplier for Hammel's and the reason why Hammel's came to his father's mind in the first place. They had not been seated very long when a ruddy-faced, heavy-set man, well over six feet tall and wearing the patch of the First Army on his shoulder and bright Brigadier General stars above the shoulders of his Ike jacket, came barging his way across the room toward them.

"Randolf Hawkins, you old son of a bitch," he shouted and almost crashed into their table in his enthusiasm. But Harold's father froze and did not offer his hand. Harold could feel the tension and the instant hostility and feared that Hammel's celebrated stained glass windows would crack under the power of his father's hate, his silent stare splintering the General's gleeful overtures, as though they shared a secret not forgotten over time. The General, suddenly so culpable, seemed fearful and stunned to realize that some old transgression was still alive, even in the crowd at Hammel's in 1945, even in the glow of his stars and decorations—the Legion of Merit, the Croix de Guerre, the Bronze Star with an Oak Leaf Cluster—his ribbons lined in a row to demonstrate his value as a man.

The shock in the General's blue eyes yielded to the thousand-yard stare of Harold's father. Their waiter stopped in his tracks as though immobilized at what would come—all of that so swift, like the sudden pain of the dentist's drill, a nerve grazed, a bolt from nowhere just as you thought that the deep drilling was through. Harold gulped and held his breath while the waiter stood a few feet away.

Finally his father spoke to the General, still standing, now awkward, not knowing where to turn. "You were the only officer who ever ran," his father said. "You ran from the line, from the First Army at Stenay, and you ended up at headquarters in Toul on the Moselle River, and if the war had not ended we would have slung your ass in a sling as strong as David's and flung you into Fort Leavenworth. Now get the goddamn hell away from me and my boy. And take those asinine ribbons and your chrome-plated General's stars with you and don't ever show your cowardly, snivel-livered self to me again. And if those clenched fists mean anything, I'll knock you into the next room so don't even try it...assuming you have found an ounce of nerve somewhere, which I profoundly doubt."

Harold heard all of this, so close to it, so much a part of it, that his heart raced in fear. He had no doubt of his father's honesty, but no one insults a General. The man was in a uniform of authority. And then the General left the table.

The rest of the meal was subdued. His father had three drinks before he was able to relax and enjoy his lobster. Harold was given three matching glasses of wine and then after dinner a cherry liqueur while his father smoked a cigar and drank brandy. Eventually they talked—of building a long pier back at the farm, a pier that would go out to the deep water so that when Harold's father bought the boat he was going to buy after the war they could dock it in front of the house. His mother would be better then, Harold was assured, and he could bring friends back from school and they would all go sailing out into the Chesapeake, and maybe someday his father would sail all the way around the world. At the end of dinner he thought of the General and how his father had told him off and he thought of his own confrontations with fellow cadets. It was clear that he was never going to measure up. He could go without Novocain for the rest of his life, he could walk a hundred tracks a thousand times, but he would never be his father's son, the son of a man who could make a General wither away in fear.

Chapter 6

In the winter of 1946 my brother married a young woman named Marion Shepard. Marion lived in New Britain, on Ten Acre Road. She was an exceedingly pleasant young woman who smiled easily. I thought she was very pretty. She had two younger brothers whom I had known as a boy in New Britain: John and Danny. As I recall, the three of us were ushers at the wedding but I, at least, had no function. Marion's slightly older brother, Billy, in all probability gave the bride away. Her father had died. How he died did not concern me and I never asked.

My sister can't recall attending the wedding. She was living in Charlottesville with her husband, Frank, and beginning a family. Perhaps she did not go north with us. I recall driving up in my father's first post-war Cadillac, purchased from General Motors through his boyhood friend Sherrod Skinner, who by 1946 had ascended the ladder to a vice presidency. My father, who often spoke of Sherrod with envy in his voice, remarked in later years that he should have gone to Detroit with his friend—two young men, each with high mechanical aptitude and a love of engines. Regrettably, he'd hung back because of "the old man," his father, and then let his life slide away. He'd look away when he spoke of Sherrod Skinner, but then he'd refocus and perk up—always the good scout—"but your mother was such a humdinger," he'd say, and that would be that. Given a choice, living with my mother and raising three children certainly carried more value than a vice presidency in Detroit. Had he gone, he would have been an eighteen-year-old apprentice instead of a freshman at Yale, an institution he'd hated. He would not have gone to war. It would have been a very different life, far removed from his family in New Britain and at Martha's Vineyard. My father would have been happy in Michigan.

Anyway, we motored north and slept at Stan and Alice Eddy's, up Lincoln Road near the Shuttle Meadow Country Club. Bill's best man was Howard ("Howdie") Eddy. The marriage took place in the Shepard living room where we were crowded together. I remember some kind of "to do" over where my mother would sit, her illness kicking up, her demeanor informed by a perpetual frown of discomfort. At last the ceremony was concluded and Bill and Marion went off to Nassau for their honeymoon. I was glad to have such a pretty sister-in-law. Just knowing that my brother could love someone made me more comfortable. My picture of him as a menace had lost its sting. From that day on he would be out of the house, belonging to someone else. I could forget about him. That was what I assumed.

As the wedding began, and we were all squeezed together in that small living room, I sensed a measure of irritation, which I attributed mainly to my mother: Couldn't Bill have married someone with money? Why wasn't the reception going to be at the Shuttle Meadow Club? Where was the music? Why wasn't there a bridal dinner? Where, in fact, were the bridesmaids? I had expected a major affair, the wedding of an aristocrat. Though my brother was tall at six feet two and handsome from years in the Army, and Marion was lovely in her white wedding gown, everything looked too homey and middle class.

The above is written in hindsight, but again I recall my assumption that my family had some prominence in Connecticut. The truth of living on a Maryland chicken farm eluded me. Something was out of kilter, though, and as events would show, my unease was prescient. Marion died three years later in childbirth. Her elder brother eventually committed suicide, and her youngest brother, Danny, was murdered in San Francisco under mysterious circumstances. John, who married my cousin Joanne Hart and sired three children, left home and moved to Florida.

Bill and Marion had two daughters, and how these innocent girls were raised remains outside my purview. I was told much later by one of them that her life had been a nightmare, filled with dark secrets, but I did not press for details. It may be less than accurate for me to say that back in 1946, at sixteen years old, I sensed a tragedy coming, but when I looked at my brother in his wedding suit I felt nervous and had vague intimations that things weren't right. While it was natural to feel relieved that by marrying he was stepping out of my life, it was in my nature by then to be alert to the slightest contrary nuance. In that crowded, bumbling, strained gathering of Shepards and Harts, everything seemed far too offhand. The house looked too small for a proper wedding, and standing, almost flattened, against the wall of the living room, I watched my mother, who was off in a corner tucked into an easy chair, grimace. I felt sorry for my mother. In the crowd, I didn't see my father at all. No, it was all wrong and jinxed and would never work out.

Truth in Fiction: Harold Hawkins #4

It was 1946 and the war was over. Harold Hawkins was almost seventeen. He drove up to school with his father in the Cadillac which glistened bright red in the hot afternoon. There was a highway now that had been built to run straight from Washington down to Cedar Point and at times it bisected the old potholed road that ran along the low spine of Maryland, pausing every now and then for a gas station or a bar like Robey's or maybe a general store with a bar in the back, split in sections so that colored folk could drink in one part and white people in the other. But if you stayed on the big two-lane highway with its nicely rounded shoulders, you would get only quick glimpses of the old road and the railroad tracks and the deep mysteries of rural life. Harold used to think that some of the large white houses that lay back behind broad green carpets of lawn or fields with a copse of trees off to one side and a barn in the rear contained in them memories of men who toiled their hearts out in the blazing sun, bending to the pathetic tobacco crop and then went to war or to the back of a general store to sit on crates as at Gerner's and drink and sometimes fight over a loose word, an insult, some cut into their dignity.

This year, Harold promised himself, he was going to fit in. He would play football and stay away from Captain Fillmore, and he would head out to Robey's and Long's Café with the rest of the school leaders. He stretched his legs and found that they had been cramped. He had grown very quickly during the summer, "shooting up," his mother had said, and was now his father's height. He had high hopes.

It was a time for hearty athletes to swagger, and though Harold had forsaken his formal studies in order to fit in with his teammates, he still kept up with his reading, including Alexandre Dumas and Victor Hugo and three novels by Kenneth Roberts that someone had donated to the Brook Hall Library. He also read Nordhoff and Hall's *Mutiny on the Bounty* and a set of novels by a man named Howard Pease which dealt with the Merchant Marine and filled him with wanderlust. His roommates, Sanderman and Enderberry, were conscientious about observing taps, so at night Harold would take his book and go into the pool dressing room and sit on one of the benches and read.

His looks had changed. By May, Harold was considering himself as handsome as his friend and company captain, Sanderman, the mirror showing him to be a tall blond with wavy smooth hair, combed back over his ears. Sanderman was still crewcut, his thin body wired tight by an inner tension and a desire to succeed. Whereas Sanderman's features were regular, Harold was developing a high forehead and bushy eyebrows. Both Sanderman and Harold fit in nicely with a new boy named Huck Woodling. Woodling was round-shouldered and tough-looking and loved to roughhouse, although he would not dare to take on Sanderman, whose scissors grip was legendary in the corps. He could squeeze a boy so tightly that he'd pass out and then either Miss Stowell or Miss Ziegler would be called for resuscitation.

All of Harold's good intentions took a turn one night in the spring when the calls of the bobwhites were indiscernible from the whippoorwills and the warm winds blew lovingly up from the Potomac and before that from the great Chesapeake and before that from the open sea miles down county, just about due south. It was a night for high humor over at Long's Café, where Harold heard again that if you were big enough to reach the bar you were big enough to drink. It was a Friday night, and the next day Harold and Woodling and Sanderman were to play baseball against St. Alban's.

That night at Long's Harold drank quickly, a rum and Coke along with too much beer. Finally, just as Woodling was heading to the bar for still another round, Harold felt ill and had to leave the roadhouse. After vomiting, he was too weak to rejoin his friends, so he started retracing his steps back to the school. When he came to the edge of the campus, though, he turned off onto an old wagon trail that went up into the high pines of the forest. He had walked that way many times, but only for a quarter-mile or so to the fork in the road where the trail veered off to run its course beyond a row of white houses that stretched behind the railroad tracks that led to Washington. The other fork veered toward the interior of the deep woods, a meandering trail no doubt as old as the Revolution and most probably used now only by the Amish.

As his head began to clear and his stomach settled, he let the stars guide him down the wooded path. Every now and again he would brush against an overhanging branch and get himself scratched, and he enjoyed the rugged test of the branches, so full of leaves. The center of the path was clear, but sometimes he would sway off to the side and feel a scratch and wipe himself and carry on. He thought he could hear an owl in the distance or a communal clucking which meant that he was near a buzzards' nesting place where maybe twenty or more of the giant birds slept perched in the trees, clucking and airing their feathers. He continued on, laughing to himself and feeling the effects of his drinking begin to diminish. He could also feel the building excitement in his chest, like the thrill of an explorer.

Before him in a clearing there appeared a gray-shingled slant-roof house, one side of the roof falling near to the ground. There seemed to be no side, just all roof and a jerry-built, primitively framed structure, probably fashioned by an unskilled farmer in a hurry to construct a shelter before some long-ago winter. At least that was how it looked to Harold. Its windows were like afterthoughts, and the chimney was half brick and half cement. Off to the right was a barn which was equally on its knees, its sides full of open cracks and the door hanging from one hinge at the top of its frame. Neither the house nor the barn was painted, although the door to the house looked black, or maybe maroon; Harold couldn't tell. Behind the barn he saw a pigsty and a chicken coop. Back farther in the gloom was a much smaller structure that turned out to be a horse stall, temporarily vacated. It was filled with hay and straw and smelled sweet, and in the half-mind of semidrunkenness Harold stretched out on the floor to sleep in a pile of hay strewn against the back wall of the stall. He could see the stars through the opening, and he sneezed once from the hay before he passed into a deep slumber.

The hands shaking him felt like Sanderman's, very sure and almost possessive. As always, he was being awakened by his company captain at the last minute in order to make reveille formation. He began to roll over but stopped, realizing he had an erection and knew that once again he would have to wait in bed for his hard-on to go away while Sanderman, unaware of his condition, would call, "For Christ's sakes, Hawk. You'll be late." Sometimes the damn nuisance would not subside and Harold would have to crawl out of his bed backward so no one could see the projection in his skivvies or pajamas. But now he realized that he was still in his clothes and the twill trousers would obscure his problem so he began to rise, and then he saw her. She was black as tar pit and wearing an old set of coveralls over white long johns, the top of which showed from under her denims and semicircled her thin neck, almost matching the whites of her startled eyes. Harold looked up into her face and thought he was dreaming. Her eyes were especially unnerving because they showed a fear that was akin to what he was feeling himself. He had no idea where he was. And who was the girl now rising to her full height after squatting beside him?

A sheepish grin spread across his face as he rose to address her. He had violated someone's private property and as he looked out through the doorway, he saw that the sun was very high and realized that he had missed reveille formation. At any moment he expected the girl's father to round a corner with a gun in his hand. For a second he thought that he should run for it. Just get out. But where was he? He still could not get a handle on the previous night.

"You're at my uncle's farm," she told him, answering his question in the same local patois spoken by the new mess boys who worked with Willa. To Harold, it sounded as if they spoke not in sentences, but just in a string of words, eliding syllables at will.

He stood before her and tried to smooth down his hair and rid himself of the hay that was sticking out of his sweater and from under his belt and out of his shoes. Finally her fear faded and she smiled at his vain attempts to get clear of the hay that was vexing him. She left him for a moment and walked over to the other side of the stall and picked up a straw basket with a few eggs inside.

"Y'all stay here," she told him, and went out.

He waited for a few minutes, trying to get every last bit of straw out of his clothing, then looked around for some water to wash his face. His mouth tasted dry and burned, as though a powerful sunlamp had been inserted in it while he slept. He shook his head to clear his mind and finally recalled Long's Café and all the beer he had drunk, plus the rum and Coke, and, just as he was about to run for it, to lope back through the woods and thence to school, he saw the big man come into the stall.

He was probably in his late thirties, although Harold could not be sure; the age of colored people remained a mystery to him. The man was also in coveralls and long johns and his skin was as dark as the girl's. But there was no fear in his huge brown eyes, and he was grinning and shaking his head. He stretched out a large hand and Harold shook it and then he said that he'd had a good many strange animals nosing about the farm but had never had a boy from Brook Hall. He made mention of a dog, recently deceased, that would have chewed at Harold something terrible had Harold come tramping in there but two months previous. But he was smiling and laughing as he spoke, and Harold could barely understand him. Then he said, at the end of one of his protracted grins, "Y'all come in."

So Harold was invited inside, where he sat ramrod straight in an unpainted chair at a table covered by a stretch of oilcloth tacked randomly, and he was given a muffin and some hot coffee. It was Saturday, he was told, and was getting on toward ten in the morning. The girl was called Cousin or Cussie and lived there with her uncle and his wife, a very thin, short woman who looked away when Harold eyed her. Apparently the couple had one teenage boy who had gone to Washington to find work. They had no other children, just Cussie, whom they'd taken in because her father was no good and in any case had run away to enlist and never did come back. Cussie's mother was dead in a car crash. As for himself, he lived by barter. In exchange for pork he got milk and bread and butter, and he raised his own eggs and turnips and potatoes. He droned on as Harold tried to catch a few words here and there in order to determine the meaning behind the one-sided conversation. The man spoke with a grin on his face, laying out an abbreviated life story, convinced that Harold would be curious. And in a way he seemed to be justifying something which Harold eventually took to be that he was illegally homesteading on land that belonged to somebody else, most probably, Harold fancied, a bank. He had squatted on land that ran for many square miles off toward La Grange, a spread of pine woods cross-stitched by thin ribbons of dirt roads that connected in a backwoods maze. Harold could imagine a whole network of scratchy farms built by Negroes and poor whites who had never learned to read or write or sign a paper.

Harold could hear the squeal of hogs and the whinny of a mule. The girl, Cussie, was back again and eating a muffin too as her uncle continued to talk. He wanted Harold to know that it was all right what he had done, that there was no need to talk of it back at Brook Hall. Apparently the man knew he had built too close to Brook Hall and that someday he would be discovered. Of course, there were some white folks down at Bowman's General Store who knew he was up there in the woods, but he was worried about Major Keller. He had the concept well planted in his head that "the Major" was a real major and that he would call on the Army to run the man off the land he had squatted on and turned to good use. So, as he explained to Harold, it would be very bad indeed for the Major to find out about him and his wife and their niece. Harold would understand. He was a good boy.

Harold did understand, and in any case, he would not have brought the matter to the attention of the Major—he himself being AWOL and in big trouble. As for Sanderman and Woodling, he would not tell them either. It was too good a thing to louse up, he ruminated during his hasty walk back to campus. If he were lucky enough to avoid full-time on the track for his disappearance, he would return to the farm. His heart thumped at the thought of the adventure that awaited him. A real honest-to-God Negro family with a pretty young girl just waiting there. He remembered her hair as being very short and kinky, lending an added attraction to her fine-boned face and delicate features. She had straight full lips that to Harold were very kissable, like Lena Horne's. She was his age, he guessed, maybe younger, because girls grew up faster and people who were very poor were the fastest growers of all. He couldn't see her figure beneath the coveralls but he'd bet she had a swell body, and he daydreamed of being with her.

When Harold finally showed himself around eleven in the morning, he was already late for the Saturday drill. A Company was practicing silent drill, which meant that there would be no vocal commands. Instead of Sanderman bawling out, "To the right flank, march! To the left flank, march! To the rear, march!" the company would perform a memorized routine, for fifteen minutes or so marching in dead silence, save for the sound of feet pivoting and the subtle noise of rifles and slings shifting upon shoulders until the time came to halt and face the reviewing stand. Then the company would present arms, still without commands but in perfect unison.

He dressed hurriedly, pulling on another pair of pants and a clean shirt, and dusted off his sweater and his overseas cap and ran, Indian fashion, behind where the main barracks came close to the football field. He could see the commandant and his two aides standing in the center of the parade ground, and just when their attention was directed to C

Company, Harold scooted out onto the field and into place at the head of the third rank. Sanderman stared at him, for a moment bewildered. The silent drill went on until 11:30, followed by inspection. The drill went well and Sanderman received high marks. Only one cadet was reprimanded, a cadet named Diddle Little who'd worn white socks, claiming he had athlete's foot and had Miss Ziegler's permission. Harold passed muster without a comment.

At lunch he told Huck Woodling that he'd fallen asleep out in the woods. "I just slept for a lifetime," he said. "I must have been really bushed."

"Or really hungover," Huck said, and then they laughed like grown-ups, like two soldiers back from a night on the town.

• • •

Early the next afternoon Harold slipped away from his room He walked quickly toward the farm, taking a straight line through the woods. It was a warm day and only a few high clouds were evident, lazily passing overhead, serving as a gentle backdrop to the buzzards that circled patiently, high above. Harold thought of his father who would be at home, probably working on his dock. His mother would be reading the Baltimore Sun and sitting in a lawn chair. Up the waterway, neighbors would be finishing a late lunch, and a woman whom Harold had ogled from afar would sunbathe while her husband studied the contents of his briefcase, working as he always did on weekends. Mrs. Cawley, down at Casa Toledo, might be with Captain Fillmore, the two of them out on the grounds checking the property, chatting like sisters. Harold felt very much at home in the woods and waved at the buzzards and wondered if the girl called Cussie was thinking of him.

She was standing by the barn. Before her was a sow that had gotten loose and she was trying to retrieve it by making strange guttural noises, bending forward in a threatening pose designed to scare the critter, who only grunted and sniffed the ground. Harold quickly joined her and copied her sounds and her posture and extended his arms as if to encircle the beast. Once he slipped, and this seemed to frighten the sow, who turned slightly and gave a short oink which Cussie took to be an opening. She ran to the animal and kicked its large round rear and then the sow half-turned and moved away from Harold and back toward the pen. Harold jumped up and the two of them nudged and shoved and kicked and finally got the stubborn animal enclosed.

They went into the kitchen and again sat at the old unpainted table with the oilcloth cover stained by coffee. There was a wooden crate of Royal Crown Cola placed by a pine bureau directly opposite the sink. Cussie opened two bottles and they sat at the table and drank. She told Harold that her Uncle Darren and Aunt Aggie were in Thomasville, at the Bluebird, which was a colored tavern. They went there every Sunday to see friends, she said. As before, her diction was hard to grasp and Harold had to imagine what she meant, following her very closely and piecing her sentences together. But they were alone and he could feel himself become aroused and wondered if she felt the same way. Often she would turn her eyes downward, and her ebony skin took on a slight reddish blush. When she lifted her eyes, he saw that they were full of feeling and were speaking to him.

Just when the tension was becoming unbearable, she told Harold she was going to bathe. She beckoned him to follow her outside, where she led him to a shower stall that stood at the side of the low-slung, teetering barn. A long pipe ran to the shower head from the water tank that loomed over the yard back of the house. Harold watched her step inside the stall and then saw one slender arm rise to place her denim coveralls and her graying long underwear over the side of the stall. He could hear the sound of the shower, which seemed to last for an eternity before she emerged, her black skin shining like oil in the sunlight, her coveralls on again but her undergarments still resting over the side of the slatted enclosure. After a moment she took his hand and led him back into the house and without speaking she took him on into her uncle's bedroom where there was a double bed resting on four Maxwell House coffee cans. They were fashioned to grip the understructure of the old box spring mattress while the sheets and the one pink blanket lay slapdash on top. As she slid onto the bed and rested on her back, Harold blushed much as she had earlier. He found himself fumbling with her denims but was finally able to unhook them and slip them off, she rising up so that they could be pulled down along her legs. Her eyes were closed and this made it easier for Harold to undress, tearing at his khakis and pulling madly at the laces of his brogans.

An hour later, waving at Cussie, he left the farm and ran down the trail to school. He loped on until he found the water tower and ran beneath it to the back of the main barracks and then across behind the old smoker and then past his suite, where Woodling and Sanderman were sitting at the table playing rummy. He showered by the pool, which was noisily in use. Some of the younger boys were swimming while the sergeant of the guard, a cadet named Flint, was keeping an eye out in case the roughhousing should end in someone getting hurt. On a whim, Harold ran to the pool naked from the shower and jumped in, feeling the warm chlorinated water fill his eyes and seep inside his mouth. He climbed out the other side of the pool and struck a pose, proud of his sexuality, strikingly on display. He wanted the younger boys to see him nude and to stare in admiration as he had once stared at the upperclassmen. He wanted confirmation of the secret that he'd carried down from the tall pine forest far up behind the school.

·   ·   ·

After graduation from Brook Hall I once again motored north with my parents. It was 1947—I was seventeen. The war had been over for two years, and the world was at last at peace. I spent the summer spotting pins and dated a girl my age named Judy. I played a good deal of softball in an informal league that had been started for the summer months. Little by little, Brook Hall and the odd sexual interludes that had attracted and vexed me began to fade away. With each kiss, with each home run, with each well-earned bottle of Ballantine Ale earned from pin-spotting at Bill Jones's Alleys, with each day that passed, I shed another memory pressed on me by that benighted school where I had spent a long five years.

Judy and I were part of a group of teenagers, liberally mixed with veterans who added panache and tall tales to our crowd. I was out every night in a prewar Dodge rented for me by my father. We were still in the bungalow while my brother had taken my late grandfather's boathouse, the same place that had been rented to the Stanleys. I no longer had to peek at Sally Stanley and Mary Lewis, even if they had been there, though they weren't. I now had Judy, whose lithe figure offered all the requisite joys.

Time and new experiences and social acceptance wiped away Brook Hall. I went to dances at the East Chop Tennis Club and swam daily at the beach club in East Chop. I was part of an assembly of perhaps thirty youngsters who partied together and sang songs into the late hours of the night. As autumn approached, my confidence grew. I felt wonderful about life. In November I would be eighteen, old enough to drink in New York, old enough to enlist. And old enough, of course, to be in college. Alas, my parents had not given any thought to that until May of my senior year. By then, with every college and university engorged with returning veterans on the G.I. Bill, there was no room anywhere for me. Somewhat halfheartedly my father drove me to Swarthmore near Philadelphia for an interview. The dean of admissions had never heard of Brook Hall, and besides, Swarthmore was overloaded. Much as he'd like to give it a try, he said, there was no way to wedge in another student. We then went to Rutgers and were told the same thing. We went no farther.

Meanwhile, back at Brook Hall a tentative feeler had been extended: if I should return as a postgraduate to play football, I could be assured of a scholarship to the University of Maryland, which was building a football team to achieve national ranking. Brook Hall already had a great quarterback, Warren Cutterly, and they needed me to streak down the field catching his spirals. For a minute or two I actually considered going back. I saw myself as a captain of the corps, taking only a few advanced courses. Then at night, Cutterly and I and some World War II veterans, who had been similarly recruited, would drink over at Dyson's or at Copsey's in New Market. There would be wild, shit-kicking country girls. I'd get my name in the *Washington Post* sports pages: Brook Hall would be a powerhouse. I'd been told we would play a ten-game schedule, mostly against the huge high schools and private schools in and around Washington. Maybe I'd get into Duke, a magical name. Or North Carolina, where Choo-Choo Charlie Justice was a star.

I had my dreams, true, but I knew very well that I wouldn't pull it off. Somehow, someway, I'd get into trouble were I to return. Now secure and happy and admired by Judy, I looked back at southern Maryland as a fearful place, a territory rife with incipient dangers—car wrecks, fistfights, unwanted pregnancy with some rural high school girl with a name like Mary Lou Steffens or Beth Ann Briscoe, soft names familiar in the Maryland countryside. I let the scholarship slip away.

It was a road not taken: Brook Hall, Maryland University at College Park, co-eds, going steady, perhaps marriage and a life in Maryland or the District of Columbia. Gradually I would have slipped away from the Vineyard. Who is to say what road not taken would have been the better path? Yet even now the image of a former football star, a mindless good ol' boy, haunts me as I construct a scenario for what might have been.

In the fall of 1947 my brother and his wife, Marion, moved down to Maryland. (The irony was not lost on me. As I was turning my back on the sleepy hillbilly peninsula of southern Maryland, my newly married brother was accepting what I had rejected.) My father had purchased a strip of land at the entrance to Smith Creek, down where the Potomac opens wide to enter Chesapeake Bay. Along with the land came two old farmhouses and a couple of rickety docks. The Smith Creek Boatyard at Ridge, Maryland, was born. Along with Bill and Marion came my first cousin Howdie. Howdie had served in the Marines, and when he returned, he found that his wife, the willowy and very sexy-looking Ginny, had sparked rumors. We all knew that she had been friendly with Navy fliers in our great-grandfather's house in Harthaven which she and others had turned into an unofficial officers' club. Later, they were divorced.

While I was still up north, Bill and Howdie began a tortuous partnership. They were stuck with each other in this place far down toward the very tip of Maryland. I, who had turned my back on Maryland, had no interest in their adventures—or, as it happened, misadventures. I stayed on at the Vineyard, hanging about into the fall when my uncle Foster Upham took me to live with him in Cambridge. This side of the family, my mother's side, had begun to interest me. They were an odd bunch, peculiar, disturbed tradition-clingers who clung to their oddball, Old South history in order to establish self-worth. They were poor, big-oted, and, except for Foster, stuck on themselves.

There were five of them. My mother's eldest brother, Uncle Frank, was a blowhard New York City lawyer who slid into alcoholism and emphysema, from which he eventually died at sixty-eight. For a consid-erable period of time he lived like a kingmaker as the chief counsel for the Chrysler Building, New York's second-tallest skyscraper. During the Depression he had a chauffeur to drive his always new Chrysler. Uncle Frank had two sons, Bourne and Hayward. Both died of alcoholism in their forties. His wife, Pamela, was a friendly woman though she talked "hoity-toity." She harbored pretensions of being upper class. She floated in and out of our lives, gushing on about the latest hit show that had just opened on Broadway or whoever they had had dinner with at the Cloud Club, a semiprivate restaurant on the top floor of the Chrysler Building, where, no doubt, Uncle Frank was routinely treated like the man who owned New York. Pam was warm but seemed phoney. In the end, she outlived both her husband and her two sons by many years. She died in humble straits, practically living in her old Chrysler station wagon packed with boxes and fixtures and some antiques. In her way she'd become a mobile bag lady. Her sons, Bourne and Hayward, went first to Rye Country Day and then to Deerfield and Wesleyan. Both served in the Navy. Bourne was fourth in his class at the University of Michigan Law School. Both young men had it all and had nothing and the nothing part won out.

Now, with all four of them gone for so many years, I stroll by their graves. They are all buried near my parents. I see their faces when I look down at the earth. The truth of their lives is beyond me, although I can guess at it. The truth in my head is that I miss them all. Even Aunt Pam. The Frank Uphams were part of my youth. They were invariably overt with their affection, genuine or not. Sometimes when I read their head-stones, I wonder how I dare probe beneath the veneer of their lives. But without probing, I shall never understand my own life.

Uncle Foster, a handsome World War War I naval officer, died at sixty-one from heart failure. If he had a strong point it was his geniality. We all loved it when Foster came to call. He sailed with my father on his schooner and was often at dinner. He was always broke, and his sister Fannie and brother Frank gave him money for rent and food. Being broke did not inhibit Foster from owning fancy automobiles. In the '50s he bought a Studebaker Avanti, but could not make his monthly payments. Before long my father took possession, paying off the dealer or the bank. Undaunted, and perhaps buoyed by my father's aid, Foster went out and bought a Jaguar. Again my father came to the rescue. In later years I was the beneficiary of my father's good nature, happily driving both cars while on the Vineyard.

Foster pretended to be a salesman and actually worked at times, on commission from some firm, supposedly selling kitchen appliances or fixtures. By the mid-'50s, though, he was in desperate straits, living with his golden retriever in Oak Bluffs, having long discarded any notion of work. Penniless, he scrounged food from George Munroe, who owned a steakhouse in Oak Bluffs called the Boston House. Munroe would leave "scraps" out for Foster's dog—half-eaten steak dinners, baked potatoes, salad, rolls, chops, and even some gnawed-at bones actually intended for the dog.

Somewhere during that period Foster had carried on with a divorcee named Ruth Blakesly, who eventually married my father's cousin Ted Hart. This suited Foster just fine because it gave him access to Harthaven. Earlier, he had been more or less expelled by my mother. She'd become ashamed of her brother during the Avanti-Jaguar period and finally told my father that Foster could not visit them anymore. Alas, before anyone knew it, Foster was back in Harthaven, staying at Ted's. All winter, when Ted and Ruth were in Barbados, Foster stayed in their house, protecting it from nonexistent burglars and sponging off Ted, who paid for his food and drink.

Some years later, in the early '60s, just before Foster died, my father apologized to him for the ostracism enforced by my mother. After Foster died—he sort of withered away from a weak heart—my father told me, "I'm glad, damn glad, I went up to find Foster. I told Fos how sorry I was. I'm damn glad I did that," as though he had made everything all right. My mother had kept the two of them apart for ten years. Foster was my father's closest in-law and perhaps his best friend, someone he'd known since World War I. I loved Foster, as did my father. He never lectured me or suggested I do anything with my life. I suspect he just enjoyed me as I enjoyed him. What else mattered? That would have been Foster's way of looking at life.

Anyway, back in 1947, on the loose, with no college to enter, I spent the fall with Foster in his one-room apartment in Cambridge, just off Harvard Square. We spent many hours driving back and forth between Cambridge and Martha's Vineyard. We dined on chicken livers and not much else. I lost weight and grew nervous about my future. On the Vineyard I'd run into a pal named Dick Bache who introduced me to Tiger Tilton and Buck Legg. I began hanging about with them on the island, listening to Frankie Laine records and drinking large quantities of beer. I was often tipsy and would struggle back to Foster's small house above Waban Park in Oak Bluffs. Though worried, I did nothing to address my future. No one ever suggested that I actually do anything. Therefore I languished, going on eighteen, getting to know my Uncle Foster but nothing else.

Before long even my parents were able to see that hanging about with Uncle Foster was not a grand idea. Other boys were off in college. My college boards had been satisfactory in history and English but far below acceptable levels in math and science. So someone suggested that I strengthen my weak points by attending New Rochelle High School, a nice, highly ranked school for middle-class white children in an affluent suburb of New York where my maiden aunt Fannie Upham taught English.

Fannie Upham was my mother's older sister. In her spinsterhood she'd become the matriarch, taking charge whenever she could, sharing the family leadership with Uncle Frank, the New York lawyer. We called Fannie "Wad" (rhyming with "glad" or "dad"). How that nickname came to be eludes me. But Wad she was, and will remain as I write about her. She told me that she'd once had a boyfriend, but in all of my life she had been the take-charge, no-nonsense older sister, the unmarried woman who gave short shrift to men. Like her brother Frank she was opinionated, and most of her opinions were riddled with bigotry. Although she was never explicitly racist or abusive, she exuded an attitude of disdain toward those who would never get a fair shake. She could turn a phrase so it cut. Certain people were "those people," "people like them." Certainly she needed to feel superior to those she thought were the masses.

I cannot put exact words in her mouth, but I remember her haughty contempt for Catholics and Negroes. For most of her adult life she had taught English at New Rochelle High, though by the time I arrived to brush up for my college boards, her classroom duties were seemingly nonexistent. What I eventually learned, to my horror, was that she had developed the habit of turning on a small radio once the class settled down, and each day banal radio programs issued from her desk in front of the blackboard. In the early afternoon she tuned in the melodrama *Our Gal Sunday* and then sat back to enjoy the fun. Years later I asked her about it, expecting her to deny the practice. Not at all. She told me it was a good way to keep the class quiet and let them hear narratives, get the feel of English as it was written and spoken. By 1948, when I came to New Rochelle High, my aunt was a tenured teacher who didn't teach.

Wad had inherited her parents' home in Mamaroneck, on Barrie Avenue next door to Frank and his family. Foster was often a visitor. Wad, living alone, welcomed me and put me in her furnished basement apartment, called "Texaco" because it had a clean restroom, which in the late '40s was the theme of an ad for the company's gas stations.

I moved in right after Christmas 1947. I was just eighteen. I didn't care a hoot about my college boards. All I cared about was that I would be forty minutes from Grand Central Station. Wad was fifty-two or fifty-three years old, a strong woman with a merry face and blond hair turning gray. She had a formidable bosom and muscular calves. Not yet old in any way, but aware that youth was finally gone, Wad emitted an aura of sexual tension. Often I saw her looking at me and I would become aroused. Once she stormed down into Texaco when I was daydreaming of some sexual possibility that awaited me in New York and she caught me off-guard, exposed and excited. A day or two later I could feel the tension in her living room and I saw her rise from her chair and go to her bedroom, just off the living room, where she left the door open and stripped. I saw her through the open door, a wondrous body flushed as mine was, but I did not move. Eventually she shut the door and called good-night. We never said a word about what I'd seen. During that winter I often wondered why I didn't go into her room, and the answer remained: Wad is my aunt.

Whenever Foster showed up, he'd take the room that had once been the dining room. I always suspected sexual goings-on between them, but from my quarters down in Texaco I had no evidence. Once Wad told Foster off in front of me for having undressed at a picnic back on Martha's Vineyard. Everyone could see him. "You just stood there drying off and posing," she said. Foster smiled a bit, knowing he'd gotten Wad jealous. The incident had happened many summers before, back during the war, when we all went for a picnic at cousin Carrie's beach on the Atlantic shore, the same place from which I had wandered as a very young boy and come upon the woman sunbathing, naked, on her back. When Wad spoke I remembered seeing Foster remove his bathing trunks and just stand there, and I knew what Wad meant. But Wad spoke with a sense of ownership, and the way Foster smiled in response set my mind to wondering. My imagination worked overtime as I tucked myself in, down in Texaco.

I learned nothing at New Rochelle High School. What I did learn was my way around Greenwich Village, Times Square, and the Grand Central Station complex, including the Biltmore Hotel, where preppies and college kids drank. In the Village I met longshoremen who wore Henry Wallace campaign buttons and college professors who were of a similar stripe; it appeared that everyone in the Village was behind the Progressive Party candidate. I ran into homosexuals in the nightclubs and in bars such as the San Remo. I was not surprised by their overtures, my Brook Hall experience still clear in my mind. I elicited attention in Upper East Side movie theaters and, oddly, in the men's bar of the Biltmore. It became amusing for me to rebuff overtures from longshoremen, professors, entertainers, musicians, and lonely white-collar workers who would sidle up alongside me at a bar where I'd stopped for a beer. Lonely, I was prey, and there was an allure to the taboo aspect of overtures from men. But then I'd hear father's voice: *Don't be a fool, don't be a fumblefinger, don't be a fathead.*

Mostly I listened to jazz at Eddie Condon's. There was a train to Stamford around 3 A.M. that stopped at Mamaroneck. On a snowy night in the winter it was a long walk from the station to Wad's house on Barrie Avenue. Once I got caught in a blizzard and almost had to knock on a stranger's door to find shelter. But I persevered as was my habit, learned at Brook Hall, where I'd spent so many hours walking the track and where I'd slipped and slid through five years of military life. I adjusted to Mamaroneck and Texaco and my strange position as a postgraduate at New Rochelle High School. It was my way of moving on by flowing along on the tide.

The youngest Upham brother was named Phillips. We called him Uncle Phil. I disliked him intensely. He was weak and obnoxious. He was the only Upham who never went to college. Phil sold phonograph needles. "Did you know, Buster, there are more phonograph needles manufactured than there are razor blades? Just think of that!" he'd say. He once told my mother he was going to rent part of our beach at Harthaven for a hot dog stand. I cheered when I heard him say that, not because I'd changed my mind about Phil but because I loved hot dogs, a "common man" kind of food we were denied at home. My mother burst into tears and fled the dining room table—Phil's declaration was made on one of the infrequent occasions when he'd been invited to dinner—and I heard her go directly to the phone in her bedroom to call my father in New Britain. "He's going to start a hot dog stand," she cried, "and Bussie"—her nickname for me—"is cheering him on!"

Shiftless as Phil was, amazingly, he was so conceited that he even went out to Hollywood to try to become a movie star. He changed his name to Phillips Webb and struck a debonair pose for publicity stills, copies of which he showed me. As far as I know, he never made a movie. I stayed clear of Phil. Drunk, he used to come into the bowling alley where I spotted pins and would try to bowl. I viewed him as a fool: loud, dumb, and full of himself. Sometime in the 1960s I heard that he'd died in a car crash on an overpass on Biscayne Bay in Miami. He left a wife and three children, first cousins of mine whom I never see and of whom I have lost all track.

•   •   •

The Uphams, like the Shepards—the family into which my brother married—were star-crossed. The Uphams were attractive but badly twisted, flawed by their upbringing, which had led them to believe that just being an Upham was somehow very special. I suspect they'd inherited my grandfather's view of himself as a "man of God." Added to this was my grandmother's southern heritage and her belief that she was descended from antebellum aristocracy. An overpowering presence, she often argued with my grandfather, sometimes reducing him to tears. Emotions rode on the air, were rich in every loaded comment, and whenever Uphams assembled there would be the cries and wailings of Christian souls in torment, or southern aristocrats in torment, or a combination of both. I recoiled from the Uphams.

Nevertheless, it was Uncle Frank Upham who got me into Wesleyan University in Middletown, Connecticut. An egotistical campaigner, he'd had himself made a trustee of that estimable college. Foster, too, had graduated from Wesleyan right before our entry into World War I. My grandfather had earned a Phi Beta Kappa key back in the Gay Nineties, and both Bourne and Hayward Upham, Frank's boys, went there. As it turned out, so would I. My father, psychologically impotent, or perhaps completely indifferent, when it came to forms and procedures, had shown no interest in my academic future. Nor had my mother. Frank, therefore, stepped into the breach. Against the better judgment of the dean of admissions—"We're taking a real gamble on you, young man"—I was enrolled for the fall of 1948.

My freshman year at Wesleyan was difficult for me. For the first few weeks I had no idea what people were talking about. The turns of phrase, the endless allusions to names and concepts of which I was expected to possess some passing knowledge kept me in fear and in silence. In class, everyone seemed so bright. Who the hell was Beowulf? What was *The Divine Comedy*? Even democracy as a political concept gave me pause. I was far out of my depth.

Football saved me. I went out for the freshman team, but I was terrible. I'd lost my confidence in my year away from the game and I could no longer call forth feelings of aggression and violence. The old joy I'd felt at Brook Hall when I realized that I loved to *attack* an opponent—that was gone. I flinched, and a flincher is a loser in football. I did make the squad, however, and eventually became the guy who ran back punts. I played some defense on the secondary. In practice I could intercept passes with some deftness, but my cowardly flinching did not desert me.

Football made me feel I was one of the fellows, and my turning out for the team suggested to the fraternities that I might be a good catch. Much to my surprise Psi Upsilon pledged me, and I joined one of the three most lauded fraternities on campus. Suddenly a very shy, introverted, frightened youngster from nowhere had been accepted into a crowd of grand young men wearing tweed sport jackets and gray flannel trousers, young men with straight handsome features, poised to grasp the brass ring that awaited them in places like Chicago, Manhattan, San Francisco, and Philadelphia. The all-time flounderer, there I was with a group of lads between eighteen and twenty-five who seemed destined for meaningful careers, who were going somewhere solid. Down in my soul I rejoiced. Ever since leaving our large house on Lincoln Road in New Britain, I had been waiting to return to a status I fancied would suit me. Harthaven was fine, but it was not something I had earned, nor was it embedded in my heart as New Britain had been. I had begun to excel in New Britain, but just as I was about to grow up, it was taken away from me. Now, thank God, I was back in Connecticut where I belonged, at an exalted liberal arts college among the right sort of guys who liked me.

Gone were the oddball faculty members and the dullards with whom I had consorted in Maryland. I'd found my own kind at last. I was enjoying a brush with the way things worked at the top in America. I went to parties at Yale, and Wesleyan on its own attracted more than its share of beautiful young women. Off-campus I gladly tasted whiskey sours, martinis, and manhattans. At Psi U. we would drink punch amply laced with brandy. Occasionally on weekends we'd go down to New York and stroll into the lobby of the Biltmore Hotel looking for young women with whom we could flirt. I loved it all. For a time, Wesleyan held me in thrall.

By the end of the year I even enjoyed my classwork. I was beginning to catch on. I was getting reasonably good marks, playing freshman baseball, and hanging about with what I thought to be the best guys in the whole world. I'd arrived.

• • •

That summer I fell in love. It was late June, and though I was still friendly with Judy, we weren't "going together" anymore, though I did take her to the first dance of the summer at the East Chop Tennis Club. By 1949 Phil Edmonds and his big Tivoli Band were no longer playing on the island. Phil Edmonds had always concluded the dance with his rendition of "All of Me," sung in a raspy voice. Now we had what would be called a society band, a smaller group led by Ralph Stuart. This was Lester Lanin-style music—or rather Meyer Davis, as Lester Lanin had yet to ascend. We danced to bouncy Rodgers and Hart and Cole Porter ballads as well as current hits. For some reason the lyrics to "Mountain Greenery" ("where God paints the scenery") stick in my mind. But no matter, the dances were held every Tuesday night, and with a year of college behind me I invited Judy to the first one of the summer.

As was the custom in our crowd, Judy and I slipped out to the car, the old Dodge, for a few beers, as drinking was not allowed in the clubhouse. We sat in the front seat and drank and vented our affections, so to speak, even though Judy and I knew our teenage romance was over. I remember how I would nose my Dodge into a grove of pine trees where you could smell the pine sap and the needles and see the bright stars up in the sky, shining through the clear Vineyard air. We'd nestle together, and with the help of a few beers our inhibitions would melt away. That particular night, as we reentered the club, off to my right I noticed a young girl, perhaps seventeen, whose long black hair and prominent dark eyebrows caught my eye. She was sitting under a lamp, and she looked lustrous with the light falling upon her. I'd seen her at the beach club and wondered about her. Carrie Robertson was her name. You couldn't help but notice her figure in a skintight one-piece black Jantzen. She was new that summer, coming up from Pensacola, Florida. Her father, we were told, was an admiral.

Now there she was, unattached and smiling at me. I do not remember what became of Judy that night, but I left with the girl of my dreams and together we rode to the seawall in Oak Bluffs and I kissed her. I was in love from that first kiss. From the first time I touched Carrie Robertson I lost my heart, and as the summer wore on I became obsessed with this dark beauty who dazzled me. For one whole summer I lived like a young man helplessly in love.

Although I looked to be the picture of health, I was emotionally needy and was not mature enough for falling in love. My sense of self was nonexistent. When I met Carrie I was transported into a realm of feelings that overwhelmed me, but they did not obscure the physical aspects of love which were too dear to describe…to put into words, then or now. I thought of her all the time. She was a radiant young woman, responsive and adorable, and when she was not with me I wondered where she was and what she was doing. On occasion she'd slip off with a girlfriend and I'd become very jealous. I didn't want her to have any friends other than me. Young males were drawn to her looks and the enthusiasm that showed on her face. She was game and moved easily toward a good time. She may have been only seventeen, but older guys, veterans, would give her the eye. I absolutely adored her, and just the thought of other men looking at her caused immense pain that dug into my heart. I viewed her simple interactions with our crowd as displaying herself. All evidence to the contrary, I could not believe in my heart that she loved me. I knew she'd leave me, that day, that hour. Some handsome fellow with much more élan and a well-rounded education would wrest her from me. My feelings were so sharp they cut me to ribbons.

All of my jealousy and insecurity made me frantic, and in this welter of emotions I would hold her in my arms and weep, heartbroken without knowing why. All my life I had buried my feelings. Now I was beside myself, open to the world, my emotions written all over my face and in my eyes. I was tortured by love. At nineteen real life came to me, and I was woefully ill-prepared.

• • •

I returned to Wesleyan in the fall of 1949, a young man sick to death with love. In order to get by I had to pretend that my love affair had never counted for much in the first place. In order to save my self-respect and keep myself from going mad, I pretended that I could get by without Carrie Robertson, and gradually I slipped away. I denied my own feelings in order to save myself. I would not learn for twenty years or more that when you deny your feelings, in the end your feelings will chew you up.

During the early winter we threw a big fraternity party. One fraternity brother was expecting his girlfriend to journey up from Virginia. I was looking forward to meeting her. I don't remember the girl's name or the reason for the party, but we were all excited by the prospect of another festive Saturday afternoon and night. A band was coming up from New York. Most of the guys had dates; not I, of course, for by this time I was carrying a torch deep down in my psyche, the victim of a love that I pretended did not exist. But my fraternity brother was aglow. He'd been unable to see his girlfriend over the long football season because every Saturday he'd been playing for Wesleyan. In accordance with the honor system, he was not allowed to drink at post-game celebrations, and his self-imposed regimen had put a damper on his social life. She, a livewire party girl, had apparently decided to wait for the end of the season before coming north. Then that Saturday morning I heard the bad news. She wasn't going to make it. Some emergency was keeping her in Richmond.

I vividly recall what took place late Sunday night, after all the dates had gone home, when some of us were sitting in the dining room eating sandwiches that we'd scrounged from our vast kitchen in the bowels of the fraternity house. There may have been a whiskey or two, but we were all sobering up; the next day held classes starting at 8:00 A.M.

As we were unwinding, recalling the weekend, in came two fraternity brothers who had eschewed the party and gone instead to New York City. They couldn't wait to tell us of their success. They'd hardly settled in with their drinks at the Biltmore when two beautiful young women took a table right beside them. Very soon they'd joined up and become a foursome—laughing, drinking, and flirting through the evening. They'd eaten dinner somewhere, heard jazz at Condon's, and then before the night went too far they'd found rooms in a hotel where they fell into their respective beds, each with a luscious and responsive young woman. "She was a living sex machine," one of them said, and then the shocker: he was speaking of a busty girl from Virginia whose father had "tons of money," and as he described this sexy woman it became obvious that she was the date who couldn't make it to Wesleyan, our good friend's girlfriend.

We looked at our wounded fraternity brother who was hearing a tale of sexual gymnastics with someone he'd thought was his true love. I was stunned and felt empathetic shame. I glanced at my friend and could feel his heart drop into a dark hole. If a woman could do that to him, what chance did I have? Little wonder that I was backing away from the girl I loved. Right close at hand I had reason to rationalize my actions. That was why I affected an indifference to love and to life. If nothing really mattered, you could make it through unscarred. It was immaterial that Carrie Robertson had done nothing to suggest deception or any lack of fidelity. One woman's treachery, described in lewd detail, gave impetus to my growing fear that I could not hold on to Carrie's love. Therefore, nothing much counted anymore.

Indifference as a way to cope with life did not start with the tale of sexual mischief by an errant date. I'd begun to question myself as early as my sister-in-law Marion's death the previous summer. By July of that year, 1949, Marion was experiencing difficulties with her pregnancy. I did not care about the details; all I gathered was that for some reason Bill's second child would be delivered not in Maryland but in Connecticut, where it was assumed that Marion would receive top-notch attention. In August the baby was born but, unbelievably, Marion died. She'd had some condition in which her body was poisoning itself. I knew nothing more.

I'd always loved Marion. She was pleasant and warm-hearted. "Sweet" was the word everyone used once they became acquainted with her. Two lonely people brought together by Bill, we crossed paths occasionally on my return trips to my father's farm, and whenever I saw her in Maryland she was especially kind to me, recognizing my loneliness as she may have thought I recognized hers.

But now she was gone. I should have wept and grieved and let her loss wash through me. Two little daughters, one a newborn, were without a mother. This was an immense calamity. My reaction, however, was to avoid the whole mess. Grief was not for me. I was becoming an emotional escape artist. The smarmy emotionalism that I fancied would inhabit the aftermath of death was anathema to me. I was in love with Carrie Robertson. Nothing else counted. I would avoid anything that might interrupt my single-minded pursuit. Indeed, minutes after the funeral, held on Martha's Vineyard in the lovely Chilmark graveyard, I slipped away, sneaking off to the East Chop Beach Club for a rendezvous with the object of my heart. I cared nothing for the tender post-interment scene back at our Chilmark camp. I would push out of my mind the lovely words intoned by our first cousin Norman Eddy, a young minister with a parish in Harlem.

Far back in my memory I keep a picture of my brother kneeling at Marion's grave, crying as the rest of us walked away; my brother Bill, so flawed. Yet on that day he was very vulnerable, very human, and very much in love with his wife, whom he had worshipped even though in his confused way he had often treated her with disdain. So much hurt. I quickstepped out of the graveyard. I had a chance then, and only that one time, to hug my brother, but I did not even consider doing such a thing. Nor did my father, who must have seen him kneeling and weeping. Like father, like son. We left him alone and I drove away.

PART III

Work and the Air Force

Chapter 7

My sophomore year at Wesleyan was shabby, and I behaved contemptuously toward the college and life in general. I blundered through the fall and into the winter, when I was suspended for a month for participating in a break-in at a delicatessen: a friend confiscated a mountain of beer, and I, knowing it was stolen, drank it with him. I did little studying and cut classes with regularity. Every time I did try to study, my mind wandered. Having willed myself away from Carrie Robertson, I once again grew obsessed with sexual daydreaming.

Once suspended, I was able to persuade my father to pay my way to New Orleans. In an explosion of joy and sexual release I celebrated in the French Quarter. I met a pretty girl who was just starting out in one of the leading whorehouses. With this winsome young lady I loved away the pressure and for a few days I felt absolutely wonderful—only twenty, leading a life of controlled decadence. To this day I can feel the immense relief that came in those days of youthful debauchery in a city full of music and heat and temperament and flesh.

But I could not stay in New Orleans. I returned to Wesleyan, where my life began to collapse around me. My stammer by now was so intense that I couldn't even ask a clerk in a drugstore how much a tube of toothpaste cost. I was unable to answer the telephone. I was sinking, and always in my mind was the extraordinary young woman whom I'd loved so much and let slip away. I knew one thing with certainty: if I had persevered in our romance and found her to be disloyal, I would have killed myself. Such thoughts led me off in desperate flight and I tried to pretend that she had never mattered to me one whit.

Partying and trips to New York became commonplace, and by spring my permanent departure from Wesleyan was ordained. I was considered a bad influence. All I did was drink, and dodge class, and plot ways to get into Manhattan. I lived with a constant wanderlust, and fidgeted and suffered through the dour months of a Connecticut winter in Middletown. In the postwar era, the town's factories were still belching smoke into the sky, and its streets were clogged with darkened snow and slush, and a perpetual chill ran up the Connecticut River and spread over the area. Whenever I went into town to grab a beer, it was bone-chilling cold and I was tempted to lose myself in some Sicilian barroom, cashing in my chips, saying the hell with college life.

It was a rainy May afternoon when I left college. I still had the old Dodge, and with a heavy heart I pulled out of the fraternity parking lot. I did not go directly home to Maryland; I drove to New Britain instead and stayed with my cousin Larry Pease, a couple of years older than I, who was taking a course at a local business school. His parents were in Florida, so we were on our own. In the afternoons we played golf and at night we drank at the Shuttle Meadow Country Club, where not too many years earlier my parents used to take me on "maid's night out"—Thursdays—for the buffet. A mounted moose head welcomed you as you entered the vestibule at the club. There was a small bar manned by a middle-aged fellow named Caddie. Everyone liked Caddie, including the younger waitresses, with whom he was having relations. You could sense it sitting alone at the small bar and watching Caddie's eyes roam the contours of a passing waitress. I charged all my drinks to my father, who was still a member, as I idled away the hours, feeling the loneliness of a young man without a woman.

My days were filled with a desire to escape, to return to New Orleans. I rose late, Larry long gone to school. But the moment I went downstairs into the kitchen, I moved into a room of fear. I lived in terror of the telephone. My shame in being a stammerer was all-encompassing. I was unaware that this unbearable depth of embarrassment was an indication of a plunging self-image. I had not bothered to figure out that when I was full of myself on the golf course or having a drink at the club, I had not the slightest trace of a stammer. When I was unsure of myself and battling the knowledge of how I had so thoroughly sabotaged both college and my love life, I was a fearful person and vulnerable to the slightest wound.

By late spring my restlessness had taken me home, briefly, to Maryland. My friend Louis ("Wink") Winkelman and I planned to head west for a few months in the new Chevrolet station wagon my father had just purchased for the farm. My mother had noticed how I kept fidgeting. I couldn't seem to sit still and read anything. Eventually she came to the conclusion that I needed to have my eyes examined. It wasn't natural, she said, for a young man of almost twenty-one to avoid books and newspapers, to be so restless.

One Wednesday in early June I had my eyes checked by an optometrist. To our surprise, on our next trip we were scolded. "Your son," he said, looking accusingly at my father, "cannot read. He is so farsighted as to be blind as a bat with letters and images placed close before his eyes. It is a miracle that he survived even a month in college with such eyesight. I don't doubt that he had to leave," he added, obviously aware of my history. Chastened by the doctor, my father bought me two sets of reading glasses and suddenly I could read again as I had at Brook Hall when I'd worked my way through the small library, always looking for more novels by Dumas and Conan Doyle.

Thinking now about my eyesight, I am appalled that not once in a lifespan of twenty years did either parent think to have my eyes examined. So tied up in knots by their own circumstances, they never pondered the possibility that my eyesight had anything to do with my floundering. All of a sudden, with reading glasses in hand and a new style to my comportment, I must have given my parents pause. Had they failed me as parents? How could they not have noticed that I needed glasses? If either one ever thought along such lines, a drink would cover such discomfort. If I'd left college because I couldn't read, it was a minor lapse on their part, something best forgotten. With drink in hand my father would exhort, "Oh boy, oh boy, Lu. When things get better, we'll take the schooner and sail around the world." And my mother would cock her eye at him and smile, warming to the dream that lived in his words.

Wink Winkelman and I returned to the Vineyard by August 1. We'd seen the United States, Tijuana, and a good chunk of Canada. We'd done it without a hitch, camping out, laughing and singing our way along the interconnecting network of winding roads and the few superhighways that existed in 1950. Somewhere in the middle of the country we read about Korea. I sensed that I would be affected, and I played with the notion that sometime soon I'd be in uniform. Images of military school that I tried to keep out of my mind rushed back. Once in the Army, or Marines, or Navy I'd be crisp and rugged and precise and have a mission. Shiftless, I yearned for a cause, and far out West some-where, as the news from Korea grew ever more serious, I began to daydream of boot camp and getting in shape and rising to reveille once more.

•   •   •

My mother was getting weaker with each passing month. By the summer of 1950 my parents had moved into the boathouse on Harthaven Harbor, turning the bungalow over to my sister, Bideau, and her husband, Frank, who were raising Bill's two little daughters along with their own three children. My brother, when he visited the Vineyard, stayed with us in the boathouse or in a hunting camp next to the old bungalow. In addition we had a small house that we called the shack—not more than a cabin overlooking Chilmark Pond. Both my brother and I used it for sexual liaisons, and wondered if my father did as well. For by 1950, Kay Radford and Claire Dent were traveling north each August to visit us.

My father would take the women sailing on his schooner along with my mother, sitting askew in the cockpit, uncomfortable in a red beer jacket from Abercrombie's. It would not be long before she'd be unable to go on the boat at all. The walk down the dock and the angu-lar and cramped quarters of the vessel were far from commodious. Using the toilet was an effort for her, and often she was incontinent. Also, I imagine that she hated contrasting her infirm fifty-year-old body with the long-limbed and limber Kay Radford, who was twenty years younger. Dentie was a perfect cover. All four of them were so close, such good pals.

Whenever my father took Kay for a drive on some pretext, Dentie would stay home to keep my mother company—and, I suspect, get her a drink or two, as drinks were supposedly proscribed during the so-called working hours of the day. I can see them now: Dentie and my mother having stiff highballs at three in the afternoon while Kay and my father were out together driving through Chilmark or out on the schooner, my father pretending to show his guest how to varnish or repair something. Below decks they'd find a place for intimacy.

I spent that August on the Vineyard awaiting events prescribed by others. My uncle Stan Hart had inherited from my late grandfather a directorship at Fafnir Bearing and the top position at Tuttle and Bailey/

Great grandparents with assorted grandchildren. Author's father at bottom right.

Lucy Upham, 1919

William Hart, 1940.

Author with his dog,
1939.

Max Eastman with the ladies on the beach at
Chilmark, 1938. *(Collection of Yvette Eastman)*

Three Wesleyan students at the Yale Bowl, 1950. Author is in the middle.

Author aboard his father's schooner, 1953.

Brother, Bill, in cadet
training, 1942.

Sister, Bideau, 1939.

The Uphams. Author's mother
at far right, 1935.

Harthaven Harbor. *Stormy Petrel* at the
end of the family dock, 1953.

Author in military
school, 1947.

Author's parents at Harthaven, 1947.

Author in the Air Force.

Author and Wink
Winkelman having fun
in New Orleans, 1950.

Sam Barnes in Paris, 1957.

David and Rosalee
McCullough, 1955.

Author in Europe, 1957.

Author with Madame
Cognac and Sam Barnes,
Nice, 1957.

Author with Joan Johnson, 1956.

Author with Burl Ives aboard
Tibby Dunbar, 1958.

Author with bride, 1960.

Author's children, Ward and Hillary, 1969.

Ned Bradford, editor-in-chief
at Little, Brown.

Senator Edward W. Brooke
with Arthur Thornhill, Jr., of
Little, Brown, 1966.

Rose Styron on the author's boat after publication of Lillian Hellman's *An Unfinished Woman*.

Author and John Heminway in a Manhattan saloon, 1966.

Lillian Hellman,
1967. *(Permission of
Corbis Images)*

The informal Vineyard way
of life: Kathy and Alfred
Eisenstaedt with Max and
Yvette Eastman and uniden-
tified man, 1950's. *(Collection
of Yvette Eastman)*

A new beginning:
author, 1969.

Bideau, 1969.

Cousin Al Pease and writer,
Gerry Kelly, a Vineyard friend
of the author.

Hart and Cooley Manufacturing. He was now a well-established manufacturer with two companies under his direct control. Uncle Stan had
two daughters as did Bill, and maybe that was what drew him to my
brother. Without a son of his own, he turned to Bill. In the aftermath of
Marion's death, and with a sudden swiftness, Bill departed a rotting,
dilapidated Maryland boatyard and moved north to become a young
executive. He was twenty-six. In a year he'd be president of Tuttle and
Bailey/Hart and Cooley and a director of Fafnir. People said he was a
fast learner. Now there was talk of my working for him. With no college
for me to return to, no job, and no interest in anything tangible, my
father and my brother eventually decided that I should go to Canada to
begin a career in manufacturing at the Hart and Cooley plant in Fort
Erie, Ontario. I shrugged my acceptance. I had no choice. Other than
spotting pins at Bill Jones's bowling alley, I'd never worked. I knew how
to drink, play softball, and work in a bowling alley. I could take out girls.
My résumé was brief.

Naturally, I looked for Carrie Robertson even though I vowed
that I'd stay clear. The trip around the country had given me some
respite from my troubling fixation with her. Though not yet nineteen,
Carrie had a year of college behind her. Bright and popular she went on
to Southern Methodist University in Dallas. In August, with some dis-
passion, I was able to watch her with other young men, her tan face
aglow as always, her enthusiasm so captivating, primed for adventure. As
was my custom, I told myself I didn't want her anyway. Yet I studied her,
surreptitiously noticing her curves in her Jantzen and the dark eyebrows
that reminded me of the forest of her sex. I ached for her but I kept my
distance. I knew she was dating a swimming instructor. If I let my imagination run free, jealousy would drive me crazy.

Vexed as I was by my continuing love for someone who was quite
obviously enjoying herself with others, I suffered as always with my
brother. Back and forth from New Britain, he kept entering my life as
though I were his friend. Six years older, with children whom he never
saw, with the exalted position of corporate vice president, with a war
behind him…what did he want with my company? If I went over to
our cousin Maxine's for martinis, he would surely follow. Were I to slip
off to a party on a Saturday night, somehow he'd get wind of it and
appear. Large of body and broad-faced and fleshed-out from drink, he'd
loom over us and press his awesome and, to me, objectionable personal-

ity upon the group. I shuddered whenever I saw him, and each Sunday when he returned to New Britain I breathed a sigh of relief.

Truth in Fiction: Harold Hawkins #5

He saw the big fella come in through the screen door, letting the door slam behind him. The spring was broken and the door made a loud slap when he pulled it hard. The big fella was Harold's older brother, one of those men always ill dressed, a man who refused tailor-made clothes that might actually fit his irregular, lumpy frame. Instead he wore trousers that were too long and a sport jacket with sleeves too short. He lumbered like someone who had trouble comprehending where he was and what was happening. He was always rubbing his forehead, indicating inner confusion: What were they saying? What were the secret messages? Who in the crowd didn't like him? What girl could he approach? Who couldn't he whip if there was trouble? Who should he look out for? Where was there a drink?

They were at a party at Beverly Clauson's house downharbor, and sometime near midnight they had Charlotte Hanley in a circle. They were tossing her from man to man. Harold sat on the edge of the circle, straining for views of Charlotte's panties as her skirt flew over her hips with each toss. The men tossed her from one to the other as everyone cheered. It was a dumb game, just something to do, a chancy thing should someone drop her. Charlotte was a good sport. Somewhat drunk, she cried in glee as she went flying through the air from one swain to another, the dark patch between her legs more alluring with each toss.

Then it happened. Harold should have foreseen it. On a toss from Robbie Feeney to the big fella, the big fella dropped his arms and the flying Charlotte landed flat on her back. Everyone looked on in shock and then Charlotte began to scream in a delayed reaction. She wailed as the others scurried to help her. Eventually they loaded her into the back seat of Robbie's new Oldsmobile and drove her to the hospital. She hadn't been able to move her legs, and Barbara Thompson who had served as a nurse in the war warned the group not to disturb her. She was overruled amid the anxious movement of people ashamed of themselves. Harold, too, was swept along in the need to get Charlotte out of the house, into a car, and away to the hospital. The big fella left the room and drove off.

Someone had said: "It was an accident, right?" Wrong, said Harold to himself as he looked away. Wrong, dead wrong. In his soul where honesty lived, he knew he had revisited the evil of his brother, always so overbearing and violent. In succeeding days Harold would look at his brother with a troubled skepticism. He'd never improve. He was over six feet two and sloppy with an expanding girth. Imprisoned by his body, he had a wide waist and broad shoulders and long loose arms and when he stood up he looked rectangular and without a graceful line to his form. He'd never been well coordinated and always failed at athletics. It must have irritated him to be so big and awkward and so bum at sports. The big fella was easily ruffled, too. With strangers he was haunted by fears that someone would lead the conversation toward art, the cinema, the latest well-received novelist.

Harold had always avoided his brother, but on the night when the big fella let Charlotte fall to the floor, he felt something deeper than dislike. *How,* he thought, *could I have a brother who could do a thing like that?* Harold left the party feeling responsible for Charlotte's fall, since somehow he'd been responsible for his brother's presence at the party.

The crowd that had been assembled that night at Beverly Clauson's never spoke about the wretched breach of conduct they'd all witnessed. Though Charlotte had recovered with only a bruise, for Harold, the sound of the thud as Charlotte hit the floor and her screams would trouble him throughout his years. It was as if he himself had withdrawn his own arms to let the trusting, vivacious Charlotte fall to her pain.

• • •

During that August on the Vineyard I was troubled by the daunting prospect of going to work in Canada. I knew it awaited me sometime in September and was unavoidable. My brother had arranged it with our Uncle Stan. Indeed, plans had progressed so far that I was invited to a party for company executives held at Uncle Stan's house across from our place in Harthaven. Once a summer my uncle invited his vice presidents for a week of fishing, drinking and male companionship. Thus far I had been excluded from man-talk, my father having no truck with either tall tales or dirty jokes. Back at Brook Hall we'd talked incessantly about sex as images of naked, wanton girls danced in our heads. But except for one or two experienced cadets, there was little bragging. Of course we posed and postured and strutted about, but that sort of adolescent behavior didn't count as man-talk or qualify as what would become known as male bonding, a term unheard of in 1950. At Wesleyan we were always in motion: rushing to class, to the library, the movies, New York. We had bull sessions but as I recall them, there was an intellectual base that justified everything we said; we were relating to one another in a world of ideas.

At my uncle's I met five or six men who were red-faced from fishing with Uncle Stan on his boat. They had the egotism that comes from managing a factory. Competitive, they talked loudly and thumped about; a back-slapping group, loud in their laughter and hearty to the core. Har-de-har-har's filled the air.

For an hour I drank with these worthies—men of means, men of advancement, men to notice. It occurred to me that I'd joined the business world and I shuddered at the thought. I'd never really contemplated a life among businessmen; my father, who'd retired in his forties, could reduce their bragging with a snort. But I hung on for another hour, observing how these middle-aged men deferred to my brother. I grew aware of my brother's power in that room. Bigger and louder than the others, he dominated them. I was appalled, yet in spite of myself I was proud of him. It seemed like just yesterday that Bill was thundering around a shabby Maryland boatyard. Now he had everyone's attention as he told a dirty joke, one sure to inspire a chorus of ho-de-ho's and thigh slapping.

Eventually I left the house and went looking for friends my own age. During those weeks I'd continued to avoid Carrie Robertson, though I was desperate to see her, to glimpse her out of the corner of my eye, feeling my heart drop when I caught sight of her in the arms of another man. But I played the game; I shrugged and the days flew by.

Then one evening in late August I ran into her. She took me aside. She seemed shaken and wanted to tell me something. We stood in the shadows outside the tennis club, standing beside my old Dodge. It was the first time we'd really talked that summer and she held me by the arm as she looked into my eyes. I could hear the pain in her voice. "Your brother, Bill," she said, "we had a date." She paused and I felt myself go weak from the shock. *Bill took Carrie out! How could he? How could she? Didn't she know I loved her?* I stumbled backward, not wanting to hear.

"He's very, you know…I'd never gone out with a man who'd been married," she said. "He was so forceful," she said not wanting to say the words, the right words to describe what my brother had done to her. She said she'd never go out again with a man who'd been married. Her brown eyes were pleading for sympathy.

"Oh," I said and continued to stumble away. I broke from her grip. I couldn't hear any more. The girl I adored had been with my brother! I knew Bill, what he was like. He was a bully who had taken advantage of this precious girl.

I was full of shame. He was my brother and I was somehow responsible because that was why she went out with him in the first place. Carrie was using Bill to get my attention; a gambit. And Bill? He wanted what was mine and had taken it by force. It had been that way since early childhood when he'd hidden my toys and leered at me like a villain. As she tried to tell me what had happened, I closed off her words that stung my mind. I brushed them away like a swarm of insects and stumbled backward; I was no help, no strong shoulder to lean on, no friend. My pain was too deep. I pushed her beautiful, beseeching face out of my mind and retreated into the darkness. I drove off, alone in the old Dodge, the same car in which we'd embraced. I was completely heartbroken. My only recourse was to pretend that I'd heard nothing. That day, though death did not come, a part of me died.

Loving her had once cut me to ribbons, but that was the madness of being in love. Now I was destroyed and my stomach went hollow. How could my older brother have taken advantage of her, the only girl I would ever adore, a sweet, joyous college girl? I raved: An eighteen-year-old girl! *My* girl! She didn't have to go out with him. Why did she expose herself to assault? Bill was my opposite; didn't she know that? She'd gotten trapped in his car. She'd been humiliated. I could kill him, I thought. But then, in the tradition of my family, I drank it all away. By the next day I'd put aside what was unbearable. What remained would be forever wanting. My heart was broken and would never work again.

•   •   •

On September 15, 1950, General Douglas MacArthur unleashed his counteroffensive and landed at Inchon on the west coast of Korea. I was not monitoring the Korean War, but I was aware that as a college dropout I was vulnerable to the draft. Now, with a major turn in the action, I could relax. It looked as if the war would end very soon. In my shyness and essential reticence I had not been in touch with my draft board in Middletown. As far as I knew, they still had me listed as a student. I should have been a junior that year. Instead I was in my car, a 1948 Plymouth my father had purchased "as a spare," driving up to Canada to start a job in the adult world.

Somewhere in upstate New York I recalled the affirming hours I'd spent spotting pins at Bill Jones's in Oak Bluffs. I could go on spotting pins; it gave me confidence and I was good at it. I could hang back and let adult life pass by. What the hell…why not? But now it seemed too late for hanging back. My father and my brother and even Uncle Stan were pushing me toward responsibility. *Good God, how did I get caught up in this?* I asked myself, all the while closing in on Fort Erie, Ontario, and a new life.

Technically I worked for Burr Clark, who was president of Hart and Cooley Canada, Ltd. Beneath him, my immediate boss was a scruffy, ill-kempt chain smoker named Jack Parr, who could never be confused with the TV personality, Jack Paar, who was just beginning to attract some attention in the media. While Parr was difficult, everyone liked Burr Clark, who had a way with his employees, a regular-guy approach to leadership. I worked in the outer office near his small quarters. Often, it seemed, he would shut the door for private sessions with a secretary, and in short order I guessed that intimacy was in progress. I could sense their movements, and when the secretary emerged I looked at her with longing. As I recall, she was an attractive woman, solid looking with nice curves and brown hair. Thus fantasizing, I got the notion that Canada might not be as inhibited as the United States. My hopes soared.

Burr Clark actually worked under my brother, who had ascended to the presidency of the corporation. I do not think he cared about me one way or the other. I was assigned to the time and motion department under Jack Parr because doing time study, as it was called, gave me an overview of the total operation within the plant. Parr, for his part, was a patient teacher and taught me how to use a slide rule and a stopwatch. Hour after hour I'd stand beside him timing people at their work in an

attempt to set a fair standard. Production performed beyond the desig-
nated standard earned the worker a bonus. Below-standard work could
eventually get a worker fired. Naturally the union detested time study, as
it took control away from the union and returned it to management.
Management, of course, felt it reasonable to expect a minimum rate of
production—a standard—from each worker. It seemed fair to me, too,
and I went into the plant every day assuming I was doing something
important and to the benefit of both management and labor.

After two months, trouble came to our factory and it centered on
Jack Parr. The men in the shop had long argued that Parr's standards
were too high. They didn't oppose the practice of time study, but Parr
had achieved a reputation for setting standards so high that bonuses were
few and failures rife. As I listened to their discontent, I started to side
with the men. Parr had a narrow way about him. A limited man, he was
stuck on being white collar, part of management, and the power he
wielded with his stopwatch was palpable. Standing beside Jack Parr, I
could feel his pleasure in control and authority. A worker bent to his
task at a large press, just knowing Parr was behind him, timing him and
subjectively arriving at a conclusion—too slow, too many movements,
too devious, trying to make it look harder than it was—would bristle.
Parr was disliked because he personalized his work. Using the stopwatch
was like using a whip. It was Jack Parr versus the rabble in the shop, and
the so-called rabble felt that Parr got a perverse pleasure by sticking it to
them with his high standards.

Parr, meanwhile, had made overtures of friendship toward me. He
was a bachelor who lived out in the country in an unheated house on a
tiny salary with an empty refrigerator and a small radio. He needed
companionship, and he saw me as someone to pal around with—someone who also just happened to be the brother of the big boss and a
nephew of the biggest boss, both down in Connecticut. *This guy, Stan,
can give me a leg up.* Chain-smoking and hacking and wearing a five
o'clock shadow all day long, this scraggly man tried to befriend me and
I rejected him. Maybe it was a result of my years at Brook Hall, but caution stirred within me, and I began to side with the men in the shop.
They were the good guys.

I joined the company bowling team and went to parties with
union members. Whatever was in the air relating to the union didn't
deter me. Johnny Crowell, the union boss, became my friend. He'd call

me at my rooming house suggesting a beer or two. I'd met a young woman who appeared receptive to my furtive advances. The fall began to pass with beer drinking and bowling and parties in dark basements where I could look for a kiss or a caress.

I liked Canada. I began to think that, with time, my shyness would evaporate. I seldom said a word to anyone in the office and was positively mute with my landlord and his wife. But Johnny Crowell and his gang of workers were drawing me out. Self-centered as I was, my self-imposed prison was cracking.

Although I gave occasional thought to the Korean War, I was not reading the American papers anymore and had no access to a radio. My draft status was of no concern to me. I simply forgot about it. Gaining confidence, I looked forward to each day at work and was enjoying the informality of Canada when, all of a sudden, at about 9:00 A.M. on a workday, the great presses in the plant stopped running. I poked my head into the shop, now silent except for the shuffling of feet. I heard Burr Clark mutter "strike," and we began to gather our paperwork to file away. Out in the driveway as we tried to leave, an angry mob lined our path. I was right behind Jack Parr as the mob upended his car. Unscathed, he clambered out. I picked him up, and drove around the half-overturned vehicle, and took him home.

With work at a standstill, I was transferred to the Hart and Cooley factory in Holland, Michigan. Prior to leaving, however, I had been contacted by Johnny Crowell, who told me that the strike, though ostensibly about a raise in wages, could be settled swiftly if Burr Clark would get rid of Jack Parr. Parr was the problem, he said. A nominal raise for the men and the firing of Parr would satisfy the union.

Just before heading west toward Michigan, I called my brother. The strike was getting expensive. Back orders were piling up. Hart and Cooley produced ducts and grilles and grates for air-conditioning and heating equipment, and the marketplace was impatient. I told Bill that if they wanted to get back to business, they'd better let Parr go. My brother, taken aback by my emergence as a labor negotiator, said he would consider my information. In the meantime I was to report to a man named George Copeland, president of Hart and Cooley in Michigan.

It was December when they fired Jack Parr, and true to his word, Johnny Crowell brought the union back to work. By then I was living in a large bedroom in a Holland rooming house directly across the street from the factory. On Saturday nights I'd drive to Grand Rapids to see a movie. Once George and Sally Copeland took me to dinner at a club on the outskirts of Holland. They served liquor, which was an exception for that area dominated by the Dutch Reformed Church. I drank too much that one time and felt some relief. My work was unbearable, as I never learned the time study system in Holland and I suffered from tension. The freedom I'd felt in Canada was missing in Michigan. Secretly I thought I was going crazy.

By Christmas the war in Korea had turned against us. Chinese regulars were pouring across the border and our Army and Marines were in retreat. The draft board would have checked at Wesleyan by now and surely I would be listed as missing, a draft dodger. Strangely, I didn't care. I was too confused and too lost. I was isolated in my bedroom wondering about old friends and young women I'd known. Nothing mattered anymore.

And then I heard about Jack Parr. After being fired by Burr Clark, he'd quickly disappeared. Apparently he'd gone back to his cold, porous house out on a rutted road and hunkered down, ashamed to show his face in town. Then one dark day, the story went, he shot himself, a suicide.

I heard all of this, sketched for me by George Copeland, who had heard it from Burr Clark. As was my habit, I deflected the news with a shrug and a clamp on my mind. I refused to think about it. *Who gives a shit*, I would have said had anyone asked how I felt. That was how the cookie crumbled. Jack Parr was dead.

Years later I was on my honeymoon when I saw the "real" Jack Paar in the lobby of the Rock Hotel in Gibraltar. I paused for a moment, recalling the man I'd been responsible for getting fired. Not that I put it that way to myself even then. It was much easier to think about the man who stood before me in the lobby of the Rock Hotel than it was to suggest to myself, even for a second, that I'd caused the other fellow's suicide.

I'd known him only slightly when I was twenty. In my sixties now, as the end seems to loom ahead on every curve and thoughts that I may be running out of time begin to make their worrisome inroads, my views on Jack Parr have taken on a different cast: I should have gone to him first and told him what Johnny Crowell had told me. I could have said, "Jack, I'll have to tell my brother, but I wanted you to know first so you can protect yourself some way. Go see Burr Clark and tell him that you might be the problem and strongly suggest that you'd be pleased to change to suit everyone, even loosen up the standards, which probably are too high." Clark was a taciturn man but fair. Something could have been worked out. Instead I informed on Parr to Bill, who summarily sent down the order to fire him. "Stan could be right. Get rid of Parr." I can hear his voice on the phone, talking to Burr Clark. "Get rid of the son of a bitch."

My father would have shaken his head. On the one hand, a whippersnapper of a lad had blown the whistle on his supervisor and triggered a suicide. On the other hand, all I'd done was transfer important information to my own brother, my boss. My father would have been uncomfortable over what had happened, but in the end he'd have had a drink or two and said to his wife: "Lu, that fellow Jack Parr, the man Stan says killed himself, was not Stan's look-out in any case, was he?"

•   •   •

The story of Jack Parr's purported suicide was the first of two shocks I had to endure that year. Although there is nothing more final and fearsome than death, what my brother chose to tell me ignited a rage that was impossible for me to bury in the dim chambers of my mind as I had buried the news of Jack Parr. What he related tore at me, firing dreadful, heated images and attendant fury.

He had flown in for a meeting in Holland. Thanks to my intercession the strike in Canada was over, and there may have been talk of my return to Fort Erie, but of course my situation was only tangential to the purpose of the meeting. Bill and George Copeland and others in management had decisions to render, policies to analyze, various reports to scrutinize, and while they clustered in an office upstairs, I was out in the plant trying to get a handle on the time study system. At the end of the day my brother came to my office. He suggested that we take my Plymouth and drive down to Chicago for a night on the town. Naturally, I agreed. I'd always looked at Bill with a combination of loathing and awe. Now he was my boss, outranking everyone except my Uncle Stan.

The night in Chicago was a night of drinking and listening to jazz at a place called Jazz Unlimited. By the time I closed my eyes I was more than half-drunk and reeling, not just from the alcohol but also from my brother's account of having his way with Carrie Robertson.

"It was in the car," he said, "down at Katama, behind the dunes. She was a hot number who really wanted it," he said, describing with macho glee how she had succumbed to his charms. He was blunt and vulgar. Inside I felt a terrible anger. Had I a knife...?

On the way back to Holland, as he drove the car, I reviewed his comments, painful as they were. He must have known that she'd tell me what had happened. Maybe she'd even warned him: "If you don't stop now, I'll tell Stan." The trip to Chicago could have been a setup designed to give him the opportunity to tell me his side of the story, to let me think that there had been no force, that indeed she, so hot to trot, had seduced him. He wanted to be blameless in my eyes. A business leader, he had a reputation to protect. Also, he would be around next summer to pursue other young women on the Vineyard. Should there be talk, he'd need me to stick up for him.

But he should have known that his words would cut me to the bone. In emotional turmoil, I was nevertheless in a very touchy position as I heard his tale. If I responded like a wounded animal, he would have the satisfaction of knowing he had hurt me. I had to pretend that his conquest by force of a girl I loved more than anything in the world didn't matter. Like a coward, I shrugged away his words and pretended that his disclosure meant nothing to me at all. Underneath I died, and in dying I sank into a pit of shame and helplessness. Back at the nightspot where with slurred words and hateful eyes he'd bragged of his supposed seduction, I'd wanted to slam him in the face, to see his blood pour onto the table. But I did nothing. Any last vestige of brotherly affection, though, had soured forever and turned to unrelenting detestation. I felt then that for the rest of my life, whatever I would grow to treasure would be in jeopardy because of him, and life itself would be forever unsettled so long as he was alive.

●   ●   ●

I returned to work in Holland right after Christmas after spending a couple of days with my family on Martha's Vineyard. My parents had finally moved north from Maryland. With Marion dead and Bill gone and cousin Howdie's brief stay just a fading memory, there was little to keep them there. Or so I was told. Closer to the truth was my mother's growing suspicion of Kay Radford. They'd sold the chicken farm quite suddenly and had everything packed into a Mayflower moving van, and soon their belongings (and mine) were in storage out at the Martha's Vineyard airport.

I passed a day or two with them over Christmas and even managed to find a tree in the woods to chop down and trim on Christmas Eve. My sister and her family were there, too. Bill was present, but his visit was brief. Uncle Stan was giving him more responsibility. He may have been chairman of the board by then; his rise was the talk of New Britain and elsewhere in Connecticut.

When I returned to Michigan I had only one thought: *escape*. No one seemed interested in sending me back to Fort Erie, and living in Michigan was intolerable. Since the age of fourteen I'd used sports and sex as ways to express myself. In Holland I had access to neither outlet. I was terribly lonely, beyond the customary meaning of the word. I was isolated and turning in on myself. I had not yet discovered the joy of reading for pleasure. I saw one movie a week. I took no walks and made no friends. I daydreamed constantly. Back on the Vineyard, I'd been a lively, popular kid. Now Michigan was a prison. In my loneliness there was only me and myself. Soon I would begin talking aloud to myself in my room and in my car. I was wracked by inhibitions. My stammer was a constant nuisance, it taxed me as I tried to find synonyms for words that stymied me and held up discourse. I couldn't relate to the people with whom I worked. Though I had thought often of the Korean "police action," with a suddenness I knew my time had come. Just before the end of the year, 1950, I walked across the street to work, ascended to George Copeland's office, and told him I was quitting. In a moment of great inspiration I had decided to march off to war.

Copeland understood me. I think he knew how bound up I was. I think he sensed that I was going mad, living alone as I did with nowhere to turn. To mark my departure, he invited me to his house. It was New Year's Eve and they would be going out, but we'd have a couple of drinks together, he said. We'd celebrate my pending enlistment.

It was snowing as I drove over to the Copelands'. But I was young and agile, and a snowstorm was a blessing. I drove to George's house feeling the excitement, anticipating cocktails with my soon-to-be ex-boss and his attractive wife, Sally. The town was aglow with lights arcing over snowdrifts, and snowflakes were caught in the beams of streetlamps. Crisp was the word for it, and I felt civilized and grown-up. Buoyant was another word for my feelings. Crisp and buoyant—that was the ticket, as my father might have said. I was free of the dreaded time study work and about to enlist for a grand adventure. As for now, I'd hoist a few with management in a large house on the right side of town where people had money and position.

I drank heavily, as did George, whose capacity for alcohol was well known. My brother had warned me, "If you are invited out with George Copeland, don't try to match him drink for drink," but on that night I was reckless. *Let it rip.* Around 7:30 the elder Copelands left, leaving me with a half-filled martini. Sitting across from me in the living room was their daughter. She was about fifteen at the time. She had been in and out of the living room all evening, probably waiting for her own big night to begin. Surely a young man was scheduled to pick her up. Was he late? Or...was she waiting for me?

Blurry from martinis I began to leer at her. She tried to talk to me, playing the role of hostess, but whatever she said was obscured by the fact that we were all alone. Twisted by drink, my mind settled on the notion that she wanted my attentions. Quite literally, I began to circle her like a hunter closing in on his prey. But then she slipped out, skipping quickly toward the kitchen as my language became intensely suggestive. I went to pursue her. Then I heard her voice from upstairs. She was on the phone talking to her father. I was embarrassed. I felt like a thief in the night who'd been caught and was being reported. Yelling good-bye, I quickly pulled on my arctics, grabbed my overcoat, and fled the house.

On the way back to my own quarters I skidded into a snowbank. Standing by the Plymouth, puzzled and covered with snow, I stared helplessly at the car, wedged into a sizable drift of snow. Down the road came a sedan, shining under the streetlights. It was George Copeland, grinning broadly, obviously relieved that whatever alarms his daughter had raised were groundless. There I was, halfway home and stuck in a snowdrift. Hardly a rapist or a threat to anyone, I was a young fellow needing a hand. Copeland was a strong man, and he was able to push me out as I gunned the engine.

The very next day I was driving south, heading for Connecticut. If I got thrown in jail for draft evasion, so what. Nothing could dampen my glee at escaping the nightmare of my non-life in Holland, Michigan.

•   •   •

My draft board was astounded to see me. I was given one day to enlist or else I would be drafted at once. But the woman in charge was a kindly soul; she reassured me that now that I had shown up, all charges would be dropped. The point was to get me into uniform, not punish me. *Amen*, I said, under my breath.

I told my parents that I was going to be gone for four years. I'd joined the Air Force. I had tried the Navy but was rejected by a recruiter in Bridgeport because of my stammer. The Marines were my first choice, but I'd been scared off by stories of the wretched cold in Korea—Marines were losing body parts to frostbite. I shuddered. Someone said that in the Air Force I'd always be warm and well fed. That was enough for me. I found a recruiting office back in Middletown. Four years seemed like nothing to me. And I could be a hero in the Air Force. I would be a tail gunner and shoot down MIGs. I had my heart set on it as I was sworn in.

I affected a bravado for my classmates at Wesleyan, whom I visited right up to the moment when I went off to the troop train in Hartford, a bravado that embraced a profound sense of relief that coursed through me and lifted my spirits. I was enlisting for four years, but I was at the same time at last free.

Heading down to Texas on the troop train, I thought of my evening at the Copelands'. I kept wondering what I would have done had their daughter been receptive to my initial overtures. Sex-starved, almost beside myself, I would have taken her in my arms and would have pressed on to the end. I would have told myself that she wanted it. She would be "a hot number" whether she was or wasn't. I would have used the same words my brother had used about Carrie. We were just alike. I too was vile and repulsive.

As was my custom, I banished such thinking from my consciousness and rolled along on the rattling train, whizzing through the black night toward Texas. There were men all about, a thousand or more of us on our way to do our part. The Korean War was saving me from myself. I knew that much as I pressed against the pane and saw the darkness out there in the night.

Chapter 8

In January 1951 the wind whipped a wide swath down the face of North America, starting in Canada and then roaring its way to the Mexican border. Whether you were standing outdoors in South Dakota or in Oklahoma or in Lubbock, Texas, you'd feel its fierce, cold power. It was a wind to turn life into something raw, to crease faces into rawhide. I could feel my own face weather as I stood in the chill, facing into what they called the Canadian Express.

That's how it was for the many thousands of us who were stationed outside San Antonio at Lackland Air Force Base. We were supposed to be taking basic training, but the weight of numbers overwhelmed the base and most of our days were spent hanging about, moving our limbs, trying to stay warm. We slept in tents in light civilian clothes, waiting for our uniforms to arrive. Other than attending a few lectures on military justice and sexual hygiene, we idled, lining up for food or the PX. Sometimes we marched, and because of my five years in a military academy, I was made leader of our flight. I stepped out briskly and the others followed along. We waited in the tents for almost a month before uniforms arrived and we were processed out, sent on our way for training deemed appropriate to our respective abilities.

Our troops in Korea were dying and suffering extreme frostbite. MacArthur was eager to attack China. *Hooray!* was my response. I wanted a real war so I could enjoy the consequences of victory. I hungered for celebration and all the medals that came with such a great accomplishment. Had anyone asked me, I would have told them I wanted to fly in combat as a gunner and shoot down MIGs, and when the war ended and China was leveled by either conventional armament or by nuclear force, we would march into San Francisco in a victory parade with MacArthur at the head, like rebel troops following Stonewall Jackson through Frederick or like the great parade after World War I when the Rainbow Division marched down Broadway. I was barely twenty-one and I had romantic notions that would run my life if I let them.

Beyond heroism, another aspect of my romantic nature focused on kissing. I was extremely lonely in a crowd of men, and I often thought of young women and how I would like to kiss a girl. I longed for affection and the communion that takes place when two people kiss each other and love passes from one set of lips to another. As a recruit I suffered mild buffeting from authority figures; I had no rights and felt insignificant. As a beleaguered enlistee, I had affection on my mind more than carnal knowledge. When people who love kiss, they become vulnerable. They can sense a giving, a receptivity in the lips. Strong, passionate, forceful kissers effect the opposite sensation. They appear aggressive and as a result they can frighten away desire. Hard, driving kisses work only in the movies. In real life, passion rises with titillation and tenderness, or so I know now. Back in 1951, however, I was just lonely and desperate for a woman's softness and thought constantly of kissing and what it would mean.

I still place a high value on kissing, and when it is right I remember the experience forever. An occasion back in 1948 still burns in my memory. I was standing in front of a fraternity house at Yale when a girl I had seen on the Vineyard walked by, stopped, and said hello. We'd both been drinking rum punch, and with a loosening of inhibitions we began to kiss. I never got her name. I only remember the longing I felt in her lips and the sensation of being desired, a sensation that went straight to my heart. We kissed for what must have been a half-hour and then she left to search for the boy who had invited her to Yale.

Another episode involved Ava Gardner. I was nineteen and she was in her prime, probably twenty-six or twenty-seven. I'd been invited over to her table at Eddie Condon's in Greenwich Village. We must have kissed for ten minutes with tenderness and great feeling. She was very beautiful and a wonderful kisser. She told me that she had a crush on Choo-Choo Charlie Justice, a football All-American at North Carolina. He's cute, she told me when our lips were not together. She'd go *Brrr* and shake herself whenever she mentioned his name. I consoled her over Choo-Choo Charlie and went back to her incredible face, which I was kissing at will. I kept Charlie Justice's name in mind, thinking that someday I'd meet him and tell him that the most beautiful woman in the world was crazy for him. We never met, but I never forgot kissing Ava Gardner at Condon's. Later on I invited her to attend a big weekend at Wesleyan and she accepted. I lost her address, though, and unable to confirm our date in Middletown, I languished, knowing that she would never appear. She didn't, undoubtedly being on location or off with a man her own age.

•   •   •

There must have been thirty thousand men and women crowded into Lackland that January. By then we were mobilizing for an all-out war in Korea; everyone knew that the term "police action" was a euphemism. Also, as we were reminded, wars of the future and the present, meaning Korea, would be won or lost by the Air Force. The cream of the crop, we were called. Hardly the cream of any crop, I was wandering about that huge base when I ran into a college fraternity brother and classmate, Don Kipp. He was with a fellow named Tom Chapman from Sandusky, Ohio, who had gone to Bowling Green. For a moment, as the three of us chatted, civility and good humor reentered my life, and I was transported back to the civilian world I had left. The loneliness I'd felt ever since quitting college in May disappeared. Just seeing Kipp and his friend, who was to become my friend, gave me an immense lift. Now it seemed that all of us were in this thing together. My type of people, people who looked and talked like me, were joining up, too. I was delighted. Though I was at Lackland for about a month, the only thing that stands out in my memory is meeting Don Kipp and Tom Chapman. I grabbed on to them with desperation and affected a familiar collegiate pose in their company.

Tom Chapman was shipped with me to Keesler Air Force Base in Biloxi, Mississippi. As it happened, Don Kipp and a friend of his from Hartford named Art Stedman were also transferred to Keesler. Artie had dropped out of Brown. So there we were: two Wesleyan dropouts, one ex–Bowling Green student, and one Ivy Leaguer. Until Kipp and Stedman were processed off to other bases, we were nearly inseparable. Chapman and I remained buddies until he rebelled against visiting a whorehouse I knew of in Gulfport and broke off our friendship. But that was at the end of our training. Within days of our argument, he was shipped out and soon he was serving in Korea. I stayed on at Keesler for a few more weeks. I never saw Tom Chapman again.

•   •   •

One Saturday night in the summer, Tom Chapman and I met some girls at the Aquarium Lounge on the Gulf at Biloxi. They had driven down from Louisiana State University for some excitement. The weather had been sunny and hot and the young women were looking for fun, looking for the beach and a chance to meet some young men. They met Tom Chapman, Artie Stedman, and me at the Aquarium.

One was named was Polly Sawyer. She was a junior at L.S.U. Healthy and bouncy, she was a warm-hearted young woman, quite pretty and very friendly. More than that, she liked me right from the start. I promised her I'd come up to Baton Rouge by train, spend the night in a hotel, and take her out. Her friend, a trim brunette, would be with Chapman. Artie was not in our plans, quite possibly because he was heading north to Otis Air Force Base on Cape Cod.

One thing I always loved about Keesler was the marching. Every morning, except Sunday, at 5:45 we marched past a reviewing stand, our squadron in a row of squadrons, all stepping out syncopated with the "Colonel Bogey March" that cut into the sultry air from the public address system. A group of officers watched us pass by. The sharpest squadron received a ribbon. Squadron Commanders made a great fuss over this as the garnering of ribbons testified to their abilities as commanding officers. Once or twice we earned the prize. But what counted to me was the sense of pride I felt as I passed in front of the reviewing stand, my khakis pressed, my body tight from exercise and good lean meals often containing local seafood. I remember hearing the "Colonel Bogey" again in 1958 when Sam Barnes, a friend, and I saw *Bridge on the River Kwai*. I nudged Sam and said, "What the hell! I used to march to that." He told me to keep my voice down. All it was was the "Colonel Bogey". "Everyone marched to that," he told me, but my heart flew when I heard it. I had not heard it in seven years. Twice a day we marched, tramping back again at 12:15. My legs pressed the sandy earth and my back went straight as a board.

Coming as I was from Keesler, the war on, and I assuming a part in its heroics, it was with no little vanity that I and Chapman bused to New Orleans and took the train up to Baton Rouge. In those days the best hotel was the Heidelberg, where we secured a double room. Once in the hotel room we dallied and enjoyed the clean freshness of our quarters.

I was in the best condition I'd ever been in—almost six feet and 160 pounds. I felt reborn after my dismal days in Michigan and the confusion I'd felt in trying to work for a living. It was midsummer and I'd been playing in the base softball league. We practiced in gym shorts and glistened in the subtropical heat. Whereas months ago in Holland, Michigan, I had felt flabby and lonely, now I was hard and tan and sculpted by exercise. This was as close as I'd ever come to looking great, and after my shower at the Heidelberg, I strode from the bathroom into the bedroom wanting to be seen.

Within a short time we'd be with our girlfriends, but at that moment I felt a strong homoerotic urge, surely a flashback to Brook Hall Military Academy and the striking cadet leaders who strode naked in the open lavatories, to the preying teachers who would pad their way down the dark hallways at night, entering rooms to fondle priapic youths, erect in deep dreams of movie stars.

More than anything, however, it was the hotel room. After months of confinement and military life there we were, alone in a hotel room dominated by two double beds. Strutting was enough, however. The sheer vanity of nakedness produced a high that temporarily fulfilled me. I dressed slowly and soon was ready for the hotel bar and the evening ahead.

Looking back, it all seems so natural—my pride in my body and my desire to strut, feeling full of myself, trim and good-looking. Sexual expression is an endless enterprise, and I have grown very lenient in matters related to human sexuality, understanding that it lies at the base of all the arts, work, sport, and in the flourishing of one's personality and talent. I had been frustrated in Canada and especially so in Michigan. Had it not been for the Air Force, I, a solitary man, would have turned so far inside myself that I would have ceased to function in any kind of reasonable manner. Back in Michigan I did not have the wherewithal to expose my being or my mind or my essence as a young man.

At the Heidelberg I was ready to bust loose, to walk the walk, to hold a woman and to kiss her. Polly Sawyer was waiting, and now, over forty years later, I still think of her. While Tom Chapman drove, Polly and I hugged, but maintained her virtue, extending affection like a million teenagers were doing that exact moment elsewhere in America. Over the next two years I would see her again and again. We never went "all the way," which was not an option in the early '50s or at least not an option for a middle-class southern girl, even though she was so very lovable. We were just together, enmeshed and enjoying ourselves.

Early that Sunday evening the girls dropped Chappie and me off at a small country store with one gas pump on a cement slab outside and a bar inside with a jukebox against the wall. Sooner or later a car would swing in and someone would holler, "Fill 'er up," and maybe we could hitch a ride. We tarried inside for a while, the girls now gone, and played the jukebox while we drank Falstaff beer. "Because of You" was the hit song of that time and we listened to Tony Bennett sing it over and over again. His voice struck my heart. I was sentimental and feeling loose from the beer and the attention I'd received from Polly Sawyer: I was an airman going off to war. We would write each other, and I would return someday to Baton Rouge.

Eventually we hitched a ride down to New Orleans and got ourselves to a bus station, and finally on the bus we fell asleep on our way to Biloxi. We arrived just in time for the 3:30 reveille formation, followed by mess and our inspired marching past the reviewing stand to the beat of the "Colonel Bogey March." I loved it: I loved having a girl to love, the hitchhike down to New Orleans, the fact that I was so young and durable. And that is why I recall it now: I really loved being twenty-one, unable to forget Tony Bennett's romantic ballad echoing in my soul as I stood near the Spanish moss on the soft shoulder of a back road in Louisiana.

•   •   •

No one wants to read about someone in the armed services unless there is warfare on a grand scale, some element of derring-do or comedy. In my case there was no war or derring-do, nor much humor, just a series of human encounters that had little to do with the military. I was often in civilian clothes, and for a time I lived like a civilian in an apartment. To some degree I was bankrolled by a savings account that had been building since birth, and when I turned twenty-four, my father released dividends to me so I could receive quarterly payments from Fafnir Bearing, General Motors, and General Electric, money to buttress my meager Air Force salary.

So when one considers the military and the tough life that it supposedly embodies, my Air Force experience fell short. Most of the airmen I knew were soft, noncombatant, nonmilitary technicians. We spent so much time in school that I found myself wishing I were back at Wesleyan. Studying the cathode-ray tube was a bore compared to reading the "Great Books" at Wesleyan, which seemed to hold such bright promise. I thought of my father. He always had a sparkle in his eyes and his face would light up when we met. His look if not his words spoke of his love, and perhaps he was pleased that I was somewhere safe, attending classes, marching, partying on Saturday nights, just as I would in college. But there would be scorn in his heart, too. How could I wear a uniform and not be heading into battle or returning from some horrible conflict wearied from the terror combat holds? I wrestled with this, and three times while I was at Keesler I tried to transfer overseas. Once I even tried to get into the Army paratroopers, pursuing a rumor that the Airborne was low on men while the Air Force had too many. I was turned down. My schooling had progressed too far. In time I'd be a specialist in a demanding role.

In those days I did not view my father as flawed. I think I knew he was a bigot and terribly opinionated, but I saw him in context and did not think badly of him. I grew up in a world of heavy drinking, of men going to the office, a good deal of camaraderie and a pecking order that involved family prominence (the old families) and money.

The women my mother's age rose late if they wished, attended to the servants if there were any, tried to monitor the children, often lunched with each other and passed the afternoon hours awaiting the return of their husbands. Surely some did volunteer work, especially during the Great Depression. But my memory of women in the 1930s through 1950 entails a mindless lassitude, gossip with other women and a good deal of drinking. At Keesler my fantasies were more up-scale as I dreamt of women in tweed skirts and nylons, driving to country clubs and cafes, women older than I, already bored with bilious husbands, women my lean body could excite. Older women I fancied lived a life depicted in the pages of *Town and Country* magazine and would desire a fellow like myself. They shopped at Lord & Taylor and drove station wagons and went to the theater.

In October I received my orders for California—Mather Air Force Base near Sacramento. On my last trip to New Orleans a whore I knew actually wept when I said good-bye. I'd been going to Dora Russo's in the French Quarter, an ornate Victorian house for gentlemen, as well as the Silver Dollar Club in nearby Gulfport. This girl had journeyed to New Orleans from somewhere in Tennessee. It was my understanding that she left Tennessee because she had become pregnant. In those days a girl "in trouble" would leave town. In her case, I supposed that she left in disgrace and said the hell with them all and, once the baby was aborted, she took up the oldest profession. She was bright, amusing, and attractive. She might have been twenty, no older. On Sunday afternoons we'd lie about on her queen-sized bed and drink and enjoy each other. Dora Russo herself selected this girl for me. The estimable madam told me the girl was just starting out. Because of the way we enjoyed each other, I believed her.

There was another woman in Gulfport I later used as a model for Gail Schuyler in my novel *The Martha's Vineyard Affair*. She was quite pretty, a dirty blonde with a thick mat of pubic hair that ran in a strip up to her navel. I was wildly excited by her, and afterwards we would drink together at the bar of the Silver Dollar. I think her name was Sharon. What I recall with some pleasure is her body and the atmosphere of decadence that hung in the air at the Silver Dollar. She reminded me of young women in Greenwich Village, bohemians I had first seen in 1948. Sharon drank like a trooper and loved sex. She laughed with gusto, and in the half-light of the club she looked pretty. I never knew why she became a whore. I suspect now that she was hooked on drugs, perhaps heroin, which would have been rare in 1951 but possible.

In December 1951 I made my last visit to Dora Russo's. Dora greeted me with her usual good humor. I paid only twenty-five dollars for the services of the house, which included all the liquor I could drink. I think I was allowed inside the door for such a paltry sum because Dora liked me. I was a change from the diamond-studded older men who were her usual customers. In all my visits I never saw another man under fifty. I always felt like a prince when I left Dora Russo's.

•   •   •

I did not stay in Sacramento very long. At Mather Air Force Base, which was part of the Training Command, I was a private first class without much of a clue as to my capabilities. I'd had almost a year of intense schooling at Keesler—six hours a day, six days a week. What I remembered best was making my own oscilloscope, the forerunner to television. I was supposed to know all about radar but I didn't. In fact, I'd gotten through Keesler by memorizing just enough to pass the biweekly tests. I hated electronics and hungered for gunnery school, but was always denied. At the same time, I was ever fearful of flunking out because if I did I'd be sent either into food service or the Air Police or the motor pool, three lines of work for the non-academic, mechanically oriented serviceman. Had I actually flunked out and gone into the old M.P.s, now called Air Police in our service, I would have repeated my brother's experience. I had reason to persevere.

Mather was a blur of adjustment. During my first tour I worked on B-25s, the Mitchell bomber. Six mornings a week I went onto the flight line in the dark, just before dawn, to pre-flight the radar equipment that was being used by airborne operators in those storied bombers. I often thought of the Doolittle Raid and fancied that the very plane I was working on had flown in combat and felt the sting of flak. I also thought of the comfort my former classmates enjoyed, sleeping cozily in the fraternity house back in Connecticut. Were I still with them, I would be a senior.

By March I was gone. The base was overstaffed. Sacramento itself was historic and alive with possibilities. One felt a sense of the West, the Gold Rush, and Sutter's Fort. When I returned a year later the city was spreading out and growing at a fast clip. But in 1952 there was still a sleepy quality to the big park in the center of town and in the bar of the Hotel Senator, and the name on everyone's lips that winter was Honeybear Warren, the Governor's attractive daughter.

I recall the Hotel Sacramento and the Cluny, two watering holes where a young man might meet a secretary who worked for the state. The best place for meeting young women was the Capitol Tamale Café. Often at the piano bar, good-time women sat with drink in hand, looking for a handsome officer. In civilian clothes and keeping my mouth shut about what I did, I could pass for a lieutenant. In that winter of 1952, however, I was unable to meet anyone who would take me home. I rose before dawn, did my work, and let the days pass until I was transferred. In April I was on my way down to Waco in the Chevy Bel Air my father had purchased for me, buying it off the dealer's floor on Van Ness Avenue in San Francisco. There was little doubt in my mind that I was a rich kid, taking it easy in the Air Force while the war raged in Korea.

I had two other fellows with me and we drove nonstop. We had several days to get to Texas, and once I'd let the others off I drove up to Baton Rouge. Luckily, Polly Sawyer was still available and was in fact looking forward to a job in Dallas—an easy drive from Waco—once she graduated from L.S.U. I stayed at the Heidelberg and saw Polly and then drove down to Waco.

•   •   •

It was poor planning: the Air Force had taken too many of us, most of us trying to avoid the Army and doughboy drudgery. The Air Force was oversubscribed, there really wasn't much to do. In any group, there are enthusiasts who take on as much as they can. So it was at Waco. There were some men who genuinely enjoyed electronics and the complexity of radar systems. I had no interest at all in my work, and so I put in my time removing malfunctioning units and then replacing them as I twisted about in cramped quarters, wiring and clipping and bolting the units into place. I often found myself standing on the flight line, longing for Wesleyan, where I would have been close to graduation. I missed my college friends. Still a private first class, I went through the motions with vague hopes that before long I'd be sent off to war.

Most of the time I stayed on the base, but once I went to Galveston, where I was robbed by a Negro whore on Post Office Street. I slept in the Hotel Panama and watched a large ceiling fan make circles above me. I drove back, low on gas and broke. Another trip took me to Villa Acuña to watch Pat McCormick, the vaunted female matador. Later at Mrs. Crosby's, a notorious bar and hotel across the border, I sat beside her. She'd been knocked to the earth six times and was bandaged across the abdomen and chest from the several gorings I had witnessed. We were drinking toward drunkenness, and our conversations spilled over into each other's areas. She was the first gutsy woman athlete I'd met and I was immediately attracted to her androgynous sexuality. She was so much one of the macho crowd that clustered around her: a survivor of a dangerous sport, and still tantalizingly female. I thought of her as a woman guerrilla working with a band of hombres. Had I kissed her it would have been an adventure. She talked with assurance, like Ava Gardner, though she was not as pretty. She looked supple and durable in her bandages, like someone Ava Gardner would want to play in a movie.

For some time, as the tequila flowed I sat near this enticing woman. Days later, back at the base, I saw her picture in *Life* magazine; much was made of her goring and her courage. We'd hardly spoken at Mrs. Crosby's, but my eyes had been on her the whole time.

By May I was on the move again, off to Lowry Field in Denver. It was all top secret, but we'd been flown up for six months of training on the K-system, a network of computer units that sprawled within the turboprop six-engine B-36 as well as the B-47, our new jet bomber for the Strategic Air Command. The K-system was designed to drop the hydrogen bomb. It would be our job to assist the bombardiers and navigators who would have to use it. The K-system delivered the bomber to its target, where it would release nuclear havoc. All of us were impressed. For me almost anything was better than Waco, and the prospect of a six-month tour in Denver seemed a lovely idea. Although the business about a top secret security clearance and hydrogen bombs played in my mind, it didn't cause a ripple in my behavior. We were at war and I was going to yet another school, this time five hours a day, and at night I'd think of women and sometimes find one.

Outside Denver, in the town of Aurora, there was a watering hole called the Beacon Supper Club. On Saturday nights I would drive over to the Beacon and drink at the bar. It was always crowded; single women, often in pairs, sometimes alone, drank into the late night hours. In 1952 it was rare to see women without men drinking into the night at a bar. But the Beacon Supper Club had a homey neighborhood feel to it. They played music from the Gay Nineties and a man sang like Phil Harris: "That's What I Like about the South" was a Beacon favorite. I could hear them singing along in the supper club while I drank at the bar, shoulder to shoulder with local folks and Air Force officers.

One evening I showed up, as was my custom, around midnight and was immediately approached by a tipsy woman in her early twenties. She was tall with long brown hair and a whimsical sparkle in her brown eyes. Just to look at her and hear her talk brought a smile to my face. Two years later when I saw the British actress Kay Kendall in *Genevieve* I was reminded of her...Victoria Klein, called Vicky. She came from St. Louis, Missouri, and worked up at Boulder. She said she was somehow related to Andrew Jackson. She was very good-looking and very much her own person. That night she was with an Air Force captain who bored her, and spying me in the crowd gave her reason to leave. "I'm getting out of here," she said as she took my arm. We hung back in the corner of the club away from the bar as Phil Harris's double sang "Darktown Poker Club." I finished my drink and we stepped quickly to my car.

We had a fine late summer and fall together. Once over Labor Day we drove to Mexico and subsequently got arrested in El Paso for speeding. Unaccountably, Vicky was thrown into a big cell full of streetwalkers and I was transferred to Biggs Air Force Base and locked up with wetbacks who had been caught trying to sneak into Texas. Her trumped-up charge was disturbing the peace. Mine was speeding and maybe being AWOL. Eventually I paid our way out of the mess I'd gotten us into and cleared myself of AWOL charges and at last we were able to start back to Colorado.

I never forgot her. Once, in 1987, I tried to call her on the phone. I wondered if she was still in Boulder. She was, but the operator said that her number was unlisted. Through an acquaintance who lived in Boulder I was told that she had two unlisted phones, both under the name of Vicky Klein. My friend, who had contacts with the telephone company, said that his contacts were of no help beyond that point. Her numbers and her address were not obtainable. But she'd kept her name. I was sure that she'd never married, and I wondered what it would have been like to see her again.

● ● ●

In Denver I remained a private first class, but I enjoyed a felicitous freedom. At night, I saw Vicky and, during the daytime hours, there was golf. Each day after a light breakfast at the PX I'd take off for one of the semiprivate golf courses scattered in and around Denver. One lovely summer day I was alone with my new set of Spaldings slung over my back. I hit a drive off a tee out toward the fairway that ran along a fairly busy street. My drive flew up into the air like a jet fighter and then began to curl to the right. The errant drive sailed far beyond the edge of the fairway, arcing toward the street.

I shrugged and hit a mulligan and then stepped away from the tee. I was playing alone, enjoying six or seven more holes with alacrity. As I approached still another tee, I saw a woman streaking across the fairway. She was holding a golf ball. "Is this yours? Is this yours?" she was shouting. "What is it?" I asked, taken aback. She was approaching quickly, narrowing the distance between us. "A Spalding Dot," she yelled. "Yes," I answered. "It might be mine. I boomed one out of the fairway," I volunteered, trying to be helpful, wondering why she was racing toward me, going to all this trouble to return my ball.

"You killed my father," she said, and then standing right before me she positioned herself like a prizefighter. Her legs were apart. Her arms were taut.

Stunned, I heard her words that struck terror. My golf ball had soared into the path of her car and struck the windshield. Her father, a man in his sixties, was sitting next to her in the passenger seat. The shock of the windshield shattering caused a heart attack. Now, almost an hour after the accident, he'd been pronounced dead. Stepping along like a man without a care in the world, I was suddenly accosted with the cry, "You killed my father! You dumb son of a bitch, you careless young…" Her voice trailed off in rage.

I gave her my name, then walked quickly to the clubhouse. I was able to find my car, and I slipped away from the parking lot without notice. Back up the street I saw a knot of cars, including a police car. By now the ambulance was gone. Any minute a policeman would find me, I thought, but no one did, and in a short time I was safe behind the gate of Lowry Field. I never mentioned the incident to anyone. Quick to rationalize, I figured the old man would have died anyway. What kind of a heart couldn't take a little shock like a pellet hitting the windshield? Now that I am in my sixties I feel differently, but there is no way to redeem the past. Two years earlier in Canada, Jack Parr had died because of my intervention in a labor dispute, and now in Denver it was an old man with a daughter beside herself with grief. You could call it carelessness: carelessness with words that brought Jack Parr to suicide. Carelessness at sport. Carelessness in just about everything. But in 1952, enjoying a grand Colorado summer, I reassured myself that I was doing my part in our war against communist aggression. I was able to maintain a buoyant attitude that overruled all private annoyances. I shied from anything that might cause me embarrassment or shame, and I kept on playing golf.

After six months at Lowry Field I returned to Waco and remained there for four months. Polly Sawyer was up in Dallas and I saw her once in awhile. My conscience was bothering me over Vicky Klein in Colorado, but I did not go back for her. She wept when I drove off; she was standing on the sidewalk and I *should* have gone back and scooped her up and taken her with me. But in the early '50s a young man from New England didn't do that unless he had marriage on his mind. I had no such plans. It was still too close to the time when I'd fallen in love and fallen apart. Marriage was not an option at all, and Vicki, I was sure, would not be enthusiastic about illegal cohabitation in some converted motel room or efficiency apartment in Waco. After all, she had a good job in Boulder, connected to the university in some fashion. As I drove away from her apartment, these concerns did not interest me for long. What had my attention was the drive ahead and the excitement of the open road.

•   •   •

In the summer of 1953 I was back in Sacramento and the Korean War ended, and for us in the military, everything began to relax; we could live like civilians, though without civilian pay. I moved off base and took an apartment with two airmen. Back on the base we idled away the hours playing a game called "Distance." We bet money on Coke bottles, hoping to pick the bottle that had traveled the longest route from its bottling company. We plugged coins into the big red Coke machines and clustered around waiting for each thick bottle to thump into position. Once I got a bottle with Taunton, Mass., embossed on the bottom and beat out a fellow who drew San Antonio. Stacks of Coke bottles piled up as we wagered in a chain reaction of small sums.

There were other games as well. I played both tennis and semiprofessional softball in the Superior Softball League of California, which included a team from Folsom Prison. Twice I played inside the walls of that nightmarish place. In order to hit a homer, you had to belt one over the wall and watch it fly to freedom while spectator-convicts, many in for life, cheered.

At tennis I wore civilian clothes and looked like I was playing for some California tennis club. Above me in rank were one sergeant, two lieutenants, one heavily-decorated captain who had flown for both the RCAF and the US Eighth Air Force in WW II, and a major named Watson who was our chief weather officer. John Watson and I became great pals and drinking buddies. We traveled to San Francisco together and on our tennis trips we always found a few beers. With Korea over with, the Air Force was becoming, for me at least, a sports center. I left work at random, heading for a playing field, my top secret work on the K system just a reminder that I was still an airman.

I continued doing my bit, too, making the long trek on the flight line, often servicing the system that was ready to drop nuclear bombs on

Russia. I had nine months or so to go until my discharge when the news came from Margaret Kelly, back in Hartford, that I was to become a father. This hit me like a cannonball and the joy in my life vanished.

But, I'd made my decisions. When the child, a girl, was born, she was whisked away by adoption specialists. Sadly, the baby had severe disabilities and was never adopted. She remained in the care of the state of California until she died at an early age.

To be twenty-four years old and living as aimlessly as I was, this should have been a jolting wake-up call. I should have gone for counseling, collapsed, asked for advice, broken down in shame. Perhaps I should have married her, a concern that has vexed me for forty years. Instead, I stifled my guilt and took on a merry demeanor. I upped my drinking to dull the awful thoughts that crossed my mind. No one knew of my trouble. I quit the softball team, which was not easy. My teammates could see that my life had become slipshod and almost out of control, yet they needed me in center field. There I was, torn between real life with its adult complexities on one hand and a game on the other. It is stunning to think that they did equal battle for my attention. I'd hang out at Cisco's near the base or at the Capitol Tamale Café and weave my way home. On weekends I'd go to San Francisco. I drank to get sedated. Life had turned into a horrid mess. I lived daily under great pressure, feeling in my heart that I had done wrong.

My conscience told me to cave in to the pressure and get married. What kept me from the altar was a lifelong fear of incurring my father's profound disappointment. Although my mother was by now an overt alcoholic and my father was continuing his affair with Kay Radford, I nevertheless feared their scorn. I simply couldn't return to them with a wife and child. Though my father was aware of my predicament, such awareness was a long way from approval. Because no one in our house ever talked about personal matters, I was operating in the dark. All I had was my intuition, which told me that I would be letting my parents down in some serious way. I could hear my father's admonition: "Don't be such a fumblefinger." I'd fumbled a big one now, and I couldn't go home.

• • •

For a while during my disaster with Margaret, I lived alone in an apartment off base. I had plenty of women friends, including Annette Yarborough, who lived in the same building. Annette was the city's foremost barroom party girl, and, of course, Evelyn Slade, whom I saw off and on. Annette had long legs like Cyd Charisse and a full bosom. Her underbelly was matted with bushy hair that excited me. She stood about five feet six with a straight-on ranch hand face. She should have been a star and may even have given it a try. She told me that somewhere along the line she had an affair with Dinah Washington. There were others, including the actor John Hodiak, who had come to Sacramento to act in *The Caine Mutiny Court Martial.* Annette and another girl went down to the bar at the Hotel Sacramento, where they had heard the actors were staying. Sure enough, after the show Lloyd Nolan, Henry Fonda, and John Hodiak came in for drinks. Nettie's friend went upstairs with Fonda. Nettie went with Hodiak, who was married to Anne Baxter—an actress after whom I hankered. About 2:30 in the morning, Nettie knocked on my door and came inside to be with me. Hodiak hadn't done the trick, she said.

Annette Yarborough was ahead of her time. She'd left a husband and child in Macon, Georgia and now she was out on her own like Thelma and Louise and could well have died as they did, driving over a cliff. But she possessed frontier glamour—great legs, wonderful earthy charm, stamina, and enthusiasm. She loved sex. She had ecstatic orgasms and figured such was an essential part of her life, her just due. She was living on her wits and her looks, like Ava Gardner but without the stardom and the money. Nettie was a grand Hollywood-style girl who took baths with the door open, inviting you in to sit on the edge of the tub while she arched her pubis above the water and floated her ample breasts and held a strong drink in one hand, balancing herself with the other. In another room either Frank Sinatra or Johnny Edwards sang from her new hi-fi system. She wove herself into the pattern of my life, a stitch here, a stitch there. It could have been more, but I shied away. Events had made me wary. In one way Annette Yarborough was too good to be true; in another way I feared serious trouble. I was nervous around so much personal freedom.

I finally moved back to the barracks, deciding to leave downtown Sacramento because, as I told my pals, everything had become "too peculiar." First and foremost there was Margaret's pregnancy, yet to be resolved. Second, I was courting even more trouble with women. Nettie was one case in point. Sylvia Stone was another, a WAF on whom I had developed a crush. She was very pretty and, like Vicky Klein back in Colorado, zany. She drove me crazy as I pursued her, my love unrequited. Finally she ran off with a lieutenant and got married and pregnant and left the Air Force. Three days after my discharge my friend Red Daly and I, both driving east in our own cars, stopped somewhere in New Mexico for lunch. There was Sylvia, sitting at the counter. Befuddled, I could not speak to her. Red nudged me and said, "Stan, that's Airman Stone, the WAF." I agreed it was, but I was too immobilized to speak. I am sure she saw me and remembered, and perhaps she expected me to recognize her, to approach her and say hello effusively as you do when you are surprised by a friend you meet by accident and out of context. But I did nothing and she left the café before we did. I mention this to illustrate how neurotic I was becoming. I had little control over my feelings or actions other than when I followed orders. I had very little ability to put things together and make them work.

The oddest experience involved my neighbors. In the apartment next door to mine lived the bartender from a local hotel, a cocktail waitress from the same bar, and her fourteen-year-old daughter. Every so often the two adults would go on a three-day binge and stay inside, just drinking. Afterwards a clutter of whiskey bottles would appear on the landing outside the apartment door. I noticed this and did not understand; in 1954 I knew a good deal about drinking but nothing of binges. But I could hear their loud drunken voices whenever they began their mutual bender.

Then one afternoon after I returned from work at the air base, there was a knock on my door. The bartender, a rangy guy with big hands and a loose build, wearing a western shirt with snaps on it instead of buttons, asked me over to his place for a drink. I knew they were at it again, though he didn't look drunk. He looked like a man who was always a bit pickled yet could hold his liquor. I followed him into the next apartment. His girlfriend looked like a very tired Maureen O'Hara. She had long, dark red hair and was tall and well built. She probably garnered good tips at her job. Both of them already had a drink, and I was given a gin and tonic. We sat at a little table and then the man rose, went back to the bedroom, and returned with the daughter.

The girl stood still, staring at me, maybe frightened. She had green eyes set in a nondescript trailer park face with a blankness to it as though she was trying hard not to comprehend. With a hairbrush and a different attitude she would have been quite pretty. Her mother went to her and slipped the straps of her jumper over her shoulders. She undid her blouse and showed me the girl's chest to assure me that she was developed. I nodded, having no idea what was happening. I drank quickly and looked toward the door thinking that the bartender could stop me if I tried to leave. He could crush me with his big hands. I was sitting beside the window and I decided, if I had to, I could crash out of the apartment through the window. The ruckus would bring help.

"Do you want her?" the man was speaking.

"Want her?"

"Look," he said. "The two of us are leaving the state. Mexico is where we're going. We can't take the kid. Too dangerous," he allowed.

"Oh," I said, still not getting the point.

"We want you to have her. She'll fuck you and tend to your cooking. You can cook good, can't you, honey?" the man asked, looking at the girl.

"Yes," she said, dropping her eyes. Her breasts were still exposed.

"Shit," I said. "I can't do it. I'd sure love to help you out, but my transfer is in," I lied. "I'm heading to Kansas to a SAC base."

"Damn," he said, and he looked over at Maureen O'Hara. "It's all your fault, calling for *her*," he said, pointing at the fourteen-year old. She'd been with them only a little while. Where she'd come from was anybody's guess—an errant father? a grandmother? a foster home?

I rose from the table. "I've got to get packing," I said. "The Air Force will be after me."

I turned in my apartment key a day or two after that encounter. I did not want to run into the bartender again. I think I actually feared that he would just foist the girl upon me, dump her in my lap, commanding, *You take care of her,* with a threatening cast to his eyes. To my credit, the idea of "owning" a fourteen-year-old girl with a woman's body was never an option. Had I been drinking or on my way to getting drunk, though, I might have taken her. The couple would have been long gone by the time I came to and wondered how I was going to talk myself out of a charge of statutory rape. I was two different people: when sober, I was sane and shy and athletic and I kept to myself; when drinking, I was lusty with a lascivious mind. When I drank heavily, I wanted to immerse myself in the smarmy side of life.

•   •   •

There are veterans who, when they talk about their military experiences, recall the rigors and bravery of combat. A minority of humorists will see the absurdity of war and military life and lampoon what they witnessed. Then there are those, like me, who never got near combat, saw very little that was worthy of satire, and are content with memories of friendship and their first exposure to the human condition. You grow up a bit in the service, away from home, being treated like just another body. Ideas of privilege and uniqueness fade, and slowly you become one of many. What was a private bedroom becomes a barracks. The toilet is now a latrine. The shower is open. Your body has become the property of the government. People watch you use the toilet and observe you in the shower. "What you see is what you get." Pretension vanishes. How can one remain spoiled living in a barracks, doing K.P., taking orders, getting yelled at? For me the four years I spent in the Air Force were a godsend. Even the people I didn't like I can still look back on with fondness. They all played a part in keeping me interested, amused, and sane. The Air Force marked the end of my isolation.

I was always in the Training Command. The only time I saw death and destruction was when a Mitchell bomber went out of control on a landing approach and with one engine out banked the wrong way, away from its power. It began to fall and crashed into the base stockade. Several prisoners were killed along with the crew of the bomber, and one fireman died when he was blown into the sky, having climbed up on the smoldering fuselage just before the plane exploded.

All that happened in the winter of 1952 on my first tour at Mather in Sacramento. I was still agitating to get into combat, to transfer to gunnery school, to go to Korea in any capacity. Alas, no one ever took my requests for combat seriously, and by the time I had spent a year in electronics school, any such requests were thrown right in the wastebasket. The plane crash fit my mood. I was shaken by it and for several days I had horrible visions of the fireman exploding into the sky. But down deep I was pleased that something terrible had finally come my way.

Personal experiences became my métier. I looked for them, nurtured them, exposed myself to as many people of all kinds as I could. The first time I drank at the bar at the Cal-Neva Lodge in Tahoe I ran into Ginger Rogers, with whom I flirted. I began to fancy myself as her lover and new discovery—the two of us an item. My father adored Ginger Rogers as she appeared in the movies, and I took pleasure in being so close to the apple of his eye. Unfortunately a young man with a foreign accent approached us. He cast an angry look my way and slipped between us. I assumed it was Jacques DeBergerac, a marginal actor whom she had befriended.

Nothing came of that encounter, but it was enough to bring me back to the Cal-Neva. Not long afterward I met a woman who was an amateur tennis champion who had just completed a tournament in San Francisco. I do not think I ever got her name and if I did I forgot it almost at once. We were both drinking steadily at the piano bar. Around midnight she turned to me and said, "I won't lead you on with false hopes. You may rest assured you can sleep with me tonight. Also," she said, "I want you to know I am wearing falsies. I have no bosom. I am like a man. I didn't want to mislead you."

An amazing woman. I think now she was someone I should have pursued after I left Tahoe. As it was, we did sleep together, myself too drunk for intercourse at night, but we made do in the morning. That afternoon we found Red Daly, my sidekick, and she threw herself down on the bed of our cabin

with invitation in her eyes. I drew Red away. I wanted her to think only of me. I would have forgotten her completely had I not seen her picture in a tennis magazine two or three years later, just after my discharge. She was standing beside Pancho Gonzales, and for a moment I thought of her in bed and at the bar. I had liked her. Now it bothers me to think that I was so diffident and so passive in those days, that I didn't even have the emotional wherewithal to get a lover's name, to get a phone number, to show some ability to pursue a woman. Why wouldn't she have thrown herself at Red Daly? She probably thought I didn't like her. And, as with many encounters, I was amorous and adventurous with liquor in me but the day after, once out of bed and back in life, I would retreat and shy away. My shyness often gave the impression of indifference. Our insecurities could have forged a common bond, but I let it all pass me by.

•   •   •

My parents began coming to California in the winter of 1952. They stayed at the Smoke Tree Ranch in Palm Springs. Stationed in Sacramento, I was invited down to join them. My father had not yet bought me my car, so I went down by air and train.

In 1952 Palm Springs was still a small town. It was ballyhooed as a playground for the movie colony, which it was, and some wealthy businessmen not connected to Hollywood made their homes there as well. Palm Springs was very Californian in feel. It was a Garden of Allah in a valley between beautiful mountains on the rim of the desert, where ravines extended away from the lush greenery that grew everywhere in town. The Smoke Tree Ranch offered reciprocal membership privileges for both the Tennis Club and Racquet Club for tennis and the Thunderbird for golf. On Saturday my father gave me a tour and we had a drink at each place plus a few others. (The previous afternoon after I left the old adobe train station I was supposed to call the ranch where my father was alerted to come and fetch me. I was so nervous that I went into town and drank at the bar of the Chi Chi Club. I had four or five Scotches before I dared telephone my father. I did not wish to shame the family by stammering and I knew that in any telephone confrontation I would stammer hopelessly unless I was relaxed with drink.) My father and I went out for a drink in the late afternoon and when we returned, I made my exit. I had my eye on a young woman at the desk at the Thunderbird.

She was quite pretty with long, black hair and thick eyebrows like Carrie Robertson which made me take note. She appeared to like me as I flirted with her at the reception desk. The next night we went out for dinner and then to a saloon where cowboys glowered at me. One false move and I was a goner. For months they had been eyeing my date who had kept each one at arm's length. Brazenly she showed up with a ten-derfoot and I could feel their ire burn into me as I stood at the bar.

When it got too uncomfortable, I led her outside, the music from the jukebox following us out the door, music I had heard in Mississippi and up at Baton Rouge with Polly Sawyer. Hank Williams was singing "Hey, Good Looking" and that was how I felt about the young lady who was soon to be in my arms. Eventually we found ourselves far down a right-of-way out on the desert. We stripped under a full desert moon. It was a moment I would not wish to forget: I had never seen female beauty that way. We kissed and fondled each other for hours as the moonlight streamed down upon us. How could anything in the future compare with this? Naked in the desert under the moon and with a few stars sparkling over the mountains we held each other and let our feelings flow with our kisses and her body was as I had imagined it to be.

The next day around noon I stopped by her quarters down the road from the Thunderbird. She was waiting for me in her tiny studio apartment. She was sitting on the edge of her bed in a nightgown. I lay beside her and we undressed each other, she fumbling with my pants. As I slipped her nightgown over her head, exposing her total body which was so sexually stunning in its beauty and youth and full figure, I felt in awe of her and now, so much in the daylight and without a drink, I felt awkward. Finally I, too, was nude and both of us were the way we'd been in the desert under the moon with the mountains looming in the distance, and then suddenly in her bed and ready for intercourse I fell victim to a horrible phenomenon, something I'd never experienced nor heard about—premature ejaculation. I ejaculated with no pleasure, almost as though I had an overflow of sperm and it spurted from me like from a spigot. I was horribly embarrassed. I'm sure that she had never considered such an eventuality either. There was a look of utter amazement on her face, and my own face turned crimson with shame. How could I? How could I? What an awkward ass I was.

I dressed hurriedly and began my retreat from her room. "Don't leave me here like this," she said, pleading with me, her eyes so confused but so full of desire to indicate that she, too, would explode with but a touch. But my shame led me to the door. I retreated, mortified and of no use at all.

Back at Mather I wrote her once asking her if I could return and see her. She answered saying that she was afraid to see me—she might fall in love and she had plans to return to college and eventually enter graduate school. She was afraid to be derailed by a serviceman. She was sorry.

I would never know what she thought about when she thought of me. Was it true that she was afraid of falling in love or was she being kind? Was she really returning to a university? In time I lost her address and her name.

I was immensely pleased with my parents' choice of a winter home. They rented a small house at Smoke Tree Ranch for twelve or thirteen winters, until my father died in 1963. In the '50s one could ride horseback far off toward the foothills of the San Jacinto Mountains. Coyotes howled at night and jackrabbits bounded across the prairie. Movie stars rented horses from the semiprivate stables, almost against the wishes of the ranch residents. Flashy actors were discouraged: once a well-known movie star and a male companion checked out two mounts and were espied naked down in a gulch, or arroyo, engaged in some form of sexual activity which rendered the riders from the ranch speechless. "I can't say what they were doing," said my father, shaking his head. Actors like Clark Gable, George Montgomery, and Cary Grant, however, were most welcome.

I met Cary Grant on a breakfast ride one morning. I was with my father, and we were about to sit down to one of the huge breakfasts served on a long wooden table. A chuck wagon stood nearby. The smell of bacon and sausage and flapjacks with syrup made my mouth water. Cary Grant kept eyeing me. He was darkly tanned and extremely handsome, in his late forties at the time. He was wearing a tight set of Levis, both jacket and pants fitted to his wiry body. I'm sure his boots cost more than my monthly wage.

He kept giving me the eye and it made me feel like a girl. I had my father with me, and maybe my sister or one or two of her children, so I was protected. But once again I sensed that I was on familiar territory, being eyed by an older man. Years later, when I thought of it, I could imagine myself going with him. Later in life it became clear to me that sexuality is not absolute. It is blurred. Who's to say what I really am? Homosexual conduct was not an option for me then because of taste, not desire. At Brook Hall, when I was a boy, events had overpowered me, and my lust was not to be contained. Still, I'd had that exposure, and Cary Grant could sense it. He kept his eye on me until I turned away.

•   •   •

Nineteen fifty-four neared the end with my getting stopped in Sacramento with a friend at the wheel of my car, eluding a motorcycle cop, careening through side streets. Christmas itself was subdued. I thought about the baby, born badly malformed and, now in an institution. I thought of the baby's mother living in San Francisco, looking for a new life. I read from a Marquand novel, *So Little Time*, and stayed quiet. Between Christmas and the New Year, as I was being mustered out, I went into town twice for drinks. The rest of the time I did my work and went to bed early, and in bed I longed for Margaret Kelly, the baby's mother.

Although I tried hard to avoid the full implications of my affair with Margaret, my cowardice tortured me. My dereliction of duty as a man became etched in my mind on those nights. I was fairly sure I had been disturbed since childhood, as witness my nightmarish stammering, and now this cowardly act on my part added spice to the turmoil in my soul. In daylight, every time a dab of spicy guilt dropped into the gruel of my conscience I turned faint and almost quivered until I found physical action or a drink to break me free. At night I could not escape.

Between Christmas and the New Year, as I kept to the barracks and awaited my discharge, I began to assess my family and the myth that threatened to drown me in it. The myth had to do with the class system and the false notion I had of being in a higher rung. Although we were not exalted like the Rockefellers nor snooty like the rich people in Edgartown on Martha's Vineyard, in the New Britain of my youth I always thought Harts and Stanleys were special. When I'd enlisted in the Air Force, I'd felt like a student prince who had gone slumming.

This myth of unwarranted superiority had done me no favors. Thinking I was above the rules, I often broke them. Margaret's pregnancy and the birth of an impaired child had left me badly shaken. Refusing to marry a girlfriend who was "in trouble" was a major breach in the mores of that time. On nights when I rolled from side to side in my upper cot, I'd see Margaret's face full of alarm turning to rage: *You won't marry me? You fucking son of a bitch. You won't marry me?*

All my upbringing had led to this moment and to my cowardice. I rationalized that Margaret wouldn't fit into my family. My family? I did not know how benighted and dysfunctional my family was. I said to myself, *I will not marry a woman I don't love,* when in truth I did love her. In truth, the deciding issue was not love; it was my own weakness as a young man. I could not face what I perceived marriage to be. I would not know how to raise a child. I'd be forever dodging phone calls and confrontation because of my stammer. I'd be forever jealous because Margaret was so passionate in bed. I would not be able to hold on to her, and so I denied her. That was the truth, and it gnawed at me night after night. The truth was that she was too good for me and not the other way around. The truth was that I had been very lucky to have a girl like Margaret. She would have helped me grow up. All I had to do was trust her, but now it was too late.

I had one last night with her after the baby, after things settled down. The next morning I reached for her again. I wanted more than ever to stir her incredible passion as I had done during the night. Instead she rose from the bed, tall and naked, her pussy full again after pregnancy, her small breasts delicate and taunting and her stomach flat. She stood before me giving me a last look. Her eyes told me, *No more.* She turned and walked into the bathroom and shut the door. She called out at me, "You can go now. Last night will never happen again. Don't come back."

I left her small apartment feeling smug. What a man I was. Then suddenly I realized that *she* had used *me,* and when she was done I'd been dismissed. She knew that in time—a week, a month—I'd begin to see what a fantastic treasure I'd let slip through my fingers. At the height of her allure she had told me to go. She was ready to trade up.

On January 5 Red and I were discharged, and with hardly a wave of the hand we were gone. We followed each other until I left him in New Mexico in the town where we saw Sylvia Stone in a cafe. It still puzzles me...Sylvia Stone had been a friend and so very amusing. Why didn't I speak to her?

• • •

I never retained anything from my Air Force education in electronics. I was disinterested from the start and able to pass exams by memorization. I could never visualize a watt or picture how an electron acted or why a cathode ray tube did what it did. The only thing I can recall now is the general idea behind radar and the computerized navigation system that was so secret. I know no more. When directed, I followed what was called "standard operational procedure." In this state of workaday ignorance I found challenge in the world of people rather than science. I specialized in little interactions—a chance encounter, a conversation in a barroom, a night with a woman who appeared to like me.

Korea was a dreadful battle zone. It was lucky for me that I never made it to Korea. Some 53,000 Americans died there while I chased girls and played softball, or went on tennis trips or browsed in a library. Fifty-three thousand people died while I was servicing highly-complicated, top secret electronics equipment designed to deliver the hydrogen bomb. And soldiers were dying while I marched to class, stepping out to the "Colonel Bogey." I owe much of my attitude about life and human beings to what I learned from the men I bunked with and conversed with over coffee at the PX or on the flight line. I will always remember cups of coffee out on the freezing cold tarmac at 6:30 or in a line shack somewhere. Older men in fatigues with master sergeant stripes who had served in the old Air Corps in World War II...I venerated them. I imbued them with extensive personal histories though we seldom spoke.

I left the Air Force, driving east away from the pull of men in service. There was so much back there: memories piled upon memories of a team at work and play. Amazingly, I'd passed an exam that allowed me to advance to warrant officer status. I thought of this as I drove toward San Antonio, where my sister and her doctor husband, a captain in the Air Force waited for me.

As I drove along, deep forebodings told me to reenlist. I felt protected in the Air Force. After five years at Brook Hall, almost two years at Wesleyan, and four years in the service, I was sure to flounder as a civilian. Lord knew I detested the inhibited, secret life which had shackled me as a kid. But I recalled Brook Hall and the corps of cadets and what it had felt like to step out proudly in formation. I hankered for the barracks and the flight line. The Air Force had been good for me. There had been days on end when I didn't even stammer. In civilian life I would be embarrassed again. I visited my sister and in due time I was back in New England. Habit ruled, and I'm sure I felt the call of my father to come home, but all the while I thought of the Air Force, where I'd been safe and where excitement welcomed me on every weekend, where the big bombers carried equipment that somehow I was able to maintain, where life was often sloppy yet sometimes crisp, and when it was crisp the neat cut of my khakis made me think I was a man who could get the job done, and where the drop of my tie at the bar of the St. Francis pointed to my martini and the odds-on expectation of romance.

PART IV

The Adult World

Chapter 9

Lately, when I think of my father, warm thoughts move through my mind. He was always my conscience and my support, and I was his charge. As a youth I knew that no one equaled him. My father was better than anyone else simply because of who he was. I continued to feel this way even though, as I grew older, I began to recognize his faults and weaknesses. But it was imprinted on my mind that he was the best person in the world, and no accumulation of shortcomings would ever tarnish that impression.

During my years at Brook Hall we spent many Wednesday afternoons and evenings together when my father drove me to Washington to go to the dentist. Often on the way back to school we'd stop at the Imperial Cafeteria. It was the first cafeteria I'd ever been to, and just to look at the long, hot, steaming counter compartmentalized with great heaps of mashed potatoes and beets and peas and a pile of succulent chicken breasts, southern fried, and hot rolls and pitchers of juices and even soda pop...my eyes bulged. This was during the war, and I was awed by such an abundant outlay of food—such pungent and juicy items to consume. It's been over fifty years since I last visited that cafeteria, but I still think of it when I think of my father. It was something we did all by ourselves. We'd be riding along in his Buick, and then there it was: my stomach turning over in hunger...the Imperial Cafeteria. The woman who served us was brown-skinned, and I remember how she would beam at us after our first few stops. "Here you are again, you two," she'd say as she began to slide along the rail behind the succulent array of treats. "Another chicken dinner, my oh my." My father and I would take a rectangular table big enough for four and sit across from each other and dig in. He loved it as much as I: the two of us on the town and welcomed by strangers to a place where, to my astonishment, we could go back for seconds or even thirds. All you had to do was go through the line again, fill up your plate, and pay the wonderful woman who smiled so readily.

She could have been from Trinidad and I often thought of her in terms of the song of that time, "Rum and Coca-Cola." I could imagine her on the beach waiting for a G.I. As always, my mind turned to romance and sex. I was thirteen when my father and I began pulling over in front of the Imperial Cafeteria on the way out of Washington. I would be seventeen when we made our last stop.

Once in a while we tarried in Washington late into the night. After the dentist, we'd go to the Earle Theater to watch the stage show and the movie. I remember seeing the Spike Jones Band at the Earle, which pleased us both. We saw a parade of war movies there and slowly I built up a lust list of young actresses: Lizabeth Scott and Gail Russell, Eleanor Parker and Ella Raines. My favorite was Alexis Smith, whom I pictured in the nude and yearned for. I wanted so much to grow up and have such a woman for my very own.

But my father and I never discussed sex or growing up. We did talk about the war, but only in the most general terms. Once in New York I asked him to take me to the documentary *Desert Victory* in Times Square. It was an intense hour-long newsreel on the British victory in the North African desert, but my father's conversation afterward in the cab was clipped and short.

In Washington on those late evenings we sometimes dined at Olmsted's, a small restaurant where we were seated at a table for two on the second floor. My father always drank two manhattans before dinner and I could see him relax and warm up. And yet I recall no dialogue. I suspect that I chattered on about the movie we had seen. I never chattered about school, however; to do so would have caused great embarrassment. What went on at Brook Hall was not for my father to know. He never did learn the truth about that strange military school he'd chosen for his son. I never wanted him to visit, and when he dropped me off on Wednesday evenings, sometimes late at night, I would hurry from the car and hope for his quick departure.

Twice we dined in a rather adult restaurant called the 440 Club. As with Olmsted's, we had to go up a flight of stairs to the dining area, but in the stairways and the foyer we'd see women in slippery dresses and high heels. The men at the 440 Club were mostly officers, and I had the impression that the ladies lounging about with the high brass were ladies of the night or mistresses or sexually loose secretaries or in some way scandalous. They appeared too sexy to be anything other than women who were trading their looks for money and advancement. I could see that my father was uncomfortable at the 440 Club but we went there two times before we stopped going, and I think my father returned without me, looking for one of those slippery women. I think that was why he rejected my last suggestion to dine there a third time. I guessed we ceased patronizing the 440 Club because he was going there on the sly hoping to pick up women, himself.

My father was easily embarrassed. He was reticent and steadfast. No matter what, he stayed married to my mother even though she was alcoholic, emotionally unstable, and suffered from multiple sclerosis, and her intensifying instability made her increasingly unattractive. He liked women. He offered high praise like "She's a peach" or "She's a hum-dinger." In his silence at dinner, I felt his mind move in ways I could not put into words, though I knew they were adult.

Once I got him to take me to a baseball game in Baltimore. It was May 1946 and the Montreal Royals were bringing a black man, Jackie Robinson, with them to challenge the color barrier. Enlivened by the drama of it, I got my father to take me out to Municipal Stadium for the game. All I can recall is sitting in right field and hearing racial slurs and sensing an ugly tension. By the seventh inning the effusion of banal racism thickening the air had made us very uncomfortable and my father suggested we leave. Things may have turned ugly afterward; I am not sure. What I do remember is being beside my father and feeling secure even with meanness all about us. What my father thought about Jackie Robinson I would never know.

My father loved my mother, his children, the Yankee Division with which he served in World War I, and to a degree his memories of Hotchkiss, a boys' preparatory school in Connecticut. He was a very good carpenter, a good mechanic. He greatly appreciated the lovely lines of wooden sailing vessels and in particular liked mahogany planking. He was also a bigot who denigrated Jews and belittled Catholics. But he also had his own idea of fairness. I suspect that he was on Jackie Robinson's side that day at Municipal Stadium, even though he would never expect Mr. Robinson to come calling at his front door. He was a

man of his time and place, a Connecticut Yankee from New Britain. As
time passed, I took my father for granted. I never knew what he really
thought about and never even tried to guess until I was well into middle
age. He was my father, which was more than enough.

Years later, in the summer of 1955, my mother received a letter
from Kay Radford. Kay, still employed at the naval base, had planned to
visit my parents as usual at their home on Harthaven Harbor with her
ever-present sidekick, Claire Dent. A few days before their scheduled
arrival the letter came, a letter that explained so much to me about my
father. Here I paraphrase. *Dear Lucy*, it began. *I cannot go on any longer
with this deception. I am in love with your husband and unless Bill and I can be
alone together, free from guilt, with everyone aware of our love, I cannot bring
myself to return to your home on Martha's Vineyard. Please do not feel you have
to reply unless you will allow Bill his freedom with your blessings. Sincerely, Kay.
P.S. Dentie and I won't be visiting this year unless we hear from you in accord
with my fervent wish that you will understand and step aside.*

The letter was read to me by my mother as my father sat across
from her, looking very uncomfortable. It was obvious that they had been
arguing, my father defending himself, my mother accusing him of fucking Kay Radford. Her language was harsh, and, over drinks, she could be
very crude. I was staying in our camp in Chilmark and wandered in
around 10 P.M., probably to have a drink with them. They must have
been fighting since the noon mail. In any case, I rushed to the aid of my
father. I told my mother that the idea that he'd been having an affair was
a preposterous notion. Dad, I said, is way too old for Kay Radford. "Dad
is in his late fifties; Kay only thirty-two or thirty-three. And Dad loves
you," I said, looking into her eyes, still dark with anger and astonishment.

This calmed her and she looked across at my father, now buoyed
by my words. "You see," he said, "I'm way too old. I can't help her infat-
uation, can I now?" he asked.

In time it all blew over. I think my mother came to believe that
my father might have kissed Kay Radford or shown some affection, but
nothing more. True to how our family worked, unpleasant matters were
swept under the rug. I do not think that my mother was ever able to
reconstruct all the Wednesdays from 1942 to 1951, when my father
would load up the eggs from his chicken farm and take his time in
Washington.

•   •   •

In February 1955 I reentered Wesleyan. I was still on probation, my academic status unchanged from May 1950 when I had quit. My 1950 grades had been abysmal, my attitude had been self-destructive and I'd seldom attended class. But I'd left with the understanding that if I ever became serious I could return, and so I did. I believe I was given this leeway because I had had a good freshman year. Also, my uncle Frank Upham was still a trustee. Had it not been for those two factors I would have been told good riddance.

I remember the winter of 1955 as gray and bitter and, at least in Middletown, dirty with soot from a local factory. I was very lonely. A veteran at twenty-five, I was uncomfortable living with boys eighteen and nineteen, and beyond that, I continued to suffer terribly from my stammer, which returned in full force when I came back to Wesleyan. It had been very apparent, back in 1950 when I quit college, and, for a short time, lived in New Britain. My paralytic stammer was with me in Holland, Michigan, when I worked at Hart and Cooley in an office, prior to enlisting in the Air Force. I did not know it but it would return with its dreadful power after graduation when I attempted law school. In all, Wesleyan depressed me, and I turned inward, twisted around within myself like a snarl of rope, stammering and feeling too old and out of place.

Beyond my unease, my age, and the prevailing winter gloom, there was something else—the youths into whose lives I had entered were subdued, studious, colorless. The Beats and good-time women I'd known in California were night people, carefree and offhand in their discussions of Nietzsche, Heidegger, Sartre, Camus, Beckett. They traveled to Mexico and smoked marijuana and wrote poems. They had casual sex lives. Wesleyan was sexually arid, and its intellectual chitchat seemed pretentious. There were rules, too, and the endless rush of homework. I hated the pressure and longed for the bar talk in San Francisco. I had read Faulkner and Hemingway and Fitzgerald—the big three of my time—as well as Marquand, Cozzens, O'Hara, Irwin Shaw, and Thomas Wolfe. I always had a book with me and once attended an opera in Mobile. In San Francisco I had gone to hear Bea Lillie and Reginald Gardiner. I sat in the audience in my Brooks Brothers suit secretly an Airman First Class, in stitches over their humor; surely I was a sophisticated member of the San Francisco elite. Later I went to the

Buena Vista for Irish coffees. I had been reading and thinking, but more, I had been experiencing the life that writers like the popular novelists wrote about. Now I was living with kids and fussy professors. I did poorly, barely managing to be readmitted as a junior. That June I started summer school at Harvard, which was a smart move: it showed the administration at Wesleyan that I was trying. In the meantime, I had my parents and my family and my constricted life.

My parents left Maryland while I was in the Air Force. My brother Bill and our cousin Howard "Howdie" Eddy had long left the state and no one wanted anything to do with Maryland anymore; everyone moved back to Connecticut. Howard Eddy married and resettled in New Britain as did, eventually, my brother Bill. Bill married Toni, a nineteen-year-old Christian Scientist who scorned drinking and medicine. My father had to resolve a lawsuit related to my brother's actions at the boatyard. "It cost me a small fortune," he would repeat to me. In disarray my parents moved north.

My brother had arranged for my father to buy a pre–Revolutionary War house on a hill on the wrong side of the river in Mystic, Connecticut. The smart set—architects, lawyers, Broadway producers—all lived on the south side of the Mystic River or elsewhere. We lived in a rundown area, definitely déclassé.

Bill, who had found the house and steered my parents to it, had erred. He knew nothing of the social dynamics that obtained in the Mystic-Stonington area. The up-scale, tweedy crowd were loath to journey into such a tawdry neighborhood. My father laughed at this. After all, he had his other house on the harbor at Harthaven. My mother, however, was upset: "Why don't people call on us?" she'd ask. Then, after she'd actually got some people over for dinner, she'd complain: "We had four couples for dinner and not one has returned the favor and invited us to their house."

Mostly what I recall about Mystic is the drinking and my mother's terrible raging at my father. Their stay in that ancient New England house was a disaster. They had brought their bodies and possessions from Maryland but had also brought their temperaments and addiction to alcohol with them. It would not have mattered where they settled; their lives were so set in drinking by the time I returned from the Air Force that I recoiled at the thought of staying at home with them. I could not stand being with my mother, who got drunk at every lunch and dinner, while my father kept his counsel. When pressed he would say, with drink in hand, "It's all right, Lu. When things get back to normal, it will all be peachy fine."

. . .

My brother had been after me to leave college and work for him. He'd managed to insult Uncle Stan and as a result had been dethroned from his executive position. By the time I was discharged, he was heading up a tiny conglomerate called the Gibraltar Corporation. He'd go about New England with a pal named Rob Crandall analyzing small, oddball manufacturing companies. When one appeared favorable, he'd buy stock in it and "take a position." The seed money, as always, came from my father, who was cowed by his son. No one ever wanted to argue with Bill or deny him anything. To do so was to run the risk of an explosion. With my father's financial backing he set up his office on the second floor of a nondescript office building in the neighboring town of Berlin. There he and Rob Crandall met to expand their chests and huff and puff and then go out for drinks.

Having read Sinclair Lewis, I viewed this tawdry scene with distaste. Wesleyan, with all its academic pressures and pretensions, was surely a better alternative in the short run, and over the long haul it was my way out. My father was mute. I really think he wanted me to work with Bill. When I forsook my brother, running against the silent wishes of my father, I saved my life. The joy of having a mind that contained knowledge was becoming known to me. I would not give up the excitement of being able to think.

. . .

That summer I ran into a young woman I had known superficially back in my teens. Her name was Joan Johnston, and she had by then been a model, a showgirl at the Copacabana, and in the chorus of the musical *Wish You Were Here*. An only child, she lived with her parents in Maplewood, New Jersey, and in Vineyard Haven in the summer. She had been around, and in many ways was much older than I, although we were the same age. At twenty-five she was extremely curvaceous. Joan stopped conversation whenever she walked into a room. "Who the hell is she?" was a question I was to hear many times. *Look at that* was the expression I read in the eyes of both men and women.

Joan darkened her red hair so she'd look more like Rita Hayworth. Indeed all allusions related to Joanie, as we called her, are from show business. She read the tabloids in the mid to late '50s—long before the media began to rage through our lives with a force so strong that by 1980 a whole generation of young people wanted to look and act like rock stars. In our day one listened to Frank Sinatra or Peggy Lee, but it never occurred to us to want to look like Frank Sinatra or Peggy Lee. Joanie was different. She copied the stars and saw her name in lights.

I dated Joanie for three years or so on a fairly steady basis. When people asked me what we talked about I could not come up with an answer. Though Joanie seldom got beyond the *Daily News*, her extraordinary good looks and easy style and fetching naïveté coupled with her Hollywood body were quite enough to turn my head. Still slightly starstruck (as a kid I'd read and collected movie magazines like *Silver Screen* and *Photoplay*), I easily drifted into her dreamworld of actors and glitter, and I was excited about dating a girl who had danced at the Copacabana. At the Copa she undressed before other girls—dancers naked in front of wall-length mirrors with big round light bulbs. Introverted and shy as I was, my imagination went wild when I thought of beautiful women in various stages of undress backstage at the Copa. In my mind I was dating a star.

As for sex, to me sex meant mating with a woman. I avoided other kinds of sexual activities, pushing them into the recesses of my mind, but Joan had had experiences that interested me. For example, she had been dating one of the actors in *Wish You Were Here*, a handsome older man named Paul Valentine. He'd take her to the New York hot spots, displaying her like a trophy. When they were alone, he'd have her strip while he masturbated into a sock. Detecting a line of red fuzz running up her stomach, he had her shave, and every time it began to bristle up, he'd tell her to shave it again. Eventually over the run of the show she developed a nice strip of pubic hair that extended up from her triangle to her navel. Paul Valentine was excited by this, and in later years so, too, was I. Joanie told me that Shirley Jones's husband, Jack Cassidy, was Valentine's friend and sometimes they'd go out as a threesome. There was a good deal of drinking and familiarity and theater talk.

Joanie and I started going together the day I took her out on my father's Palmer Scott powerboat for a picnic off the beach at Chappaquiddick. I was sleeping up in our camp behind Chilmark Pond, but I was often at our house on the harbor at Harthaven. We had our own dock where my father kept his schooner, and the Palmer Scott lay alongside the T-shaped pier. On the golden July day I took Joanie off to Chappaquiddick, I was beginning to wonder if we would become lovers. We'd kissed after a movie or a dance but that was all. By two in the afternoon, however, my hopes were soaring. We had concluded lunch, consisting of several gin and tonics and probably a couple of egg salad sandwiches. Joanie jumped over the side for a dip, swimming a slow Esther Williams crawl in great circles around the boat. Eventually she made it to the port side where I had a ladder, but she did not climb aboard. I looked down at her and saw she was naked, holding her two-piece bathing suit in her hand. She tossed it into the cockpit and then, bending her head backward, performed a splendid back flip, in the process of which she displayed the entire front of her body.

It was a view that almost took my breath away and I was speechless: suddenly there before me on this splendid afternoon the most beautiful of women had put herself on display. She was stark naked, with an ideal configuration of red hair and a deep tan except for her full bosom, white as a sheet, with two pink nipples waiting to be kissed, and her flat stomach, equally white, like new Vermont snow, now and forever marked vertically by the Paul Valentine line of fuzz. She looked extraordinarily receptive as she positioned herself on the long seat that covered the stern of the boat. She reclined, grinning at me as she let the sun dry her, her bright red pubis glistening in the sun and her vulnerable breasts picking up sunburn almost before she could dry off.

I was hooked. I had never seen anyone who looked so good undressed as Joan Johnston at twenty-five. That day we made love in her fashion, which did not include sexual intercourse. Any penile penetration caused her pain and she'd tighten up and grimace. One could toy with her and produce pleasure, but entering her with an erection was only for a rapist. Just twice over the years did we fully consummate our affection for each other, and each time when entry was achieved, her pain ruined it for her.

She told me in sketchy detail that her father had exposed himself to her. From this she had developed a fear of being sexually violated, which led to a most bizarre phobia. She had seen shorn chickens and ducks in markets, and a bird denuded of its feathers triggered horrible memories of her father's genitalia. As a result, she suffered from a fowl phobia in which all cooked birds engendered terror, and if forced to eat one she became ill.

Joanie's basic problem with sex should have sent me on to another woman. That it didn't tells me quite a bit about myself. Certainly I was struck by her good looks and her access to good tables in restaurants and bars in New York City. She was affectionate and it was delightful to be with her, watching her and feeling her hands caress me. As for intercourse, I was off the hook. I did not have to worry about pleasing her. Although I'd had my share of experiences, I sometimes felt a sense of tension when a woman undressed and became ready for me. Usually I would be drinking, which negated my anxiety but in total sobriety I could clutch. Without drink I had to know the woman fairly well and be playfully relaxed in order to please her. I was always a worrier about most everything and my affair with Joan Johnston was a blessing as she soothed me without any demands at all. Naturally, I was hungering for other young women and often I strayed, but between the summer of 1955 and late 1958 we kept seeing each other regardless of my other involvements and her dalliances in New York City while I was in college. And I might add that with Joanie I did not have to concern myself with an unwanted pregnancy. After what happened with Margaret Kelly, this was a major ingredient in our affair.

(True: With Joan Johnston, I could not get in trouble. However, during 1959 I had a one-night affair with my aunt's masseuse. She came up to the Vineyard for a short stay to attend my aging aunt who lived next door. I took her out one time on our powerboat for a picnic. Later, when the summer was over, I saw her in New Haven where she lived and worked and where she was attached to a hospital.

Sometime in the fall she telephoned me and told me she was pregnant. I erupted: "No, you can't be, no! Just one time," I hollered into the phone.

She spoke calmly. "Yes, I am. There is no doubt."

At first I fled the news. Later on I told myself that I would have to marry her. I thought optimistically: *Stan, this is a blessing in disguise.* If pressed, I would assent; otherwise I would wait and see.

I hemmed and hawed and saw Joanie, and I almost told her about my situation. Though there was only one course open to me, I wanted her brand of advice. I wanted Joan to tell me that I could avoid marriage. Joanie might have given me a name of a doctor in New York, garnered from some showgirl she knew, who had once been in trouble. I waited, and after a month of silence I received a letter. She had found a supportive doctor who "took care of everything." There is no longer anything to worry about, she wrote.

But my mother knew: Sometime, not too much later, on a weekend visit, I'd spent the evening with Joanie and did not return to my parents' home until 2:00 A.M. My mother was still awake. She called out from her bedroom, the door ajar: "Won't you ever learn?" she hissed. "Are you too stupid to learn?"

My father, lying beside her, said nothing. I knew to what my mother was referring. My aunt had been told and, in turn, told my parents. I had screwed up again.)

•   •   •

Time moved on. My parents, going nowhere in Mystic, decided to relocate to Woodbury, Connecticut, to be near my sister who was raising five children. Mystic had turned into a nightmare of drinking and social ostracism. A new house was built to my father's taste on a vacant lot next to my sister. Everything would be "peachy fine now," my father must have said a hundred times or more. As I went on into my senior year at Wesleyan, my parents brought their alcoholism to Woodbury, Connecticut. As 1957 rolled across the horizon, this is how we stood:

My sister Bideau, now thirty-five years old, was unhappy. It seemed that her doctor husband of fifteen years was inattentive. Her own sexuality, bursting from within, was ignored. Frank Abbot was still setting up his practice in nearby Waterbury. Beyond that he had taken up hunting. I gathered that he had become a very busy man with interests outside the home.

By 1957 my brother was exhibiting a perpetual red glow to his face from drinking and there was a load of hate in his eyes. No one could stand him; yet he was always *there*, or *here* which was worse. The closer he got to me the more I worried. There always appeared to be an angry mob living inside his head.

My sister had taken care of brother Bill's two daughters, born of his first wife, the lovely Marion, who died in 1949. When he married his second wife, Toni, he took them back to live with him in New Britain, and according to optimistic letters from my mother they were all leading normal lives. Soon Toni had a child named William Howard Hart.

The next thing I knew it was all over. When I returned from the service, Bill had lost his job, started a new business, lost his wife and son, was arguing with everyone and becoming drunk at the country club, bragging when there was nothing to brag about. He had ended his second marriage to Toni and was still living in the house my father paid for when he moved to New Britain to take on the presidency of my uncle's manufacturing company. In time he would come across a small oil exploration company out west and hit up my father for a sizable investment. All in all, he was so oppressive a force that I avoided him as I would a dangerous forest fire or the tumult of a tornado.

•   •   •

In 1957 I read Eugene O'Neill's play *A Long Day's Journey Into Night*. I saw my family in that play: O'Neill came close to describing my parents, my brother, and me. Suddenly I saw my family in bold relief, full of hurt and broken plans and wishful thinking and self-deception. I was shaken and clung to Joan Johnston and other women, and began drinking to excess. I read from a wide range of books and developed a patina of intellectual pretension as a dodge. I figured Bill and my mother were partners in a disaster. I still viewed my father and sister as healthy people. It took many years before I began to wonder about my father and the way he evaded the awful truths that slithered in and out of our family. For him life just had to be grand. Discomfort and dismay would always be fleeting.

If my father was steadfast in his behavior until his death, I did not have long to wait to observe the unraveling of my sister. She had begun to hunger for something beyond domesticity. Woodbury, Connecticut, where the Abbots lived, was located in an arty area for those who wrote, produced plays, ran publishing houses, and tended to a genteel retirement. West of Waterbury and north of Danbury one found thick woodlands and rolling hills and quaint little towns with village greens, general stores and white churches with dominating steeples that spired into the skyline. Rustic villages—New Milford, Sherman, Roxbury, Woodbury, New Preston—beckoned the tweedy New Yorker who could put a book-lined den to good use. Along with the genuinely productive people who lived in Woodbury and sought a quiet conviviality there and in neighboring villages, a gang of marginally creative men and women lived on the fringes of theater and writing, and these people formed an arts and crafts community. Doomed to reside forever on the outskirts of New York, these locals performed plays, molded pottery, sold trinkets, painted, and wrote novels and poems that never got published, or at best found a home in the "little magazines" and "small presses" that took chances with unformed talent or rough writing that needed polish. Into this amorphous community of bright people with vague talents moved my sister, looking to find an outlet.

Her story would make very familiar reading two decades later when women joined a universal crusade, but back then she was still an exception. The family dysfunction that began with my mother's multiple sclerosis, far back in the middle of the Depression, was seeping through the seams of our family, oozing like some poisonous oil leak. We denied our culpability, our weaknesses, our deceits and conceits. My sister lived like a woman on a wire once she had taken her first tentative steps away from home, working in local theater. In the rush of camaraderie and excitement, she began to feel appreciated. Going back to infancy, I believe that my sister always felt the sting of disapproval from our mother and perhaps our father. The idea of being awkward, inept, not measuring up in some way haunted my brother and me, and I think it haunted her as well. Now her deep sense of failure was beginning to vanish. How heady it must have been to meet a crowd of interesting folk, all living nearby in western Connecticut, who liked her just fine the way she was, who could laugh at their imperfections and create a world of make-believe and build sets, sell tickets, and put on a show. Considerations of family and marriage slipped away. She whipped in and out of her house like a zephyr. Her husband and children learned to adjust to a wife and mother who was discovering herself.

Later on, when she fell in love with a musician, her need to be free found a focus and became full-blown. Seemingly beside herself, she drove my parents, who had moved to be near her, into depths of dismay. Typically, my mother took her behavior as a personal affront: *How could she do this to us? We paid so much to have our house built so we could be next door to Bideau and then she leaves home and runs around with that man...*

I will call him Conrad. He had been married, since the war, to my sister's friend, our cousin. He excelled in his field of music, composing a symphony which would be published and performed. He taught music at a nearby prep school. To everyone's delight, he played piano with esprit and could accompany a band or entertain at sing-alongs. Beyond his talent was his considerable wit and his ability to talk far into the night, always with humor and intelligence. There was not a chance that my sister, so long bottled up, would not fall for such a bright, free spirit. Seduction was imminent the moment Conrad brightened to her smile.

By the summer of 1958, they were carrying on, first in Connecticut and then on Martha's Vineyard as Frank stayed behind, practicing medicine. I felt sorry for both Conrad's wife and Frank, people I liked very much, but I was caught up in the excitement of Conrad and Bideau, Bideau and Conrad.

• • •

By the late 1950s I was drinking more. As my belated graduation from Wesleyan approached, I needed something to take me away from my family and from Joan Johnston, whose frigidity was contributing to my instability. In a flash it seemed like a good idea to go abroad. I had never been to Europe, so I applied for a passport and laid my plans.

I had been to Cuba twice and enjoyed a taste of the international high life. Havana in 1956 and 1957 was as hot a city as I could envision. Beautiful women graced fine continental and Cuban restaurants while in Oriente Province, Fidel Castro carried on his revolt, which only made Havana seem more intense and sexy. Upper- and middle-class Havana was having its last party. Music poured from every portal, and the sweet, heavy odors of rum and tobacco floated on the tropical air. Bars stayed open all night. The prospect of sexual liaisons played on my mind as I visited nightclubs and strolled along the boulevard. I stayed at the Nacional, where I ate Spanish olives at the bar and felt like a foreign correspondent readying himself for a sortie into the mountains to find the rebels.

A young woman named Camilla Rodriguez, whom I had met at Idlewild Airport, showed me about. Once we had sex in the stairway to her apartment in the Vedado section of Havana. I remember hurting my back leaning against the steps. Camilla was slightly built and very pretty. She possessed the hauteur of an aristocrat, and I gathered that her family was rich, powerful, and cosmopolitan. Camilla and her brothers had been educated in Switzerland and France; she spoke three languages. With Castro pressing on, there was a heightened anxiety among the well-to-do. I could sense it in the nervous babble of Spanish overheard at corner tables at the better gathering spots. Camilla introduced me to some family members, and I could feel the fever pitch of worry; there was so much that they could lose. They were hoping to protect their assets through arrangements in America and Europe. Soon the revolution would take much of what they had.

While I was there, a friend of Ernest Hemingway's son, Jack, told me about an exhibition starring Superman. We were by the pool in the Hotel Nacional. Apparently Ava Gardner had become steamed up over the size of Superman's equipment and took him on while her two male companions and a Cuban girl watched. Because I had been with Ava Gardner at Eddie Condon's in New York, I felt destined to visit where she had been. When I heard of Ava and Superman, I resolved to go there as soon as the sun went down.

Superman and a young whore joined me in a small room where I sat waiting. He wore a Superman cape and with a mighty thrust he bared his body. The girl oohed at his size and laid herself naked upon a round bed. Superman, exhausted from a thousand exhibitions, had to play with his member in an attempt at an erection. Somewhat flaccid he managed to enter his accommodating partner, only to withdraw in failure. He gestured at me and I quickly took his place, a youngster now reasonably aflame from what I'd been seeing. When we were done, Superman tried to caress me but I pulled away as the girl giggled. We had a drink and in time we got dressed. I never said a word about his show of affection and the look in his eye.

Cuba had been a sexual playground, and now that I was at last a graduate of Wesleyan, it was natural to think of Europe with a leer in my heart. I hankered for adventures that would exceed the frustrating limits of my affair with Joan Johnston and the brief flings with other women whose paths had crossed mine. Remembering Cuba, I eagerly awaited the autumn of 1957 when I would go abroad.

Chapter 10

Almost everyone I knew had been to Europe, and in that autumn of 1957 a friend of mine was in Paris studying at the Sorbonne. When I left New York on the *Liberté*, I felt that my time was past due. I wanted to experience firsthand what I'd been seeing in the movies and reading about in Hemingway, Fitzgerald, and a book that particularly moved me, Malcolm Cowley's *Exile's Return*. I was too exultant from drink and merriment to see myself as a young man trying to escape the turmoil that had swept over my family. I was looking for fun.

I was slender in those days: tapered from walking up the beach from our little cabin behind Chilmark Pond to Ray Cox's. Ray and Margaret Cox lived west of Windy Gates, high on a hill above one of the world's best beaches. The sun baked us that summer of 1957, hot and heavy with heat, and I courted languor, eating sparingly and drinking vodka at night, enough to feel comfy and affectionate. Joan Johnston and I would end up in bed and listen to the night sounds of herons rustling their feathers at the edge of the pond. Sometimes a bird would fly overhead, flapping its wings in the starry night, off course, now late and flying home, long after others had nested in their roosts. We lay atop the sheets, completely free with each other as though we'd grown up together and had always played house since early on.

I'd been given license to loaf because in early summer I had been diagnosed as having Hodgkin's disease. One night, drunk and threatening, my brother lurched toward me and said I was going to die. "You're standing here thinking you are just fine, a college graduate," he spit the words out. "And all the time you're dying. Right now, minute by minute, you're dying from Hodgkin's disease," he yelled, looming over me with his six feet two inches of bulk, his face red as a mottled beet. As it turned out, I suffered from something called sarcoidosis, not

Hodgkin's disease. In time—it took all summer and great quantities of penicillin—I regained my health. In the meantime I welcomed the languor and looked forward every day to the long walk up the beach.

Ray Cox was unbearably conservative but he was a jaunty fellow with a trim body who fancied the opera, a high-class entertainment, and enjoyed looking fit. He had a well-stocked wine cellar in his house and drank quite a bit. I spent many long sunny days lying on the beach naked beside Ray and Margaret. About half the time, Joanie would join us, retaining her bathing suit except when she went swimming. Then she would go down the beach fifty yards or so and strip and swim her Esther Williams crawl out past the breakers, arm over arm down the coast and then back again. Margaret Cox, who stammered and was very thin, never saw her naked and Ray wouldn't have cared.

I felt myself turning from a frenetic college boy or serviceman looking for girls into a mannequin, a model, a man on display like a lazy animal on a ledge in a cage. Surely Joanie, already a model in New York with the summer free, abetted me. The two of us were stretched out like figures painted on a canvas. We could have been photographed and hung on the wall.

Before boarding the *Liberté* that fall, I spent the night as Ray's guest at the Hotel Drake. Ray and Margaret were in a suite down the hall. As a going-away present, he gave me a very brief bikini and then took me to Trippler's to buy me nylon undershorts. Later he had me join Margaret and him in his suite. I was invited into his bedroom to lie on the bed. "You look tired," he said. "Why don't you lie down?" I knew the line: I'd used it on women in Sacramento when I was in the Air Force and picked up girls at the Capitol Tamale Café. I rejected his offer for a nap and left the room and the suite. After weeks of nudity on the beach, he'd been at last bold enough to make an overture. Margaret, who appeared indifferent to her husband's attempt at seduction, never said good-bye as I left. I hardly ever saw either of them again. I knew that Ray and Margaret were serious business. To me they were very cosmopolitan and naughty. Lewdness with taste is what came to mind once I'd left them in New York. I liked the thought of it. *Lewd* was a good word for what appealed to me.

●   ●   ●

Europe was aswarm with tiresome Americans, but the post–World War II period in Paris was over. There had been a time when every

American in Paris was either writing a book or learning to paint, or at the least carried an aura of mystery. When my turn came to see Paris, I saw tourists and students and I kept meeting businessmen with wives who had gone to Bryn Mawr. Try as I might, I could find no survivors of the Lost Generation—rich Americans of independent spirit who mingled easily with expatriate artists and writers, all of them mingling with native Parisians and burgeoning bohemianism. As far as the World War II crowd went, I was awkward and probably drank too much to find them. I could have tripped over James Jones or Irwin Shaw or someone at the *Paris Review* and not known it. I drank in tourist bars and nightclubs and attempted to take women home to bed. I wandered about the city having a good time, to be sure, but in truth, I squandered my time in Paris.

Fortunately, all was not lost. An old friend from the Vineyard met me as I departed the boat train from Le Havre. Sam Barnes was a Yale graduate and a naval officer, still in the reserve. In 1957 he was living in Paris with a Swedish girl who was pregnant, though not by him. I saw him on and off during my first visit to Paris.

On the journey across I had met a Canadian woman whose husband was high up in the Foreign Service, posted in London. She was tall and formed in a way that brassiere companies called "full-figured." She enjoyed me, but I was afraid that she could cause trouble down the road. She asked me to meet her in Rome and travel through Italy with her after she rendezvoused with her husband for a second honeymoon in Florence. I had no wish to travel with someone else's wife and I had begun to feel sorry for her husband.

On my own, I looked for action in the bars and elsewhere, spending inherited money as though it held no value. Raised on the movies, I searched for romance everywhere I went. Briefly: there was Madame Cognac in Nice, a sly, slender woman of color raised in Martinique. She was a woman of the cafés, clearly a creature of pleasure who became my friend and never asked for a dime. We drank by volume and toured the surrounding villages in a small Citroën, eating couscous washed down with bottles of table wine. We drank gin at Bar O'Connor, a sailors' hangout for the American Sixth Fleet, headquartered at nearby Villefranche. She called me Monsieur Stanley. She had soft black hair and shapely legs, especially when she stretched out on a bed, full of affection. Her skin was brown but sometimes showed a glint of yellow and reminded me of the term "high yellow" for a mulatto woman, which I'd heard used in New Orleans.

In Nice I studied the salesgirls in their shifts and fell under their spell. One girl worked in a record store where I visited her every day. At last I brought myself to ask her out for dinner but was refused. She had seen me with Madame Cognac. The amusing mulatto, with the brown eyes that sang and a fresh laugh to go with a dash of insolence learned back in Martinique, was not unknown in Nice. I was tainted by our friendship. The young salesgirl shrugged and threw back her soft chestnut hair. She spoke the words "Madame Cognac" and pressed two fingers together to indicate that we were as one. I had never seen anything as fetching as she, so unattainable and so winsome.

In Nice I ran into Bill and Nana Allis at the bar of the Negresco. They were from Milwaukee and we became fast friends, drinking together, even up at Bar O'Connor where Bill and Nana thought Madame Cognac to be charming. I saw the Allises again in Rome and later on in New York and Milwaukee. I used to call them when I was drinking. In recent years we have lost touch.

At the casino in Nice I met an assertive Zsa Zsa lookalike playing chemin de fer. Her last name was Hagerty. I thought she was a shill as she tried to keep me next to her spending my money. Finally I extricated myself from her, and as I left she told me to come by in the morning; she'd leave her door unlocked at the Negresco. I don't know where Madame Cognac was, but that morning I arose and went to the Negresco, up to Zsa Zsa Hagerty's room. The door was unlocked and I entered. She was in bed wearing a flimsy nightgown which I lifted over her stomach. Like my Canadian friend on the *Liberté*, Zsa Zsa (as I kept calling her) was gamy and verdant and quickly responsive; she had been waiting for me, full of anticipatory excitement. When done, I left her in bed and went directly to the Ruhl Plage to swim away the unclean feeling. For me, and I suspect for most men, sex was localized. For women like the Canadian and now Zsa Zsa, their sexuality was total; it ran through their whole being, spirit and body indivisible. I suspected such women invested heavily in their ability at lovemaking. As I sat by the Mediterranean, I wondered how it would be possible to retain such a woman's love, the love of a woman who had no investment in monogamy at all.

I remember that morning, walking away from the Negresco. It was early October on the Riviera. The summer sun was lingering, its warmth washing over the rocks on the beach and brightening the rich blueness of the Mediterranean Sea. Nice was quiet; the tourist rush was now over, yet the good weather persisted and as I quick-stepped along the Boulevard d' Anglais I kept up a jaunty pace, thinking of the Canadian and Zsa Zsa Hagerty. I carried a very clear vision of Zsa Zsa with me. She was a large woman with dyed blond hair set up on her head and her lower belly had an expanse of dark curls. Her thighs were very full and she had a roll on her waist...all those images played in my mind, my vision was bright with memories of a woman soaking and emotive. Surely if sexy meant a shortened hem line and a seductive look in the eye, sexuality was another matter. It was an eruptive totality that scoffed at sexy and could transport its possessor and lover far off into a nether world where there were no rules. In the long run I preferred decorum and girlish teasing as much as the female animal, perhaps more.

I saw Zsa Zsa Hagerty again. It was in Paris, as Sam Barnes and I were having a drink in the bar of the Hotel Georges V. The George V was an American hangout and like Harry's New York bar, I tried to avoid it. Perhaps it was an illusion but I fancied that I was on my own, experiencing Europe and accordingly the last person I wanted to see (other than Sam) was her familiar face. As we ordered our drinks, I looked across the room and there she was. She was drinking with an American Army colonel and a man in civilian clothes, both middle-aged. NATO, I thought. I pointed her out to Sam, and we caught her eye as we walked out of the bar. She looked at me long and hard, as if to say to herself, *There goes that son of a bitch.* She was sore at me for avoiding her in Nice after our brief morning in the Negresco. Hanging about with Bill and Nana Allis I would point to Madame Hagerty whenever I spotted her in a café and then the three of us would take evasive action. The Allises and I snickered behind her back. She could have known this and she detested my dodging her, she trying to establish something based on one early morning together.

As I strolled the boulevard, I continued to ponder the difference between sexiness and sexuality. I had learned to settle for sexiness and Joan Johnston was sexy in her good looks and teasing affection. The Canadian woman was absolutely sexual. How would a man make do with her over the long haul? What I gave of myself was a fraction of my being; from the Canadian woman came something infinite. It seemed to me that the rush of male orgasm hardly compares with the maternity that is innate in women's sexuality. The origin of a woman's gift to a man, and to herself, resides far down where instinct rules and life itself is on the line. It dawned on me as never before that women carry babies, give birth and nurse, and are responsible for life. For women, the act of love was a naked expression of some deep vulnerability from which springs the reason for living: the "maternity of sex," I decided to call it. How could a fellow like myself match up with that? I shrugged: it would not do for me to probe any further. I was only some half-person in France to see the sights. Leave it at that, I thought.

I needed a woman—not a Zsa Zsa—who was less earthy than the passionate women I had been with, a woman like the one I would soon meet at the outdoor café of the Hotel Royal. I was having tea—I hated French coffee—and a croissant. Next to me—unbelievably—sat the Duchess of Windsor. She was alone, and for some reason, she spoke to me. She averred that she was "very bored." "It is so tedious," she continued, "what with the Duke away and we can't use our apartment in New York." As she explained it, the State Department had made the mistake of offering the only presidential suite at the Waldorf Towers to two different heads of state for the same dates. As a result of the snafu, the Duke had graciously offered his own suite. Dispossessed, the Duke was off shooting grouse while the Duchess idled out of season at the Royal in Nice.

She was very unattractive to me...too severe-looking, far too lean in appearance, coiffed with iron hair and not a soft line in her face. It was about eleven in the morning and both of us were lonely, sitting at our respective tables. She had a small dog at her feet. She seemed to be looking me over—checking my diction, placing my background. As I finished my tea she asked me if I had any plans. She did not introduce herself, assuming I knew who she was. I sat speechless for a moment and then lied about meeting someone at the beach. I paid and left. She didn't watch me leave, but looked straight at her newspaper. She was too old for me and too hard. As I departed the Royal, I wondered what on earth the former King of England had seen in Wallis Simpson.

Much later I chastised myself for being so cocky that I could spurn the Duchess of Windsor when I knew what she was suggesting. It rankled me years later that I had chosen to walk away simply because I had found her unattractive. The Canadian and Zsa Zsa had dulled my appetite. At the time I had no stomach for yet another controlling older woman. And yet, imagine the Duke upon his return. It would have been the Duke, the Duchess, and me and it tickles me to wonder what might have come of such a trio.

•   •   •

After Monte Carlo, where I gambled in the private casino, standing like a playboy alongside faded aristocracy and eventually winning, and where I was able to find a young woman my own age who took me home for a night, I left for Rome. In Rome I reconvened with Bill and Nana Allis who got me a room at the Hassler. They left soon after I arrived and I rattled about, walking the city, until I was caught up in John Ringling North's entourage. With him was a second-rate movie actor named Bruce Cabot, who spouted racist remarks everywhere he went. Much to Cabot's distress, John included the black Harlem singer Thelma Carpenter in his group. Thelma's boyfriend, at least for a night or two, was the middleweight champion of Europe, a boxer roaring with machismo. Others came and went. I remember a fortyish woman with blond hair who said she was Will Rogers's daughter. A pretty Italian woman whom I'd first seen with Lex Barker at a bar called Gerry's was on the fringe of the crowd, and when Barker dumped her, she took me home. So it went, around and around from bar to bar and nightclub to nightclub. In a way it was like getting caught up in a festival at which no one sleeps. John Ringling North was tireless, and since he picked up all the tabs, we went along with him. Sleepless in Rome, I soon became ill and had to find a few days of quiet. Though I blamed it on the flu, I know now that alcohol had made me sick. I drank so much—too much—and got so sick that even a pick-me-up didn't work. I lay in my bed at the Hassler and shook through my withdrawal, thinking I was suffering from a terrible chill related to the flu. John Ringling North stayed at his brother's apartment and wanted me to join him there for ever more roistering. I remember back at his brother's after one all-nighter, he matter of factly changed clothes and announced he was going to the Rome Country Club for a round of golf.

Mostly, though, I was lonely. I avoided the tourist bars; I went to Harry's Bar in Venice only once. In Florence, at the bar of one hotel where I stopped to drink, Arthur Godfrey came in, very redheaded, very drunk, and very loud. By then, I had no idea what I was doing in Europe. In Venice there had been no gondola rides with a barefoot con-tessa, no visits to the private studio of some aspiring Italian artist following in the huge footprints of the masters. I was all alone in the midst of artistic treasures. In Florence I stood beside a young woman my age, the two of us admiring Michelangelo's David. The graceful lines of the body reminded me of young men at military school. The girl was breathless. I wanted to tell her, *Look at me, look at me; I'm like David*, so desperate was I to connect with someone, to be noticed, to be loved. I never said a word, though, and left her there staring at the nude figure while I ambled away.

I was much younger than my years and I asked myself too many questions. I knew this and didn't trust myself and quickly I was back in Nice with Madame Cognac and then went on to Paris to find Sam Barnes, who by then had shed his pregnant Swedish friend. Sam reminded me that President Eisenhower was visiting Paris, checking on NATO, renewing ties. "Eisenhower always goes to church on Sunday, right?" he asked. I agreed. "Therefore he will go to the American Church in Paris," he said. "If we want to see Eisenhower, all we do is go to church. Tomorrow," he added. "Tomorrow is Sunday."

So we met the next morning and wandered off toward the American Church. At 10:10 A.M. we simply walked in and found a pew in the middle of the church on the right side. Within an hour Air Force General Lauris Norstad, Secretary of State John Foster Dulles, and President Eisenhower were praying at our side. There was but a handful of Secret Service men in attendance. No fuss at all. I'd rejected the Duchess of Windsor and now I was reciting The Lord's Prayer with Ike. I remember smiling as I mumbled my prayers in Paris.

•   •   •

I withdrew some more money from savings and took Sam on a slapstick tour of Switzerland, Austria, and Spain. When we returned, we regaled Sam's sister Rosalee and her husband, David McCullough (who had yet to write his first book), with story upon story of our high times and indiscretions. Our journey, so described, lasted almost until Christmas and took us to St. Moritz, Vienna, Madrid, Toledo, and back to the Riviera to reunite with Madame Cognac and her friends at Bar O'Connor. Eventually we returned to Paris and took a Vineyard neighbor, Kit Farrow, for drinks at the Ritz Bar.

As for the Ritz Bar, on my first trip I went to a different bar at the Ritz and ran into a woman I'll call Cheryl Goodyear. Like me, she was alone. She was drinking hard and had surrounded herself with newspapers. The bar was hardly open and she and I were the only patrons. The French bartender was eyeing her as he shined the glasses and sliced limes and readied the bar for its formal opening. I had a vodka and tonic but soon followed with a Ritz Bar Special—a drink combining Cointreau, champagne and orange juice. Cheryl Goodyear was buying.

A rather basic problem with Cheryl lay in her unkempt appearance. She looked as though she had slept in her dress. Her dirty blond hair was a mess of snarls and she insisted on brushing it to the annoyance of the bartender. Her newspapers took up two tables. I almost suggested that the two of us go somewhere but she looked insolent as she continued to brush her tangled hair. Finally the bartender ushered her from the bar because she would not desist in her brushing. This was a gauche breach of etiquette; she was another American who didn't know any better.

Later on, just back from Europe, I was drinking in New York at the bar of the Sherry Netherlands Hotel when I noticed to my left the one and same Cheryl Goodyear. I saw the bartender shut her off. "She has no more credit with us," he told me. "She's staying in the hotel. Always a problem," he added succinctly as he moved away down the bar.

A year later in the winter of 1958 I ran into her again. Of course she was drinking, as was I, and she was with another woman. We were in Palm Beach and they had checked in at the Brazilian Court. We met in a bar and eventually the three of us went back to the hotel. Cheryl's friend told me that they'd been arrested and jailed in Miami. They had just been released. The two of them smelled like meat left to rot. The stench in the hotel room was so horrid I left them even though my interest in Cheryl Goodyear was more than a little piqued. By then I was starting to flirt with self-abasement, with overt scandal, with losing myself to the foul elements of life. By then I was thinking of living "down and out" on the Bowery. I wanted to trash my life and live with trash. I began to think what it would be like to live with Cheryl Goodyear.

Sometime soon after my short visit in the Brazilian Court I rejoined Joan Johnston who was seeing General Ted Landsman, Bob Hope's old pilot who captained many flights into war zones in World War II with Frances Langford and Hope and his entourage. Speaking of Frances Langford. Back in college in 1950 a classmate showed me nude pictures of Frances Langford, or so he said. They were taken on the North African desert. She struck many poses but the one that inflamed me showed her lying on her back with her legs apart. My classmate's father was with some other officers and they took the singer-actress out into the desert for a wild wartime party. Those naked poses haunted me and when Joanie had gotten into the Ted Landsman crowd that included Frances Langford who had married an outboard motor manufacturer named Evinrude, I was instantly interested in her again. By extension, I was now at last connected to the lusty woman who had taunted me in idle moments for a long, long time.

When I think of those carefree days in Europe with Sam Barnes, I am struck by my innocence. Although I had my personal demons, nothing in the outer world could trouble me. Within context it was all good self-indulgent fun, and we talked about our adventure for years. And I give Sam credit: it was he who got us into church with Ike and it was he who talked me into attending the opera in Vienna and who insisted that we travel up from Madrid to Toledo to see El Greco's museum-home and the striking town itself on a commanding hill, so impressive in memory.

In Toledo we missed the bus and took a cab built in 1938, bumping along back to Madrid. In Vienna we went to the Cafe Mozart, picked up a couple of young women, and the next day on the way to the opera Sam looked at me with concern. "Geez," he said, "things really happen fast in Vienna." When he sold his golf clubs in St. Moritz, he got some pocket money and didn't have to keep borrowing from me. He saved his putter, however. It was a "lucky putter" and the Yale golfer revered it and guarded it zealously throughout most of our journey. Alas, somehow he misplaced it on our train trip from Madrid to Paris, and when he realized he had lost it we were already on the boat train to LeHavre, ready to board the *Liberté* to go home. Sam wrote to the National Railway in Spain and miracle of miracles they had it and mailed it back to him. This bit of kindness seemed typical of Europe and Europeans.

•   •   •

Once home I defended my inattention to high culture by claiming that I'd been soaking up the atmosphere. While in Europe for three months I did manage to read some Thomas Mann, but mostly I read the *Herald Tribune* Paris edition. I never bought a guidebook. I visited many museums and gazed in admiration at great works of art, paintings I'd seen in art books and studied at Wesleyan. I noticed certain architecture and ventured into cathedrals of historic importance. But nothing in-animate moved me, for I was totally inspirited by simply being an American abroad, a human being among other humans, waking each morning eager to seize another day. I lived with the aura of being in Europe, the sexuality of the women, the hustle-bustle of people speak-ing languages I did not understand. Walking all alone about Florence, for example, stopping for a beer or a coffee... *just being there* was what got to me. The great masterpieces I stood before had no beat. The people were the excitement, and the din of their voices and their laughter and the way that they looked drew me to them. Once I was home, I knew I should have stayed abroad.

I drank in cafés with a newspaper and a pack of Marlboros. Once home at my parents' house in Woodbury, Connecticut, I had Art Sted-man and his fiancée, Wendy Williams, for dinner. They drove up from New York, she very educated in an assertive way, a junior year Phi Beta Kappa at Vassar. I showed them my slides. Never once did I say a word about art or politics. Instead I spoke of how it felt to be walking on the Lido beach outside Venice, drinking in the grand lobbies of imperial hotels in cold war Vienna, ice skating in Davos or finding a German girl in Cannes.

Wendy Williams thought I was a Philistine. She was right, of course. I really didn't care about art. I didn't care much about anything except other people who would befriend me.

• • •

Back in Connecticut I was bored beyond endurance. I still had Joan Johnston for venting my frustration, though by the winter of 1958 she was in Palm Beach. Along with Sam Barnes, I headed south in my red Chevrolet convertible with a white Dacron roof and a chassis shined to a fine luster, or what my father would call "a fare-thee-well." "Snappy" was a useful description for my car, but perhaps not too useful for describing Sam and me.

To give us credit, we did not idle too long on the beach. We job hunted. I was offered a sports reporter's job at both the *Palm Beach Post* and the *St. Petersburg Times*. I almost accepted the latter offer, but we'd been in town long enough to know that there were no local sports that would interest me other than two months of spring training at the Yankees' camp in Clearwater. While in Florida I received a call from CBS. Through a friend of David McCullough I'd submitted a short story I'd written in college to their story department. Now in St. Petersburg the words flew at me from the receiver. They could use me. I should report for an interview at once.

In 1958 CBS was producing live dramas on television. They always needed material, and they needed script readers and rewrite people. I met an executive, who offered to hire me. I told him that I had to think it over. To sweeten his offer and impress me with the collegiality of the department, he introduced me to another man about my age who had recently been brought on. I shook the hand of this thin English-looking chap whose name, I was told, was Michael Korda. A moviegoer from five years old, I'd seen several movies produced by Alexander Korda, Michael's uncle. The name alone was terribly exciting. But then here was this aesthete, a fellow who would no doubt embarrass me with his bookish ways and his knowledge of Western literature. The thought of this Korda chap, the sort who I fancied could quote at will from *Paradise Lost,* intimidated me, and I flew back to Florida. I left word via David McCullough, "Thanks, but no thanks." I couldn't work at CBS. Michael Korda went on to become a well-known writer and editor at Simon and Schuster. Fifteen years later I met him at a party on Martha's Vineyard. He looked pale—no threat—and I was mortified that I had let him frighten me away from CBS.

• • •

That spring, leaving Sam Barnes in Florida, along with Joanie, still sunning herself on the beach, I pulled up stakes and headed north. It was April when I pulled into my parents' driveway in Woodbury. My father greeted me with a trace of annoyance. As I reconstruct it, he was deeply perturbed by four situations he could not dodge:

One, my mother was drinking far too much, turning ugly at dinnertime, making both of their lives a nightmare. Every day she would harp on the subject of Kay Radford and other suspected lovers. Anyone attractive and healthy was an object of envy to my mother. I can still hear the sting in her words whenever she got drunk, a daily occurrence. The tension escalated.

Two, my sister had not cooled in her love for Conrad. She was often absent from her own house next door. We all worried about the children. My mother scowled at her whenever she came by. My father, for his part, could not abide the thought of his daughter's carnality. It made him furious and he steamed inside. My mother's brother, Uncle

Frank Upham, a New York lawyer, had sent off a letter to the fashionable prep school where Conrad taught. Did they know that their music teacher, *who tutored young ladies alone in his home*, was a lecher, a womanizer, a destroyer of homes, was carrying on with the wife of Dr. Frank Abbot? As a result of the letter, Conrad was fired. Distressed as they were, my parents appeared helpless. They dared not raise a direct complaint against my sister lest she become furious and...do what? So they worried and struck out at each other instead and wondered aloud if Uncle Frank's moral posturing and intercession had been the right thing to do, even though Conrad's dismissal seemed fair to them.

Three, my brother, for some time quiet and out of sight running his curious conglomerate, had married for a third time, a cheery, buxom nurse named Lyn Molet. They'd moved to San Francisco so he could be near one of his enterprises, an oil company, taking along both daughters from his first marriage. My parents worried over the well-being of their granddaughters, fearing that the two girls were being ignored and were likely to be looked at as obstacles in the way of a new marriage.

And four, they were worried about me. I was going nowhere. I'd spent the inheritance left to me by my grandfather on trivialities. My travels, which were supposed to broaden me, didn't impress my parents. My father knew what I was doing: I was getting drunk and finding women far from home where I could get away with immoral behavior. I'd been to Cuba, Europe, Florida, Puerto Rico, and Nassau, and now I was back. I'd turned down jobs at two newspapers and CBS. My father was not happy with me. I think he saw me as enfeebled. My Air Force career and college degree did not mean much anymore. I could talk a good game, and I claimed to be educated. But my father was not a talker, and he distrusted education. He was a maker of things, and he valued common sense. I was a sore disappointment.

By 1958 my father had become lumpy and old-looking. He was bald now with a rim of white hair around the sides of his head, with only a light wisp on his crown. He was always ruddy in the face but otherwise white-skinned, and when he worked on his schooner, moored at our dock in Harthaven, he wore a white undershirt covering a sagging, pale torso.

My mother would sleep until noon. She awoke to be walked into the living room, helped along by her husband. Once established in her

chair she'd ask for a scotch, and thus would begin her slow downslide
toward night, when my father would slowly coax her back to their bedroom, where they shared a double bed, the two of them still drawn
tightly together, perhaps tied tighter than ever now owing to the adver-
sity they were encountering.

In May 1958 my father decided to sell his schooner, the *Stormy
Petrel*. My mother always complained that he spent too much time on it,
and she was now too infirm to go along on day cruises around the
Vineyard. My father loved that boat, and so did I. I had taken her out a
few times without my father, always with my cousin Al Pease. Sometimes Sam Barnes would be with us, or Joan Johnston. We had fine times
cruising Nantucket and Vineyard Sounds and Buzzards Bay. We'd drink
ourselves numb at night, and I would lead Joanie to bed in her stateroom. I'd sleep across the way on a bunk and then slip back to see her in
the early morning. The smell of coffee and bacon would waft through
the cabin and before long we'd all be on deck, beers in hand, raising the
sails, heading home. So much was going out of my life along with the
schooner. But then my father announced that he was selling his boat to
Burl Ives, and suddenly my life took a decided turn for the better.

•   •   •

Burl Ives was forty-nine years old, six feet and almost three hundred pounds of entertainment. All of a sudden in 1958 he was a star. His
long-playing records were moving briskly. Just prior to selling him the
Stormy Petrel, my father had purchased an album of Burl's, a com-
pendium of ballads including the popular "Blue Tail Fly" ("Jimmy Crack
Corn"). Burl had become a star on Broadway in 1955 when he played
Big Daddy in Tennessee Williams's *Cat on a Hot Tin Roof*. When we met,
he had just completed a movie for which he would win an Oscar, *The
Big Country*. He was full of himself and enjoyed talking about being on
location with the director William Wyler and the other actors, notably
Charlie Bickford, whom he liked very much, and Gregory Peck, Charl-
ton Heston, Jean Simmons, and Carroll Baker, who were also in the
movie. I could see he relished being a movie actor: when he spoke of *The
Big Country*, his eyes twinkled as he remembered good times on location.

A couple of years before I met him he had written his autobiography, *Wayfaring Stranger*. A leftist balladeer, he was enamored of the labor

movement out West that took on the banks, the land barons, and the timber interests. He hated the far right and denigrated Henry Fonda for something related to the House Un-American Activities Committee. He fancied himself a man of the people, a rough-and-ready sort who slept under the stars and sang for his meals on the doorsteps of grim farmhouses out on the plains in Willa Cather–Grant Wood land. I thought he was very naïve when it came to politics, but that didn't matter to me. He was very likable and was wary of people who wore fancy clothes and had it easy all their lives. He was a man of the Depression, but at the same time, like so many newly rich, he was very money conscious and kept tidy accounts of everything he spent. Somehow he'd rationalized that cruising on his newly bought schooner, which he'd renamed the *Tibby Dunbar*, was part of his job and everything related to it was a legitimate deduction. Royalties were pouring in from record sales and his book, and there may have been residual payments from Hollywood and Broadway. In any event, he lived in princely fashion but watched his money and railed against the IRS like any Republican industrialist.

In an effort to control his weight, Burl took what he called "pisser pills" which made him urinate with increased regularity. He drank heavily. My heart soared the first time I walked down to the dock to meet him just as a delivery man was loading supplies onto the schooner. By "supplies" I mean cases of Beefeater Gin. My face broke into a broad smile as I went aboard and climbed down the companionway, stepping around the cases of Beefeater, piled in the cockpit. Down below was Burl, an immense man with round metal-framed glasses, studying the charts. He shook my hand and introduced me to a seadog of a fellow named Joe Myron. Joe had a large gold earring shining from the side of his head, and he wore a horizontal-striped pirate shirt. I thought that this was going to be the time of my life.

During that summer we sailed together up and down the coast as far as Annapolis and around Long Island Sound, the Chesapeake, Block Island, and the Vineyard. Joe Myron couldn't sail a lick, but he looked great and was a good bartender. We had another fellow along whose name I've forgotten. He wore a strange Robin Hood hat and looked like Will Scarlet, but I got my names mixed up and called him Allan-a-Dale, which pleased Burl no end.

Burl's publisher, Charlie Duell, boarded the boat in Woods Hole for our cruise down to City Island near Manhattan. Duell was over fifty then, a short, wiry fellow who ran a book publishing company, Duell, Sloan and Pearce. He'd published both *Wayfaring Stranger* and *The Burl Ives Songbook*, as well as Erskine Caldwell, W. H. Auden, some John O'Hara, and Dr. Spock's original baby book, but not much else with staying power. Everyone liked Charlie, including me, especially because, like Joe Myron and Burl, he liked to drink. Our evenings were merry ones. The three of us (and later Allan-a-Dale, whom we picked up on City Island) reclined in the cockpit with the sails furled and the anchor down, or, what was more likely, snugly fast against a dock. Burl always felt that while on location out west for *The Big Country* he had been with real men, and that's how I felt during those precious hours once the ship was secured. I was with some unusual men. I was accepted by them.

I'd spent four anonymous years in the Air Force and over four years at Wesleyan which I endured, wrapped like a mummy, my only explosions of freedom occurring when I drank too much. On that precocious campus, applause was a click of the fingers rather than a clap of the hands, and students were referred to by the insufferable sobriquet, "Wesmen." The president of the university, who was a serious, troubled, thoughtful educator named Vic Butterfield, was called by one and all "Vic." At Wesleyan at that time there were no women. The skies were always gray and at dusk from the church tower came the sound of the carillon, a sing-song melody tolled by a youth on scholarship, and its haunting tone echoed down the hill throughout the campus. One trudged toward dinner in a bleak world, almost medieval with the bells tolling overhead. It was God-awful lonely for there was no dropped handkerchief on the carpet, no door to open for a woman showing a flash of thigh, no tube of lipstick left on an end-table, no radiance from a woman in love, indeed no love songs, no soft edges to inspire dreams. I'd often asked myself why I had endured four years of the cold war, attending Air Force classes and working on icy flight lines or on tarmac so hot it would melt, just to reenter a prison full of young men who had committed no crimes, whose only singularity lay in their high intelligence. Finally by 1958 I was with Burl Ives, with adults who spoke without censure, who laughed from the bottom of their bellies, who knew women, who got erections and mated and laughed and loved in an open world…I was at last with people who had seen a good deal of life and produced enough on their own to be independent and secure enough to follow where their own minds told them to go.

•   •   •

Burl was married to a large woman with no interest in sailing, who joined us for only a few days. About his marriage Burl said: "We give each other a lot of leeway. Anything goes so long as we don't embarrass each other. That's our credo." In amazingly short order Burl was able to put his credo into play. One night we had the *Tibby Dunbar* in a slip at a yacht club along the coast of Long Island Sound, and Burl and I went ashore for our evening repast. We'd had our round of martinis on the boat and, feeling like kings, we settled into a delicious steak dinner with Caesar salad. As we contemplated our dessert course, now drinking Heineken's beer, a most attractive woman in her mid-thirties came over to join us. I was used to people dropping by because everybody, no matter where we went, recognized Burl Ives. His round face and beard and his bulk and his wonderful voice made him a familiar figure to the whole nation. But seldom did someone just sit down with us as this woman did. Naturally Burl bought her a drink, and I, at my peak in looks and health, assumed that she was going to make a play for me. The woman was very tan and sexy, with brown eyes and dark blond hair. She was jaunty and full of herself, and I kept thinking of her undressed, assuming she would be repelled by the grossly overweight celebrity who was intent on charming her. It never occurred to me that this lovely woman would prefer such a fellow, especially when I was there for the asking.

We drank beer and Burl paid the bill and we sat and we sat until finally I came to understand that she was not interested at all in a svelte, twenty-eight-year-old such as I. She was interested in fame and stardom, embodied in an obese balladeer-turned-actor. "Jimmy Crack Corn." I hummed his anthem as I walked away from the yacht club.

Back on the boat I curled up and quickly fell asleep. But then— was it two or three in the morning?—I heard them descend the companionway and, giggling, make their way into the saloon where Burl had his bunk. They kissed and teased each other and soon I heard her ask Burl what it was like to kiss Elizabeth Taylor. "Oh, she is a very good kisser," replied Burl.

"Kiss me the way you kissed Elizabeth Taylor," she begged, and Burl obliged. I heard them kissing, the young woman oohing and aahing as he held her. Unable to take it anymore, I emerged from my bunk and coughed my annoyance into the saloon.

Later that morning Burl returned to wake me again and give me a detailed account of their lovemaking back in some motel on Route 1. Jealous, my ego bruised, I roused myself and went off looking for coffee. I'd learned that the star always gets the girl—even if he's fat. Fame attracts bed partners, and Burl's adventure that night was my first intimation of star power.

Burl told me later that he intended to keep seeing the woman and had decided to come up from Manhattan on a regular basis to carry on their affair. "She is something," he said. *Maybe they are in love*, I shrugged, and put the thought in the back of my mind. Someday I'd read about them in a gossip column. Leonard Lyons would spot Burl Ives at Costello's or Danny's Hideaway with a doe-eyed blond, a mystery woman, and I'd know it was the woman from the yacht club who should have been with me.

That would be my last unfettered summer; I had been loose and natural with Burl and Charlie and Joe Myron and Allan-a-Dale. On the Vineyard, besides Joanie, I had for a companion a stunning young woman with a lovely bosom; she was a blond and when we lay together on the beach, I would just stare at her body, amazed at how beautiful she was. This would be my last whirl, my last tango. It was my last summer of looking good and feeling rich every minute of the day and night. And that was a feeling in which I luxuriated. If ever there were anyone "entitled," it was I. That summer of 1958 I took it all for granted: women, the sea, the sun, the *Tibby Dunbar*, my new friends. I was so very much at ease in that self-centered life. I remember how I felt riding the Shore Line, sitting in a rattling coach of the New Haven Railroad, flying along through Connecticut, having left Burl in Stratford on my way home to spend a day or two on the Vineyard. People looked at me. *Who is that guy?* they said, or so I fancied.

That guy was me and I loved it.

PART V

Publishing and the Time of My Life

Chapter 11

Sometime during that summer with Burl I took an aptitude test for law school. I rode the New Haven down to New York, leaving Burl and Joe Myron at a slip in Mystic. I stayed in Burl's apartment, a duplex on West End Avenue, where the wife of MacKinlay Kantor, the Pulitzer Price winner, was also ensconced.

I spent a sleepless night, uneasy with Mrs. Kantor so close by, and the two of us alone in the apartment. I was painfully conscious of her presence. The afternoon after the exam Burl came into town to pursue a project over lunch. Ignoring my law school plans, Burl had decided that I should become a movie actor. On my behalf he'd arranged a lunch at Sardi's with the film and stage director Elia Kazan, who had directed Burl in the Broadway production of *Cat on a Hot Tin Roof*. We were to meet for lunch at the late hour of 3:00 P.M. By 1:30 I was hungry and worried about the test, and thoughts of Mrs. Kantor kept intruding. It was odd, but I felt as though I had let her down by not knocking on her door, that I'd been a fool not to pursue her. And thinking this way made me wonder about myself. Quite simply, I was still not used to women, and they stole my attention all of the time. I couldn't even accept the thought of Mrs. Kantor as just a fellow guest asleep down the hall. I had to think of taking the risk, acting badly, giving it a go…who knew? The prospect of seduction haunted me even as I saw myself clearly as someone unhinged by sex. In Hollywood I would be devoured by circumstances beyond my ability to control or orchestrate. Thus conflicted, I began to waffle about our forthcoming lunch.

Burl had told Kazan about me, and "Gadge," as he was called, readily agreed to meet me and arrange for a screen test on the coast, followed by a contract with a studio. It was assumed that I would pass the test. I think Burl and Joe Myron saw me as a troubled young man, with an appeal made popular by James Dean. As the '50s were coming to an end, the "boy next door" was now a cliché. *Angst* was a word employed at random. To be interesting you had to be somewhat disturbed, and my subterranean pressures must have been apparent to Burl. At the last minute, unready for Hollywood, I backed out. I told Burl that I had set my heart on becoming a lawyer, which made him gasp. Who in the world would prefer lawyering over acting? "Don't you want to be a movie star?" he shouted, in shock.

For years afterwards I told people that I turned down Elia Kazan and Burl Ives, thereby giving up the prospect of movie acting for law school. Often I embroidered my story by saying that I had actually lunched at Sardi's with the great Gadge Kazan. Sometimes I believe it, and even now I see myself at a table against the wall with Kazan on one side and Burl on the other, telling them I'd think it over, but all the while knowing I had opted for law school. It sounded like fun, I said, being a star, but I had taken the law school test. I'd wait and see how that came out, then I'd let them know.

The sleepless night wondering about Mrs. Kantor was not all that changed my mind. Worse than death I dreaded the thought of disgracing myself in the eyes of my father. I could picture him hearing word of me carrying on with some starlet. And down deep, too, lay my fear of stammering. When I drank I did not stammer, but I couldn't drink all the time. Sooner or later a movie director would catch me dead sober and I would stand petrified, my eyes tearing. By now I'd learned how to avoid situations that might ignite my affliction. Acting was sure to expose me, and if the night life didn't kill me, being exposed as a mortified stammerer would be dreadful in its own right. Naïvely, I thought law school was the answer.

As I write this I am still amazed that my parents allowed me to go through my youth and early manhood without even once mentioning my stammer. Never did they allude to it; never did they suggest that I go for help or that I try to do anything about it. My schoolwork, my social life, all relationships were tainted and limited and I was acutely embarrassed. I view such an error of omission on the part of my parents as neglect. Although I was given so much that contributed to my material comfort, my emotional life was ignored. I know that they were very absorbed with each other and my mother's illnesses. I know that, but why couldn't they have seen that I needed help?

I lasted three months in law school. After weeks of humiliation in which I dared not speak lest I stammer, I walked away. The large amphitheater classes at Boston University Law School were unbearable. I felt like an idiot standing up and trying to recite before over two hundred students. I'd been accepted at Duke, and in that law school's smaller classes I might possibly have overcome my terror at speaking. Harvard would have taken me as well, if I'd been willing to wait a year. Instead I chose Boston University because I'd heard it was easy, which Harvard and Duke were not, and because I could return on weekends to the Vineyard and see Joan Johnston.

•   •   •

Back on the *Tibby Dunbar*, Charlie Duell had told me that anytime I wanted to work in publishing I should give him a call. He'd make room for me at a moment's notice should I decide to move to New York and join Duell, Sloan and Pearce. It now seemed the obvious choice.

The founding partners of the firm were Charles A. Pearce (called "Cap"), Sam Sloan, and Charlie Duell. They had purchased a brownstone building with three floors and a basement on what insiders called "Publishers' Row." Their East Side offices were just off Fourth Avenue, renamed Park Avenue South, in the district of Manhattan known as Murray Hill. Grand Central Station was just up the avenue where the great commercial hotels were still in operation: the Biltmore, the Roosevelt, the Commodore. Larger publishing houses had already moved out of Murray Hill, but there were still quite a few in the neighborhood; Harper Brothers was around the corner. W. W. Norton and William Morrow were nearby.

Charlie was thin and tough like pemmican, hard beneath a quick smile. He wore the standard Publishers' Row uniform, consisting of a Brooks Brothers suit and an oxford shirt with a button-down collar. Near New Haven, I'd seen him nearly assault a harbormaster twice his size so I knew he was tough, and I admired him. Sam Sloan had died but Cap Pearce was very much alive and kept to his large office on the second floor, always on the phone, occasionally editing a manuscript. Cap affected a continental look. He wore dark blue or black tailored suits with wide lapels and spread- or straight-collared white shirts. His face always looked scrubbed. He sported glossy black shoes and was very trim and dapper. I told Charlie that I thought of Cap as a natty fellow, and Charlie, rumpled in a Yale alumnus Brooksie pose, said, "Yes, he is, and I respect that in Cap."

But the way he said it sounded to me as though he was leaving out an important consideration as in "I respect the way he looks but...." In a short time I learned what Charlie had left out. Cap was a bender alcoholic. Every so often he would disappear for a week into the city, drinking himself to oblivion, and finally holing up in a hotel where he would dry out. Eventually, with his nerves stabilized, he'd get a shine and a shave, buy a new shirt and tie, and return to his office, jaunty and cheerful. During his absence we'd all cover for him. His wife, who was the daughter of the illustrator-artist Rockwell Kent, would call throughout the week. It was painful to have to deflect her anxiety with "I'm sure he is fine, but I don't know where you can reach him."

Charlie was in charge of the business end of the firm, and all editorial matters were left to Cap. Because Cap was gone so much (toward the end of 1959 his sober intervals became shorter and his drinking bouts more extended), I took up the slack and became an editor.

I'd actually begun my career as an editor over the Christmas holidays in 1958. While at Smoke Tree Ranch in Palm Springs where I was visiting my parents, I read the manuscript of a novel the firm eventually published, *The Sound of One Hand*, by Lawrence Savadove. Charlie wanted my opinion. Cap wasn't interested in it, but Charlie's secretary, Bette Schacter, was. Larry Savadove was her brother-in-law. I read it with growing enthusiasm. I made little notations around the margins of the manuscript and, during my first day on the job in New York, I wrote a report praising the book. Amazingly, I was given the novel to see through to publication and, almost immediately, I became an editor for a New York book publisher. Miraculously, my stammer began to leave me.

I always assumed that Charlie and Cap were independently wealthy and that they drew no salaries from the company. I assumed, also, that they shared in the profits, if there were any. But with a list dependent on military books such as a history of the Strategic Air Command, a history of nudism, a romantic novel by a strange lady who lived far up on the West Side named Rubylea Hall, and a novel, *The Night Cometh*, smuggled out of Africa that never even got reviewed, the list was devoid of best-sellers, and I knew that sales figures were meager. We did have Dr. Spock in hardcover, but, as Charlie said, the big money for Dr. Spock was in the paperback edition. Our backlist trickled along: some Erskine Caldwell, a request here, a request there.

Margaret Wilson, a woman in her fifties, handled all royalties and contracts and subsidiary income and coordinated her efforts with Bette Schacter. She was a tireless, nervous woman who lived up in the Bronx and stuttered. She had her own glass-walled office where she kept her ledgers. Like Bob Cratchit she would bend to her task. She kept tabs on all the money and where it was to be allotted, and when there was a glitch over royalties and an irate author called in or an agent began to complain on the phone, Margaret, despite her stutter, would have to deal with it, defend her obsolete accounting procedure, research the mistake, correct everything, and placate her adversary. Margaret ran Duell, Sloan and Pearce. No one went against her wishes lest it hurt her feelings, and she was very protective of Charlie and the company. She was the sole person who had any clue as to how business was progressing. The rest of us spun around her while she sat glued to her statements and ledger columns of royalty percentages and payments.

Nancy Mazocco was Cap's secretary. Nancy typed Cap's letters and did his filing, but her most important job was to cover for him when he disappeared, and no one knew exactly when that would happen. In time I learned that it happened whenever Dick Harraty showed up or when General of the Air Force George Kenney stopped by. Both were Duell, Sloan and Pearce authors. Harraty was a red-faced New York Irishman who had made a career in journalism. He wrote a travel book for us and once I carried copies of it to a Madison Avenue travel agency where they were placed in the window. As payment, Dick Harraty sent me a case of Carlsberg beer. Often he came by the office just before lunch, and sometimes Cap was out. When that happened, he took me to lunch at Costello's up on Third Avenue.

Harraty's next project was a photobiography of Franklin D. Roosevelt, titled *FDR in Pictures*. He arranged for serialization in *Look* magazine, which meant a goodly sum for him and increased sales to Duell, Sloan and Pearce. Whenever he found Cap at work, they would retire to Cap's upstairs office and close the door. We knew Cap had a bar up there, and before long we'd hear the guffaws and the har-de-har's as the two men told each other stories and roared with glee. Nancy

Mazocco would raise her brown eyes to the ceiling and almost shiver. So would young Joan, a twenty-two-year-old who worked in an ad agency and was often in our office going over my copy or talking with Betty Schacter. And so would I raise my eyes. All three of us would stare at the ceiling over which stood Dick Harraty and the editor in chief, drinks in hand, tales and jokes flying.

George Kenney was another trouble spot. He was a four-star general, a genuine hero. During World War II he ran our Air Force in the Pacific. MacArthur lauded his work. A short man, he'd stride briskly into our office, neat as a pin in a dark suit. His book on the legendary Pappy Boynton, *Baa Baa Black Sheep*, was probably one of our few publications that had a crack at the best-seller list. He was a cold warrior—a stern, no-nonsense anti-communist. He seldom spoke to the staff; he'd walk straight up the steps to Cap's office. And after the customary har-de-har's and knee-slapping ribaldry and tinkling of ice cubes, the two of them would leave together, out into the city. "Good-bye, Mr. Pearce," Nancy would call weakly after the departing editor. And then the door would slam shut.

Joan, whom Charlie called "Miss Innocence" was a bit more than that. I took her out for drinks and dinner on occasion and we slept together. A girl from Illinois, she was a hippie before there were hippies. She had a pad near the Chelsea Hotel. We all liked her. She was a real blond with soft pubic hair that I liked to pet. I enjoyed her, but I was still on-and-off-again with Joanie Johnston, who was usually in town, and there were others as well. I don't remember but I think Joan left New York before I did to go off and study art. I have no idea now—I just recall her as a good sport and a good drinker.

Cap was supposed to be brainy and had a reputation as a hot editor from his old days at Harcourt, Brace, where he edited John O'Hara. "He helped write *Appointment in Samarra*," people would say. Although he could be prickly, Cap and I got along, and as the months went by, he gave me more and more editorial responsibility. My title was "assistant to the president." I also wrote all the ads for Charlie and did any odd job he might come up with. It seemed that I was forever carrying things over to our shared sales department at David McKay Company. Another function was to hand-carry review copies to the desks of the book review editors at the *Herald Tribune* and the *New York Times*—Maurice

Dolbier and John Hutchens on the *Tribune* and Charles Poore and Orville Prescott on the *Times*. My little excursions were very exciting. I'd wind my way through the halls of power to the appropriate offices and, *plump*, I'd lay the book on the desk, often with Prescott or Dolbier or whoever it might be sitting before me reading. I loved it. Occasionally a book even got reviewed. I know *The Nudists* was, and a book of political philosophy by Edgar Ansel Mowrer.

As for Mowrer, he was an old newspaperman, and we were able to get him onto the *Dave Garroway Show* to talk about his work. Charlie asked me to meet the distinguished man and take him over, which I did. We went and sat in an anteroom and, while we waited for airtime, Jack Lescoulie came in. Lescoulie was the sidekick who shared on-air time with the great Garroway. I recall Lescoulie entering our waiting room at 6:30 A.M. wearing a tuxedo. His eyes were red, and he appeared quite ravaged. His face looked like a campsite for the Mongol hordes, all pocked and bruised and criss-crossed with the lines of excess. He was given some coffee and disappeared into a dressing room. Thirty minutes later he reappeared. He was tall and straight, out of his tuxedo and into a tweed jacket. All lines and creases and pockmarks were gone. There in a flash stood a new man. I looked in amazement, for before me was Dorian Gray.

The Lescoulie incident stayed with me for years and years. I patterned myself after him. To debauch at will yet look fine within minutes was my ideal. A shower and a change of attitude, that was the ticket. Mainly it was the change of attitude. Given time and a good outlook, one could will away turpitude.

Dave McCullough and I would lunch about once every two weeks. One time he brought a classmate he thought I should meet—a chap named Brian Hollingshead who worked for Oxford University Press as an editor. I'll never forget my embarrassment when he asked me what our "big book" was that year. I probably answered, "Our African novel, *The Night Cometh*," which I liked very much but in my heart I knew it would be overlooked by the mainstream press. Brian then informed us that *his* big book was Richard Ellman's *James Joyce*, a grand biography, an intellectual feat the publishing world was anticipating. I realized how trivial was my candidate and also my job. We had nothing important on our list, nothing essential…certainly nothing *big*. Nor would we. At lunch that day I foresaw toiling forever in the minor leagues. It did not dawn on me that if I stuck it out I'd be able to transfer to, say, Random House, that I was developing a fine curriculum vitae. I was working with a minor company, but I was involved with many aspects of publishing.

. . .

For my first six months in New York I shared an apartment with John Walther, who was working for the Hanover Bank. He had graduated from Wesleyan with me in 1957. I liked him a lot but, alas, he fell in love and quite often he and his girl would take the bedroom while I slept on the couch. No matter, I was not interested in sleep anyway. Joanie was in town whenever I wanted her. The young woman I'd been seeing on Martha's Vineyard and taken to the beach was also in town, working for American Express. So was Samantha Crichton, who worked for an advertising company, and Sheila Morton, in sales at NBC.

The Vineyard beach beauty, whom I will call Ramona, was someone I should have adored. Unfortunately I thought of her as being too young and naïve. Whenever I said something that I thought was of great interest, she would nod as though she understood me. Perhaps she did, but I held the notion that she didn't have the foggiest idea of what I was trying to say. She looked terrific and had a classy job at American Express, but I saw us as having no interests to share.

In order to know her better, I took Ramona up to the McCulloughs' home in Connecticut. She volunteered to bake a pie. As we were sitting in the living room, having a drink, the McCulloughs' dog began to bark. A canine smoke detector, the collie alerted us to a kitchen engulfed with smoke. I asked Ramona if she really knew what she was doing: "Do you know how to bake a pie?" She nodded. This stroke of fallibility might have made her beauty even more fetching, but in a very short time our friendship foundered.

Joan Johnston, who had been able to raid my life when she wished, decided to lay claim once again. She was with Catalina, modeling bathing suits, and seemed to know a good number of people, and as always enhanced her personality with a touch of glamour. For me, she was familiar territory. I was comfortable with her. I drifted away from

Ramona, and for a while I was back with Joanie. Of course that didn't last long; her frigidity always created tension. I may have given a thought to getting back to Ramona, but another woman intervened.

Sheila Morton was slender and had straight black hair that fell down her neck in lustrous tresses. Her body was perfect in a neat, curvy way. She had expressive brown eyes that were very alert and then danced brightly when she discussed books or painting. She was a native New Yorker with a good job at NBC and seemed to me quite clever. Also, she loved to drink. We drank like troopers, once celebrating my birthday at the bar of the Fifth Avenue Hotel with the movie actress Veronica Lake and a fellow named Chuck Hershey who said that it was their birthday, too.

One thing I'll always remember about Sheila Morton is how she would undress and then don a sweater of mine and stroll about my apartment in the Village, her perfect legs extending from below my sweater, the hem of which cut enticingly across the very top of her thighs. We should have become serious but we didn't and eventually she left New York. By then I'd gotten her fired from NBC by keeping her up too late and hugging her too long in the morning. When she moved out, she moved all the way to Rhode Island. I never saw her again.

Stitched in here somehow was Samantha Crichton. I began seeing her in the spring. She was slender like Sheila Morton but was very much a blond. She had soft light blond hair and, as I recall, a kind of cockeyed smile. In June I took her up to the Vineyard and we fell for each other, going alone to the barren Atlantic beach at Zack's Cliffs.

We never consummated our love, however, because for me Samantha was too delicate, too fragile. She'd been raised in New Zealand, the daughter of a career diplomat. She seemed uneasy with herself, having been lugged about as a girl, not having a real home. Or at least that was the reason I gave myself for not wanting to hurt her. Though I pretended that nothing could hurt me, I was sick of hurting others.

I broke up with Samantha, sending her from my bedroom. I couldn't have intercourse with her because I knew what that would mean: we would become serious lovers for the long haul, and I was not going to get married. She was far too nice and too vulnerable to lead on and then bail out. There was a wonderful, trusting spirit in her, and I dared not tamper with it. When a perplexed Samantha Crichton left my apartment, I tried to understand the confusion in my life but gave up. Everything seemed out of kilter. Before long I'd be en route out of the city.

• • •

By Christmas of 1959 Fidel Castro was winning the revolution in Cuba. On Christmas Eve I was drinking heavily at Joe Allen's, a bar on the East Side, with "Miss Innocence," Joan the junior ad saleslady. Suddenly I had the urge to link up with Castro and march into Havana as part of his entourage. I left Joan and took a taxi to Idlewild Airport, bent on Havana, but I missed the last plane. By then I was so irrational I shudder now to think what Castro's men would have done with me. I probably would have been shot.

Out at the airport, with the last flight to Havana now airborne, I had to take stock. It was almost Christmas morning. I'd turned down a chance to visit my parents in Palm Springs. I did not want to see my sister, whose own life was a mess of family and lover and her ability to rise above it all. My brother, who now lived near San Francisco, was never an option. As my addled mind rolled on, I suddenly thought of Bill and Nana Allis, drinking partners from Europe. I caught the last flight to Milwaukee.

The Allises had a most fetching house guest visiting them from London. Her name was Sonia. Her husband had been a bomber pilot. She was splendid to view, and a riot of humor and quick retorts, and when her husband flew off to Canada for business the day after Christmas, she became allied with me. After a marathon of drinking and revelry, we flew back to New York together, drinking champagne all the way. Sonia's husband, Thomas, had reserved a room at the Ambassador East on Park Avenue, the same hotel my parents used to stay in years ago during the Depression. Thomas wasn't due to return for another day. We ascended to Sonia's room, where we ordered drinks from room service. We were just getting undressed when we heard a key in the lock. Thomas had come back a day early. Surprise.

Thomas, a master of British *sang froid*, never directed a word of criticism toward me as I awkwardly dressed before him. Later I gathered from Sonia that he did not upbraid her either. He flew off again and in two days' time she felt free to see me at my place in the Village. Before she left she gave me a photo of herself that I placed on the wall. She had told me of how she skied nude across the glaciers of Europe. It was a vivid description and I thought of her that way for a long time.

Off and on I asked Nana about Sonia but never got any news except that eventually Thomas divorced her. Finally, in 1988, I asked again and was told that she'd traveled into grimmer venues, a victim of a party that never ended. It has been forty years since we last met. Sonia was a wild, beautiful, antic woman, and she is probably gone from this earth. I hardly knew her, yet she remains, very vivid, in my memory.

•   •   •

In late 1959 Charlie Duell decided to sell out to the Meredith Publishing Company. This was a nice merger for him, since he would become executive vice president at Meredith, a very profitable company famous for the successful magazine *Better Homes and Gardens*. Meredith was developing a line of trade books, and Duell, Sloan and Pearce, with its peculiar backlist and current publications, appeared attractive: balladeering books by Alan Lomax and Burl Ives and works by Dr. Spock and Margaret Bourke-White and Erskine Caldwell and now the popular Dick Harraty and General George Kenney. The merger looked good for everyone.

Cap Pearce would trail along filling a role as senior editor. But what pleased me was that Charlie wanted me to go as well as his executive assistant. I'd get a big raise and benefits. I would be on my way in "big time" New York publishing. Even with all of my drinking and flirting and traveling back and forth to the Vineyard, I had been dependable and bright and good-natured. I'd done what I was asked and was never out sick. What mattered to Charlie was that he was giving up the old brownstone and a million memories. I'd only come in on the tail end of it, yet I felt the impact. I'd stayed late so many nights, sitting at my desk near Margaret Wilson's office as she toiled at her job. The old brownstone seemed to breathe when I walked through the doorway out onto Fourth Avenue, a silent partner to so much roaring laughter and joy and craft and edification.

As I considered my elevation in a much bigger publishing company, I shuddered at where it might lead. I saw phoniness everywhere, and though in some respects I was drawn to it, it also repelled me. One time I'd taken Estes Kefauver's sister for drinks at the Stork Club. I'd met her somewhere up on the West Side, where she was a teacher in a public school. I was so struck by this plain, anonymous woman whose brother had run for vice president that I took her out on the town. At the Stork Club all I had to do was mention that she was Senator Kefauver's sister and management extended its arms. "Anything for you, Mr. Hart. Why, of course, come right this way." My success at name-dropping was so appalling that we laughed at it over drinks.

Amusing in its sick way, the effect of dropping Estes Kefauver's name was symbolic of New York City. The more I thought of the smarmy toadiness of the city, the more I detested it. Once when I stopped at the Russian Tea Room to idle for an hour before meeting Sheila Morton, I ran into an actress I thought was Barbara Rush. She was weeping next to me at the bar. I could not console her. Running off to Sheila's, I felt like weeping myself. The city was indifferent and there was too much pain everywhere. Even for movie stars. I'd had it. When Sheila moved to Rhode Island, I decided to move out too. I told Charlie Duell that I could not go on to Meredith with him. Astounded, the old Yale man told me that I was turning my back on a great career in book publishing. The clubs: Dutch Treat, Coffee House, Century…they were his and they would be mine. Interesting people and exciting projects. I was mad not to see what lay in store, he said.

I couldn't make it in law school because of my stammer. Now in New York, with my stammer almost nonexistent, I was once again looking for an exit.

Chapter 12

In the summer of 1958 David McCullough was working for *Architectural Forum* and living with his wife, Rosalee, in Wilton, Connecticut. I'd known Rosalee McCullough since she was fourteen, when she used to be Rosalee Barnes. She was a very pretty spectator at the softball games on Martha's Vineyard when her brother Sam and I played. I'd always loved Rosalee, who was totally adorable. Everyone knew that David, who was presented to us as an artist—he was excellent with water colors—would go places. He'd started out at *Sports Illustrated* right out of Yale and then moved on within the structure of Time Inc.

That summer I took Joanie and David and Rosalee over to Nantucket on my father's small powerboat to spend the night. We checked in at the Nantucket Yacht Club for a drink and spotted Roy Larsen, the president of Time Inc., sitting near us. To my amazement, David left our table and walked over, extended his hand, and introduced himself. A toiler from the lower depths had just said "hi ya" to the top man in the executive suite. Such aplomb. I looked over at Rosalee and then Joanie. He had confirmed what we knew in our bones: he was going places.

In February 1959 David called my office to tell me that he and Rosalee were planning a trip to St. Croix for a short vacation. Why didn't I fly down for the weekend? I had only been on the job at Duell, Sloan and Pearce for a couple of months, but I rationalized that two months in Manhattan for me was half a lifetime for anyone else. I was already frazzled from the pace and chilled by the winds that blew down the cavernous avenues, and my feet were always wet from hustling about on sloppy streets. I told Charlie Duell I was off for a long weekend and he told me to get going.

The three of us booked rooms at the old Comanche, owned by a former Navy carrier pilot named Ted Dale. There was a pool and a bar. I drank heavily for three days and became sunsick, the tropical sun turning me pink and blistering me. I'd been in the tropics before, to Nassau and Puerto Rico, but of late I had let myself get soft and white as porcelain and the sun bore into me. Most likely the weekend would have meant nothing had I not met an assertive woman named Elizabeth Birmingham.

Raven-haired Liz lived in Manhattan, where she was a gallery owner. She was very proud of being a woman who knew Willem de Kooning and Jackson Pollack. She was a woman entitled to the best, and her presence in St. Croix contrasted with our discovered paradise of Cruzans, laid-back black people who beamed their happiness at us. The aquamarine water lapped on sandy beaches and the palm trees swayed in the trade winds. Set against this beneficent world of love and nature was the pretentious Elizabeth—hard-edged, if not rapacious. While I intoned on the unspoiled beauty of St. Croix, Liz saw an island ripe for development and in need of a good gallery to attract the elite in the art world. Getting to know her made me ponder my career in New York City. Getting to know her made me yearn for St. Croix and natural beauty.

Out of curiosity I dallied with Liz after I returned to New York. I had never met anyone so money-oriented. Liz was a harbinger of the upscale yuppies I'd meet thirty years later. To me, she epitomized the bad form, the excess, the pushiness of New York.

One evening Liz produced a brother, and the brother produced a blue Rolls-Royce. We drove up into the country west of the Hudson River and dined, la-di-da, on pheasant in a grand country inn. When the check came, it was passed to me. "After all," said Liz, "we rented the Rolls. You can take care of this little matter." With that, she edged the tab toward me. Luckily I had brought along a blank Hanover Bank check. But I had been taken. No one had mentioned the Rolls, the restaurant, or the Hudson River. Charlie Duell was paying me $50 a week, gross. I took home $37.50. The huge tab at a restaurant where I'd surmised I'd be treated to dinner rankled me. A few evenings later she had me over to her small apartment and quickly undressed, positioned herself in bed, and waited for me. By now I had begun to consider backing off, not only from Elizabeth Birmingham but from everything she represented. I looked at her body, all white skin with a black patch, and I simply walked away. Her flat stomach looked like the underbelly of a skate, and the wiry black triangle no longer held any allure. I told her I didn't feel well and I skipped out the door and kept walking.

• • •

I would return to St. Croix in March 1960. But just prior to that I went down to the Vineyard and bought an old building in North Tisbury, a little community within the rural village of West Tisbury. I paid $10,000 for a winterized structure that had once served as the home and ice cream parlor of Ole Bergen. When I was a small child, my father or grandfather would drive me and other children to Ole's for his homemade ice cream. We always stopped there on the way back from Cousin Carrie's beach and bought chocolate soda pop bottled by Tashmoo Springs in Vineyard Haven. Ole had a stuffed owl, and that, along with his Old World Scandinavian charm and the ice cream and cold soda pop on a hot July day, made the experience of stopping in North Tisbury indelible. Other than Harthaven and our camp in Chilmark, my warmest feelings rested in the very house I was lucky enough to purchase.

My idea, plotted with enthusiasm in New York, was to own two bookstores. I'd operate one in St. Croix where there was none and another in the old ice cream parlor on the Vineyard, in competition with a highly eccentric operation in Edgartown, the Borrowdale Bookshop. Borrowdale's was a small, understocked shop squeezed in the back of a carelessly maintained house owned by a prep school headmaster. He and his daughter served the whole island in a haphazard fashion. But by the beginning of the '60s a literate public was emerging and the island needed a real bookstore. I aimed to furnish the Vineyard with a bookshop and coffeehouse or café in combination, and I'd run it in the summer months. In the winter I'd be in St. Croix managing the sister operation. I would call them both Red Cat after Joan Johnston whose red pussy had been an unceasing delight to me.

• • •

St. Croix and Martha's Vineyard were very similar. In 1960 both islands had yet to be developed, although word was beginning to seep out about their beauty and people were moving to them and constructing resort homes at an ever-increasing rate. But each island was still in the shadow of a sister island, respectively, St. Thomas and Nantucket. St. Croix and the Vineyard were roughly the same size. They were informal. Back then, each had wide open spaces to explore and miles and miles of beaches not yet claimed as "private property." On both St. Croix and the Vineyard, if you knew your way about you could pretty much have the run of the place and you'd never have to wear a tie again or even a sport jacket. In the last days of Eisenhower's presidency both islands were unspoiled by commerce, but that would change. The Vineyard soon fell prey to developers and lost much of its charm. St. Croix would also fall prey to "progress," but back then, when I first landed on St. Croix, I thought I had landed in heaven.

At the bar at Joe Allen's on New York's East Side, I had met a fellow about my age named Center Hitchcock—"as in the center of a circle," he said, leaning against the bar. Center, as he quickly told me, had a guest house and a Jaguar, both in Frederiksted on the west side of St. Croix. "Be my guest," he said, and I answered that indeed I would.

Center was a hard-looking guy with a slightly pockmarked face and a thin body that could be graceful. His late uncle was once America's premier polo star, Tommy Hitchcock. Center elided his syllables like a true blue blood from Long Island. I had trouble following his sentences. He shared a house with a handsome guy named Geist Ely, the two of them offering their friends a twenty-four-hour, day-in, day-out party. As women in bikinis strolled about, all vestiges of modesty went out the window.

They allowed me to stay on, and before long I was able to lease a building in Christiansted for my store, the Red Cat Bookstore and Bar. I acquired a liquor license and began ordering books—best-sellers and useful handyman books.

Back in New York, my pal Sam Barnes was getting married. I flew up to be an usher and attend him at the Little Church Around the Corner. There was a woman who attended the wedding, a friend of the bride, named Marie Zoll. I was struck by her friendly nature, and caught up in the spirit of the wedding, we went back to my apartment on West Twelfth Street where I was still locked in by a lease. We romanced each other in New York City and I even took her to New Britain and, inspired, I asked her to marry me.

After Sam Barnes's wedding I flew back to St. Croix to attend to business. Now unofficially engaged to Marie, I was not in St. Croix for more than a couple of days when I met a vacationing college girl, Wendy Smith. She was staying at a wild restaurant-inn called The Reef and Sand, where Richard and Claire Sherman ran an outcast-of-the-islands hostelry for drinking yourself silly and eating gourmet cooking prepared by either Claire or the angular Australian woman, Bettina. I had gotten to know them through my cousin, a New Britain, Connecticut, transplant and architect, Allen Moore. His wife Jennie was Wendy Smith's best friend. Both Geist and Center could be found at The Reef and Sand and one time I passed out there to awake and find myself nude with Bettina who was caressing me and telling me I had the greatest skin she'd ever known. Sam and Joy spent their honeymoon at The Reef and Sand and they were joined by me for drinks and hi-jinks. All the while Richard Sherman piped Lester Lanin's society dance music in over the loudspeaker. Songs such as "I've Got You Under My Skin" and "In A Mountain Greenery" (where God paints the scenery) suffused the area. The general ambiance was tropical Jazz Age with merengue joining Lena Horne and Louis Armstrong and the prevailing society bounce of Lester Lanin interceding at will. Sometimes in the mornings you'd awake to Lester Lanin's "Just In Time" or "Just One Of Those Things" and looking out into the courtyard you'd see Bettina asleep, tangled in the limbs of a Eucalyptus tree.

Into this insane atmosphere came a very young Wendy Smith. She took a room at the hotel where the Barneses were staying and I moved in across the hall. During the day we played golf and went to the beach, driving to Sandy Point where there was no one but us, just sand and sea. Eventually we became quite friendly, and the night before she was to leave she mentioned marriage.

There I was, nearly thirty years old, already an alcoholic if not yet a drunkard, thoughtlessly engaged to a Marie Zoll whom I hardly knew. I had no prospects other than my idealized life of matching Red Cats and a tropical/Vineyard lifestyle of drinking, bookselling, beachgoing, and an early death. And on that score the prospect of dying at age forty-five from cirrhosis of the liver did not bother me a bit. I was having such a grand time. Nothing dire dared to cross my mind.

Wendy Smith was twenty-two. She had soft brown hair and possessed the allure of a woman athlete. I'd always been attracted to such women: I liked the look of outdoor women. Girls who could keep up and "run like a boy" I imagined to be lifelong buddies. Wendy was a superb athlete. She was an Olympic-level skier, an excellent golfer, and decades later would be ranked number two in the nation in senior squash. We were both Connecticut people, and her chummy ways enchanted me. She would graduate from Sarah Lawrence in a couple of months. I took her mention of marriage as a proposal and I thought it over and then I thought, *yes, why not?*

Down deep, far below my cavalier attitude about an early death, lay a desire to live. I had a yen to be returned to normalcy. I simply knew in my bones that I'd drink myself to death or die in a car crash or fall off a boat and drown. In its casual acceptance of libertine impulses, St. Croix was like the vision of Hollywood I had rejected back when Burl Ives and Elia Kazan had offered it to me. Wendy represented a return to Connecticut, not as the son of my troubled parents but as a husband who had taken a prize for a wife, a girl who projected a glint of old-family class, money, a good golf swing—a way of life that ran deep within the establishment that ran America. She would please my father: he'd note her schools, Westover and Sarah Lawrence, and view them as solid like his own, Hotchkiss and Yale. I, too, liked what she represented. Of course I did not know the woman at all.

"Why not?" I said. "Let's get married." It was clear to me that she'd dropped in from the heavens to save me.

But what to do with Marie Zoll, who was flying down to visit Sam and Joy Barnes and me the day after Wendy flew back north to return to Sarah Lawrence? For a few days Marie and I stayed together in the room next door to the honeymooners, Sam and Joy Barnes. I drank very heavily trying to wash away my guilt, for I had decided that I simply had to choose Wendy. Life with Marie would be the same old thing—a very dangerous party life. Marie Zoll was wonderful to me. She was slender and blond and kissable and would have made a fine partner as I led the two of us into the jaws of death. I talked this over with Allen Moore, and his wife, Jennie, who was Wendy's best friend. They assured me that I had to choose the preppy girl from Farmington over Joy Barnes's friend. "Wendy is rich," said Jennie. "You'll love the family," said Allen. "They are drinkers," which was a comment that warmed my heart. Weakly, I agreed, and then I went back to Marie and told her our engagement was off. There was someone else. She seemed heartbroken, but in time she married a far nicer and saner person than I, and, as I understand it, had a fulfilling life.

• • •

I stayed on in St. Croix until June, when I flew north to open my Vineyard store. By now a ton of books had arrived. The shop needed work. I had furniture in storage, and Dave McCullough helped me cart it up to the store, where we furnished the upstairs with a bed, a dresser, and some chairs. I was expected to attend Wendy's graduation later that month. There was also a huge engagement party at her parents', at which Russ Hart, my cousin, hit a golf ball that traveled so far off the lawn that it landed on a passing car, far out of sight. Days later an injured party traced the ball back to Olcott D. Smith's house on Mountain Spring Road. There may have been a settlement of some kind. I was not in the litigatory loop, being down on the Vineyard at the time. With a shudder, I briefly recalled Denver and the woman whose father had died, though in the glow of my engagement such an errant thought did not last more than a minute.

My St. Croix bookstore-bar was being run by a woman named Anne Riley. Anne was a free spirit who had once lived up in St. Croix's mahogany jungle, where she ran with abandon over the green grass in the lush countryside. I could have lived out my life with her up in the backlands of St. Croix, and I gleefully hired her. Unfortunately, the cash register seldom rang. The local folks enjoyed it: there was chess and cheap rum, but no one was lining up to buy best-sellers.

On the Vineyard business was better. I opened the Red Cat Café and Bookstore with a full stock of books and hired my sister, Bideau, to run the kitchen. I also took on Kim Hart, a cousin, and Bideau's daughter, Lucy. A brunette named Nancy rounded out my staff. We turned out full-course lobster dinners at night and lobster rolls for lunch. Customers brought their own liquor and wine. Wendy was usually in Connecticut, while I spent a good portion of my summer days swimming in Gay Head with Alfred Eisenstaedt and his wife, Kathy. No one wore bathing suits, and though I was engaged to be married, I could not help but notice some of the lovely girls, lying supine on the beach. I wondered about my capacity for fidelity as I studied the women up at Zack's Cliffs. How could I be faithful? Every young woman I saw, I wanted.

As it turned out, Wendy did not like Martha's Vineyard, disapproved of my drinking, never cared about the store, had no use for my family, and was positively leery of my sister, who seemed so liberated.

Wendy preferred the Connecticut shore, her summer home at Fenwick on Long Island Sound. On the Vineyard I sold books and served food to Katherine Cornell and her crowd who would drive up from her house at Tashmoo, or to Leonard and Felicia Bernstein and Lillian Hellman and all kinds of bright, creative people who loved the idea of a bookstore-café. Certainly the people who worked for me—my sister and Kim and Nancy—were more spontaneous and quicker-witted than the folks at Fenwick. Wendy looked displeased, and I could imagine her frowning over anything that disturbed her. Though caught up in the idea of an engagement, she entertained second thoughts about a wedding, and I could see that the way I lived on the Vineyard irritated her.

As for me, I rolled through the summer, trying to avoid weekends at the Connecticut shore, working instead to improve my new enterprise, using the Red Cat Café and Bookstore as a shield against the banal existence of conforming people in Fenwick. As the summer bore on into late September, we were married. On that day both bookstores were doomed. For a brief moment I had been my own boss, doing what I loved doing, living the way I wanted to live. I had tried and almost succeeded in overcoming the limiting forces that ruled my childhood, once so obvious in my stammer. With my marriage, pressure and limitations came tumbling back.

I sold for $7,500, an inherited house in Harthaven, one which I seldom used. I sold it in order to pay for a first class cabin on the *Leonardo da Vinci* to Gibraltar and a grand tour of Spain and France by rented Opel. The wedding was huge—the guests all said the same thing: she was *Olcott Smith's only daughter, you know*—and my father danced up a storm. The ceremony took place in Hartford at St. John's Episcopal Church. We had to wait for my sister, who arrived almost an hour late. The service was held up so she could sit up front beside my father. My mother was far too incapacitated to go to the wedding. Her sister, Fannie (Wad), took her place. My brother, whom I had dutifully asked to be my best man, stayed in California and never even replied to my offer. I assume now that he feared seeming out of place in Farmington. His social graces were so ill formed that he avoided the whole matter without a word of explanation.

My ushers were Al Pease, my cousin, whom I sailed with; Art Stedman from my Air Force days; Sam Barnes; and David McCullough. Wendy's three brothers were ushers as well. My best man, Don Kipp, had been a Wesleyan classmate and fraternity brother. He had also been with me and Art Stedman in the Air Force. I thought it was a stellar group of friends. Unfortunately I found it increasingly difficult to see them once I got married. Wendy, after all, had come from "the first family of Connecticut," a statement from her lips that gave me pause. Her mother's family, the Brainerds, had been major stockholders of the Aetna Life and Casualty Company. There was money in insurance, but to me insurance was a nuisance one had to endure, and hardly a candidate for prestige. When she spoke of her "first family," I let it sail by. When I began losing contact with my ushers, I felt a sadness that rankled me on and off for our entire marriage.

I should have seen my error in this match, but the truth is that I loved Wendy Smith. She looked so wholesome, and it was her wholesomeness that I fell for. I refused to see her conflicts that wrestled below the surface, as she refused to see mine. I could not imagine a mean streak in Wendy. She was fresh as a meadow, and I was drawn to her glow, although her father, Olcott, tried to warn me. Just prior to our wedding he took me aside and led me into the study of their large brick house in Farmington.

"Wendy is like me," he began. "She has my temperament, my ways, my outlook on things." I brushed him off. As far as I could see, Olcott was a wonderful chap, a good tennis player, an apparent success at the law, someone who had married very well and sired four reasonably attractive children. He lived as a millionaire should. He had a three-story house with a pool, a tennis court, and a paddle tennis court. He owned a house and grounds, big enough for the largest of weddings. Olcott drank as I would if his daughter would allow me: he drank for relaxation, not to get tight. Certainly I liked that about him. If Wendy Smith had a nature similar to her father, so much the better. We left the study arm in arm. He'd warned me, he said. The only trouble was, I didn't see it as a warning at all. I liked Olcott Smith.

Just about one month into our wedding trip I suffered a terrible nervous breakdown. We were sleeping at the Hotel Continental in Nice, and in the middle of a violent thunderstorm I awoke screaming in terror. The previous afternoon Wendy and I had walked past the Bar O'Connor, where I'd done so much drinking with Madame Cognac. That period of my life seemed a decade in the past, but it had not yet been three years. Madame Cognac could have been inside as we paused on the street. I was anxious to go in for a drink. Indeed, my whole system, my history, my future, my life itself was pushing me toward that barroom door. Thus far on our trip I'd felt constrained. Now, I so much wanted to introduce my wife to the "real me," the person who belonged in a bar just like the one in front of us. I wanted her to share my life. There was no one in the Bar O'Connor who would embarrass us. Madame Cognac would be understanding: she'd seen it all and she would welcome Wendy with approval written on her face. Monsieur Stanley, she'd called me...I was proud to present to all the familiar hangers-on, my wife.

Wendy exploded: she saw me leaning toward the door, a wistful look in my eye. "That filthy *bar!* You want to go in there, don't you?" she cried, gasping in fright. "That *bar!*" There were two words she always underlined—*drink* and *bar*—and this was not the first time I'd noticed it. I shrank back like a shriveled penis. I cowered and turned my head. We walked on, but I trembled in my soul. My life was in the hands of a censor. I had hoped for an ally. I was the last person on earth who should be living with someone who hated drinking. I stumbled through the rest of the day and the evening meal like a man with no name, someone suffering amnesia. I knew only one thing: I was a lover of life who needed drink to pull it off, and I'd married someone who was taking my life away.

That night a wicked thunderstorm struck Nice and I fell into a fitful sleep. Soon I was dreaming of Tony Perkins at the Bates Motel. I saw him dressed like his mother and I saw him stabbing at Janet Leigh. I awoke screaming and turned to Wendy, who was wearing an ugly beehive of a bonnet to protect her hair, rolled in curlers for the night. At this frightening sight of my wife in a bonnet full of curlers, I again saw Tony Perkins dressed as his mother and I screamed in terror and couldn't stop screaming. Finally I wept for what seemed the entire night. A doctor was summoned. He had to make his way to the hotel through a torrent of rain, beneath God-awful bolts of lightning cutting apart an angry sky. He came into the room carrying a black medicine bag like a mad doctor in a horror movie. I lay there convulsed in deep sobs, totally absorbed in stark fear. He gave me a shot and prescribed pills. Soon I slipped into a drugged sleep.

If we were to go home ahead of schedule, I alone would have to arrange for a change of tickets at American Express. Wendy told me she would have no part of this: what would she tell her family and her friends? How could we properly explain an abbreviated honeymoon? The morning after my breakdown found me in line at the American Express counter, shaking and ashen-faced. Gregory Peck was behind me. He looked sympathetic, as though he understood there was something the matter with me. I did not think I could hold out, and I wanted to speak to him. Desperate, I wanted to tell him about Burl Ives and our sails on Long Island Sound, about June Havoc and John Houseman and other people Burl had introduced me to. Both knowing the same people would make us friends. It would be a way to stop my shaking and to keep me from falling apart.

Mr. Peck and I spoke only when I said good-bye. At the counter I was able to change our tickets. As I left the large office, other Americans were beginning to fall in line to pick up their mail, as I had done in the time of Madame Cognac. But I could not afford to remember those free and easy days lest I collapse again. I held our new tickets in my hand and quickly walked back to the hotel. My wife was waiting for me. She kept repeating: How could we tell her friends and her family that we just quit our honeymoon and went home? It wouldn't do to describe a husband crying hysterically into the night. She stared at me as I presented the tickets. We flew home that same day.

Earlier, there had been a close call when I almost killed my wife. We had taken the ferry from Alicante to Majorca. From Palma we drove up to Cape Formentor, a stunning promontory at the opposite side of the island. We spent the night in a fine hotel, the Palace de Formentor, into which I had to talk our way. Apparently they screened all their guests—Leslie Caron and her husband were there—and they knew nothing of us, two newlyweds arriving with no reservation.

The beach was a pleasant strip marked with beach umbrellas, but the fall winds were bringing a chill. I remember sneaking two gin and tonics at the bar before dinner. At dinner we shared a bottle of wine, and when we went to bed I felt fairly relaxed, but by the next day Wendy was criticizing me again.

Often she complained about the way I had lived my life, my friends, of whom she was leery, and my family, whom she viewed with dismay. Once she berated me for having been an enlisted man: Why weren't you a fighter pilot? Why didn't you fly jets? I tried to explain that those who worked on the flight line also served. I told her my work was *top secret*, maintaining the system that would drop the hydrogen bomb should war erupt, but I was overruled. Perhaps I was overly sensitive. I was, after all, an alcoholic looking for a drink in order to relax. But it did seem that I was always defending my checkered life and as we stopped to look at the sea from atop the promontory, I had my chance. We had parked the Opel and walked across to a tremendous drop. She was on her toes, looking down a giant plunge of a thousand feet to the shore, awash with a crashing surf. There was no one near us, no one for miles. I felt a compulsion to push. No one would ever know the truth. My wife had tripped and fell. But...I still loved her. I thought, *she is probably right in finding fault with me.* I turned and started walking back to the car, thankful that I had come to my senses.

•   •   •

I have always deflected thoughts of my first marriage. For me it was an endurance test and too difficult to describe. Now, as I face my memories, I can see that much of the tension in our marriage came from me. My drinking and my outlook, focused on pleasure more than responsibility, made it extremely difficult for Wendy. As an alcoholic bent on having a good time, I was a poor partner in marriage. Especially with someone who deplored heavy drinking. I could not conceive of not drinking heavily, and it was inevitable that I should upset my wife and elicit her scorn. When our marriage was filled with misery, it was so because of my drinking. Whenever I felt her sharp words, and when her agitated demeanor was manifest, I should have looked inward. I never did. I found fault with Wendy when it was I who was triggering the despair and the vituperation with my own scandalous behavior. I believe I thought I was humorous and lovable. The opposite was the case, as far as my healthy and hopeful wife was concerned. And that was how it remained, year after year.

We moved down to St. Croix in October, where I rented a house in Frederiksted. Allen and Jennie Moore were nearby, living above an apothecary. At the other end of Cricky Dam Road on the north shore lived Anne Riley with her husband, Karl. The Nelthrop brothers, Cedric and Douglas, were new friends. I was writing a novel (which I completed but never got published). I'd write in the mornings, go for a swim with Wendy, and then the two of us would drive over to the St. Croix Tennis Club for doubles. It was a wonderful way to live. For a while she was content, or so it seemed. Because of my novel I felt fulfilled—I had a mission. I kept my drinking to wine and beer, an occasional cognac or stingers. We both were healthy, and in my mind I felt that we were accomplishing something. I had asked Douglas Nelthrop to build me a house on some land I had purchased, and my architect cousin, Allen Moore, produced a design. I couldn't imagine anyone wanting to leave St. Croix.

Attitudes can change with the passage of time. When our first summer came, Wendy was very pregnant and very interested in leaving. It wouldn't do, she said, to have a child in St. Croix. Since we had to journey home to have our baby, why not just stay there? Reluctantly, I agreed. I wanted to stay married, and with a baby on the way, I had no choice. The house, now half-built, was left like a dream that could never come true.

Soon we were at Fenwick, and I was dispatched to New York to look for work. A man named Ward Cheney, who was venerated by Olcott Smith, offered to help. We lunched at two of his clubs, the Lynx and the Brook. Quite rich, he had connections in book publishing. He was a friendly patron, but his attempts at securing me a job in the publishing world came to naught. Caught up as I was in Ward Cheney's efforts, I never thought to ask Charlie Duell for help until the end of the summer. When I did, he told me I would be unhappy at Meredith, but he thought I would do well at Little, Brown in Boston. He'd heard that young Arthur Thornhill, the vice president, was looking for help, and he offered to write a letter on my behalf.

And so, without Olcott Smith or Ward Cheney, I found work in Boston. At least Boston was near the Vineyard. Had I found a job in New York and settled in, say, Westchester County, as I write this now, I realize I could still be there, in New York—or dead.

We had a son at the end of July, named after me. In time we moved to Dover, outside Boston, and then later into Needham, where our daughter joined us. Finally we moved into a very large house on the Sargent Estate in Brookline. I started work at Little, Brown in September 1961. St. Croix was a thing of the past even though I now owned a house there, completed at last, perched on the top of Mount Welcome with a spectacular 270-degree view of the Caribbean. Neither I nor my wife had mentioned the house as it was being constructed. Even in its beginning stages, it was best not to broach the subject. I think I knew in my heart that Wendy would never live in it. The house, which had a small swimming pool, was to be our home in the tropics, where I would write and, at night, we'd entertain. We'd raise a family there. We'd have children who would take to the sea and become scuba divers, sailors, children of the out-of-doors. But that was my dream, not hers, and it had to go.

When I flew down to sell the house, I met a married woman I'd slept with once in my island days at Center Hitchcock's. I took a ride up Mount Welcome to say good-bye to the house in which I was never allowed to sleep. I had the married lady with me, and as the house was completely furnished, she saw a bed and plopped herself down on it. She lay there and looked at me. I read her mind: we might as well initiate the bed and bedroom before everything was sold. I turned her down. I refused to be unfaithful, although by then fealty to a marriage license had no moral hold on me. But if there was going to be a traitor it wouldn't be me, at least not then. I felt the treachery had already occurred in my wife's rejection of my dream. Without explanation it had been assumed that the life I had planned didn't matter and had never mattered.

In Frederiksted with Wendy, I'd hear the steel drums from near our house. Youngsters practiced them. Everyone loved the sound of steel drums. To me the drums went with the palm trees and the beaches and the informality that freed me from old fears.

In time I would grow wistful remembering the Reef and Sand, Center Hitchcock with his celebrity guestbook and grand parties, even the Frederiksted church on Easter Sunday with the wonderful singing of hymns, the rising voices of Cruzans which swelled from the pews. Often, flashes of dirt roads and dense foliage would cross my mind as did images of Jenny Moore and Anne Riley. I'd left it all behind before I really got to know it. In memory I imagined so much that I missed, and in my loss I was reminded, often, of the weakness of resolve that so surely defined my character.

Chapter 13

By the time I joined Little, Brown in September 1961, Arthur Thornhill, Jr., though still vice president, was running the company. His father, Arthur Thornhill, Sr., was president and chairman of the board, but by then the elder Thornhill was concentrating on book clubs and paperback companies to which he could assign reprint rights. I was aware that there was no one in the industry who could sell a hardcover book to the book trade or to a paperback house for a cheaper edition as well as "Senior" (as we referred to him behind his back). As for the Book-of-the-Month Club and the Literary Guild, these appeared also to be in Arthur Senior's pocket. As the '60s rolled on, it was my practice to bring a manuscript or project to Senior for his evaluation regarding reprint income. Then I would address the amount of the advance. When I found I could sign Lillian Hellman for $60,000, it took only a few minutes for Senior to report that our income in club and paperback sales would far exceed that amount.

"Junior," as we called young Arthur, was a slender, well-dressed bright light and a usually agreeable man. He was dedicated to the "imprint," which is how the Thornhills referred to Little, Brown. He hired me over lunch at Locke-Ober. I liked him at once. He'd flown "the Hump" in World War II, flying as a navigator out of Burma over the Himalayas. There was a touch of glamour to this fellow, I thought. Not too many years older than I, he must have been very young when he was sent into India. I did not talk about it, but I always had a good deal of respect for Arthur Junior, much of it because of his service during the war. I would have joined Little, Brown anyway, but when Junior told me that he'd flown the Hump, he had me eager to join him and become a part of his firm.

Junior sought to be a gentleman publisher of the old school. He dressed in tailored suits and wore shiny black shoes and sported a gray fedora. I never saw him mussed. His soft, wavy black hair was compressed without an errant strand. He had a mind that was quick and worked well with figures and contingencies and planning and interaction with various publishing groups. He had vision and could entertain notions of expansion. Where Arthur Junior fell short was with his product: the basic nature of books—that is to say, literature—was not something with which he was comfortable. Arthur Junior's expertise lay in operations.

His father, by contrast, was a bull in a china shop when it came to operations—after lunch, full of whiskey, he ranted and raved and could not grasp new ideas—but Senior knew books. He read everything that the trade department published. He read pre-published material in either manuscript or galleys. Hardly a single Little, Brown book went to a bookstore unread by Senior. All his life he'd been a reader, and when I met him he was nearly seventy years old and still reading on the commuter bus to work, on the bus home from work, at work, and at home. Never did I hear Junior comment on the contents of a book. His father was just the opposite. The older man loved to talk about what he'd read. In the case of Senior, however, what he read had to be marketable. His comments were overlaid with talk of sales potential.

Publishing literary works for the sake of being literary was not something either man chose to do, yet on occasion an editor at the Atlantic Monthly Press (whose books were published jointly with Little, Brown) would give us a book of quality but with little discernible sales potential. Edward Weeks, the esteemed editor of the *Atlantic Monthly*, often used his prestige to awe Little, Brown into publishing books with marginal sales potential. I remember a book he presented at a sales conference, written by Ernest Hemingway's sister Marcelline. Hemingway had recently killed himself, and both a brother and a sister were capitalizing on it. The sister's book was uneventful, uninteresting, and in the end a self-serving bore. Yet Weeks, with his towering ego and august demeanor, made it sound as if we were going to have a hit on our hands. I'd already read the manuscript, as had Senior. It was weak stuff, but no one dared cross Ted Weeks. I looked toward Senior at the head of the table as Weeks droned on and I could read his mind: *Ted Weeks has all the presence of a great editor but he is also full of shit.*

Our editor in chief, Ned Bradford, would also contract some embarrassments, as would Randy Williams, our vice president and manager of all trade operations. And I, too, sometimes brought in submissions that were suspect. A case in point: after I had been drinking heavily in New York with a long-ago agent named John Starr, I proposed a novel written by Stanley Wolpert, who had authored a best-seller on the assassination of Gandhi, called *Nine Hours to Rama*. *Nine Hours* had been a main selection of the Book-of-the-Month Club. Now, in hand, I had his next novel, *The Expedition*. I'd read some of it on the train coming back from New York and the rest at home, and when I was done, I presented it to the editorial meeting, at which point Randy, reserving judgment, took the manuscript with him to read on his own. Surprisingly, at the next meeting he gave it his approval. By then, however, I'd cooled on *The Expedition*. I'd begun to see it as a predictable, pedestrian story written for the movies; it had no literary value nor was it particularly commercial. I backed away. Randy took it on and rendered his blessing. The book was published as I was leaving the company. I never heard of it again.

Randy Williams used to go to London to talk publishing with English publishers or their counterparts on the continent. Primarily, his mission was to sell foreign rights to books of ours. Sometimes he gave additional purpose to his trips by returning with British books he thought fit for American publication. For example, he would present to us works by John Hadfield. These were collections of little sayings and oddments that Randy thought were charming. Charitably speaking, you could call them novelty books. In truth, they were horribly effete trifles of no value and very out of place in the American market.

To Randy's credit, it was he who picked up American publishing rights to the first volume of Bertrand Russell's autobiography. Not only did the book eventually sell well, but it also gave Little, Brown a cachet, a sudden intellectual gloss to signal that we were a serious publisher, not just a small company with J. D. Salinger and a long backlist including *Fanny Farmer* and Bartlett's *Familiar Quotations*. Bertrand Russell was a controversial genius, a difficult man, and, above all, an acclaimed intellectual. The world of books was stunned by Little, Brown's coup. It was Randy Williams's finest moment. For the most part he read "stock cards" and worked with inventory and was the rock-solid center of the company. He was Little, Brown's version of Margaret Wilson, but more so. Unfortunately, he was quite deaf and his hearing aid didn't appear to help. He'd miss whole conversations and then introduce a topic that had already been addressed. He wore a bow tie like Mr. Chips; he'd once taught at a boys' prep school. In my time, Randy abstained from alcohol, but I'd heard, in the old days, he could become aggressive.

Arthur Junior was very prim and circumspect. He was not inclined to hang about with the common man or common woman. His world began and ended with his devotion to work and home. On occasion he would enjoy his cocktails and allow a burst of emotion to erupt. But his constitution forbade an easy relationship with the world around him, and I did not think he was overly conversant with the subtle changes taking place in America. As the '60s bore on, the women's movement picked up steam; as a young man I was at least part of the contemporary world. Toward the end of my tenure at Little, Brown I was approached, through mutual friends, with the idea of a book by the Boston Women's Health Collective, a publication about, for, and by women. The text would not be censored and would not be filtered through the eyes of men. The "pill" was by now a fact of life. Women were at last free to find and enjoy lovers. As always, there were sexual, emotional, hormonal, and gynecological aspects of female life that were swept under the rug, to be ignored lest they embarrass someone. Women were sick to death of pretending that their sexual and emotional lives were to be discounted. Women's liberation was alive and growing, and to all of this the management at Little, Brown seemed oblivious. After I left, a colleague, Llewellyn Howland, took up the project, *Our Bodies, Ourselves*, but management rejected it. I was told that Arthur called it "too vulgar." By then I owned a bookstore, and the very book I thought I'd discovered I sold by the dozens. Simon and Schuster published *Our Bodies, Ourselves*, and it became a huge best-seller.

There was a time when I had Gail Sheehy and David McCullough in tow, either of whom we could have signed for a modest advance, no more than $5,000. I was on the trail of Joan Didion and Lewis Lapham, both writing for the *Saturday Evening Post*. All four writers were unknown to Ned Bradford and summarily rejected. It was less risky, apparently, to keep publishing A. J. Cronin, C. S. Forester, and the pseudonymous Emilie Loring. Junior's main author was a Colonel Blimp named F. van Wyck Mason who wrote outdated historical fiction. Colonel

Mason lived in Bermuda, and whenever he made one of his infrequent trips to Boston, I'd dutifully shake his hand, but inside I'd wince.

Colonel Mason was the *old* Little, Brown. I wanted a *new* Little, Brown of Gail Sheehy and Joan Didion, Dave McCullough and Lewis Lapham and Pete Hamill, who'd been referred to me by a *Saturday Evening Post* editor named John Appleton. I could argue for these exciting young authors until I was blue in the face, but all the while Ned Bradford would be staring off into space. McCullough and Sheehy and the others were, quite simply, people he'd never heard of.

The last time management backed me, to its detriment, was when I acquired a manuscript with color photographs of Jack Kennedy's scrimshaw collection. I had been looking for a "Kennedy book" because, in the wake of the assassination, America's appetite for books about the late president seemed inexhaustible. A scrimshaw book was the most marginal and unlikely of Kennedy material, and yet, filled with errant enthusiasm, I enlisted Ned Bradford's support. After more sober reflection, I saw my mistake and tried to scratch the book, but it was too late. My admission of bad judgment fell on deaf ears. I think by then no one was listening to me at all anymore. I eventually resigned while the scrimshaw book and the Stanley Wolpert novel I'd discovered were being processed. I'm not sure that I ever saw either book in print. For years I twitched with regret when I thought how my associates had taken my enthusiasm as well placed and not just a symptom of alcoholic excess. Back in the 1960s we were not yet so aware of alcohol's pernicious effects. Almost everyone drank. Someone should have suggested that my judgment was impaired as a result of drink. But I looked all right, and I had, for the most part, done very well.

During the '60s, Little, Brown was my life. There was so much trouble at home by this time that, by contrast, I found joy, humor, friendship, and relief the moment I walked through the door at 34 Beacon Street. In time it became my job to assemble our first list of softcover editions, unimaginatively named Little, Brown Paperbacks. I cleared reprint rights, attended to promotion and ran the editorial meetings. Little, Brown Paperbacks was my affair and I did well at it even though I had to find time for my other functions. In addition to managing the paperback line, I was a hardcover book editor, and I was overseeing all permission requests for reprinting Little, Brown material. Also, I sold serial rights to magazines and oversaw movie and television rights for our authors who did not have agents. By 1963 I was working ten-hour days and coming into the office for a couple of hours each week-end. As the years wore on, I began to sandwich in more and more time in New York following leads. I look back on those days now as the best of all working worlds. I could not conceive of a better job, other than being a professional athlete or a movie star. Work was play. Work was being involved with people, books, ideas, and lunch. Work was drinking with friends. Home life was something I did not think of once I left the driveway.

At the time, Little, Brown was one of the premier trade publishers in America. Not only did we have our own books, but we were also the publishing arm of the Atlantic Monthly Press, an editorial department of the *Atlantic Monthly* magazine, across the Public Gardens on Arlington Street. I was always inspirited by a brisk walk over to their offices up the street from the Ritz-Carlton Hotel.

Outstanding titles from the Atlantic Monthly Press and our own editorial department come to mind: *Edge of Sadness* and *All in the Family* by Edwin O'Connor; *Ship of Fools* by Katherine Anne Porter; *Franny and Zooey* and *Raise High the Roof Beam, Carpenters* by J. D. Salinger. We published fiction by C. S. Forester, A. J. Cronin, J. P. Donleavy, Richard Yates, and Richard Barthelme. *The Incredible Journey* by Sheila Burnford and *Russia and the West under Lenin and Stalin* by George Kennan shared the list with Cronin and Salinger. We published *The Collector* and *The Magus* by John Fowles. *Manhattan Project* by Stéphane Groueff became a best-seller on lists outside New York. Bertrand Russell's book and Masters and Johnson's trailblazing examination of human sexuality, pub-lished by the Little, Brown Medical Division, were huge successes and rid our company of its conservative aura. There were many more. And when I left, I left behind Lillian Hellman, whose four books sold well enough to compensate for all of my errors in judgment.

• • •

A word on Arthur Thornhill, Sr. He was a round man with a shiny, bald head that made me think of the golden dome on the State House next door. Like his son he wore well-pressed tailored suits and glossy shoes. He was natty in the manner of a banker, quick and always alert to the nuance in a voice, the lift of an eyebrow. He was sharp as a pin, but he was not a bookish-looking chap: no tweed jacket and striped tie over oxford shirt for him. And no pipe. No halls of academe resided in his past. He was a tough nut who grew up at Little, Brown helping his father, the custodian, stoke the furnaces at dawn, to heat the old brownstone for the high-toned editors and executives who came in to work at nine. Both Arthur and his father revered Alfred MacIntyre, Little, Brown's chairman.

He never went past high school, learning all he could instead from newspapers and the books published by Little, Brown. Eventually he was promoted into sales by "Mr. MacIntyre," as Senior always called him, and for decades roamed large portions of America carrying his display cases and reading galleys, cavorting with other traveling sales reps—the men, as they were always called. Old-timers could tell tales of Arthur Senior's bulldog tenacity. One tale I heard wasn't flattering. After a day of selling in a large town in the Midwest—it could have been Omaha or Cedar Rapids or Springfield, Illinois—the men from several of the larger houses (Doubleday, Macmillan, Harper's, McGraw-Hill) met for drinks, dinner and then an evening of bowling. Arthur, a bit tipsy, went berserk and began throwing bowling balls. Calmer associates cooled him down and ushered him back to the hotel.

To say that Arthur Senior was high-strung would be an understatement. I never saw him actually go out of control, but I often heard him scream out into the hall and then thunder down the hallway, a furious leader with whiskey under his belt. He loved the "imprint" so much that any malfeasance by one of his minions could, in a flash, become a personal affront.

There were people he didn't like, and at first I was one of them. To him I looked rich and spoiled. I looked Ivy League. When I took on the paperback project, I moved into direct competition with the old man. Selling rights to other companies for paperback reprinting was a source of pride for him. He was a master at it and spent hundreds of New York lunches courting paperback editors and publishers. Suddenly, there I was, about to withhold certain new titles from him and, further, I was going ahead with high-priced quality paperback editions of books that he had already sold to the mass market—to Bantam, Dell, and New American Library. To Arthur this was an invasion of his territory, and one day after lunch he screamed at me over the phone, demanding that I come to his office. I sat for an hour while he scolded me until I couldn't stand it anymore. I finally told him off. I don't know what I said, but I began to yell back: "I am doing my job, goddammit!" At last he asked me to leave, and soon he himself was gone, taking the early bus back to Duxbury where he lived on Boston's South Shore.

The next day he canceled his lunch plans and took me to Locke-Ober. Over lunch he unloaded: he told me his life story—how much books, the company, and his son meant to him. I told him about myself, that I'd gone to a second-rate military school, had been an enlisted man for four years. I did not go to an Ivy League college. We each had four drinks—Canadian Club for Senior, martinis for me. We parted by his office on the second floor, bosom pals. I never lost my affection for him. He became very important to me, perhaps to my detriment, as I took his friendship as a license to follow my instincts.

•   •   •

Not long before my father died in 1963 he gave me his blue Cadillac sedan. It was a 1955 model and he was partial to it, but he had bought a new Cadillac and was upset with the trade-in value and in his fashion said the hell with it and gave it to me. I liked this car. I had so many good memories of driving in it with my father. I had borrowed it to go on dates. It still looked quite grand.

To me. Not to my wife. Wendy did not want a Cadillac in our driveway. We were in Brookline by then, living in a large house with an expansive backyard on the Sargent Estate. Cadillacs belonged in Florida. I should have known she would have detested my Cadillac. Before I married Wendy I'd bought a Sunbeam convertible right off the showroom floor from Roote Motors on Park Avenue. It was dark red with a white top. Though smaller, it reminded me of my Chevrolet with a white top and a white continental kit. (I used to park it in front of the Plaza when Joan Johnston and I slept in style in New York, and the doormen let it stay there.) Anyway, I had owned a foreign car that, though a convertible, was understated and bespoke some sophistication. Once we were married, Wendy made me sell it for a Ford station wagon. That was what young couples who lived in the suburbs drove. I think the Sunbeam sedan was a reminder to her that I was not the husband she'd hoped for, that I had once owned a bookstore-café and had misbehaved in ways she didn't want to think about. So it was good-bye to the Sunbeam.

So selling my father's Cadillac was my second experience of selling a car to please my wife. But it was a gift from my father, and selling it really rankled me. It still does. I sold the car for $500 to an associate at Little, Brown, an editor named Bill Jarrett. He was delighted, but I burned inside. My father, when I told him, was startled and hurt. It was a gift, he said; he didn't expect me to sell it. But then, as was his habit, he let the matter drop.

I write this to show in simple terms how I was directed by my wife. She dictated my taste in automobiles and made me get rid of my bookstore. Certain property of mine didn't look right and furthermore bespoke a nonconformity which disturbed her. She picked our friends—dependable people who had gone to the "right" schools. With Wendy I felt I always had to watch my train of thought; at work my mind ran free, but at home or with guests I was supposed to conform. I had lived in Greenwich Village and spent my time with amusing people, but now in the '60s, just as the rest of the country was at last exploding, I had to live like a banker.

In spite of everything, Wendy probably saved my life. Had I not met her, I would have drunk myself into a bad spot, maybe so bad that there would have been no coming back. People talked about my drinking, though the label *alcoholic* was not yet applied. I could be a drunkard, a hot ticket, a pistol, a party guy…never an alcoholic. Of course I *was* an alcoholic and had been one for many years, going back to my teens on Martha's Vineyard. What kept me immune from the disgraceful label—especially disgraceful in a segment of society that respected what it called "social drinking"—and what freed me to go on so long, was my ability to control my alcoholism, to hold a job, to rebound early in the morning looking no worse for wear.

So, as I reminded myself, things weren't all bad. Wendy had saved me, and by 1963 she had given me two children whom I loved. Beyond that, she had brought me into her family—the Olcott Smiths of Farmington, Connecticut—people who often gave me pleasure. What rankled was her war on my identity, an identity that was inherently shaky but that I was working to make whole—*finding myself* was the expression. I did not wish to be overpowered by a willful woman. Apparently driven by her own pressures, I felt she was harsh in her criticisms. One slip, one faux pas and I was a goner. As for friends, she tried, though people found our marriage strained and sometimes avoided us as a couple. In my biased mind, my wife and her complaints were the problem. I blamed her censure for our unhappiness.

• • •

Going to work was exciting and offered the freedom I hungered for. I loved to be around books. I was drawn to the aura that attends a full, well-stocked bookcase. I rolled through the day like an oiled ball bearing, enjoying my job and the people with whom I worked, people like Alex Williams.

Alex had gone to St. Paul's and Harvard, where he had been a member of the Spee Club, before becoming drama critic for the *Boston Herald* and then associate editor at Little, Brown. Alexander Whiteside Williams lived with his aging mother in a large house in Needham with a tennis court and a lawn that sloped down to the Charles River. He was Yankee Brahmin rich and was a snob to such a degree that he inspired humor: *This guy can't be real.* Alex never married. His social life centered on the Somerset Club and the Tennis and Racquet Club, the T and R, to which he arranged my membership. I guessed that he was sexually repressed and perhaps homosexual in a dark, secret way.

Alex never used the communal men's room at our offices at 34 Beacon. Instead he would walk up Beacon Street to the Somerset Club. When visitors at Little, Brown asked him where the men's room might be, to their amazement he would reply, "I haven't the foggiest." Alex came to work at 9:35, took a long lunch, and left at 4:00. Fridays he left at noon, taking lunch at the Somerset Club prior to attending the afternoon performance of the Boston Symphony Orchestra. His job was to read unsolicited manuscripts, and he was already notorious when I arrived as the man who had rejected *Anatomy of a Murder* by Robert Traver. He hosted long, unbearable lunches at his mother's in Needham. Invariably, pale aesthetes from Harvard would be in attendance. Vain and fragile, they'd make silly chit-chat about Harvard while the aged Mrs. Williams stared blankly across the long table. We all drank a good deal and ate heavy meals of roast beef or leg of lamb with potatoes and hot vegetables. It reminded me of formidable family dinners at my grandfather's house when I was a boy. I had no objection to a noontime drink—"noon balloons," we called them—but I preferred to play tennis or go for a walk or work at my desk. Alcoholic as I was, and as cheerfully as I could spend hours in a bar with a good companion, I was far too active for the pretensions evinced at Alex's house.

While Alex may have amused most of us, he irritated both Thornhills. He was to the manor born and did not need to work. They never raised his pay above the $5,000 per year he'd started with in the mid-1950s. Arthur Senior abhorred the smugness and snobbery of Harvard men. Arthur Junior, however, hoped—in vain—that Alex's Harvard connections would produce a Galbraith or bring back Arthur Schlesinger, Jr., who had defected after his Pulitzer Prize winner, *The Age of Jackson*, to Houghton Mifflin, Little, Brown's rival down the street. And as Jack Kennedy had also been a member of the Spee Club, Junior hoped for a Kennedy book. Again, no such luck. An indolent, porcine Alex Williams had nothing in common with the Kennedys.

Alex's days were numbered. When he began to grouse about never getting a raise, I had to remind him that a raise came when one's performance justified it. He insisted, though, that unless he got a raise, he wouldn't do any serious work. Year followed year with Alex ascending to his office, where he typed out rejection letters in between visits to the Somerset Club or the T and R. On clear days in spring and summer, he went to Cambridge to sun his naked body on the roof of the Spee Club.

When Alex was asked to resign in 1967, he departed without leaving a trace. His only "authors" were two men who wrote banal novels for women under the name of Emilie Loring. Indeed, when Alex in his stuffy yet barbed fashion introduced the new Emilie Loring at sales conferences, we would all howl. The novel was sure to be dreadful, and Alex could be unmerciful about what he described as "drivel." But Arthur Senior would jump on Alex. "All well and good to act like a big shot or a smart aleck," he'd say. "We sell Emilie Loring and I want the men to take heed. Do not treat Emilie Loring lightly. I don't want to hear again, *ever again*, some smart aleck make fun of one of our authors."

In my early days at Little, Brown I shared an office in the basement with one of our salesmen, Harry Houghton. Harry was the scion of a distinguished publishing family, the Houghtons of Houghton Mifflin. He was a most genial fellow, and I liked him at once. Often we lunched together—martinis at an inexpensive restaurant called Haley's. A bachelor from an old Boston family with girlfriends and pals everywhere, Harry appeared to live a joyous life. He was always on the phone planning his evenings. Like Alex Williams he was a member of the Tennis and Racquet Club, and I gathered that a good deal of jocularity and heavy drinking was the order of the day (and evening) at the old T and R. When I thought of my restrictive life, I was filled with a surge of envy.

In my first year at Little, Brown the medical division was still at 34 Beacon, and most of the basement where I worked was its headquarters. There was one attractive blond secretary who assisted the director, Fred Belliveau. She had to pass by my office to use the toilet, and she'd smile at me as I smiled at her. Eventually I moved upstairs to work for Charlie Blanchard, the medical department moved to new quarters at 41 Mount Vernon Street, and the blond quit her job. A year later one of the secretaries told me that she'd quit because at first she couldn't stand being so near me, but with the advent of moving up the street she found she couldn't bear the thought of being so far away. When I first heard this I was amused. I didn't even know her name. But I was very much warmed by the woman's plight. I felt worn down from defending my way of life. The news about a lovestruck secretary brought sunshine into my life. If there was a woman who could like me and fantasize about me and carry on with a secret crush on me, then maybe I was man enough to pull myself out of the domestic nosedive I was in. I thought of her good looks and her smile and told myself that I simply couldn't continue living as I was. It was time to have an affair.

Charlie Blanchard had an office on the fourth floor at 34 Beacon next door to the copy editors, a clever group run by a very smart woman named Mary Rackliffe. There was a dark-haired beauty in the department named Ibby Ellis whom I fancied, though I didn't dare to make my feelings known. She married a Harvard graduate and left the company before I could make it evident that I was interested in breaking loose. I never had a chance to tell her that I thought she was wonderful.

Charlie Blanchard was very tall, six feet three, well proportioned, extremely sweet man in his mid-sixties. He was the opposite of Arthur Senior. Even without higher education, Senior had a way of belittling Charlie, who had been to Harvard. Both men revered the memory of Alfred MacIntyre, the chairman, and both men loved Little, Brown. Charlie, in his gentle way, tried to act in a very kindly manner toward Arthur Senior. Occasionally he'd make a comment about Arthur's fondness for cocktails, his misuse of the King's English. But whereas Charlie was a plodder, Senior was all energy, a whirlwind, and he had no use for employees in slow motion. I had been with Charlie about six months when the Thornhills lowered the boom and fired him. I was given Charlie's job. It was inevitable that Charlie would go. I could sense that his mere presence was an irritant to Senior. And it should be noted that, though mannerly, Charlie could be critical. Like a butler criticizing his betters, Charlie would get in his digs at the Thornhills. He told me about the novelist Howard Fast, whose work had been rejected by Little, Brown because he was suspected of being a communist. This was during the McCarthy era, when Fast's editor was Angus Cameron, a respected professional of strong political convictions, decidedly to the left. One way or another Fast left the company to find commercial and literary success at our competitor, Houghton Mifflin. Cameron also left, eventually landing at Knopf. Charlie Blanchard would shake his head at Little, Brown's cowardly treatment of Howard Fast as if to ask, *How could a company as respected as Little, Brown be brought to tremble before Joseph McCarthy, a loathsome fellow from the wrong side of the tracks?*

Charlie had run the permissions department and was also in charge of selling book material to magazines. He was also our copyright expert and owned a priceless copy of Emily Dickinson's poems, marked as to copyright dates for ready use. He was very proud of this because once a day at least we received requests for reprinting Emily Dickinson's poetry. Just before he left the company, Charlie sold serial rights to a book about Clark Gable by Jean Garceau called *Dear Mr. G——* to *Ladies' Home Journal* for $30,000. He'd been pleased as punch with his success.

On Charlie Blanchard's last day we gave him a luncheon at the St. Botolph Club where he was a member. He received a plaque or some kind of retirement gift—I cannot recall what it was. The room was full of Little, Brown people, including both Thornhills, and there was an attempt to make it a festive occasion, as though Charlie had simply retired from the company. He took it well and left gracefully, with hardly a trace. I remember this slow, genial man with affection because he came and went without tumult of any kind. Perhaps, oddly, that is why I write of him now. He was my opposite, and his serenity was a quality for which I hungered.

When Charlie left, I inherited his secretary, a woman called Mrs. Klebanoff. She wore glasses, was very bright, and since we were so often alone up in our office, I felt a sexual tension building. I was still too cautious, however, even to call her by her first name. For several weeks we worked side by side, and close proximity. So receptive was I to her aura—I found it almost unbearable. Fortunately, before I could create a scene—would she or would she not?—I was transferred to a better office on the second floor where I would be near both Thornhills. Mrs. Klebanoff resigned her job because of her low wages, or so it was said. (It was always considered an honor to work at Little, Brown, which was an excuse for our meager salaries.) In any event, I never saw Mrs. Klebanoff again, and yet to this day I remember what it was like to stand just inches away from her, aching for contact and guessing that she knew it.

On the second floor I was presented with Sally Carroll, who became my secretary and helpmate. Suddenly, I had a great deal to do.

•   •   •

In 1962, I started seeing a psychoanalyst. Earlier, upon returning from France, Wendy had suggested a doctor in Hartford. I visited him and I felt, for the first time in my life, that someone was paying attention to me. I was hooked. Obviously, I had been under a goodly amount of strain, and, suddenly, almost in a flash, it seemed that psychiatry was a way out.

I did not know then that much of the strain I felt came from my dependence on alcohol. Nor could I foretell that the boozy paradise I entered when I drank would upset our marriage. In fact, the doctor in Hartford did not mention drinking. He did have the good sense to insist that I enter treatment and when we were settled in Boston, that is what I did. Psychoanalysis would bring me into the light. Down deep, I knew that I had to rid myself of the sickness that was part of my family life and seek a new path. Wendy's complaints about me and my background seemed cruel, but they were accurate. I had to change.

In spite of my deeper feelings, I saw myself being railroaded onto the couch. I believed that my wife needed help, not I. I was in Happy Valley, working and playing with interesting people and getting paid for it. Yet I did not protest. For one thing, had I protested I could envision an ultimatum: *Either you go into treatment or we get a divorce.* I knew that in a divorce I'd lose my son (our daughter had yet to be born). I could not imagine my son growing up without me. It was too late to turn back the clock and flee to St. Croix. I had become an effective worker at Little, Brown, where I was beginning to assume responsibility. Already I saw myself as a great fellow soaring above the crowd: good restaurants, gilded hotel lobbies, the crisp walk across the Boston Common in a suit and tie from Brooks Brothers or J. Press. Now a member of the

Tennis and Racquet Club of Boston and the Dedham Country and Polo Club, I had access to the collegial people who ran Boston. I was part of the establishment, or so I thought. I would see an analyst as soon as possible.

From 1962 until late 1967, when I walked out of Dr. Robert McCarter's office on Commonwealth Avenue for the last time, I lay on a couch four or five days a week, excepting business trips and my analyst's vacation in August. As the days passed into years, I began filling up with a new identity. Something subterranean was stirring me. I was no longer the son of my father, nor was I the husband of my wife. Little by little I was becoming an individual in my own right, someone with thoughts and opinions drawn from his own life experience and reading. I began to feel pride in having been an enlisted man working on the Air Force flight line. And, what was most strange, my five-year ordeal in military school, which I had suppressed and certainly never spoken of, began to reassemble itself in my mind, and the flavor and the details of such an important part of my growth into adulthood re-formed itself. To Wendy's consternation, I spoke my mind. At dinner parties I would receive a kick under the table. I always said things of which she disapproved and, surprisingly, I didn't care what she thought. In analysis I was spinning free of all marital constraints. There was a person inside me that was coming to my attention. Some day that person would take charge.

The major accomplishment of my analysis was the virtual disappearance of my stammer. Within six months it ceased to be a problem— this horrific weight I had carried since I was four or five years old, since the time our maid Anna was attacked and I couldn't call for help. There had been times when I did not stammer, times when I was full of myself, such as when I played a sport. At military school, where I could excel in class whenever I chose, I could go for long periods without stammering. But when I reentered the work force at Little, Brown, my stammer returned to cripple me at any moment, and as a result I held back, grew timid and worried. I hated my stammer and hated myself when it struck and took charge of my life. Clinging to me like a wild pestilence, it led me around and shamed me terribly. Now, thanks to analysis, it was gone. In my relief I often felt euphoric. After decades, I could finally talk freely.

I tried to keep my psychoanalytic sessions a secret. Even though I saw the process as a boon, I was nevertheless ashamed. I was convinced that my father would take my treatment personally and would be embarrassed by it. I did not want him to think that my stability as a young man was suspect and that my insecurity had anything to do with him. I never told him about my analysis, just as I never told him the truth about Brook Hall. I didn't want him to think that he'd failed me. I was also convinced that associates at work would view me as unbalanced, as someone not to be trusted. It never occurred to me that my drinking had already placed me in jeopardy, that, if anything, my going to a shrink would have been a relief to them.

As I lay on the couch and spoke of myself and my feelings, patterns could be discerned; rhyme and reason came into play, and as time wore on I could explain things to myself. Instant revelations occurred more and more often. If I thought of enlisting in the Army to fight in Vietnam—which I did think seriously about doing—my motive was clear: it had nothing to do with Vietnam but everything to do with proving myself to my father, who was my conscience. If I could gain the respect of my father, it wouldn't matter ever again what my wife might think.

On this matter, two years after my father's death in 1963 I had it in my mind to leave Little, Brown and get a job in Washington. I fancied myself working for civil rights in some way, and as I was dealing with Franklin Roosevelt, Jr., about a book, I thought of enlisting his support. The younger Franklin had been Assistant Secretary of Commerce under Kennedy. He knew everyone. Fair enough; I was sympathetic to the civil rights movement. But by 1965 when this idea came about, I would have joined the Foreign Legion, I was so anxious to leave home. Even prison looked good, if I could find a cause for which I could break the law. So I started to learn about myself far down inside to the extent that I would read the hidden agenda in my thinking. Self-awareness was changing my way of living; it was freeing me up so I knew what I was doing when I did it. The clouds were parted. At the same time my private world became increasingly tumultuous. And so it went: even the littlest urges received instant examination. I was forever saying to myself: *what comes to mind*, and then holding up my response to scrutiny.

•   •   •

Neither my Martha's Vineyard bookstore-café nor my house atop Mount Welcome in St. Croix survived 1963. I sold the Red Cat to

Warren Coleman, an established actor who had been in the original cast of *Porgy and Bess*, who always wanted to own a restaurant. He changed my store-café into an eatery called the Sands of Gold. After the closing, a real estate agent told me that I had made history by selling to a "colored man." No one of color had ever owned property in West Tisbury or Chilmark. Warren Coleman seemed to be a pleasant middle-aged man. When his race was brought to my attention, I felt very odd that I'd never considered his skin color. I could be extremely censorious when I chose, but race was not an issue. Whatever their faults, at least my parents had not instilled racial prejudice in me. I was always aware of class, but not race.

As for my St. Croix house with its panoramic view and the pool and all the furniture, I sold it at cost, along with a lot I owned at Grapetree Bay. I drank heavily in St. Croix as I closed the sale to blunt the humiliation I would otherwise have felt, selling my dreams at cost.

•   •   •

By 1964 I was often in New York City. I was working hard to sell book excerpts to magazines, and I spent a good deal of time with magazine editors: Ken Wilson of *Reader's Digest*, Don Gold and Rust Hills at *Esquire*, John Appleton, Ann Bayer, and John Mong at the *Saturday Evening Post,* and David Maness at *Life*. Bruce Jay Friedman worked for male action magazines with names like *He-Man* and *Male*. I liked him, and I did sell excerpts to him as well as to both *Argosy* and *True*. I lunched with Bud Hart from *Redbook,* and I saw Phyllis Levy and Manon Tingue who were editors at *McCall's*. From *Good Housekeeping* I lunched with the novelist Lonnie Coleman. At *Ladies' Home Journal* I saw Jean Todd Freeman, whom I took out for a night on the town. Another young woman whose company I enjoyed was Susan Stanwood at the *Saturday Evening Post,* who co-wrote a novel that turned into a best-seller. As I gained experience, I began seeing agents and eventually writers, and by the end of my stint at Little, Brown, I was spending more and more time out of the home office and away from my wife and children.

As an editor I was woefully ignorant in some essential areas: Shakespeare, the Bible, mythology, science. I think that Ned Bradford, in particular, knew of my limitations but hoped that my inherent enthusiasm would compensate. I knew current events and American literature and sports, and I was naturally curious about sexuality and scandal. We were a mixed bag at Little, Brown, but by luck, or as a result of Arthur Junior's intuition, we seemed to complement one other. Ned Bradford was reserved and quiet, but he had a wonderful sense of humor. His field was history. Arthur Senior was a salesman like no other. Junior was the businessman who fought for the college and medical departments and for the acquisition of a new warehouse and an additional office building. Randy Williams handled internal affairs and was genial, a good scout, a man who could have done just as well working for General Motors. Bob Feteridge, our advertising and sales manager, could rise to moments of great inspiration, but he, too, favored his cocktails. Feteridge became dour and prickly after lunch; he was at his best at 7:45 A.M., working with Randy Williams. Both men were early risers and came to work before the rest of us.

The shining lights of our editorial department were Alan Williams and Herman Gollob. Both Herman and Alan were like stars to me and gave credence to our reputation as a classy publishing house. Herman and I became pals. I enjoyed lunching with him and seeing him in the evening with his wife, Barbara. Our managing editor, John Cushman, wore a bowler, as I recall, and looked very much like a London editor. He departed a year or more after I joined the company to become a literary agent in New York, and Charles ("Cheeb") Everett took his place. Although we all had our foibles and, I would suspect, our secrets, it was such a good-natured group that I rejoiced in my good fortune. I remember one fellow, a nice chap named Harvey Isham who worked in accounting as an assistant to George Hall, our treasurer. We often took the same train in from Needham Junction. Whenever I saw him, he always greeted me the same way: "How goes the battle?" he'd ask. "Fine," I'd reply. And each time he asked that question I thought of my job, where there was no battle, no struggle, no duress of any kind. I felt as light as a feather, floating through work with ease.

I moved in among such worthies, and in time I felt more at home than I had since I was twelve years old and had to leave New Britain for military school. Indeed, life at 34 Beacon Street became my social life. Work was a party, and as I progressed in psychoanalysis, so too did my socializing, part of which included women. I think my first act of infidelity involved an overweight, hard-drinking journalist who had visited our New York office. I awoke in the morning horror-struck at what

I'd done. After her the dam broke, and I gradually grew bolder with women who struck my fancy and who appeared to be game. The young ladies at Little, Brown were adorable, and with each passing month, temptations grew.

Through an examination of foibles one can probe character; it is the quickest route to finding out what a person is like. Some of us drank too much. Cheeb Everett, crisp in manner, cast an appreciative eye at the ladies. Bob Feteridge was ferret-like and mysterious. Feteridge (no one called him Bob) could be seen slipping silently along the hallways carrying papers. He was always huddling with Randy Williams, the two of them transplants from Macmillan. Occasionally he had an inspired thought. I don't recall the details, but it was Feteridge who launched John Fowles and *The Collector*. I think he passed out imitation butterflies at the American Booksellers' convention, symbolic of events in the novel. He had an ability to grasp a novel's potential and then fashion a winning campaign. He did the same thing with *The Cincinnati Kid* by Richard Jessup.

About the time Herman Gollob brought in *King Rat*, James Clavell's first novel, Seymour ("Sam") Lawrence presented us with *Ship of Fools* by Katherine Anne Porter. The Porter novel, as the literary crowd knew, had been "coming" for many years. Sam, who was an editor with our partner the Atlantic Monthly Press, had latched onto Katherine Anne somewhere in the recesses of time, and for years he'd nursed her along. This was the long-awaited big novel by a master of the short story and novella. When it finally arrived in 1962, Sam was beside himself. All of a sudden he was in my office. *Ship of Fools* was being published without an agent. It would be my job, working under Randy Williams, to sell it to Hollywood. "Katherine Anne and I" became an annoying opener as this dark-haired, pudgy-faced chap poked his always smiling, face around the open doorway and enticed me into his world. His world included lunches in the bar of the Ritz-Carlton. ("I'm the only one to whom the Ritz will serve meals in the bar," he would say, proud as a peacock.) And then "Katherine Anne and I" anecdotes would roll from his tongue. More than once he told a lengthy story about his trip to Barcelona with Katherine Anne and how he'd bought a suit, the good-looking tan suit he seemed prone to wear whenever we dined at the Ritz-Carlton bar. I always complimented him on his suit and his accomplishments with Katherine Anne and like a broken record we'd begin our cocktails as though the rest of the world no longer mattered. All that mattered was Sam Lawrence and Katherine Anne Porter.

Eventually I became quite sure that no one could stand to hear another word about Katherine Anne. *Ship of Fools* was nevertheless a huge success, and at lunch with Ingo Preminger, Randy and I were able to sell movie rights for $400,000—a tidy sum in the early '60s. What it had was a good title, a substantial length, and the author's reputation embellished by the ordeal of a long, hard struggle to write her master-work. Randy Williams, who was nominally in charge, sent me over to the Ritz with six copies of the movie contract to get Katherine Anne, who was in residence, to sign them. I called her at 9:00 A.M. and with her consent I hurried across the Public Gardens to the Ritz. The author, then in her seventies, greeted me in a transparent nightgown with a silk bed jacket open at the chest. Her breasts were exposed when she bent over to sign each contract. Her bottom showed through her nightgown. She smelled of perfume. She had just arisen and in a sleepy, sexy mood she greeted me.

"Will you stay awhile?" she asked, after all the papers were signed. I said I had to hurry back to work. Later on I chastised myself for miss-ing another adventure, as I had with the Duchess of Windsor. But in truth it never dawned on me to probe the nuance in her voice. What mattered was Little, Brown's commission. As she signed all the contracts, searching for each line for her signature, I felt proud of myself: I was closing on a deal. When I left the Ritz, I walked at a brisk pace as I angled back to the office across the Public Gardens. I'd just sold movie rights to a novel for $400,000.

Sam lost his job, but not because of Katherine Anne, on whose benefit he ran up considerable expenses: travel, meals, and drinks. It was his position on J. P. Donleavy's novel *A Singular Man* that got him into hot water. I do not know the details, but the story was he was driving Randy Williams and the Thornhills wild. After his Katherine Anne coup (the best-selling novel earned a small fortune for Little, Brown), he became demanding. One day he was dictating terms to management and the next day he was gone.

At the Atlantic Monthly Press, the best of the lot, in my view, was Peter Davison, who was straight to the point and talented. It was hard to find someone with artistic aptitude who was at the same time pleasant and reliable. Peter, a prize-winning poet, was a good sort. Another employee at the Atlantic Monthly Press springs from my memory: Emily Morison Beck. Wendy Beck, as she was called, was an impressive figure. Her father was Admiral Samuel Eliot Morison. The Admiral prowled our library area—really Randy Williams's spacious office—autographing copies of his books. Feteridge would snake his way down the hall and present them to him to sign. Everyone was frightened of the Admiral. His daughter was assigned to update *Bartlett's Familiar Quotations*, and she was often in our offices using our reference library. She had a brother named Peter whom I would later meet on St. Vincent in the Caribbean. I tried to get him to talk of his famous father, but he shied as if in terror at the mention of the Admiral's name.

• • •

Working at Little, Brown was like being in a movie. As I walked over from Back Bay Station on a crisp autumn morning, or as I jigged and jagged down snowy streets dodging automobiles with spinning tires, I thought of myself as a leading man. I was on the way up. I looked fit. I enjoyed a glass or two (or three). I responded enthusiastically to my surroundings, and I enjoyed the beauty of the women with whom I was employed. Publishing had a cachet and it attracted attractive women. In hindsight I can see them as they held my attention thirty-odd years ago.

First the two older ladies: Miss Page, who was Junior's secretary, and Miss Marden, who worked for Arthur Senior. Obviously, Miss Page and Miss Marden had first names but I never learned them. Boston was Boston, and the sense of propriety at Little, Brown extended respect toward women as well as formality. This attitude was coupled with a belittlement of status. To call Miss Page by her first name might suggest a notion of equality, and informality might breed a lack of rigor or a lack of respect for the men whom she served. I liked both Miss Page and Miss Marden very much. I saw a good deal of them because I held so many jobs and was always delving into their files, checking on something. They were like aunts to me, as was Helen Jones, our children's book editor.

Helen Jones was a rugged woman who reminded me of my maiden aunt, Fannie Upham, with whom I had lived in Mamaroneck in 1948. I sensed a ribaldry in her even though she acted like a headmistress who brooked no shenanigans. I could discern a naughty twinkle in her eye, and I know she found me amusing. I always liked seeing her, and one day I was drawn to her offices on the ground floor with a special urgency. She'd hired an assistant named Carrie Wedemeyer. Cheeb Everett up in Editorial was agog. So, too, was I. Carrie had an amazing 1920s persona that implied wild evenings. She could deliver sharp dialogue with funny, offbeat, nonsensical phrasings. She was very pretty with a slender, supple body, a dream of a woman come to life. As I recall, she had light brown hair and wore horn-rimmed glasses, and I think it was the glasses that did it. The thought of removing her glasses and then other items set me aflame with desire.

Carrie always looked receptive to horseplay (as, I suspected, was Helen Jones), and one morning, on a whim, I went calling on Miss Jones, just to get another glimpse of Carrie Wedemeyer, only to find the two of them in the midst of an argument. "Keep your oar out of it," shouted Helen Jones. "But, but…" said Carrie, her eyes darting toward the ceiling, her breasts moving ever so slightly under her light sweater. Then I smelled her breath. I was probably wrong, but I thought I smelled gin, and it was only 9:30 in the morning. I loved her.

Several weeks later Harry Houghton married one of our publicity secretaries, Connie Irvin. The wedding was in Sewickley, Pennsylvania. I was an usher and Carrie was a bridesmaid. At one point during the evening, as Connie Irvin's uncle Bun O'Neill blared march music over the stereo system, Carrie stepped close to me and brushed me with the side of her body. I placed an arm around her and in the spirit of the evening I moved to kiss her. At that moment, a moment I had hoped would some day arrive…at that precise moment, Wendy entered the room. I saw the dagger stare of my wife and turned away from Carrie. I hardly ever spoke to Carrie again. Everyone could see how married I was, and I felt ashamed of myself. That night, once again, I heard my wife's familiar complaints: I was no good, my family was no good, my life was no good, Little, Brown was no good. It seemed that everything I liked and loved was rotten to the core.

Other young women come to mind. Susan Gregory, whom Ned Bradford insisted on calling *Miss* Gregory, was a Vanderbilt Phi Beta Kappa. Susan was a charmer and infinitely quicker than her boss. Ned never really connected with her, and she suspected that Ned was remote and more of a figurehead than a real editor. She had a point. Ned thrived on English imports. One time I got a line on Dean Acheson. I'd been drinking with a fellow who worked at Houghton Mifflin, who told me that Acheson was shopping for a new publisher. This was a major tip, and I rushed into Ned's office with the news. It should have been my project. If Dean Acheson were writing a memoir and I discovered that he was free, it was for me to follow up with a meeting. Ned, however, decided that the stakes were too high, and because he was older and a good Democrat, *he* should go to meet Acheson and contract for his book. Ned flew to Washington and lunched with Acheson, and according to Ned they hit it off splendidly. The only problem arose when Ned asked the former Secretary of State, a career diplomat with books of significance already under his belt, to submit an outline and some sample chapters as if he were a student launching a term paper. Ned had erred badly. We never received anything from Acheson. I doubt that Ned even got a thank you for lunch. As for Susan, I took her to lunch a few times, but before long she was gone. She went to Washington, I think, for a job in public broadcasting.

Molly Thomas worked in Editorial. She was dark-haired and pretty in a reserved, New England way. She was always cheerful and attentive to duty, though I suspected there was an earthy streak lurking within her. Like the other young women, she was comely and well educated, always well dressed. She had an upper-class look to go with a low-paying job that supposedly conferred status.

Jay Williams, the pretty granddaughter of novelist Ben Ames Williams, assisted me before accepting other responsibilities. Eager, perky, extremely bright and droll when she wished, Jay had been an academic star at Radcliffe. Before that she had set academic records at the Winsor School in Boston. Jay settled in with editor Llewellyn Howland, and eventually they were married. Flirtation with Jay was never a possibility: she was too young and too smart and too socially connected, and because she worked closely with me, she rightly suspected I had dark problems at home.

Almost all of the women were so attractive that they made going to work an absolute joy. I would walk in most mornings with a jaunty step, immediately on the lookout for a well-turned ankle, the flow of a skirt, the toss of hair, the arch of an eyebrow, and in time one young lady stole my heart. She was a secretary named Saralyn Crenshaw who worked in the College Department. Saralyn had shoulder-length blond hair and, at the time I met her in 1964, was twenty-four years old. I was nine years her senior. She was absolutely luscious inside her loose clothes. At work she appeared demure, but she was quick to smile at me and I was quick to smile back. I studied her. She was strong and tall and had the gentility of a well-heeled 1940s girl next door, someone who during the war would be photographed standing beside a Buick in a camel's hair polo coat. Though she dressed casually, like a college girl, I could imagine her all dolled up in nylons and high heels and thought if she ever dressed for the evening, she'd be a knockout. Saralyn was truly beautiful although she kept her beauty under wraps.

We lunched at the Copley Plaza and dined in the evening at Trader Vic's in the Statler. I was starved for love and lost my heart to her. When I stared at her, I sensed a glow in her eyes that told me she felt as I did. Finally, one Sunday, I told my wife I was going to the office. Instead I stopped at Saralyn's apartment on Commonwealth Avenue. We undressed, and when I lay beside her I feasted on her beauty. I could sense her hesitancy, however; she wanted more time. I was relieved because I, too, needed time. I'd lied about where I was going. I felt cowardly sneaking about. And I knew that once our affair was consummated, there would be no turning back. The next day at work she told me she was sorry. "When we meet again," she said, "we'll make love all the way to the end."

The following weekend Wendy was going to be away at a wedding, and while she was out of town I could see Saralyn. Wendy planned to take a taxi to the airport in the early afternoon on Friday, and with the knowledge that soon she would be airborne, Saralyn and I knowingly eyed each other when I went up to the College Department on some pretext. I had a bit of work to do after five, and Saralyn departed ahead of me. I'd pick her up at her apartment around six. We were co-conspirators, and she grinned with great pleasure as she saw me pass her desk.

At 5:30, just as I was about to leave, the phone rang. Wendy was stuck at Logan Airport. All flights were canceled because of fog. She'd been waiting impatiently, but no luck. Exasperated, she told me to come and fetch her. I was aghast at the turn of events. This was to be a night of nights with Saralyn, who was longing for me as I was for her. I felt compelled to see her before going for Wendy. In the heavy traffic of a Friday night in a city thick with fog, I drove to Saralyn's and told her it was hopeless. I was ruined when she began to cry. I told her to find someone who wasn't married. "The hell with it," I said. I fought the traffic to Logan, a mess of regret. When I finally got there, my wife was furious. I lied and said I'd had an emergency at work. She said she'd called there but nobody answered. I told her that they'd closed down the switchboard. We ate supper at the airport and then I drove her back home.

Saralyn quit Little, Brown soon after that. Although for a brief time before she left the company I'd see her in passing, we did not speak. We both knew that I didn't have the resolve to leave my wife, though it should have been obvious to me that divorce was inevitable, if not imminent, and I did not have to lose Saralyn. Beyond being glued to a marriage in which I was miserable, I was moving deeply into analysis and was understandably befuddled by my feelings. As the blinders were gradually removed, my turmoil grew. Had I met Saralyn two years later there would have been no denying us our life together. But in 1964 I was soft like J. Alfred Prufrock: *Do I dare / Disturb the universe?* I did not possess the courage to follow my heart.

•   •   •

The girls in the office—I don't remember who—referred to Arthur Junior and Ned as "the boys." *The boys went to lunch. The boys are talking things over in Junior's office.* Neither Arthur nor Ned had a clue as to how the Little, Brown women perceived them. Feminine ideas, personal lives, attitudes meant nothing. And so "the boys" was a pay-back from a couple of the younger women in the office, a slight scoff at the self-importance of their bosses.

I had been at Little, Brown about three years when one of "the boys"—Ned, I think—started using the word "sanguine." He was not very "sanguine" about a certain book's prospects. Or he was quite "sanguine" toward some idea: "I feel quite sanguine about it," he'd say, and then he couldn't stop saying it; it became his mantra, and it spread to Junior like a virus. At meeting after meeting I'd hear the word "sanguine."

Soon, Junior was sanguine as well and becoming more sanguine with each passing day. "I feel sanguine about the future of American trade publishing," he'd say. Before long he was worse than Ned; Junior was held helpless in sanguine's grip. There was a time in 1964 when he seemed to employ the word with every comment.

Finally I spoke up. We were all seated around the shiny oblong table in the president's office: Junior, Ned, Randy, associate editors Llewellyn Howland, Harry Sions, Al Hart, Cheeb Everett, and myself. Senior, who never pretended to be an editor, eschewed such meetings.

Almost immediately the dreaded *s*-word was dropped by Junior. I looked at Ned. It was Ned's word to start with. Perhaps by now he had recognized its cloying overuse. But, no, he just nodded toward his pal Arthur, his interest piqued. I could see through the round black-framed lenses into his gray eyes. "Sanguine" was a word that prompted his attention, like the click of a trigger.

After two or three more sanguines I exploded. "I'm *not* sanguine. I never was sanguine. Why must we be so *sanguine* about everything?" I pleaded.

Arthur looked at me as though I had stabbed him. "What did you say?" he asked. "*What* did you mean by that remark?"

"Nothing," I answered, backtracking very quickly. "It's just that everybody's so *sanguine* all the time," I said, using the comforting all-inclusive "everybody" rather than the accusatory second-person singular.

Silence descended. Finally someone picked up the meeting and a contretemps was avoided. I never heard Arthur use the word again, though Ned was unfazed and was in fact sanguine about several other projects during that very meeting. He never caught the criticism in my voice. Quite probably, once I interrupted Junior, Ned stopped listening. He had a way of tuning out. I had noticed him drifting off at lunch or at meetings the moment his interest dulled. Because no one ever inter-rupted Junior, perhaps Ned thought my interruption a bit much and let his mind retreat into a private limbo. He certainly had that facility. While we all knew that Randy was much deafer than he would admit and didn't hear what was said, it was unsettling to recognize that quite often Ned, who could hear very well, would simply stop listening with-out cause.

By contrast, both Thornhills listened intently like deer in a forest. George Hall, our congenial treasurer, also listened. So did Harry Sions, who was our editor in New York. He'd had come over from *Holiday* magazine after it closed. Harry brought William Manchester into the fold with a major biography of the Krupps. Later, Manchester's books on Churchill would bring status and money to Little, Brown. I suppose others listened as well, but two key players in the trade department, Randy Williams and Ned Bradford missed a good part of what was going on. Feteridge, who was also a key player, never listened by design. He always had his own agenda and would snake off down the hall the minute I tried to tell him something.

Ned was a sphinx and easy to criticize. He was also lovable and often amused by events at work and in the world. As the days turned into years and I saw more and more of him, I grew very fond of him. I suspected he was one-half of a bad marriage. I'd seen his wife at company get-togethers when Arthur Junior would have some of his people over for drinks with Colonel van Wyck Mason. One summer I organized a tennis tournament at Alex Williams's court. Afterward, we had a party at Junior's. Ned's wife did not look like a happy camper. It was my impression that she shared with me an inordinate interest in spirits. When she got going, Ned would roll his eyes and tune out. At work he was neat, intelligent-looking, usually amused, and completely removed. I'd see him daily and was always happy to be with him. He had a special ability to develop friendships and remain ineffective. Once the *Boston Herald* columnist George Frazier referred to Ned Bradford as a great editor. He was a fine fellow, but I could not ever think of him as a great editor.

Under Ned Bradford's reign, six novels that became *New York Times* best-sellers were rejected by Little, Brown, all in one year. Admittedly, not one of the novels could be confused with serious fiction. Yet this example of being out of touch in so extraordinary a fashion bears scrutiny. I do not believe that Ned had the slightest interest in the needs, wishes, and thought processes of the average woman or man. The New York secretary racing to the subway carrying a popular novel in her hand held no interest for Ned. The Wall Street stock salesman, riding the New Haven back to Greenwich, would be reading as well. What and why was not Ned's concern. Perfectly readable novels by best-selling writers were sent in by agents and before long returned. In the '60s we were considered a strong company with a string of strong titles—many published under the Atlantic Monthly Press imprint—and we certainly could have moved into the forefront of trade publishing had Ned's department really known or cared about the reading public. To Ned, the reading public began and ended with the *The New Yorker*, the *New Statesman*, the *Economist*, and *World Affairs*. To emphasize my point, I never heard him refer to *Esquire*, a magazine that was frantic to publish all the hot writers coming along, and often did.

Among the many *New Yorker* writers we published, the most significant was J. D. Salinger. Salinger was arguably the most important creative writer in our entire catalogue. Everyone loved *Nine Stories* and

Catcher in the Rye. Salinger, by now a recluse in Cornish, New Hampshire, was a rarity: he was a cult figure with a broad appeal. Reporters tried to probe his psyche as they desperately sought interviews and were turned away. His books sold briskly from our backlist and in paperback with Bantam, and so when at last *Franny and Zooey* arrived from his agency, Harold Ober Associates, we all rejoiced.

Ned, who was Salinger's nominal editor (any real editing would have been done by William Shawn at *The New Yorker*), surprised me with his myopia. He did not see Salinger in the context of that author's popularity, now peaking to great heights. Randy in his deafness and Feteridge, so odd and remote with a mind so affected by martinis, were of no help, and I was told that in all their wisdom they had decided on a printing of only five thousand copies. Not only that, but Ned had somehow forgotten to include a dedication page to William Shawn. As the fiasco unwound, it became evident that Little, Brown was going to be out of stock by publication day. It took forever to get another printing into the stores, and when that sold out, we were out of stock again! By 1962 the men who ran Little, Brown's trade department were beginning to miss everything that America was doing and thinking and becoming. Any one of the younger women who toiled in anonymity could have told them to print at least 100,000 copies of the new Salinger on the first go-around.

Ned Bradford was a member of what I've come to think of as the liberal elite. His intelligence was undeniable, yet it was obvious that he knew very little of human nature. He was too far removed from the commonplace. In ensuing years I was to meet other people like Ned. They seemed important and often brainy. They had been caught up in the glamour of the New Frontier and then the War on Poverty. Back in the '60s I was very much in awe of this crowd; they were smarter than I and better educated, and Ned fit right into my image of a bright and civilized group of thinking, concerned leaders. After I left Little, Brown and gained some perspective on Ned Bradford and people like him, I began to view liberal elitists with considerable caution. They often appeared more social than studious, more above the people than of the people. Ned was a man who was articulate in his opinions and clever in his wit, but somehow he'd lost touch with the way almost everyone else was trying to live. There was a sizable crowd of people around the publishing world who had never done hard work for a paycheck. They wrote for one another, listened to one another, and congratulated one another, and Ned, in his tendency toward complacency, fancied himself to be part of this inner circle. He was not one to be ruffled by events. He was *above* events. And yet, when I saw him at his desk at the end of the hall, studying some report, scanning the *Wall Street Journal*, dictating a letter to London, I was drawn to him.

Once, toward the end of my tenure, he'd told me that he'd like to see the breasts of one of the younger women. As with all of us, he had a bit of the devil inside that was usually suppressed. The young woman in question had taken me to bed a few times, much to my delight, and I think Ned had an idea that such was the case, although I never told anyone. In any event, he asked me what her breasts looked like and I said that he'd have to see for himself. "Do you suppose she would come into my office and shut the door and strip?" he asked. I said, "Who knows? She might." He looked away and let his thoughts luxuriate over his image of a woman I knew intimately.

•   •   •

By the early '60s my mother, ever more enfeebled, had become bedridden; she was in and out of hospitals. We all knew that she was ill beyond hope of recovery; for multiple sclerosis, there was no cure. She had become obsessed, assailing my father with sharp, pointed language. As for my sister, she had left her lover, who had never really left his wife. Now divorced, she was alone and zestful in her enjoyment of freedom. My parents were upset with her and I was growing tired of the whole business. It was very confusing. There were children involved, parents on edge, as always too much drinking. My sister went her own way as my mother obsessed over my father, and he, in turn, obsessed over his daughter's indifference to convention. My brother with his third wife and their children, plus at least one child from marriage number one, was living in Marin County in California. He'd met Wendy and Wendy thought he was bad news. In spite of how I felt about him, I wanted to defend him. I said nothing, however. I assumed that the whole mess from which I had sprung would clear up on its own.

Before my father died, he sold the house in Woodbury. It had been a nice idea: they'd move in next door to their daughter, whose solid family life and love would nourish them into old age. But it was not to be, and so they sold—my father furious with his recalcitrant daughter, my mother seeing trouble everywhere. They began living eight months of the year in Harthaven on the Vineyard and four months during the winter at Smoke Tree Ranch in Palm Springs. Out in California, my father rode horseback every day. He lawn-bowled and took care of his wife. In the summer he would work on an old Elco cabin cruiser he purchased to replace the schooner he'd sold to Burl Ives. Below the living room in the house at Harthaven he fashioned a shop where he made tables and picture frames and repaired old wooden objects. In the evening, drinks in hand, the two of them would watch *I Love Lucy* and Garry Moore—mid-American television. My father loved *Gunsmoke* and would smile and say, "Old Festus," thinking of scenes in the long-running western.

I had been at Little, Brown just over two years when my father died in October 1963 at sixty-eight. He died of a stroke in his sleep, alone on Martha's Vineyard in Harthaven, in the old boathouse that his father had owned, where they used to haul boats from the harbor in the old days, where down below it still smelled of oil and marlin and rust. "The old days": he loved that phrase. The day before he died he had been in Boston and had stopped by 34 Beacon to meet me. He saw where I worked—all spit and polish, book-lined and almost regal and certainly right out of John Marquand, one of my father's favorite novelists. With his own eyes he'd seen that I was doing well. Somehow, one way or another, his father's grandson had finally made the grade. I was very proud to show him around, to expose him to the glow of literature and the style of genteel living that pervaded my place of work.

And then he was dead. I was in shock from his death, and I carried through with his funeral like a drunkard in a blackout. I walked the walk, seemingly coherent and sensate, and by the time it was over I had buried my father not just in the earth but in my emotions. When Jack Kennedy was assassinated a month later, I shed the impact of the President's death with ease. The news of my father's death was so fierce and so brutal to my feelings that no other death could penetrate. My analyst kept asking, "You don't mention your father's death. Why not?" Lying on my back I would twitch my head and say his death did not matter. But, for all his faults, I'd loved my father absolutely and could not bear discussing my love with another person.

•   •   •

When I was a boy on the Vineyard, my father and I used to duck out to see the movies. We'd sidle off to the Seabreeze to watch Tom Mix and Buck Jones westerns. My favorite western from those early days was *The Texas Rangers* with Jack Oakie. I liked Jack Oakie, a supporting actor who usually played a sidekick. Another sidekick actor I liked, as did my mother, was Franchot Tone. Franchot Tone reminded me of my Uncle Foster: they looked somewhat alike and both displayed the passive traits that befit a sidekick. *Mutiny on the Bounty* was my favorite, with Franchot Tone, Clark Gable, and Charles Laughton. I saw that with my father.

In New Britain my mother would join us, though I do not recall her ever going to a movie on Martha's Vineyard. I suppose it was because of her drinking, but even so it seems odd. In any case, in New Britain, back in time, we'd drive up to Hartford, have supper at the Bond Hotel, and take in *It Happened One Night* or *The Hunchback of Notre Dame*. I felt very close to both my parents on these evenings out. At the Bond a trio or quartet would play for us while we dined. The lead violinist, a man named Mixter, would come to our table to bend his bow and stoop toward us. In his tuxedo he looked elegant. It seemed such a fine way to dine in, say, 1936. I felt so much pride in my parents.

When you discover the imperfections in an imperfect person, you do not necessarily lose any of your love. Once when I was only seventeen, I drove my car into a telephone pole on Martha's Vineyard and was seriously injured. The police threw me in jail, and when I regained consciousness, the officer called my father. As he drove me to the hospital, I said I'd never ever drive a car again. "Oh, yes, you will," he said. "It will be okay. Of course you'll drive again." That's all he said as I slumped beside his right shoulder. I knew he was with me in his own quiet way, and that, quite simply, was all he ever had to do to retain my love.

• • •

On occasion Ned Bradford and I would lunch at Locke-Ober. Junior and I lunched at the Tennis and Racquet Club, at Locke-Ober, and once or twice at the Union Club. Senior and I always lunched at Locke-Ober. I enjoyed being with these men, and I sincerely liked them, particularly Arthur Senior. But this little tale is not about Senior. It is about conflicting stories told first by Arthur, then by Ned, each detailing the same experience from opposing points of view.

At lunch one day Arthur Junior was talking about Ned. As always the overhead lights at Locke-Ober shone on the silverware and the glasses, giving a crystalline sparkle to our table, and Arthur's bright eyes sparkled as he talked. I pictured him in his "pinks," back during the war, having a drink in Burma. I was drawn to Arthur Junior and I leaned in to catch his words. "Ned is very conservative. We all know that and I appreciate it. My father appreciates it. It's too easy to go off on a tangent in this business. Too easy to plunge and then you've hurt the imprint and embarrassed yourself. But I'll tell you how conservative Ned really is. We were in Paris. I'd been at the book fair in Frankfurt and Ned was in Paris to meet with French publishers. I flew in from Frankfurt as he arrived from the States. We took a suite and eventually we went out for dinner. Now, here we were, in the City of Light, Gay Paree. There is only one Paris, and after dinner Ned decided to return to his room and go to sleep. Of course, he's thinking of his meetings the next day. But I said to him, I said, 'Ned, you're in Paris. Why don't you see the sights, take in some night life?' Not Ned. Back to the hotel he goes, to sleep. Sleep! Can you imagine? On his first night in Paris. That was a good insight into Ned, I thought. And once his business was completed, he flew back to Boston. Ned never did go out other than to eat and see his contacts."

I listened to Arthur intently. No wonder we were losing best-sellers. A man with so little imagination, so short on joie de vivre. How could Ned Bradford judge the appeal of books that were selling in the hundreds of thousands, especially novels that professed to speak from inside Hollywood, inside the world of fashion, inside government, novels about men and women full of passion, angling for an illicit liaison. I could imagine Ned in his hotel room, in pajamas and a bathrobe, his feet in slippers, as all of Paris throbbed outside his window.

Maybe two weeks later Ned and I were having lunch, again at Locke-Ober, conceivably at the same table. "Now, take Arthur Junior," he was saying. "He's so apt to do things, shall I say, that are inappropriate. Like the time in Paris when we took rooms together. Arthur had been in Frankfurt at a boring book fair…what *is* the purpose of all that nonsense?…and I was arriving to set up some important meetings. We were weak in some areas. We had never published Camus, Gide, Proust, and so on. Maybe it was time to do something serious. Well, I was there and, I might say, quite sanguine about matters. I'd invited two distinguished publishers to breakfast in our suite. Coffee and croissants, juice, preserves, English marmalade. I was looking forward to it and I was sanguine about Junior being there. I had Little, Brown's president along to add impact.

"So the evening before—mind you, I'd barely unpacked—Junior suggests hitting the town. I had some notes I wanted to peruse and in any case I wished to be fresh in the morning. So I declined. Well, Junior went out alone and God knows what he did. All I know is that when I awoke and entered the living room of our suite where I was going to entertain in an hour's time, I saw clothes strewn everywhere, a chair knocked cockeyed, and I think the smell of vomit strong as battery acid eating at the air in the closed room. I looked in at Arthur, and his bedroom had been struck by a tornado. I had less than an hour and there appeared to be no way to rouse Arthur. I couldn't believe it. My trip was in ruins."

"What happened?" I asked.

"Eventually Arthur got up and took a shower. We aired out the room. Somehow we were assembled when our guests called. Arthur stumbled through breakfast. Can you imagine behaving like that? He almost sabotaged everything and negated the purpose of our visit to Paris. And, need I add, he could have brought more than a measure of ridicule to our imprint."

I did not tell Ned that Junior viewed his own nighttime shenanigans as quite differently and thought that it was Ned, not he, who had acted strangely in Paris. Amused, I often thought of the two men, so opposite and willing to tattle on each other, yet close and supportive when necessary. Naturally, I sided with Junior, for I, too, would have been out all night and I would have gambled that I could pull off a business breakfast which to my way of thinking was of little consequence when one considered the glory and sexuality and fervor of Paris. I looked at Ned with kindness. You could not help but warm to him, but in my view, he was without flair.

●   ●   ●

Upsetting as my analytic sessions were, down in my subterranean self they were freeing me, and with each revelation came a glimmer of hope, a hope that I was okay. The old scorn in my father's voice—"fumblefinger"—when I tangled my fishing line was losing its wretched power. I was free to pursue life, and although life was soaked with drink and full of what I imagined to be romance, it also was sparkling with many bright moments, and most of these shining times occurred during my editorial forays. As a fledgling editor I began courting people and situations that I could put between hard covers for Little, Brown.

The first book I acquired for Little, Brown was a biography of F. Scott Fitzgerald's role model and hero, a Princeton legend named Hobey Baker. Hobey Baker was for his time the best college hockey player who ever laced up skates. He excelled at football and was handsome and easy-going. He'd flown with the American Flying Corps during the First World War and at war's end remained in France. In an act that would enshrine him among the legends of the postwar era, just after the Armistice he took a plane airborne to check its engine and crashed to his death. Adored by young society women and an idol to the college crowd and to all college athletes, he went down, ironically, not in combat but in peace. It was all bad luck, and the irony of his death rode through the Lost Generation.

I remember the excitement of producing that book. Our New York editor, Alan Williams, who lived in Princeton, where Hobey Baker's photograph hung over the bar at the Nassau Tavern, was very helpful. Although Baker was my idea, Alan produced the author, one John Davies, who edited the Princeton alumni magazine. Eventually I would visit John in Princeton, and I would visit Alan Williams there as well. Editorial projects like the Baker book could take months to get rolling: acceptance of an idea, meeting with agents, finding a writer, acquiring an outline or a proposal of some kind, writing up a contract—visiting, talking, laughing, drinking. I loved it.

I soon began to develop a list. By 1963 I had signed Massachusetts Attorney General Edward Brooke, the highest-elected black official in America. As we were working on the book with his ghostwriter George Feiffer, Leverett Saltonstall decided not to run for reelection to the U.S. Senate in 1966. Ed Brooke stepped into the gap. We published his book, a wake-up call to the Republican Party called *The Challenge of Change*, as a work of substance that also embellished his campaign. Working with him was memorable. His café au lait coloring stirred the guilt of white people throughout the state. He rode the civil rights bandwagon without being an activist. Amid the racial turmoil of the '60s he allowed

Massachusetts to feel good about itself. A Republican, he won easily in a heavily Democratic state.

It was my understanding that the entire book was written by George Feiffer. I rewrote one chapter myself. Ed Brooke would look over the pages before they went to the printer. Later, at a New York City press conference, in answer to a direct question from a journalist, I thought I heard Ed Brooke say, "I wrote my book; it was all mine." Given what I knew about the book's genesis, I did feel that Ed Brooke's claim to sole authorship was a trifle inflated.

Ed was very charming. Everyone said he enjoyed the ladies, and I envied him his easy way with people. He had a rambling summer house on the Vineyard, once owned by a childhood friend of my mother's named Coolie Morningstar. I was pleased by the change of circumstances that brought a man of color to Martha's Vineyard as owner of a well-known summer place, once the scene of flapper-era parties. I was happy to be part of this welcome change, a revolution in society, and was proud to be involved with a successful mainstream politician of color. It was, at the very least, my gesture toward a movement whose time had come, and at the same time I thought how feeble was my gesture, so safe and without risk.

Off and on my failure to sign contracts with David McCullough and Gail Sheehy rankled. Neither was known. I could not stake my reputation on them because I had yet to achieve a reputation. Still, I should have laid it on the line: take these writers or lose me. Because of my enthusiasm, I think both writers would have gone with me to another publisher where I could have edited their first books, which were respectively, *The Johnston Flood* and *Hustling*. McCullough's huge success was inevitable and so was Gail Sheehy's. Alas, I let them go while I hunkered down in Boston. I liked both Thornhills and Ned Bradford too much to leave Little, Brown, and I did not know how to assert myself.

And so it went. One New York night, out on the town with David McCullough, I bumped into a complete stranger on the street named Florence Pritchett Smith, who proceeded to pick me up and sweep me along with her. Flo had been Jack Kennedy's girlfriend and longtime confidante. She was with a couple named Stéfane and Lil Groueff. I left David on the sidewalk and trotted along with Flo into Shepard's, a disco in the Hotel Drake. This chance encounter produced a flirtation with

Flo, and in time Stéfane, who worked for *Paris Match*, completed a major book, *The Manhattan Project*, the first detailed history of how the atom bomb was made, which I edited.

When I met Flo Smith, she was falling apart in the aftermath of Kennedy's murder. At night, full of vodka, she'd weep. Kennedy, who still lived in her mind, had been her neighbor in Palm Beach, where she resided part-time with her husband, Earl E. T. Smith, who was Eisenhower's ambassador to Cuba when Castro overthrew the government. From Flo I gathered that Smith was a myopic snob who looked down on Cubans. The only place he'd allowed Flo to visit was the Havana Country Club. The ambassador was allied with the oligarchy of sugar barons who would fall before the hugely popular Fidel Castro. Smith's leanings toward the rich and powerful may have influenced President Eisenhower, who failed to respond to Castro after his triumphant march up Park Avenue in 1959. Eisenhower should have understood that Castro could have been an ally, someone to bring along as a friend.

Earl E. T. Smith, now mayor of Palm Beach, allowed Flo to live with a maid in their large New York apartment, where I was an occasional visitor. We often dined together, and several times she dragged me off to parties where I met her friends. I remember names from the society columns such as C.Z. and Winston Guest, Earl Blackwell, Denny Slater, FiFi Fell, the Joseph Meehans, Truman Capote, and Henry Ford II and Cristina Vettore Austin.

Once back in time when she was a publicist in Hollywood, Flo was engaged to the actor Robert Walker. They never married because Walker still loved his ex-wife, Jennifer Jones, who had left him for David Selznick, head of Twentieth Century–Fox. According to Flo, the actor would get into his cups and wail about Jennifer's leaving him for the famous director. I gathered that Robert Walker died from drink and a broken heart. I think Flo worked for *Life* magazine and one way or another, at some party, she met Earl Smith, who won her hand. After Cuba, they lived in Palm Beach where they raised one child, a son. It was my impression that Flo had little use for her husband but was afraid of him and certainly did not want her peccadilloes to be relayed on to Palm Beach. Therefore we told people that she was writing a book and I was her editor, which could have been true. She was at the time finishing a book for Macmillan called *These Entertaining People*. I had got the green light from Little, Brown for a large coffee-table book she wanted

to do, to be titled *The World of Fashion*. Flo had contacted Diana Vree-
land at *Vogue* to help her, and when we met at 21 or Caravelle or Le
Pavillon we talked about our project.

Basically our relationship centered on being drinking buddies,
confidence spillers, and lovers to a point. I write "to a point" because we
drank so much that by the time we got back to her place, Flo would be
completely unraveled. Often she was very tipsy or crying over the death
of Jack Kennedy, and as time wore on her drinking grew worse. She was
fine throughout the day, but by night she'd be pickled. Drunk or not,
we'd go to El Morocco, where men would stop at our table to pay
court. Afterwards I'd take her home and caress her and tell her everything was all right. I hung on to her because she was hugely popular,
very pretty and quick-witted, and would never comment on how much
I drank. And I suppose knowing that I was going where Jack Kennedy
had been pleased me.

I was in New York on business a good deal in those days so it was
easy to see Flo. By 1965 Al Hart and Harry Sions had become our two
New York editors, plus Harry Houghton, now in the city to sell paperback rights for Arthur Senior. We had a full-time publicist, Lynn Caine,
who would write a best-seller titled *Widow*. There were two secretaries,
one who eventually married Al Hart and another who married Harry
Houghton.

One day Flo, who knew when I was in town, called me at our
New York office and told me to be ready at seven. "We're going out to
dinner with Henry and Cristina," she said.

Henry Ford looked rich. Very rich. If I had to describe this rather
short, dumpy man with average looks, I'd say *rich*. Born rich, grown up
rich, feeling like American royalty, with a name that virtually everyone
would recognize, he carried himself like a pharaoh. He was crude, loud,
and yet charming. Without his money he would have been just crude
and loud. But this true heir to the American system, this ultimate capi-
talist, was indeed charming in the sense that he owned America, was
keen to include you in his circle, and paid for everything with a grin
and a wave of the hand. He said what he wanted to say and he drank
nonstop. He adored Cristina Austin, a very beautiful woman, more
beautiful than Flo, who was lovely to look at but not beautiful in the
luscious sense of the word embodied by Cristina. Cristina, with her
long, tousled blond hair that fell so casually over her face and neck and

her ears, so professionally mussed up, her statuesque body…I could not keep my eyes off of her. I undressed her as I sat across the table from her, not paying heed to Flo, who was reminiscing with Henry.

Henry called me "Little Nigger." For some reason he couldn't remember the name Brown, as in Little, Brown. He knew I worked for a book publisher but never got its name right, and when he zeroed in on me he would call out, "Hey, Little Nigger, what do you think?" Joseph Meehan and his wife, Kay, were with us but kept silent. We watched Flo and Henry spar and laugh and drink. All five of us feasted on Cristina's beauty.

We drove about New York in a Lincoln ambassadorial stretch limousine with a bar in the back, as well as a radio and a telephone. Henry's chauffeur acted like his bodyguard. Wherever we went, we double-parked. We bar-hopped, and where we finally ate dinner I can't now recall. I do remember that we were at a corner table in the dark. Flo was on my left and Kay Meehan was on my right and Cristina and Henry were opposite me, sitting side by side. She called him "Bambino," and he called her "Bambina" and they stared into each other's eyes as lovers do. Eventually we went to El Morocco, where Henry told the maître d' to put us in "Siberia," the term for the very rear of the club, out of the limelight, where midwesterners with money but without chic were placed. Henry, from the Midwest and devoid of chic, wanted to be where no one would see him. Back in "Siberia," he was at home. Neither Leonard Lyons nor Earl Wilson nor Suzy Knickerbocker would find him there. Cristina and Flo, both of whom could stop traffic, were also happy to be incognito. The Meehans, like myself, were just along for the ride.

Because Henry chose not to dance, I danced with Cristina. Throughout my life I was always far too self-conscious to dance and had never even danced with Flo, yet I felt obliged to take this beautiful native of northern Italy onto the dance floor and revel in the gaze of so many onlookers, all of whom were wondering who was the lucky man with Cristina Austin. Vanity ruled. Riding high like the movie star I had never become, I seized the moment. That night was the first time in my life that I was center stage as Cristina and I twirled about in tight circles on the crowded dance floor. I felt very rich as both Cristina's body and Henry's money touched me and turned my head.

After El Morocco we pulled up before P. J. Clarke's, the historic saloon on Third Avenue, famous as a drinking spot. The huge stretch limo idled in front of the bar and Henry barked, "Little Nigger, go in and tell them we want a table." Instantly I caught the humor in this mission: *Nobody but nobody is going to believe this,* I thought. I had been in Clarke's many times. Though not a regular, I would probably be recognized as just another customer of no consequence, a guy who occasionally stopped in for a drink.

I walked up to the headwaiter. In the back was a grillroom that ran deep along the side of the city block. It was always dark and crowded in there. Quickly I saw the harried maître d'. I said that I was with Henry Ford and a party of six and that Mr. Ford wanted a table in the back. The tuxedo-clad guardian of the grill looked into my face. "Bullshit," he said, finally.

"No. Not bullshit," I replied. "Go to the front window and look out."

Reluctantly the man angled his way through the press of people at the bar and looked through the plate glass window out onto Third Avenue. There it was, a limo that seemed to run the length of a Fifth Avenue bus. Stunned, the maître d' swung about and walked back to me, nudging aside customers three deep at the bar. "Yes, sir," he said. "Tell Mr. Ford that we will have a table at once."

The limousine remained double-parked in front of Clarke's. We sat along the right-hand wall toward the end of the room. Tables were put together and people were displaced. Henry ordered four bottles of champagne. The Grand Pooh-Bah, America's child, and his mate had arrived.

The night ended long past 4:00 A.M. Flo gave out around 1:30. She was obviously drunk, and Henry sent her home in the limo while we were in a bar somewhere, perhaps still at Clarke's. By 3:30 the Meehans had departed. By 4:00, when the last bar was about to close, we were in some nondescript bistro on the East Side where we'd found a piano with a pianist playing to only a handful of drinkers. This was perfect for Henry. He told the piano player to keep playing and gave the manager a knowing glance. We sat at the bar on stools and then Henry and Cristina fed the piano player requests as we all sang twenty-year-old songs from World War II. By now Henry and I were drinking feverishly. We drank bottles of champagne like cowboys drink beer. There was little doubt in my mind about the bar staying open. Henry's "consideration" would be immense, enough to cover several slow nights. The three of us sang and imbibed and my arm was around Cristina's back and often she leaned into me as she'd bellow in poor English a line from "You'll Never Know" or "Moonlight Becomes You." I loved it. Though very loose, I was not drunk, and I knew that on the morrow I had a day full of appointments. Therefore, as the time neared 5:30 and Henry suggested I go with them back to his suite at the Regency Hotel, I demurred. "For Chrissakes, Little Nigger," he said. "Chrissakes, don't give up the goddam ship. Don't desert like some runaway. Where is your loyalty? We'll get room service at the Regency. Room service runs twenty-four hours a day," he offered as a bribe. "Don't leave, Little Nigger," he pleaded. But I did leave. We dropped Henry and Cristina at the Regency and his driver drove me to the Yale Club where I was a guest as the morning light began to slip into town, casting faint shadows behind the skyscrapers.

I was aware of the glitter that attended Henry and his lovely fiancée but I did not know how vulnerable I was to that form of excitement. Knowing Flo Smith intimately and being drawn into the margins of her life set me up for what would be my undoing. I often regretted not going along with Henry Ford. I might have seen him pass into sleep, and then the two of us, Cristina and I, would have been alone together. When I think of Cristina Austin, I think of my missed opportunities with the Duchess of Windsor and Katherine Anne Porter and I am beset with visions of what might have been and where it might have led.

Chapter 14

Time was running out on Flo Smith. She was growing weaker and getting drunk every time I saw her. Of late I had been taking her back to her apartment and then going out on my own. I often spoke to her about her condition. I thought it was psychological. She should see a shrink, I said. She laughed at that idea, afraid, I gathered, of letting loose a reservoir of feelings and revelations concerning the love of her life, Jack Kennedy. When she referred to Kennedy, tears welled up in her eyes. Once Flo recalled a fishing trip with Kennedy and his vice president, Lyndon Johnson. As she spoke, I heard the rancor in her voice whenever she mentioned Johnson.

"We were in Palm Beach and the President told me that though he hated to do it, he simply had to invite Lyndon down for a weekend. Jackie was absent, of course. She was never there. So Lyndon came and Jack and I and little Caroline Kennedy and a couple of the Secret Service went fishing. It was something that Jack figured Johnson would enjoy. It was nine or ten in the morning and we were out in the Atlantic when the vice president asked for a drink. Jack Kennedy never allowed drinking on the boat until the sun was over the yardarm—you know, noon. So he told Lyndon he'd have to wait. Now this big, lumbering man began to pace about in the cockpit and finally he plunged down into the cabin. Suddenly the silence was broken by Caroline, who was screaming on her way up to us—'Daddy, Daddy, this man is taking my lollipops.'"

Lyndon Johnson was a dreadful man, according to Flo, and her views were shared by Kennedy, she said. To a woman who valued style in an age when style was making a comeback, Johnson's crude gestures were offensive. Caught up in her derision, I saw her point, but I sympathized with Lyndon Johnson. That morning he needed a drink, and I knew what that entailed. If he couldn't get alcohol, then a lollipop to suck on until the real thing emerged would have to suffice.

One time Flo and I were having cocktails in the bar at Delmonico's when a Jack Kennedy confidant named Charles Spalding walked in. He told Flo to stay away from me. I was bad news, he said. I'd been to the men's room, and when I returned Spalding had gone, leaving behind a bothersome libel. Flo was smiling when she recounted his warning, but I was perplexed. Could it be that by now I was incurring notoriety? Was it possible that my many trips to New York, my encounters with women when I got there, and my heavy drinking had given me a reputation? I felt so constricted at home, I certainly wanted freedom and license in New York, where I'd always thought it was safe to let off steam.

Flo did not like Jackie Kennedy, although she admired her sexual allure. She bet me that Jackie would remarry "within five years." "She's sexy," Flo said. "She likes it." How much Jack Kennedy had told her about Jackie was not for me to know. Just tiny tidbits were dropped. Once when I walked Flo into the lobby of Mr. Kenneth's, a chic hairdresser, Jackie emerged and signed the guest register as Flo stood beside her. Neither spoke and neither gave an inch at the table where the register was placed. Seeing them side by side, widow and old friend, was heart-stopping. I waited for a scream, a hiss, a claw. There was nothing but stillness and a penetrating hostility. Afterward in the cab Flo said that the whole Camelot thing had been Jackie's idea. Jack Kennedy would have been furious about being likened to the Broadway version of King Arthur. He had no use for the musical *Camelot*. His favorite song, Flo said, was "Moon River," from the movie *Breakfast at Tiffany's*: "Wherever we went and there was a band, as soon as he stepped into the room the band would switch to 'Moon River.' *That* was his kind of song."

Flo called me in Boston and said she was coming to New England to visit prep schools with her son. I began figuring a way to leave home for a couple of days. We'd stay in country inns and drink in colonial taverns. The boy would sleep in his own room, down the hall. But Flo never called again. Her friend Lil Groueff told me she'd been taken to the hospital for exhaustion. I assumed it was related to her drinking. Apparently, not so. As it turned out, she had leukemia. She died quickly, not from leukemia but from a stroke. One day my wife was reading the *New York Times.* We were in our den at home in Brookline. "Didn't you know Florence Pritchett Smith?" she asked guardedly. "Wasn't she a friend of yours?"

I was struck with fear. How did she know about Flo? Who told her? What went wrong? I'd been so secretive…and then she spoke before I had a chance to collect myself and reply. "Florence Smith just died," she said. "It's here in the obits," and she dropped the paper on the floor and walked away.

Time was running out on my marriage, too. We both knew that it would never work because I drank too much and Wendy, quite understandably, objected to it, and I had no intention of slowing down. As for Little, Brown, my days there were numbered, too. I roared through the mid-to-late '60s like a rogue locomotive. When the director of the College Department called me "Boom Boom" after a well-known Canadian hockey star, he was not referring to ice skating. Rather, "Boom Boom" was his comment on my thrust, my *boom*, as I barged from project to project.

In my enthusiasm I was attracting authors, one of whom was Elliott Liebow, a sociologist I'd learned of from Dr. Benson Snyder one day at lunch at Boston's St. Botolph Club. Ben Snyder was chief psychiatrist at MIT and very interested in books and publications, and I had wonderful lunches with him speaking of book possibilities from his arena—the study of human behavior and psychology. He told me of a superb treatise Liebow had written on black men in Washington, D.C., who gathered at a prescribed spot—Tally's Corner—and waited for offers of work. His treatise needed publication.

Here, I thought, was a way to express my commitment to civil rights, which had been largely a passive one. Liebow's study was the real thing in its objective depiction of indignity within a system of day work forced upon Negro men. The facts spoke for themselves. The dialogue was rich with hurt, confusion, and bitterness. I had never read a book that portrayed the unfairness of life so simply and meaningfully. *Tally's Corner* became a continuing success in Little, Brown's paperback line and Elliott Liebow became very respected in his field.

Tom Gladwin was another nonprofessional writer whose name and address were given to me by Ben Snyder. Gladwin's book would be titled *Poverty, U.S.A.* In a '60s America roiled by rock and roll, sexual revolution, and protest, Gladwin wrote of very poor people far outside the swirl of contemporary living. Once again I could take pride in a serious work exposing the fragile dignity of man. Whatever social consciousness I possessed found an outlet in *Tally's Corner* and *Poverty, U.S.A.* Neither took much editing, and they might easily have found their way without me, but I felt exalted when Arthur Junior praised me at a sales conference, lauding my ability to bring in books that dealt with serious issues in America. All the salesmen were present, as well as Arthur Senior and the other editors. I had been singled out and saluted by the man who'd hired me. I thought then that my career in publishing was without limits.

•   •   •

Soon after it was published in 1962 I read *Scott Fitzgerald*, a biography by Andrew Turnbull that ignited a revival of interest in the dead novelist and his work. Some years earlier Bud Schulburg's, *The Disenchanted*, had begun it all, but Turnbull's book was the major boost. The aura of Fitzgerald was back, and for a while the life that he had led, so well depicted by Turnbull, seemed to justify my own. In a boozy, muddled kind of way I read into Scott Fitzgerald a person who could make me think that the way I smiled at my unhappy wife and drank to rid myself of irritation was perfectly fine. I was heartened and buoyed by this book about a charming and clever fellow who had been in his day the ranking American novelist. That I did not share Fitzgerald's talents on equal terms was not my concern.

It became my mission to meet Andrew Turnbull in person. He lived in Cambridge, and before long I was taking him to lunch. I tried to get him to write a biography of John Marquand but failed. Shortly before I left Little, Brown, his big biography of Thomas Wolfe came out. One day we found ourselves sharing a train ride on the New Haven, coming back from New York. Turnbull was despondent. Although *Thomas Wolfe* had been taken by the Book-of-the-Month Club, and was destined to be a best-seller, it was not getting acclaim equal to his expectations. He was morose, and though talkative, he was distracted by notions of failure. He was dispirited, and I sensed that like his idol Fitzgerald, Andrew saw himself losing touch with the present, drifting into a far corner where he would soon languish and be forgotten. When the Fitzgerald biography hit the bookstores he'd been in the limelight, basking in a glow almost as bright as that which had illumined his hero. Now it was over.

I never saw him again. He killed himself, and though I did not know him well, I was hurt by such an ultimate act. In my mind I related his death to the death of my father and, I suppose, to the death of a way of life that my father and Fitzgerald in their very different ways embodied. All the drinking and living in resorts, all the hotel lobbies and speakeasies and memories of the First World War—aspects of a life I had missed. I had always ached to be part of it, and Andrew Turnbull had brought it to life for me with his words. When he killed himself, he seemed to be telling me that he had not made the grade; the older crowd whom he'd admired and romanticized had passed on before he'd had time to join their ranks. So the hell with it: if he couldn't be Fitzgerald or Fitzgerald's friend, like Gerald Murphy or Edmund Wilson, it wasn't worth going on. Like his idol he'd failed, and now, within me, was growing a similar sense of defeat. Muddled by alcohol, I began to harbor notions of defeat and dropping out of sight, if not dying. I had seen a documentary called *On the Bowery*, and now it was haunting me. I wanted to run off and live on the Bowery. For a short time I thought again of joining the Army and going to Vietnam and becoming a dead hero. Had Andrew not killed himself, I doubt I would have been so disturbed. But he died abruptly as did my father, and in that abruptness lay a penetrating image of defeat, and it festered in my mind until I drank it away. Turnbull was a remote man with whom I had only a superficial friendship, and so it surprised me that I cared about his suicide. It was only years later, my father not withstanding, that I realized his suicide struck me so deeply because I felt I was at the end of the road.

•   •   •

While my work was becoming my life and vice versa, my family was on its own course with school and play and society. Wendy played golf and tennis at private clubs and appeared to be comfortably settled in the upper crust. By now it was obvious that I was going to be a loose cannon. I did not look bad on paper. Everyone seemed to respect a book editor, and I rather think I carried myself well. It was just that alcohol was beginning to own me.

A not so subtle tug-of-war began over where we would spend our summers, Martha's Vineyard or her family's place in Fenwick near Old Saybrook, Connecticut. On the Vineyard I was a better drinker. At Fenwick I drank faster, unconsciously trying to encase myself in booze so I wouldn't see the inanity of my time spent there. Each day had a routine—tennis, a swim, cocktails, long lunches with vodka and tonic, then golf. At the end of the afternoon we'd wedge in more tennis. After a swim, the evening was for drinking. By eleven I'd be asleep, having survived a full day with my wife and her family. It was an endurance test without flair.

On the Vineyard I had a small powerboat for fishing. In the early '60s I took friends fishing for bass and bluefish. I had merry times and spent happy evenings with a first-class fisherman, Kib Bramhall, and his wife, Tessie. I drank a lot and thought I was a hearty outdoorsman. Often during the day I'd walk the beaches up island, sometimes returning to Gay Head, to Zack's Cliffs, where I'd taken girlfriends in my bachelor days. Samantha Crichton, who flew up from New York, had gotten very sunburned one June day at Zack's. In my loneliness I longed for her, remembering her naked on a large beach towel, beginning to redden from the sun, her blondness evident and inviting to me. I thought of her as I walked and I remembered Joan Johnston, who would skinny-dip but then quickly cover herself on the beach. She always maintained that her deep tan contrasted in a sexy way with her white breasts, and I loved to watch her slip into her bathing suit, teasing me as she covered herself. And so I would walk, unconsciously looking for another Samantha or Joanie.

Once in those unhappy days with Wendy, I struck out alone and came across a sunbather, supple and slender, though older than I. She was a Danish woman married to a surgeon in Boston. We began meeting by accident in the dunes at Zack's Cliffs and I'd have furtive sex with her. Both of us were unloved. We meshed together in quick interludes and then walked away. I broke it off when it occurred to me that she was a talker; she claimed to be a member of the European intelligentsia. In her bohemian way she'd tell people about us and it might get back to Wendy. As always, I feared Wendy's wrath. Her tone of voice reduced me to infancy. I hated defending myself. I felt like a kid who had been sent home from school. I was a little boy who'd misbehaved.

Now, remembering the affairs I had during my marriage, I know I excused myself by believing that I did what I did in order to survive as a person. One-nighters were common. Some went on for several nights on and off, and I often used the Hampshire House on Beacon Street as a trysting place. I had access to a room upstairs and eventually rented a room for a few months.

In 1967, near the end of my marriage, I met Barbara Cummings in the bar of the Hampshire House. Barbara was a freelance artist who worked on the covers of book jackets. I also had Anne Wigglesworth typing away as my secretary but, as I remember it, Anne, whom I adored, was engaged to a young man serving in Vietnam. It was 1967. Her hair was brown with a light golden shine to it and she had a neat, very strong body. She was fairly short, and from old Yankee stock. She wore glasses and when she stared directly into my face her eyes stimulated feelings of tenderness that I dared not probe. I think she was twenty-two years old. I was thirty-seven and all I could do was entertain thoughts. I realized that I was crazy about Anne Wigglesworth but I never told her. Her fiancé in Vietnam and her innate goodness held me at bay and I was too old.

A Phi Beta Kappa graduate of The University of Pennsylvania, Barbara was interested in weaving and poetry as well as art and editing and she took my mind away from Anne Wigglesworth. She had a boyfriend, whom she probably married, who had found a job working in a laboratory at Eastman Kodak, two hundred miles away in Rochester, New York. Barb was a drinker and was tall and full-bodied with dark blond hair. She took the initiative in sexual matters: she told me that her record for multiple orgasms was seven. Together we produced no more than three. Ours was the sort of "liberated" relationship where we counted the number of times she came.

Once when Wendy was away with the children Barbara insisted on coming home with me. When it was time to go to bed, I led her into the guest room. I felt obliged to keep her out of my marriage bed. It would have been too disloyal, and I told her as much. In a huff, she bypassed the guest room and went into the backyard and disappeared. I called for her, to no avail. In the morning around 6:30 I looked out my window. Barbara was up in a maple tree, sound asleep, sprawled like a cheetah. I called Barbara down from the tree and then drove her home.

Once I gave her a manuscript to edit. I'd signed up a fellow named Reynolds Thatcher who was going to walk across America. I thought he would spin a good tale about America, seeing it from the side of the road, behind the doors on which he would knock, asking for a place to sleep. I told Ned, "This could be one hell of a great book."

"Could be," he said, and gave me the green light.

When the trip was over and the manuscript arrived, I gave it to Barbara. She took it home and in due course returned it to me, all edited. I turned it in to Copy Editing for that department's precise checking of syntax and any allusions to names, dates, and places that appeared in the text. A few days later I awoke suddenly and spoke to my mirror: "What have I done?" Reynolds Thatcher by profession was a mason. By avocation he walked country roads. He didn't write. I'd taken Barbara's Phi Beta Kappa key at face value. Ned Bradford would not be sanguine. Randy Williams would kill me. At the last minute I retrieved the manuscript from Copy Editing and began to read. Just as I feared, Barbara had corrected a few obvious mistakes, smoothed over some rough spots, but the whole thing needed polishing; it needed a script doctor.

I was able to improve the book sufficiently and in course it was published. *Publishers Weekly*, a trade magazine, gave it high marks, but by the time the book came out in 1967, I was reeling along in a messy situation that precluded my helping oversee the advertising and promotion on behalf of my walking mason and budding writer. Feteridge, whose only exercise was walking down Beacon Hill to Purcell's for three double martinis, failed to comprehend the charm, the nostalgia, and the adventure and let the book drop. As for Barbara, I began to lose interest in her as I blamed her for my cavalier behavior with a manuscript under contract. I'd let her mislead me. She worked as an artist and I should have known that she belonged in the art department. I felt I'd been taken in.

We had our moments though. Barbara was a freewheeler who stayed up late with me, drinking and laughing and teasing, and I liked that. She was game. In the summer, with my estranged wife in Fenwick, and at the end of a long night I'd often leave her in bed at her apartment and drive home to Brookline in my new Plymouth convertible with the top down. I'd park in front of my house and fall asleep in the front seat of the Plymouth, listening to an all-night radio program that played love songs from the '40s and '50s. I remember it was sponsored by American Airlines. I'd fall fast asleep under the stars in my own driveway.

* * *

In spite of the horseplay with Barbara and other women and my drinking, I usually showed up for work to generate projects and pursue leads. I still sold serial rights, once selling a complete novel I had edited to *True*. I made the author, Allan Eckert, a quick $4,250, which he appreciated. As a matter of fact, he invited me to visit him in Florida, which I did. We fished in the Everglades with a leathery frontiersman and fishing guide, Homer Rhode. I stayed with Homer on his houseboat moored in the glades. Homer was a serious reader of history and in thanks I shipped him a complete set of the works of Francis Parkman. I learned to catch snook from within the mangrove roots. My father would have been proud of me.

Later I met Ike's son, John Eisenhower, in Valley Forge, Pennsylvania. I had him signed up for several books until the deal was scotched by Ned Bradford. John flew up to Boston to meet with Arthur Junior, Ned, Randy, and, as always, the laconic Feteridge. We lunched at the Union Club. He wanted an advance of $45,000 over three years to write a big book on the Allies in World War II, based on his father's private papers. The lunch backfired. Ned, always a diehard liberal and an Adlai Stevenson Democrat, told me that John Eisenhower was a fascist. I thought Ned was simpleminded. I'd gone through a good deal of trouble to steal Eisenhower from Putnam and Doubleday. Before it all turned sour, I'd arranged a meeting with Ike and secured the blessings of his publisher, Doubleday, to, in effect, still the aging General's urge to write for publication. Sam Vaughn, high up at Doubleday, and Ike's son John were able to extract from the General his personal papers to serve as the basis for one, and maybe two or three Little, Brown books.

Usually I was impervious to hangovers, but on that day, driving down to Valley Forge from New York with Sam Vaughn, Doubleday's esteemed senior editor, I felt terrible. I'd been with a well-known literary agent. She was hard drinking and energetic and had worn me out. For a night or two she and I had hit it off, and I stayed with her. The drinking was fierce, and I recall feeling like death by the time I had to meet Vaughn. I had not yet resorted to the morning drink for a pick-me-up, so I suffered.

At John Eisenhower's house I finally got some cocktails down, and for a few hours I felt splendid. Riding high, the three of us took off to meet John's father in Gettysburg. We arrived in the rain at about 10:00 P.M., and before we checked into a Holiday Inn, John felt obliged to show us most of the battlefield. As I had no other clothes, nor a second pair of shoes, I felt some concern. How could I face the General the next morning in a rumpled, damp suit and muddy shoes? What I needed was a drink, not a walk in the rain. John was insistent, however, and soon we were standing, wet and tired, where Pickett had launched his famous charge. Two hours later I was back in my room. The alcohol had worn off long ago. I was wet and the bar was closed. I was in a hell of a lot of trouble and could not sleep.

In the morning, Sam Vaughn, John, and I arrived at General Eisenhower's conference room at 8:45. There were two aides there to greet us, one a brigadier general, the other a semiretired Doubleday editor, whose last name, I believe, was McCann. For some minutes we stood about the conference table, my nerves tearing my stomach apart. Then at exactly 9:00 A.M. Dwight Eisenhower entered the room. He looked very crisp and neat in a blue double-breasted suit. At once I saw him smile and felt the pervasive strength of his instinctive goodwill. It was that innate warmth which lay at the heart of his leadership. Deep inside he was saying *welcome*, and we were drawn to him.

But once past the glow of his smile, the General left little leeway for frivolity or light conversation. He was suddenly very formal, even when he greeted his son, now a colonel in the Army Reserve. The atmosphere was military, not political. In fact, he was to be called General, never President, Eisenhower. I sat terrified that the General might call on me to speak. Fortunately, Sam Vaughn did all the talking. He told the General that John wanted to leave Putnam and write a book for Little, Brown based on Ike's papers. As for himself, he was worried, he said, about Eisenhower's health and wanted him to stop writing. *You shouldn't do it anymore. Frankly, it's too much. You need to turn all your writing over to John*, was his opinion, an opinion that meshed nicely with my wishes to attract a major property.

Eisenhower listened and agreed to our plan. "I'll release everything to…what company do you work for, Mr. Hart?" he asked, suddenly staring at me. I tried to answer, but I felt a stammer overtake me. Thankfully, Sam intervened. I nodded my agreement and sat mute.

Relieved, I wondered when the meeting would adjourn. I began to shift in my seat. But no luck; Ike turned to the brigadier general at the other end of the table and began talking about a recent visit paid to him by William Westmoreland. It was the summer of 1966 and General West-moreland had reported to him on Vietnam. "Westmoreland says that in order to succeed over there it will take one million men in a line stretching across the width of the country, and this line with adequate air support will move up through the North and destroy everything in its path. That is the only way." Having delivered himself of West-moreland's opinion, Eisenhower received nods of understanding, and then he shook his head. "You know, I've always been given too much credit for my warning on the military-industrial complex, and I think I was taken out of context. But I was dead right about staying out of a ground war in southeastern Asia. A million men moving in a line…" he repeated, shaking his head, signifying that it couldn't be done and the war would be lost.

Others, including myself, now that I was sure he wasn't going to call on me to speak, urged him to go on, and so he began to reminisce. He talked of growing up and of West Point and his early days in the Army, stories he'd told in one of his books, *At Ease*. Then I remember him asking himself how he came to be picked by Roosevelt to become the Supreme Commander of Allied Forces in Europe. "I always thought that the job was Marshall's," he said. "You can't imagine the surprise when I received the orders." He went on to speak of historic battles, but I was not listening by then. I had got the okay from him—or, rather, Sam Vaughn had—and I could return to Little, Brown with a real pack-age to present. I did not for a moment anticipate that Ned Bradford would be fool enough to reject John Eisenhower and, by extension, the hero of D-day.

Maybe three months later, I was speaking with Franklin Roosevelt, Jr., whom I'd met through my cousin Tim Stanley, formerly our repre-sentative318 to NATO. Franklin and his wife, Sue, were spending the summer on Martha's Vineyard. I returned to Boston and proposed that I ask Franklin to write a memoir. I was under the impression that he had lived a very full life, and naturally he'd have some important insights into his parents. The more I thought of it, the more I liked it. Franklin had been Undersecretary of Commerce for Jack Kennedy, he'd been a U.S. Representative from New York and once ran for governor. Now he sold

Jaguars and Fiats in New Jersey. Back in 1966 the Eleanor and Franklin story was still uncharted territory. Joe Lash had not yet written his book. Elliott, another son, was as yet mute. I believed that Franklin, Jr., the namesake son, could write a hugely popular book on his parents, and in all probability a very entertaining account of his life on his own.

Ned and Arthur were sanguine but guarded. They were probably wondering how I thought I could pull it off. *How did Stan get to know Franklin Roosevelt, Jr.?* Ned would have been content with our multi-volume biography of President Roosevelt, written by the Harvard historian Frank Freidel. Why get mixed up with Franklin, Jr.? It could prove risky. The younger Roosevelt was controversial. Randy Williams, who knew the process of publishing and was by now watching me closely, seemed annoyed with the idea.

Though angered by Ned's rejection of the Eisenhower book, I began to pursue Franklin Roosevelt, Jr. I asked my cousin for Franklin's address, and then I wrote him at his office in New Jersey. "Fair enough," he said, when at last we talked on the phone. "I do have much to say, one hell of a lot," he told me confidently. "You get your ass onto an airplane and I'll have my driver meet you at La Guardia."

I was met in a new Jaguar sedan and whisked into the city. We picked up Franklin's wife near the Yale Club, and from there we drove west across the George Washington Bridge to the Palisades that rise from the Hudson River and on to his place of business. Franklin greeted Sue—rudely, I thought—and then he escorted me out to his car and from there to a rather crowded bar where we commenced to drink.

Franklin was a very large man with dark eyes, brown hair, and thick eyebrows. He looked and talked like a man who took good looks, money, and privilege for granted. It had always been thus.

He was a drinker like me—downing one after another. And, like me, he was unhappy. I judged from the way he greeted his wife that his marriage was under a strain. She was so cheerful and chatty in the Jaguar, though her husband could barely say hello. So we drank, two men trying to dodge personal turmoil, like blood brothers joined by drink. I'd seen his picture many times, usually in uniform. Our book on FDR at Duell, Sloan and Pearce, written by Dick Harraty, was mostly pictures, and I thought I remembered a shot of Franklin, Jr., in a white naval uniform. In any case, he remained imposing and handsome in a baggy-faced way. There was little question that he had presence, and I doubted that he would flinch were he back on his ship and under attack. Naturally I thought of my late father, who'd loathed the Roosevelts. If my father were looking down from heaven, he'd just have to understand. I was doing my job.

Franklin and I talked for at least two hours. I've forgotten most of the conversation. What I do recall him saying was that he'd received his Jaguar dealership through the intervention of Winston Churchill. Churchill had asked "the old man" what he could do for him after the war was over. How could Churchill personally repay Roosevelt for his actions prior to Pearl Harbor, for instance, when the old man circumvented Congress and sent ships and relief to Great Britain? His father answered that he needed nothing, recalled Franklin, but if Churchill felt obliged, he could help his children. "And that's how I got the franchise," he said. "It was Churchill's influence. Every Jaguar sold in the States goes through our lot." I assumed that he had received the Fiat dealership in a similar manner, as spoils of war, but we did not talk about Fiats. The Jaguar dealership impressed me—so many of them in rows, back on his lot. Who wanted a Fiat? I thought. My mind soared aloft as we kept ordering drinks.

Then he began talking of the war, recalling how the old man had called him and Elliott to his encampment at Casablanca in North Africa, where he'd gone to meet Churchill in 1943. Eisenhower was there too. "We'd both been screwing Kay Summersby," Ike's aide and supposed girlfriend, Franklin said. "We were getting a little break from the war, and I remember being in the old man's tent when he came back from a trip into the desert with Eisenhower. They'd been gone for hours, off to see some ruins, maybe from the siege of Carthage." He continued, "Anyway, the old man returned and right off he told me that he'd selected the man who would lead the Allied invasion of Europe, our Supreme Commander. I assumed that he and Ike had discussed it and naturally they'd agreed on General Marshall. I was wrong, of course. Here's what my father said: 'No, not Marshall. I have selected General Eisenhower. We're going to be dealing with Churchill, and whoever leads the invasion is going to work closely with Winston, and to do that he simply must know history. Eisenhower is an historian. He knows history the way Churchill does. They'll get along. Marshall wouldn't get along. Cooperation is crucial.'"

So there it was: Eisenhower over the more obvious choice of Marshall because FDR had been out in the desert ruins with Ike discussing the razing of Carthage and he'd known every detail and the strategy like a true historian. "A smart son of a bitch, Ike," Franklin, Jr., said, staring into my eyes with a dark look so I wouldn't forget that he'd been with his father when history was made.

Because I'd recently met Eisenhower and been witness to his puzzlement over why he had been chosen, Franklin's explanation was not something I would take lightly or fail to remember. And Franklin's claim to having sex with Kay Summersby—that was a thought that excited me. Wartime romance: sex and danger and the desert and the endless sky full of stars at night. I remembered photographs I'd seen of the very naked Frances Langford also on the desert, the same desert, as part of a Bob Hope tour entertaining Patton's army. In an alcoholic rush I told Franklin about Miss Langford and he smiled knowingly.

I suspect I was somewhat awestruck by Franklin Roosevelt, Jr. I was out of my league, and I could have guessed that when he sobered up, he'd wonder what in hell *that* was all about.

For whatever reason, the project never got beyond our long lunch. Franklin told me that Joe Lash was writing the story of his parents. (A few years later I threw an autographing party for Joe Lash at my Martha's Vineyard bookstore in honor of his Pulitzer Prize-winning biography *Eleanor and Franklin*.) As for his own life, Franklin let his autobiography hang fire. My impression was that there'd been too many marriages and affairs and not enough solid accomplishment. Without his parents' story to relate, his own was too steamy, too fraught with privacy issues, wartime hijinks, and political maneuvering. It was mostly the story of a man who'd led a rather hedonistic life. Ned Bradford could relax. I told him that Franklin probably didn't have a book. Eleanor's confidant Joe Lash was going to write the real story, for some other publisher.

· · ·

During my last few years at Little, Brown, 1965 to 1968, I kept on the move, pursuing leads. Some had worked out such as the lead I received from Stéfane Groueff whose own *Manhattan Project* did very well indeed. Stéfane told me about an exceptional young man, recently graduated from Princeton, named John Heminway. "He is the youngest person ever to become a member of the Explorers' Club," said Stéfane. John Heminway was a very talented young man with a writing career before him, I was told.

I met John and encouraged him to write *The Imminent Rains*, an account of the white settlers whose lives were being squeezed by the changing times and tensions of postcolonial East Africa. He had begun it as a thesis at Princeton. The book was laden with nostalgia and personal involvement by the young American. John eventually wrote another book called *No Man's Land*. He became an unusual Africanist, writing from a white man's perspective; to me this was engaging stuff that spoke of the old ways of white adventurers who'd answered the call of the Dark Continent.

John himself was likable, a tall, blond, good-looking chap who seemed to know everyone in New York. He eventually landed on public television with a show called *Travels*. He once said he owed his career to me: thanks to me *The Imminent Rains* gave him his start. John Heminway provided one of the more rewarding and sane interludes in my career. Other interludes were not so sanguine, as Ned would say.

For instance, Veronica Lake. I'd met her once, years before, when I was drinking at the Hotel Fifth Avenue and we ended up celebrating our birthdays together. Now, in 1966, I decided to find her and get her to author a book, to be called *The Decline and Fall of a Movie Star*.

When I'd met her back in 1959, she was working as a waitress at the Martha Washington Hotel, a hotel for women. To find her in 1966, I used my contacts and eventually located a talent agent named Corman who knew her. He called her Ronnie and claimed he represented her, although for the last fifteen years or so she'd been "out of work." He promised to find her and, lo and behold, within a couple of weeks I received a call: "Meet us in New York. Ronnie is very interested in a book."

Ronnie was also interested in appearing on Johnny Carson's *Tonight Show*. To that end—and as a way to launch her writing career—Corman somehow arranged to get her on that extremely unapproachable show. I flew to New York and we rendezvoused at a small apartment in Greenwich Village. Veronica asked me to go jitterbugging with her. Then she told a long story of how Howard Hughes had held her captive on a mountaintop out west. She told of her escape and how she'd fled Hollywood to elude Hughes. Great stuff, I thought, but I noticed that as she held forth in the small apartment, she was drinking. Johnny Carson was televising, live, out of New York. She had to be at the studio by 7:30 or 8:00. I left the apartment and agreed to meet

Corman and Veronica after the show to celebrate her "return." Sad to say, I met Corman, who was furious, but no Veronica. She'd managed to get drunk prior to airtime and had been rudely ushered from the studio. "After a heated exchange," as he put it, "she was banished." A day later I was back in Boston telling Arthur Junior that I'd lost Veronica Lake. I told him that I'd persevered, I'd followed her trail since our first meeting at the bar on Fifth Avenue, only to…but he interrupted me. "Veronica Lake!" he shouted. "I loved Veronica Lake. Remember her hair over her eye? That look!" he said, his eyes on fire. "But, Arthur," I said, "she didn't work out. She's a lush. Her hair is really mousy brown and she is unkempt." "Okay," said Arthur. Then after a pause he asked, "Why didn't you tell me about Veronica Lake? I would love to meet Veronica Lake."

It wouldn't have worked, I told him again, but he was lost in his memories of old movies and 1940s glamour. Veronica Lake died in 1973. She did get a book published, though it was panned and quickly went out of print. I seem to remember that she sobered up and found religion. Veronica Lake was an embarrassment for me, and chasing after her for a book shows how desperate I was becoming. I was looking for a big splash.

The Veronica Lake episode made Randy Williams turn his eyes to the ceiling. Randy, who by then was keeping a close watch on my drinking, feared that I wasn't really chasing a book. What I was after, he thought, was a good time at company expense. Hanging out with a forgotten film queen might fool people like the Thornhills, who enjoyed a good time. He was right. It should have been obvious that by 1966, for me chasing books was like chasing a party. Work was now inseparable from cocktails; a very liquid social life and my job as an editor were as one.

I used authors as excuses. John Heminway and I drank at Marie's Crisis Café in the Village, and sometimes I went on my own to Elaine's on the upper East Side, where I'd find the playwright Jack Richardson, Lewis Lapham, and a floating game of stud poker. Richardson and Lapham played with a man named Coco Brown and some others whom I have forgotten. After four or five sessions I quit while I was ahead. You played till 9:00 A.M., you could lose several thousand. It was tough sledding, staying up all night, perhaps losing a thousand dollars, and then having to get to the New York office in reasonable shape in time to start a full day in the city, making a round of magazine editors and perhaps an agent or two before finally boarding the shuttle for my return to Boston. I was thirty-six and I was getting old before my time.

Heedless of petty rules, I began to drive to work, parking my Plymouth convertible by the No Parking sign on Joy Street near Little, Brown's Boston offices. Joy Street ran up the hill beside our building at 34 Beacon. I could see my car from my window. George Hall, our treasurer, also could see my car, as could Randy Williams. Both men observed the Plymouth as it collected parking tickets. Neither knew that I had made friends with a Boston criminal court judge who was my drinking buddy at the Hampshire House. Periodically, I'd send a batch of tickets wrapped in rubber bands over to him. I paid a few fines before he gave me the nod. From then on until I left Boston I parked by my office with impunity. I think Randy thought I was crazy. George Hall probably thought I was so rich that tickets meant nothing.

Flo Smith was dead and Lillian Hellman was on the horizon, and, in the meantime, in between editing a book on China's development of the atomic bomb and another book on the Allied liberation of Rome, I let the good times roll on.

I was drinking and working madly like a whirling dervish, I had Arthur Senior giving me support—now they call it enabling—overlooking my excesses while urging me to bring in *the big book*. No more ponderous histories from England, no more "quality" novels without cachet or commercial appeal. We did have Harry Sions, former magazine editor who was quite commercial indeed, and his forgettable novels that made our list all made money via paperback and lesser book club editions. But other than William Manchester, he had not found the big author, the major writer. James Clavell, who had written the much-acclaimed, *King Rat*, had followed Herman Gollob off to Atheneum. *That* was the kind of author we needed more of. Arthur Senior saw me as a fellow with "the touch." For one thing he was impressed by Stéfane Groueff's *Manhattan Project*, a kind of *Longest Day* or *Is Paris Burning?* style of history that was obviously commercial. Ed Brooke, now a Senator, pleased him, and Senior was becoming a backer of our paperback line, for which I was the managing editor and continuously responsible. Regardless of my posture, Arthur Senior had high hopes. In early 1968, over drinks at Locke-Ober, he promised me I'd never be fired. I felt I had free rein.

And always there was Feteridge, who saw me as an alcoholic on the loose and wondered if my drinking might cast a spotlight on his own mulled behavior, which was pretty much in the closet, the worst of it supposedly known only to his ally Randy Williams. Feteridge was uneasy with me and so was Randy. Randy was used to Feteridge, but by 1966 he wanted me either out on the street with the unemployed or totally sober. Sober, I could be useful. For me, however, sobriety meant death. I'd known for a long time that I couldn't live without drink.

PART VI

Lillian and the End of My Beginning

Chapter 15

Back in 1960 when I opened my café and bookstore, Lillian Hellman and Leonard Bernstein had stopped by with a group for dinner. I gave them drinks on the house, as the town was dry and I had no right to sell alcohol. Sometime after that, Lillian came by with Dorothy Parker and woke me up. I slept upstairs, above the store. It was about 10:00 A.M. and they were on their way to the beach. I came down and had coffee with the two of them and before they left they asked me to join them at the beach. I declined. Dorothy Parker autographed her collected stories for me. Then they left.

As time wore on, Lillian's name gained a luster that went beyond her fame as a playwright. By 1966 she was a prominent figure in our celebrity culture, famous just for *being* Lillian Hellman. She was admired for her tough style and sharp wit. Ahead of the curve as the women's movement began to arc behind her, she became an icon, a towering example of the independent, sexually liberated, no-nonsense, cosmopolitan woman, more than equal to any man. I recall Leonard Bernstein referring to her as "Madam," in humor, of course, but with respect as well. Lillian Hellman was a living legend because she believed that she was, and believed it so deeply that everyone else believed it too.

When I lunched with her agent, Robbie Lantz, I asked if Lillian was ready to write her autobiography. His reply probably altered the course of my life: "She is thinking of it," he said guardedly. "However, she is under contract for just that sort of book with Random House. But wait," he said, waving a hand at me, "I think she's mad at Random House."

I asked him why. His answer was illuminating. "On the dust jacket of a collection of Dashiell Hammett stories that she had pulled together, called *The Big Knockover*, Random House had spelled her name with an extra *n*—Lillian Hellmann. "It made her cross," he said. Apparently at some point they'd also misspelled Hammett's name, in his case dropping a *t*. Such errors spelled doom for Random House.

My hopes soared. He continued: "She wants to write what she calls a 'memoir book,' not really an autobiography because she doesn't think of her life as being near its end. She doesn't like the word 'autobiography,' at least as it's applied to her." I told him I was very interested on behalf of Little, Brown. Naturally, I mentioned that I'd met Lillian when I ran my café and bookstore on the Vineyard. Robbie said he'd report back to me after speaking with her. He appeared pleased at the prospect of having Lillian move on to Little, Brown.

Before long I was in New York again. Once more Robbie Lantz and I lunched, this time at the Plaza. "She wants to see you," he told me. "She remembers you fondly. She'd like to have drinks with you, maybe dinner, before she makes up her mind."

I had written Lillian Hellman months earlier, out of the blue, and had talked to Arthur Junior about her over lunch at the Tennis and Racquet Club. To his credit, he saw my point at once. Yes, Lillian Hellman was bigger than the sum of her parts. She was news, and she worked at it so that there was this ongoing charisma attached to her, coming partly from the New Frontier crowd, who enjoyed her, partly from New York theater people, partly from her association with the old guard such as Ernest Hemingway and Dorothy Parker, who were now fading into myth, and the intelligentsia who harked back to the Spanish civil war and their fight against fascism. Just as forceful was the image of her standing up to the House Un-American Activities Committee as her lover Dashiell Hammett was sent to jail for his noncooperation. Lillian Hellman had actually told the committee to go to hell, to mind its own business. Her famous line was, "I cannot and will not cut my conscience to fit this year's fashions." Tennessee Williams had his bawdy "Streetcar" New Orleans motif and his homosexuality, and Arthur Miller maintained a crane-like aloofness that implied a very special probity regarding human character. Lillian had her life. A woman who was game, she'd been there and done it; to whom and how remained to be seen, which was part of her allure. Arthur Junior's eyes glistened: "Yes, Lillian Hellman would be a major acquisition," he said.

I took her for drinks and dinner and then she took me to bed. I am quick to admit that I was very excited about all of this. At first, becoming Lillian Hellman's lover and pleasing her sexually made me feel exalted. Now I'd been where I imagined Hemingway had been. Because of Lillian Hellman, I'd crossed the line from my brush with café society via Flo Smith into an arena filled with people of genuine talent. All manner of actors and producers and writers such as Bill Styron and Norman Mailer were her playmates. Lillian Hellman was a star, and sleeping with her made me feel important.

I was still married in 1966, although I was almost estranged. I was balancing my alcoholism with difficult hours spent in the office and at home editing manuscripts. I still had other administrative functions for the company, such as selling movie rights and serializations. I kept a regular social life in Boston and on the Vineyard and at Fenwick, and around the edges of it I was often drawn to young women, and although some might disbelieve me, I tried to be a good father to two young children. And, amazingly, there were times when my wife and I enjoyed each other.

When Lillian Hellman entered my life, I added a powerful, demanding, sixty-year-old woman to a mix that was about to boil over. That I thought I could handle her attests to the ego of an alcoholic. A functioning drinker can do anything. Lillian was already a legend, but I was a legend in my own mind, harboring a grandiosity that began to feed on my association with her.

Years later people would ask me what I saw in her as a sexual partner. She was not pretty. In fact, she was rather crude-looking, with a prominent nose; heavy, drooping breasts; a toneless white skin; a thinning pubis; and along with her fading allure came a sense of desperation. She wanted me to think she was beautiful. As a make-believe glamorous woman, she expected me to serve her, to stay on as her lover. I do not think she ever took in that I had a job, two children, and was technically married. Once, when I slipped into New York to see friends and somehow found myself at a party with a particularly fetching young woman, the word spread to Lillian. She was furious. I had no right to be in New York City unless I was with her.

Lillian must have asked me twenty times or more if I were rich. She put it this way: "You *are* rich, aren't you? I mean, you have houses on Martha's Vineyard. You are rich?"

I would nod and admit to being well-off. I knew that she did not want others to think she'd taken on a gigolo. If I had money, how could

I be a gigolo? Regardless, I felt like a boy toy, a lad who trailed behind his madam wherever she went. I was aware that she was full of herself and prized her connections to the Kennedy crowd. A CBS executive and Jack Kennedy classmate named Blair Clark impressed her, as did Richard Goodwin. "He is very bright, Stanley," she would say of Goodwin. She dragged me to parties for Patricia Neal and at least two parties at Sam Spiegel's and another one at Luchow's, where she was given a reception after the opening of a revival of *The Little Foxes*. I hated those parties because no one ever talked to me. I'd stand there trying to look like a nice guy and expecting some attention. When no attention came my way, I would drink heavily. I would get quite drunk and we'd take a taxi back to her place where we'd fall into bed. For some time, as we were getting to know each other, the last thing we did was address her work, her memoir book.

She did sign her contract with Little, Brown for an advance of $60,000—$20,000 per year for three years. This was so low an offer that as soon as she accepted I rushed the news to Arthur Junior. For tax reasons, she didn't want much money up front. The revival of *The Little Foxes* with George C. Scott and Anne Bancroft was going to be a smash hit.

Finally, we began to talk about her book. She was pacing in her apartment, chain-smoking, with a drink in her hand. "I want you to just sit here all day and read what I have," she said. It was an order. The time had come. I had allocated the whole day to Lillian in order finally to get a look at what I assumed was her work-in-progress, or in any case, what she had contracted to write. I did not know how we would proceed, and as always, I let her lead me.

She went to a closet and returned with a manuscript box full of yellow pages, second sheets from the old pre-Xerox days of carbon paper. She placed in front of me a stack of typescript that looked as if it could constitute a book. "Read it," she ordered, and so I did.

What I read was a series of essays and articles that she had written for *The New Yorker*. Each article was a unit in itself, smartly written, full of Lillian Hellman's abrupt, slightly wiseass, worldly sensibility. I loved it, and when I finished I told her so. She had been pacing on and off throughout the hours it took me to read her work. "How come?" I asked. "How come they are like this...on yellow carbon copies?"

"Rejected," she said, and that was all. Where the top copies were I did not know or ask. Perhaps they had been tossed out in a fit of pique once they came back from *The New Yorker*.

"What they need," I said, "is something to tie them together." Then I added encouragingly, "They are wonderful, so anecdotal. Each page has your mark on it, so full of your voice. But they need something to unite them, a common thread that runs through each essay." "You're right," she said, now looking in my eyes. She seemed pleased with me. I'd come to the same conclusion she had already reached on her own. Had I said that they were fine as they were, she would have been furious. What others thought about me would have been true: I was just a young body for her to exhibit, an ornament for her ego.

"Okay," I continued. "We need a thread to tie everything together, and the thread is your love affair with Dashiel Hammett. Hammett and you…*that* is the real story here." And so it was. And when *An Unfinished Woman* was published in 1969 and raced up the best-seller lists, I felt I'd contributed something that was crucial. In *An Unfinished Woman,* and particularly in her next book, *Pentimento,* in 1973, she took her long affair with Hammett and accented it, setting the scene for much talk of romance and a Jane Fonda movie depicting their love.

Dashiel Hammett himself prospered from his grave. Random House rushed out reprints of his novels. Collections of his stories and the novels were ordered by bookstores everywhere. Lillian, who always worried about money, was making money from all sides. *The Little Foxes* was a big earner. *An Unfinished Woman* would bring her a small fortune. Her plays were selling again, and because she was the executrix of Hammett's estate, royalties came to her from Random House via Hammett's heretofore dead account. Even Dorothy Parker, who died in 1967, had a reemergence, and there, too, was Lillian, once again an executrix. Money flowed, and with it came even more power. Lillian Hellman was now national news. Her charisma had always intoxicated the cognoscenti, but now she belonged to the people—people who had never seen one of her plays or heard of Dashiell Hammett. She was a celebrity.

• • •

But that was in the future. Now, with the book contract signed and her reworking of the *The New Yorker* material under way, I returned to Boston, resolved to stay there for a while. I was worn out and felt I'd "had it up to here" with Miss Hellman. The gigolo feeling I had was insupportable. But as the summer of 1967 neared, I became increasingly unstable, and I was unable to drop Lillian Hellman from my personal life. In fact she followed me to Boston, saying she wanted to be near her publisher and away from the hoopla in New York. She took a job teaching creative writing at Harvard to a small class three times a week.

I gave up drinking and tried to see her for dinner dead sober. It was an endurance test I could pass only twice. Intimacy in Boston went to hell because I was so often on the wagon and, when sober, the thought of being with Lillian made me feel cheap. I told this to Arthur Junior, who knew all about our affair. He smiled and said, "I think you've gone beyond the call of duty." In his smile there was pleasure as well as pity. Lillian's contract was safely in our vault. I had acquired an author of magnitude.

Once when I was still drinking, and before she settled into her Cambridge apartment, I spent an evening with Lillian in her room at the Ritz-Carlton. She had been very expressive, and she cackled in glee and was quite humorous and almost girlish fooling around in the bedroom. All of a sudden she stopped and grew alert like a dog hearing the rustle of a footstep. Then I heard what she was hearing, a loud, theatrical voice coming from behind the wall, in the next room.

"It's Lenny!" she exclaimed. "Leonard Bernstein. I'd know his voice and laugh anywhere, as he would know mine. He heard me. He heard *us*," she said, her face now furrowed with anguish. "He heard me," she repeated. Then, "Oh my God...," and to my great amusement she hurried into her clothes and began to shush me with her forefinger against her lips and the tip of her nose.

I tarried, smoking cigarettes and drinking, waiting for the room next door to grow quiet so I could slip out into the hallway and drive home. We heard muffled laughter occasionally interrupted by Bernstein-style histrionics. "Afterplay," I said to Lillian, but she shushed me again and told me to be serious. She did not want it known to her old friend that it was she who had been crying out her pleasure through the wall.

Around 1:00 A.M. I went to the door and opened it and stepped into the hallway. I'd said good-bye. I had to get home. As I shut the door to Lillian's room, the door to the next room opened and Lenny himself walked into the hall. He said nothing to me. I, with Lillian Hellman on the other side of her door, said nothing to him. In dead silence we walked side by side to the elevator and, once inside the lift, we stood shoulder to shoulder and neither of us spoke a word.

•   •   •

In June 1967 I suffered delirium tremens. I'd been getting drunk when I didn't expect to; my tolerance was erratic. One Sunday night, after a disturbing telephone call from Randy Williams asking me to get in touch with Svetlana Stalin, who had recently defected, I collapsed in bed having made what could be construed as impetuous telephone calls to New York. An hour later I awoke; there was a bear in the room, its claws extended, a hateful light in its eyes. No matter what my wife said to defuse the terror I felt, I retained my vision of the bear and shrank away in panic. Later on I reasoned that my DTs related to Lillian. She had been pressuring me two or three times a week with arch comments and demands. She kept calling and complaining: Why wasn't I taking her to dinner? Where was the limo when she arrived at the airport after one of her frequent trips to New York? Where were the flowers that should have been sent to her apartment attesting to her fame? Why wasn't she being treated better?

I was ruing my prostitution. I saw her as an old bag. I hated both her and myself. She'd called me a day or so before I saw the bear in my bedroom. She was furious that I had written a letter to a friend of hers in Paris, Donald Ogden Stewart, suggesting that he might wish to write a biography of Dorothy Parker. It was she who'd suggested I write him in the first place. As was her custom, she had been drinking and was trying to be helpful. She was giving me a tip: Mr. Stewart could do a good job. "He knew Dottie," she'd said.

Now the phone rang in my office and a venomous Lillian Hellman was screaming at me: "How could you write Don Ogden Stewart behind my back? He called last night from Paris. It took him forever to find where I lived. He was inconvenienced…he spent days trying to get my number. He was furious. I am the executor of Dottie's estate. You go through me," she ordered.

After I hung up, I told myself that it was over. No more Lillian. I couldn't stand her anymore. She was too much at odds with herself. She adored the Kennedy crowd and would purr at them when in their company, yet once, in the middle of an argument over labor unions, I asked her whom she respected more, Jimmy Hoffa or Bobby Kennedy. Her response was immediate. She snapped her answer at me: Jimmy Hoffa. It seemed obvious that though she liked the attention from a glamorous family, down deep they made her feel awkward. She probably resented their ill-gotten gains. She appeared enamored of the workingman. "I've been with labor all my life," she said by way of explanation. But Lillian Hellman didn't give a hoot for the worker. She loved to be with the rich and the important.

On another occasion when she was pacing her living room, a cigarette in one hand and a drink in the other, I asked her who she would rather be, a beautiful blond actress with no brains or a distinguished playwright, and she answered instantly—she'd rather be the blonde. Her response was unexpected, after her complaints about actors and the theater. "They are all so self-centered," she'd say. "A bunch of unbearable egotists," was her comment and I recall it vividly because she had just lunched with Warren Beatty who spent more than two hours talking about himself while Lillian writhed in her chair.

Lillian had a great deal of unfinished business with her father. She told me that she had broken off her psychoanalysis when they'd got into transference and she began seeing her father in her psychiatrist and what she was seeing was too disturbing. As for her mother, in the time I spent with Lillian she never mentioned her mother. Nor did she ever mention children. The overwhelming interest of her life was her life. Even her plays paled beside the drama inherent in the way she had lived since she first came to New York and was hired on as a reader for the publisher Horace Liveright.

Being intimate with Lillian Hellman drew me away from my own life. What Lillian never understood, however, was that I rather fancied my own life, and it was inevitable that in time I would return to it. We drank so much that the events of her world to which she alluded, always with a drink and a cigarette in hand, blended into a hazy montage of faces, places, and ideas; and our dialogues for the most part blurred into oblivion. Drink made our friendship possible, but it dulled my mind; there was not the slightest chance that I'd ever become her Boswell, retaining pearls of wisdom. She saw herself as a magnificent woman who could give good counsel to presidential advisers—Dick Goodwin, Arthur Schlesinger, Jr.—and as a grande dame of the theater, but she never gave me any precise definition of our relationship. She responded to me sexually; the rest was too amorphous to grasp.

If Lillian thought of me at all, it was as a trifle, a temporary whim. I was too young to be in her crowd, and I had not done anything to earn her respect. I had not been on the barricades. She'd been to Spain during the civil war, to Russia in World War II, and had told the House Un-American Activities Committee to go to hell. From the first, I knew that the only thing about me that pleased her was my youth. I brought her pleasure in a way that let her think of herself as a femme fatale. Surely that was what she always wanted to be: a woman whom men found irresistible. With me she could kid herself that she was, after all, quite a dish. Even in her mid-sixties. She was a canny woman and she saw a quid pro quo: Little, Brown gets her and makes a bundle; she gets me and gets laid. That was the deal.

After I saw the black bear in my bedroom, I took sick leave and went off to a hospital. For a short while I forgot Lillian Hellman, and my wife took my hospital stay as a time to file for divorce. It was early summer 1967 and the crowd in Fenwick knew at once of my turmoil. On the Vineyard there were rumors. My mother, who lived alone with nurses in attendance, did not know I had gone away. I did not want people to know that I had gone off to the Institute of Living in Hartford. For one thing, they might think I was crazy. More important, once I got out I might not be offered a drink. Clear-eyed I emerged from my short stay at the institute, but I did not stay clear-eyed for long.

·   ·   ·

At the beginning at Little, Brown I'd led a crisp life: early to work, early to bed, everything in focus. I see a man entering his thirties with a welcoming handshake, a smile on his face, and an assured future in a wonderful line of work. Although a dependent drinker, I was not yet a drunkard. I drank to relax and release inhibitions; I never drank to get drunk, and when drunkenness occurred, it was an accident that offended me. In those years my marriage was unfriendly at times and always difficult, but on balance I enjoyed myself, and as my son grew and my daughter came along, I was a passable father. Certainly I loved them, and I thought I loved their mother. Wendy could be warm and pleasant. If those times when she welcomed me with her heart were few, I can blame myself. My personality, my line of work, and my drinking kept her on guard. She'd never known what it was like to socialize with wild, imaginative people, the kind of companions I craved. The more I followed my cravings, the more guarded and vituperative she became. And my cravings carried me along into a series of situations, some of which were embarrassing, some of which were joyous.

In the spring of 1966 Lillian was planning a dinner party. She had a problem with her conscience and wanted my advice. Jackie Kennedy was coming to dinner and had asked if McGeorge Bundy could come as her escort. Lillian said of course, but was now thinking of canceling the party. How could she entertain Mac Bundy, a hawk on Vietnam? She tortured herself with worry. She didn't want to lose Jackie, a social coup of considerable magnitude. Though they knew each other slightly, the young widow had not yet been to Lillian's apartment. *Damn, why did Jackie have to bring Mac Bundy?* I suggested to Lillian that she could suspend her protest for a night. "It is a matter of principle," she replied, but in the end she did not renege on her offer to Mrs. Kennedy. One assumes that in Jackie's glow, Mac Bundy's support for our presence in Vietnam became irrelevant. When I asked Lillian how the party had gone, she said it had been fine. She said she had enjoyed McGeorge Bundy.

And speaking of Lillian's "matters of principle," she used that term another time. She had always liked Henry Wallace and was his supporter when he ran for president in 1948 as a candidate on the Progressive ticket. I remembered hanging about the Village in the spring of 1948 and noticing the odd mixture of longshoremen and academics, all sporting Wallace buttons. Though I was only eighteen, it seemed shortsighted to me for anyone to the left of the political center to be wasting his or her vote on Wallace, perhaps helping to ensure Dewey's victory. Almost twenty years later I still felt the same way and told Lillian so. "Don't say that," she said. "It's a matter of principle. Of course I would back Henry Wallace. You do what you know is right to do. You follow your conscience." Or so she said.

Several years later, in *Scoundrel Time*, Lillian's third book for Little, Brown, she recounted her visit to Henry Wallace to break the news to him that she had decided to vote for Truman. Everyone had to vote for the candidate who could beat Dewey. She was sorry, but that was how it was. So much for principle, I thought, as I read her words. Then I realized that she had twisted fact. She'd taken my comments to heart, and when it came time in her memoirs to write of Wallace, perhaps it was better to lie a little and say that she had defected and voted for Truman. Given her incredible ego, she was sure we all cared about her choice for President and, if she was going to make a point about whom she had backed in 1948, it would not reflect well for it to have been Henry Wallace, a candidate with no chance whatsoever. Lillian never wanted to look stupid.

When I write of Lillian's politics in 1948, I am aware that all of us rewrite our own histories to some extent; no one wants to look stupid.

But it's more difficult to excuse Lillian because she made such a point of being an uncommon woman. Her pronouncements and opinions were gravid, trenchant, always to be taken so seriously. She gave the appearance of being a straight shooter. Like a Hemingway hero, she projected an image of being true, reliable, tough. One saw her with Hammett, the Pinkerton man, the two of them as honest injuns—in Hammett's case, going to jail on principle. One saw Lillian telling the Congress to mind its own business. She threw me a curve when she lied about Henry Wallace. As for her dinner party, I was disappointed when she opted for glitter over her celebrated position as a woman of strong principle. I really expected Lillian to hold fast on Mac Bundy. She was so vocal a critic of our actions in Vietnam that I expected her gladly to forgo her chance to embrace Jackie in her own home.

I am older now than Lillian was when I was seeing her, and my view of her has softened. I can see my present physical self in the way I described Lillian then. Surely were I to take up with a woman only thirty-six years old, there would be occasions when she would look upon me as a codger, a bald man whose body has fallen, whose sexual drive lives in the mind and not where it counts, someone long over the hill. Mixing ages in sexual union is a risky business. It hurts the older partner whenever shame and revulsion occur in the young lover. Thinking along those lines, I am haunted by Lillian's comment that, if given a choice, she'd prefer to be a good-looking blonde rather than a respected playwright. She wanted men to like her, and she needed an ongoing sexual relationship—a love affair with all the trimmings. Beautiful women accomplished that, not ugly ducklings, which is how she saw herself. I suspect that over her long, exciting life she seldom found a man with whom she could sustain sexual intercourse on a continued basis. I see her with artists and authors and actors, all in a jumble of dramatic gestures and interests and creativity. I do not visualize an enduring heterosexual love affair. Dashiell Hammett did not provide the answer. He was her drinking buddy and mentor, a "catch" in that she had as her companion the man who wrote *The Thin Man* and *The Maltese Falcon*. Hammett was Nick Charles and Sam Spade, and Lillian made much out of having lived with a real-life private detective, a vaunted Pinkerton man. But Hammett drank himself to sleep and reportedly went into Harlem for his sexual adventures; he did not turn to Lillian. Her husband from the old days in New York was a producer named Arthur Kober who, she told me, was a good person and still a friend, but there had been nothing between them in terms of romantic love.

Once she called me in Boston and actually spoke softly and suggestively and lovingly over the phone. She said that the day before, when I had been with her in New York, I had pleased her as only one other person had ever done in her life. My competition, I guessed, was a Harvard student in her creative writing class, a youngster she had slept with and at times talked about. Now, to my delight, I had achieved parity with him. What matters here, however, is that she could say that in all of her life, some Harvard student and I were the only partners who pleased her completely; who, I gather, made her feel loved and desired and thoroughly sexual. I had a vivid picture of the previous afternoon, and to me we had done no more nor less than what ordinary lovers do all the time. It was then (and I reach for it now) that I began to understand her temperament and her crustiness. Her life, when reduced to basics, was so unfulfilled. All those men over the decades and all the smart talk in the smart set in which she traveled never made her feel adored as a woman. Indeed, Lillian would have traded her talent for looks because she thought good-looking women had what she wanted more than anything else: adoration. As much as she derided the condition, she was starstruck and always wished that she'd possessed movie star glamour. If you were a knockout, some attractive man would fall for you and want to make love to you for the rest of your life.

Before the summer of 1967 ended, Lillian took me to one final party. Kenneth Tynan and his beautiful wife were on the Vineyard and Lillian's group gathered to welcome him. I seem to remember the party was at Kingman Brewster's house. Lillian's crowd included Robert Brustein, Rose and Bill Styron, Richard Poirier, Jules and Judy Feiffer, John and Barbara Hersey, and other writers and academics and theatrical types who visited the Vineyard for the summer. Once again I felt a terrible unease. I stood beside Lillian listening to the gush of theater talk and loud name-dropping, the conversation sprinkled with acid comments about Lyndon Johnson and the war in Vietnam. My anonymity made me conspicuous as I stood by, a mute figure in the middle of the room. These gushing people had no interest whatsoever in what I had to say or how I might think. I recall Kenneth Tynan going on and on about the Beatles, who at the time were of no interest to me, even though I'd read that Leonard Bernstein had recently journeyed to Liverpool to study the source of their music. To me the Beatles were English adolescents singing away on Ed Sullivan's television show. I suddenly realized that I was never cut out to be a passive listener in a room of chattering luminaries. I'd had it and I began to yearn for people who worked for a living and bought their food at the A & P.

When Kingman Brewster dated my sister, he would come to our bungalow in the summer—tousle-headed, leather faced, and windblown from sailing. Thirty years later he refused to recognize me. I shifted my feet in his company as an unwanted stranger. No one ever asked me what I thought of the Beatles. I said the hell with it and drove home. Lillian could find a ride.

Back in Boston she summoned me to her apartment. This wasn't working. She said, "I can't have an editor who behaves like you do. I have met Billy Abrahams, who is an editor at the *Atlantic Monthly*. He's agreed to become my editor."

I feigned disappointment, but could hardly contain my glee. In the morning I burst into Arthur Junior's office with the good news. "Lillian and I have broken up," I said, grinning. "She's going to let Billy Abrahams be her editor." *Whoopee!* I almost shouted, and Arthur smiled. His concern was with the promise of a best-seller. Now the reshaping of her material could commence. "Billy Abrahams won't get personally involved," Arthur said. "He'll be good for her." My ordeal had ended.

An Unfinished Woman and *Pentimento* were published to much acclaim. I read both books with considerable pleasure. However, when she died in 1984, I wrote a letter to the *Vineyard Gazette* lambasting the flood of praise that had attended her funeral as mourners read their thoughts over her newly dug grave. John Hersey, among others, was upset with me, but most of the merchants and blue-collar workers on the Vineyard who had chanced into Lillian's line of fire applauded me. For a brief time I was caught between the sophisticated summer colony of writers who had one view of Lillian as a hostess and raconteur and those who'd been expected to do her bidding and who viewed her as a mean-spirited harridan who treated ordinary people with contempt. I'd been on both sides: I'd heard her stories and felt the sting of her censure.

Lillian Hellman lost all interest in me the moment I walked out of her apartment. A couple of years later she brought the writer and academic Robert Coles into a bookstore I owned, and the two of them browsed about looking for a book to take to the beach. This woman who had welcomed me into her bed no longer cared to recognize me. She stalked my book shop, hacking, and ignored my eyes; she treated me like a clerk of limited interest. If she and Dr. Coles actually found a book to buy, perhaps then I could be of some use. In the meantime I was to be ignored like someone from the lower classes.

What Lillian had meant to me was star power. I shudder to confess this, but the path of my entire life was aiming me toward a person like Lillian Hellman. The blue Bakelite Monarch radio in Anna's room next to mine was on every night and in the late afternoon and early evening she kept it playing in the breakfast nook off the kitchen. The Monarch brought Walter Winchell and Broadway to me. On and off through the day and into the night I heard Bob and Bing Crosby, the Boswell Sisters, and Lanny Ross. My favorites were the *Lucky Strike Hit Parade* with Bea Wain and the Mark Warnow Orchestra. The "boy singer" in those pre-Sinatra days was Barry Wood. The *Manhattan Merry-Go-Round* was a program that took you to the supper clubs of New York: Leon and Eddie's, LaRue, the Copacobana. Lying in bed or hunched over the radio next to our kitchen, I would let my pre-pubescent mind flow to settings I'd seen at the movies: glistening bars with shiny glasses and limes and olives and bitter bottles just like the ones my father had in our rathskeller, and soft lights and sexy women. I resembled millions of girls dreaming of bright lights and looking grand. I was probably like some boys, too, but no boy I knew would admit to the thoughts I harbored. I saw myself as Franchot Tone or William Powell, a woman on my arm, checking my topcoat and her mink with the hat check girl who looked like Ann Sheridan or Joan Blondell.

This all led me to Lillian Hellman. Step by step, I was on course from Anna's kitchen and bedroom and that little Bakelite radio to Lillian, the preeminent female luminary-playwright of her time.

Chapter 16

By 1968 I had been at Little, Brown for seven years. I'd started out with a young wife in a rented house in Dover, west of the city. I ended my employment sleeping in a small basement apartment on Marlborough Street in Boston. Before that, for a few months I stayed in a hotel room at the Hampshire House on Beacon Street, an establishment that was 70 percent barroom, 20 percent dining room, and at best 10 percent hostelry. Sometimes I was lucky enough to entice a woman to leave the bar at closing and go with me to my room. Once I spent the night with a lady reporter, and in the morning we showered together in a bathroom with no curtains covering a rather large set of windows. She stood at the window wet and dripping, exposing herself to the young women at the Katherine Gibbs school next door. They looked up from their typewriters and ogled this woman, naked as Venus, glistening with water. Playfully she gestured to the young ladies that love had held sway through the night. I never knew her name. All I recall is her body and her sense of humor, at once risqué and free-spirited.

Eventually my analyst threw up his hands and "fired" me. My drinking was obscuring matters to the point where I couldn't continue in analysis. A gap was widening between what was happening to me inside and the way I was living. There seemed to be a distracting distance between the "new Stan" and the old habits and fears and adjustments to which I was still clinging, and I was slipping into an abyss. My doctor wanted to send me off to a mental hospital, but I refused. Exasperated and with tears in his eyes, his voice breaking, he said: "I hate losing. I do *not* like losing a patient, but I have lost you. Please leave my office. You are out."

With no home and no psychoanalyst, I slid through my days. My relationship with Lillian was in the past. Book projects were still aborning, but I was unable to give them proper attention. Often I overslept. Sometimes I stayed with a lady architect who had a loft down on the harbor, or with a psychologist who lived in Cambridge, and one time with a blind woman who lived out in Newton. I was forever arriving at work after 10:00 A.M. I had to sneak up the stairs to my office. Ned Bradford would look away in embarrassment. I'm sure the secretaries whispered about me, though the young woman who worked for me, Anne Wigglesworth, was loyal to the end. She tried to cover for me when I was late and drew criticism from Arthur Junior. By now Randy Williams had given up on me. For a brief time he had taken the responsibility for watching me swallow an Antabuse pill from a bottle in his desk. Antabuse precluded the probability of drinking: to drink on Antabuse was to become very ill. I soon switched the contents of his bottle with a large supply of similarly shaped unmarked aspirin. A bewildered Randy Williams wondered how I still managed to drink. Why didn't the Antabuse stop me? He never suspected me of treachery. I wondered how long it would take before he exploded in anger.

As an editor I often went outside the safe and easy channels. I spent much of my last three years at Little, Brown scouting for material among the citizenry. I would read of some incident in the papers, track down the participants, and then approach them with the idea for a book. I did that with a fashion model who had been named Model of the Year. She agreed to write the true story of her life. When I met her, she gave every indication of drug abuse. She kept insisting that Mickey Rooney had just murdered his wife. She seemed frantic as she made ready for the funeral, convinced of dire deeds in Hollywood. We had a few drinks and then I left her, a woman of fragile beauty, seemingly deranged. I couldn't imagine that I'd be able to slip her past Ned Bradford or Randy Williams. She was reed thin; an alcoholic and a supposed heroin addict, we would not have made a happy pair.

Coffee, Tea or Me, a rather sanitized autobiographical account of what it was like to be a stewardess, had come out and was selling briskly. Following a hunch about stewardesses, I got myself introduced to Chet Huntley of the *Huntley/Brinkley Report*. A new drinking pal, he produced two stewardesses who had scandalous stories to tell of sex in the cockpit at thirty-thousand feet and so on. We shared a three-hour lunch with them, drinking and listening to their stories. Liquored up as I was, I knew that once again, as with the fashion model, what I was hearing was too wild and scandalous for Little, Brown. After lunch Chet Huntley went off with the young women. I do not know if their book ever appeared.

Brenda Fraser was another person of whom I read and then pursued. She was the first celebrity debutante; in the '30s her picture had appeared in *Life*, her face in the newsreels. Prior to World War II, Brenda Fraser had been all the rage. As Debutante of the Year, she traveled in an exciting crowd of rich, young Americans for whom New York City was hometown. As the Great Depression drew to a close, millions were hungry for news that signaled the return of prosperity. It pleased us to know that parties were once again rolling along into the night, as were the Cadillacs and Lincolns and an occasional Rolls-Royce. Things *were* getting back to normal if the rich were starting to have so much fun again. Of course, all through the Depression the rich had continued to have fun, but they kept it under wraps. In the late '30s and early '40s it was out in the open again, and Brenda Fraser symbolized high times among the young and the wealthy.

Now, years later, I read her name in the *Boston Globe*. A fiftyish Brenda Fraser was living alone in Medfield, a distant suburb of Boston. I eventually acquired her phone number and called. She invited me to her house, and with some trepidation I drove out to Medfield. I knew nothing about debutante balls or that rite of passage referred to by society matrons as "coming out." But I was curious. Perhaps Brenda Fraser could offer an objective look at society before the war; nostalgia to be sure, but also some solid criticism of a vain convention now very much at odds with the social tumult of the '60s.

She lived in a huge house chock-a-block with memorabilia. Photos of herself were hanging on every wall: paintings and caricatures and framed newsprint. She appeared to be proud of her life, and I could tell right away that it would be impossible to elicit any objective look at the nonsense and immense snobbery of "coming out." I wanted an indictment of a custom, not self-promotion.

Nevertheless, we made a date to meet at the Ritz-Carlton. The idea was that I would tape her story to see if "there was anything there." I left her house dazzled by her vanity and wondering about her health. She was very thin and completely disconnected in her talk. But then, the decline and fall of a debutante was what I had in mind; I was still working the same idea that had begun with Veronica Lake. I was ever hopeful that readers would respond to books written by people who had scaled the heights only to fall. This idea appealed to me for obvious reasons: I nursed an image of myself as someone who had been riding high, only to lose his grip and tumble down. "Rise and Fall" stories were to my taste.

I thought, too, that for people my age, reading about Brenda Fraser would be like reading about Scott and Zelda Fitzgerald. Social history, nostalgia…that was what I wanted, as well as an indictment of high society. As it turned out, I wanted too much. At the Ritz, Brenda drank several bottles of nonalcoholic sparkling grape juice and talked haltingly into a tape recorder, recalling times with Shipwreck Kelly—called Ship—one of her husbands. She seemed to be quite fond of Ship, as well as Hemingway and Winston Guest, with whom she and Ship had spent much of the war. She claimed that they'd chased Nazi submarines off the coast of Cuba, having a gay time drinking and carousing once they were back in Havana.

Though her mind wandered as she talked, I was able to pick up a cynical edge to her voice. The whole Nazi submarine operation was a joke. Hemingway and his crew made sport with government officials, and only once did they actually see a submarine. At a reception for the British ambassador, Hemingway presented him with a present. It was a large box with a series of ever-smaller boxes inside, each fitting inside the preceding box, until at the end there was a tiny box, just right for a ring or a pin. A gleeful ambassador opened it and found a folded piece of paper. He unfolded it and read the message which was all that remained after he'd opened at least six boxes of diminishing sizes. The message read: *Fuck you.* Hemingway and his crew roared as the ambassador's face grew crimson. "The poor man had actually expected a gift from Ernest Hemingway," said Brenda Fraser, her thin, aging face all smiles.

I do not recall what happened to the tape. We parted with a handshake and I left her at the Ritz. She was very much a woman alone, seemingly ravaged by pills and drink and a life lived for pleasure and a most fleeting fame. I was certain that she could not write a book, and I knew of no ghostwriter who could take on a project involving someone so steeped in the lost celebrity of self. It was a long shot that hadn't paid off. When she called me a few days later, I said I'd changed my mind. I tried to soften the blow, but she knew she'd been rejected. A part of me envied the life she had led, but to transform Brenda Fraser's life into serious literature was, in my final judgment, an impossible task.

During this time I came very close to bringing in a "big" Book-of-the-Month Club book that would have pleased Arthur Senior. Hellman's memoir *An Unfinished Woman* had not yet been published. I imagined that all eyes were on me to produce the big one or else. Without a commercial success, I wasn't worth the concern I was causing.

One day at lunch, eating alone at the counter at Locke-Ober, I suddenly thought of Bing Crosby. Although very much out of phase with the '60s, Bing Crosby was nevertheless still a megastar. Even the hippies knew who he was. Quite probably I had not thought of "der Bingle" for a very long time. But there he was, staring at me from inside my own head. It was obvious! Forget Veronica Lake, Brenda Fraser, or some skinny Model of the Year. Go straight to Bing Crosby; what a life, what a story to tell!

I got the address of his office and wrote him a letter lauding his talent and, I assume now, overstating his place in the sweep of American culture. Within a matter of days he answered. He wrote me that Bing Crosby's story wasn't worth the paper it would be printed on. What counted, he said, was the life story of one Harry Lillis Crosby. I replied, restating my interest in Bing. Again he answered on the heels of my letter: Harry Lillis Crosby was the man. Forget Bing. Bing Crosby was all superficial nonsense. Once more I wrote to Bing—it was now "Bing" and "Stan"—and disagreed with him. Bing Crosby's story was the story of America. "Surely you can see that," I wrote. "Bing Crosby is a name known to all of us, not only here in America but all across the globe." His last letter arrived: "Do not write to me about Bing Crosby. If you want the real life belonging to Harry Lillis Crosby, please let me know." I filed away my correspondence. My great idea for a runaway best-seller drifted out of my mind.

In 1977, when Bing Crosby died, I read that "Bing" was a nickname for Harry Lillis Crosby. What he'd been trying to tell me was that his desire was to write an unvarnished account of his life, not the stuff of press agentry but rather the gritty story of how he had worked his way to the top. The book he'd wanted to write was exactly the book I had wanted. How I could have been so dense as to misread his letters amazed me then. It doesn't amaze me now. By 1967 alcohol was eroding my ability to think. I still had my desk and the wonderful Anne Wigglesworth at my side, but my judgment was losing its acuity; I was becoming stupid.

•　•　•

Lunch was always a problem. If I didn't drink at lunch, I felt nervous and I performed poorly. If I did drink at lunch, I drank until I was sedated. Whenever I lunched with Arthur Senior we both became sedated and would walk back across the Common from Locke-Ober like great pals, feeling a warm glow.

One time I "lost it" at lunch with Stephen Birmingham, who had written the best-seller, *Our Crowd*. We were at the Four Seasons in New York with Little, Brown's publicity director, Lynn Caine. I became drunk and insulted Birmingham. He ran to his agent, who telephoned Junior to complain. I talked my way out of it. I did not like Stephen Birmingham's writing, and I admitted to Junior that I had shared my displeasure with him. It wouldn't happen again. I'd learn to control my feelings.

But it did happen again, and very soon.

The first book I edited for Little, Brown involved the charismatic Princeton football and hockey star Hobey Baker. That was six years prior to what would become my last lunch on behalf of Little, Brown. John Davies, the author of *The Legend of Hobey Baker*, called me about a young man who wished to make a movie based on his book. As Little, Brown held motion picture rights, and as I was still handling potential movie deals for the company, I quickly struck out for New York to meet John Davies and the young filmmaker. The filmmaker brought a lawyer and the four of us had lunch. By lunch's end everything was in shambles. I'd gotten drunk again; unexpectedly, like a windswept plague, drunkenness assaulted me out of nowhere. One minute we were smiling and discussing the sale of rights to our enterprising young screenwriter; the next I fell into the grip of a terrible drunkenness and began insulting the fellow. John looked aghast, but as Little, Brown held all rights, he and the others were compelled to pay me heed.

So many terrors were at work. I'd lost two children, a home, a psychoanalyst. I'd felt shamed by my prostitution with Lillian. Alcoholism was running wild with my life. The following day, back in Boston, I telephoned John Davies and the lawyer. I apologized and told each of them that I was quitting. The lawyer advised me not to be rash. We all "lose our cool" at times. Davies said nothing. I had called from the bar at the Hampshire House, where I was again in my cups.

Eventually I made it back to Junior's office. "I resign," I told him. "I can't go on anymore. Eerything is in a mess." He nodded sympathetically and accepted my resignation. At that moment he and all my friends at Little, Brown and all the days that had made me so extremely happy, so much of my life that I cherished, ended. I had loved—really loved—going to work. Now work was over. I'd never have that life again.

The last thing I saw when I left Little, Brown was the shiny brass doorknob, glistening in the sunlight as the door closed behind me. I quickly said good-bye to Anne Wigglesworth, not wanting to linger; I feared her tears. No one else said a word. The whole building was filled with my embarrassment. The brass doorknob was no longer mine to grasp.

•   •   •

Two days later I was on the ferry heading to Martha's Vineyard. I was thirty-eight years old and would soon be divorced from a wife who deplored me. Formal employment at Duell, Sloan and Pearce and at Little, Brown was over. I rather fancied the term "burnt out." I recalled my last abortive attempt to be a father. On December 24, 1967, I drove across Massachusetts and down to Farmington to spend Christmas Eve and Christmas Day with my estranged wife, our two children, her parents, and a brother or two. I had my car loaded with presents. I thought I was on reasonably good terms with my wife. Sometimes we dated. Once I took her to a movie and later we were close again, if just for a few hours. And so it hurt when I heard my mother-in-law tell me I was not welcome in her house. There I was, my presents delivered, my son and my daughter aglow with Christmas glee. I had driven all that way to share in the love of Christmas, only to be banished in front of my children, who appeared very puzzled and shamed by what they were witnessing. Later on, when my incipient ex–father-in-law asked me to go back to his daughter, I was tempted because of our children, but I declined. When I declined I thought of that Christmas Eve, of standing in the hallway in Farmington not believing what I was hearing. Why hadn't they told me before I left Boston? Why was I allowed to see the bright faces of my children only to watch their faces fall and their eyes well up as I had to turn, stunned, and walk back to the door?

For some time after I left Little, Brown, I blamed Lillian for my collapse. I thought she'd suckered me into a terrible compromise. I felt that I'd been had, but in truth I relished the idea of being Lillian Hellman's editor and confidant while attending to her in private. I'd in fact volunteered for the very compromise I would, with the passage of time, lament. I was too soft and too dependent on alcohol to see that I had erred. Lillian was much stronger than I and was just being herself: I was the undefined, mushy young man slowly falling apart as I tried to do my job, have an affair with someone I was beginning to detest, all the while being pulled by my love for two innocent children. I could not maintain a balance.

On the ferry heading to Martha's Vineyard, freed from marriage and employment, I wondered if I was a failure or if this was just a bum interlude and my life would right itself in time. I recalled my father's words, used so often when he spoke encouragingly to my sick mother: "When things get back to normal, Lu, everything will be peachy fine." I went to the concession counter and bought a vodka and tonic and took it out onto the deck and stood by the rail: *It will all be peachy fine.* In the meantime, I was a free soul. The thought made me very happy. I said the hell with the mess I'd left behind and kept on drinking.

EPILOGUE

The first half of my life ended when I left Little, Brown. By then I was far off course. That I did not founder is a miracle. In retrospect, I believe my survival instincts were well honed in military school where, as a youngster, I kept a sharp eye on the odd events that transpired, always alert to the subtle pressures and signs of duress and castigation.

Now that I have written the story of the first thirty eight years of my life, I want to add that I am deeply sorry for the heedless behavior that characterized my style of living. I was oblivious to the notion that I came from a family rife with dysfunction. For many years, I was quite unaware of my dependence on alcohol.

I feel some sense of disloyalty to my family of origin, and particularly to my brother. But I decided to tell my story as I remembered it. Alas, there is no rebuttal from the grave.

I am ashamed of how I must have appeared to my young children back in Brookline, Massachusetts. They must have felt I deserted them. From their point of view, they are correct.

I describe my book as "true fiction." I disguised and embellished where it seemed appropriate and necessary. To use Lillian Hellman's words, I just kept "clip-clopping" along through episodes that came my way, not in any hurry. My story was not of success; it was more a story of what might have been. Weakness and indiscretion gripped me as would honor and rectitude grip a saint. As such, my story is not the stuff of conventional autobiography. However it reads, I hope my readers find it of interest and worth their while. Perhaps they will see some of themselves in these pages. In my way I was just a young fellow trying to get along. But I didn't have a clue.

Martha's Vineyard
March 1999